FOR ORGANS, PIANOS & ELECTRONIC KEYBOARDS

E-Z PLAY® TODAY

17

Fires[illegible] Singalong

3rd Edition

ISBN 978-1-4234-2125-2

7777 W. BLUEMOUND RD. P.O. BOX 13819 MILWAUKEE, WI 53213

In Australia Contact:
Hal Leonard Australia Pty. Ltd.
4 Lentara Court
Cheltenham, 3192 Victoria, Australia
Email: ausadmin@halleonard.com.au

Visit Hal Leonard Online at
www.halleonard.com

4 After the Ball
6 Ain't We Got Fun?
8 Alexander's Ragtime Band
10 Amazing Grace
12 Auld Lang Syne
14 Baby, Won't You Please Come Home
16 Beautiful Dreamer
18 A Bicycle Built for Two (Daisy Bell)
20 Bill Bailey, Won't You Please Come Home
22 By the Light of the Silvery Moon
24 Careless Love
25 Carolina in the Morning
28 Chicago (That Toddlin' Town)
32 Chinatown, My Chinatown
34 (Oh, My Darling) Clementine
36 Cuddle Up a Little Closer, Lovey Mine
38 The Darktown Strutters' Ball
40 Down by the Old Mill Stream
42 Down in the Valley
44 For He's a Jolly Good Fellow
46 For Me and My Gal
48 Give My Regards to Broadway
50 The Glow Worm
31 Good Night, Ladies
52 Hail, Hail, the Gang's All Here
54 He's Got the Whole World in His Hands
56 Hello! Ma Baby
58 Home Sweet Home
53 (There'll Be) A Hot Time in the Old Town Tonight
60 I Love You Truly
62 I Wish I Were Single Again
63 I Wonder Who's Kissing Her Now
66 I'll Be with You in Apple Blossom Time
68 I'm Always Chasing Rainbows
70 I've Been Working on the Railroad
72 If I Had My Way
74 If You Were the Only Girl in the World
76 In the Good Old Summertime

78 In the Shade of the Old Apple Tree
80 Indiana (Back Home Again in Indiana)
82 Kumbaya
84 Let Me Call You Sweetheart
86 Little Brown Jug
90 Meet Me Tonight in Dreamland
92 Moonlight Bay
94 My Buddy
96 My Wild Irish Rose
98 Oh! You Beautiful Doll
100 Paper Doll
87 Play a Simple Melody
102 Pretty Baby
104 A Pretty Girl Is Like a Melody
106 Put Your Arms Around Me, Honey
108 Ragtime Cowboy Joe
110 The Red River Valley
115 Rock-a-Bye Your Baby with a Dixie Melody
118 Scarborough Fair
112 Schnitzelbank
120 She Wore a Yellow Ribbon
122 Shine On, Harvest Moon
124 Smiles
126 Swanee
128 Take Me Out to the Ball Game
130 There Is a Tavern in the Town
132 Toot, Toot, Tootsie! (Good-bye!)
134 Wait 'Til the Sun Shines, Nellie
136 Waiting for the Robert E. Lee
140 When Irish Eyes Are Smiling
142 When Johnny Comes Marching Home
144 When My Baby Smiles at Me
146 When You Wore a Tulip (And I Wore a Big Red Rose)
148 While Strolling Through the Park One Day
150 Whispering
152 The World Is Waiting for the Sunrise
156 You Made Me Love You (I Didn't Want to Do It)
154 You Tell Me Your Dream
159 REGISTRATION GUIDE

After the Ball
from A TRIP TO CHINATOWN

Registration 5
Rhythm: Waltz

Words and Music by
Charles K. Harris

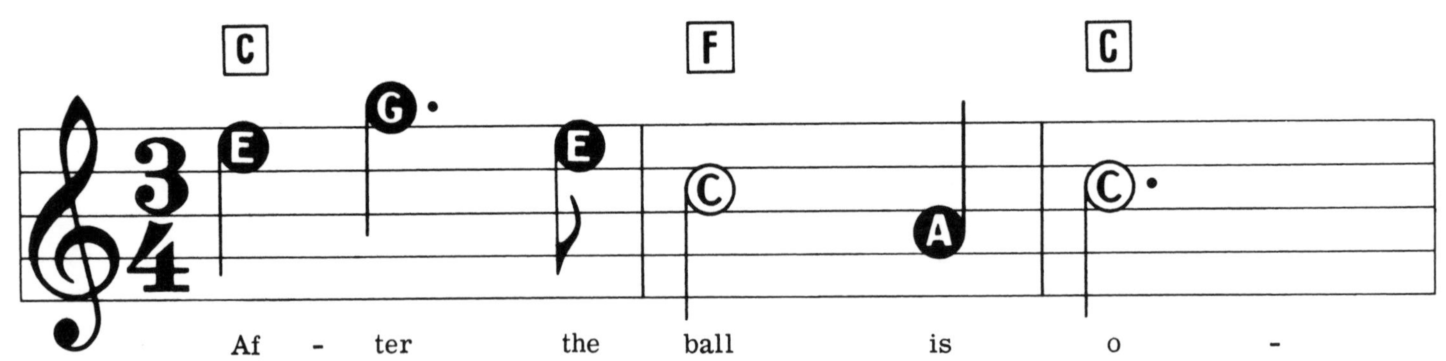

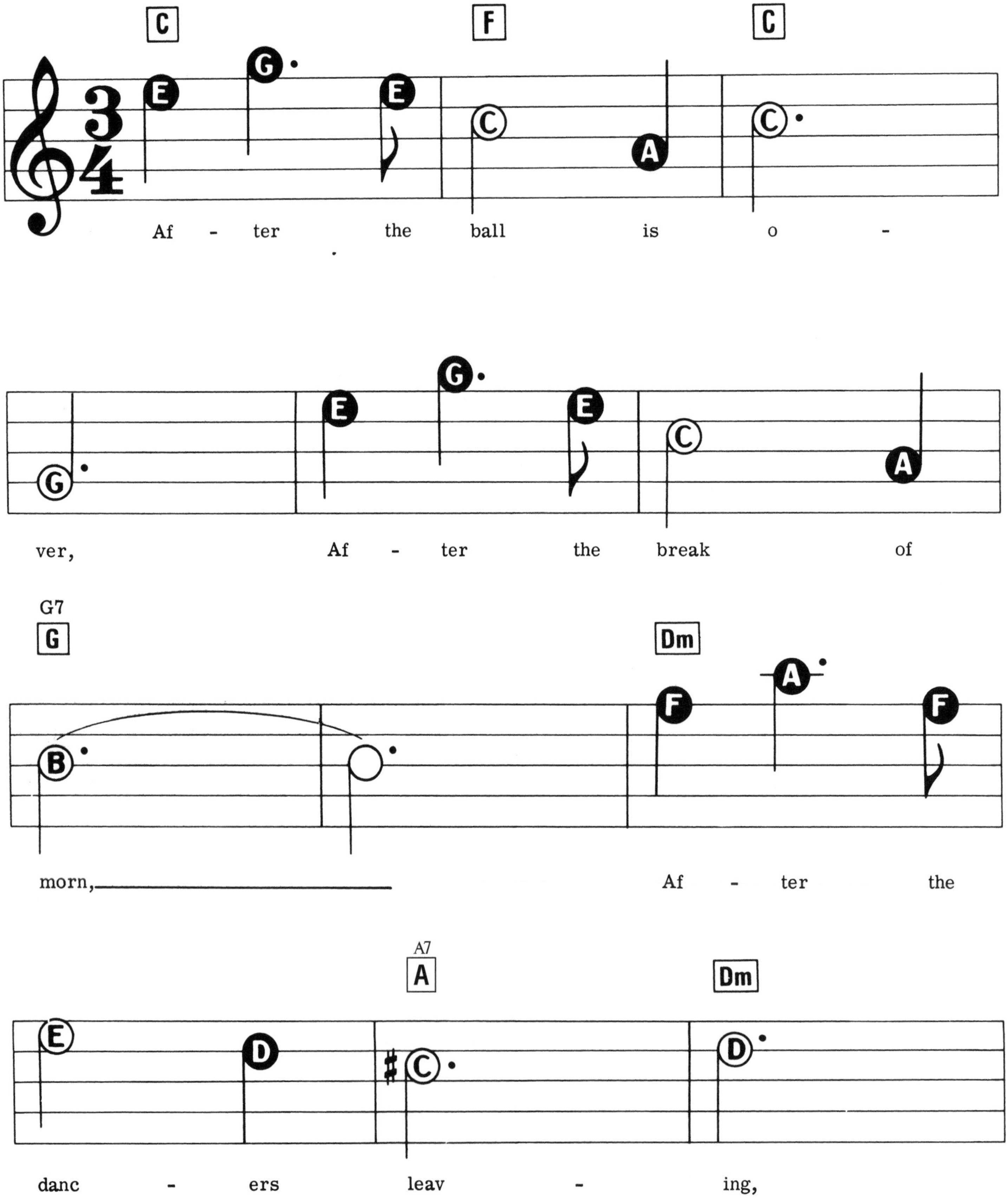

ver, Af - ter the break of

G7
G
Dm

morn, Af - ter the

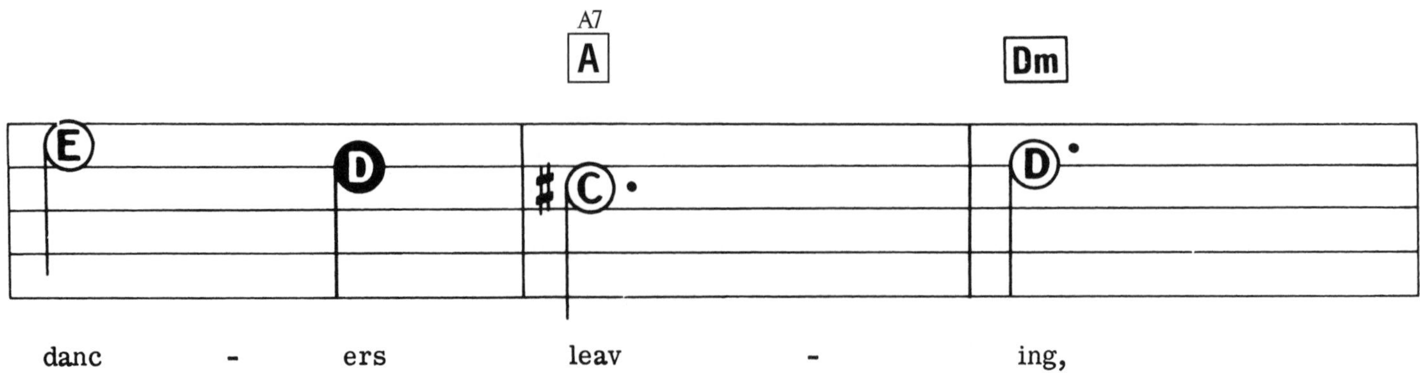

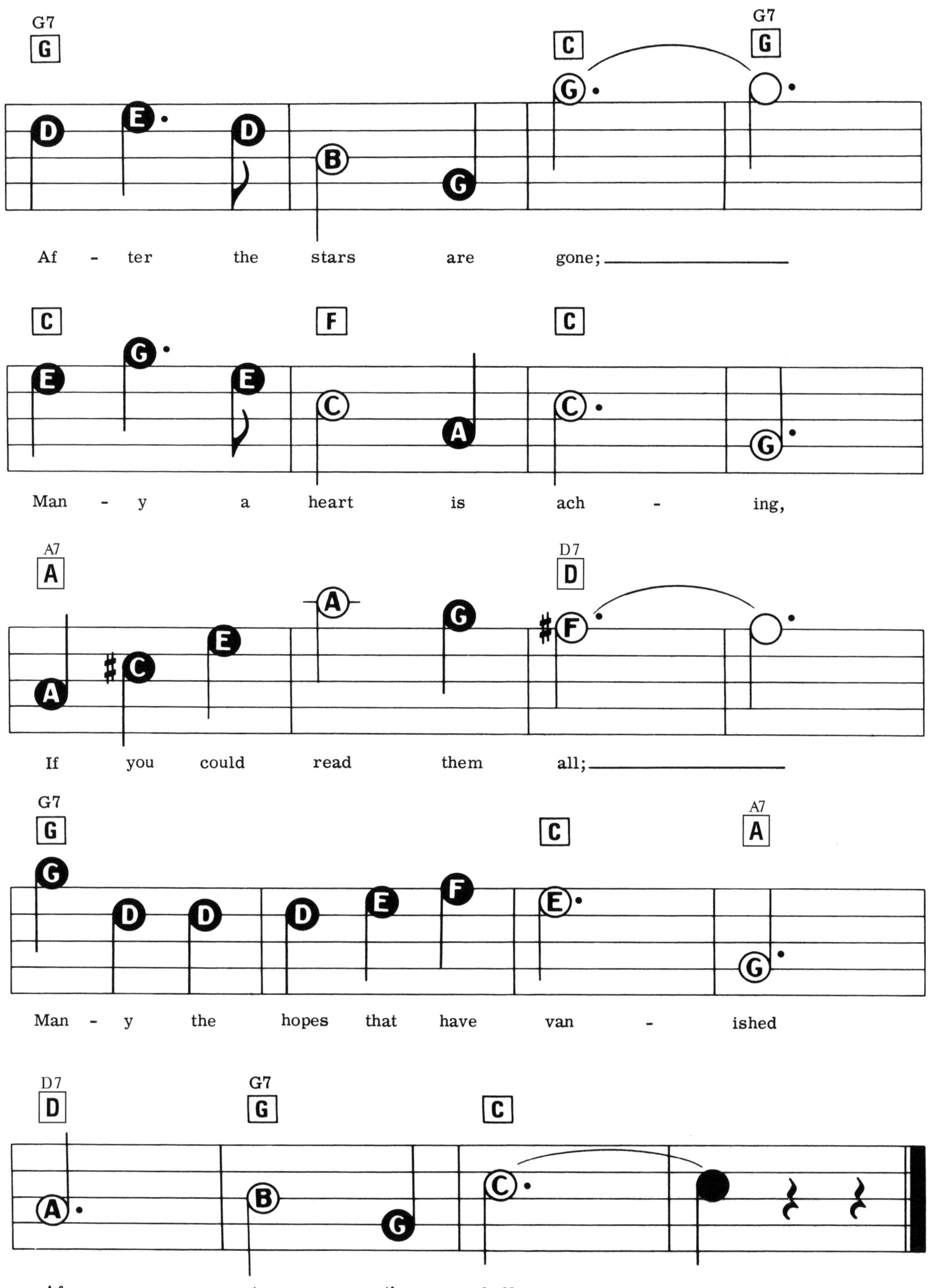
G7
G
C
G7
G
Af - ter the stars are gone;
C
F
C
Man - y a heart is ach - ing,
A7
A
D7
D
If you could read them all;
G7
G
C
A7
A
Man - y the hopes that have van - ished
D7
D
G7
G
C
Af - ter the ball.

Ain't We Got Fun?
from BY THE LIGHT OF THE SILVERY MOON

Registration 5
Rhythm: Fox Trot or Swing

Words by Gus Kahn and Raymond B. Egan
Music by Richard A. Whiting

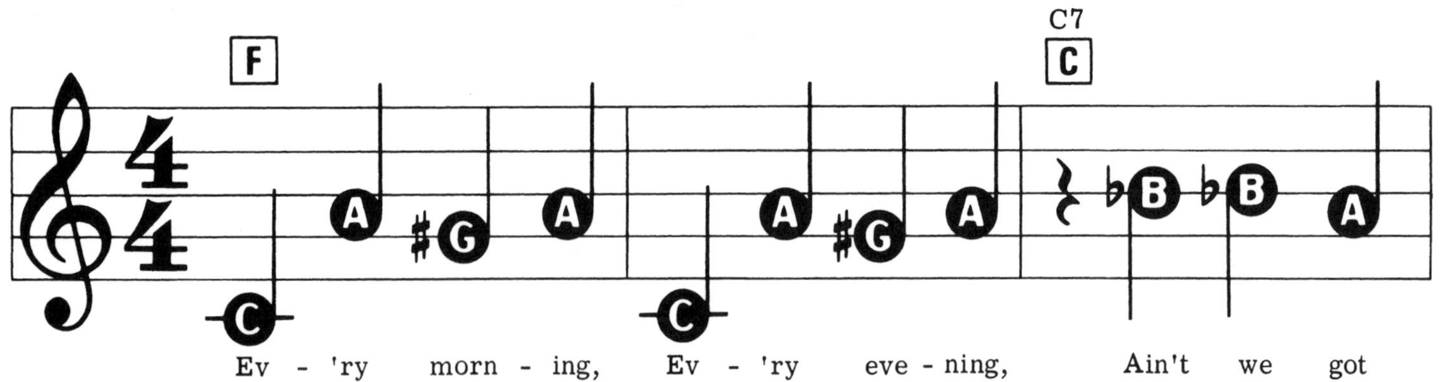

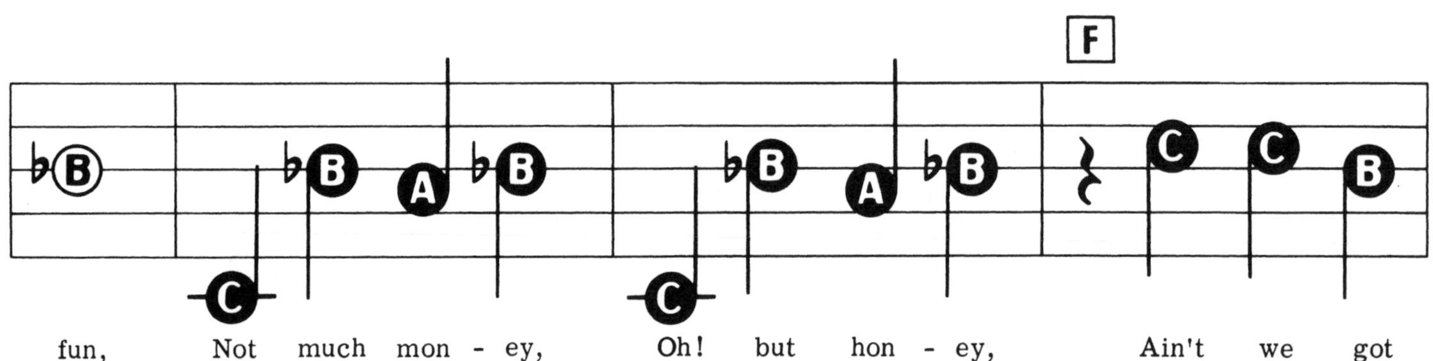

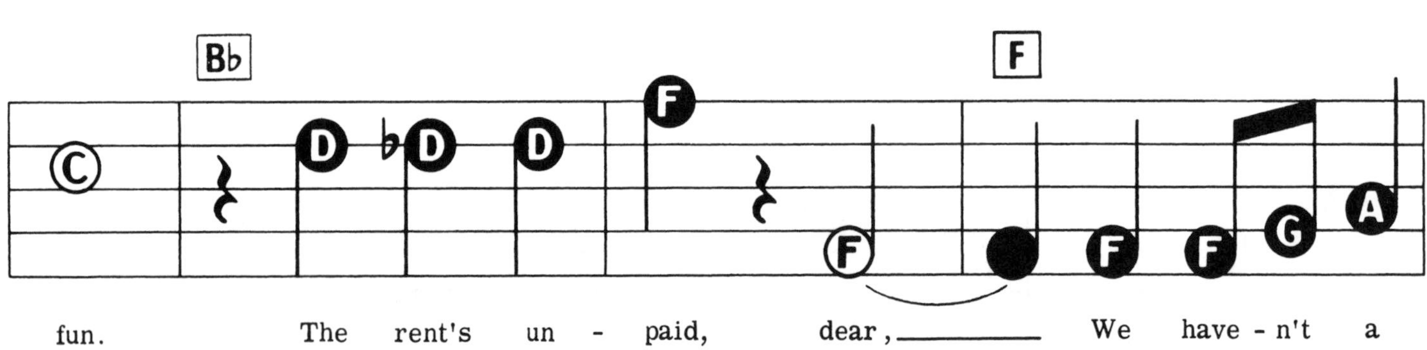

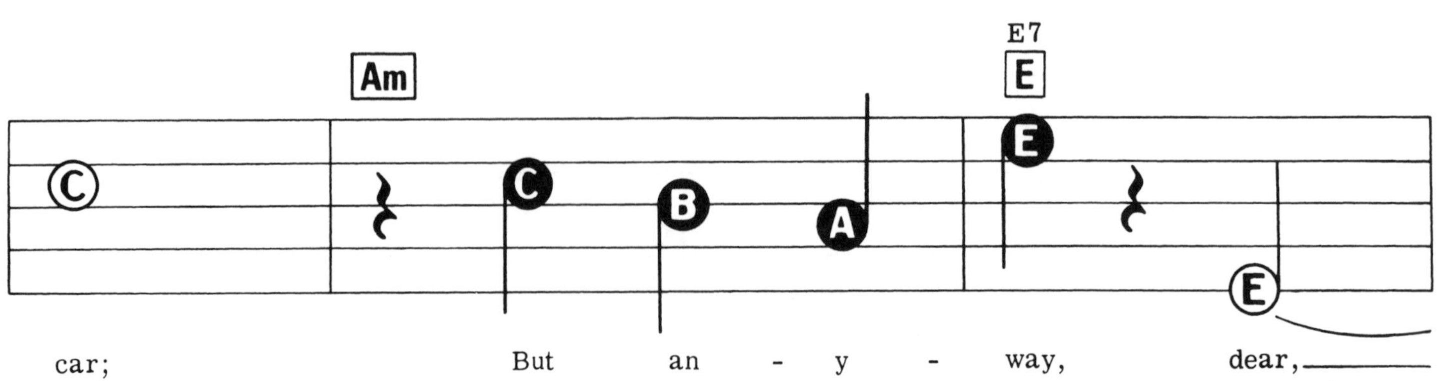

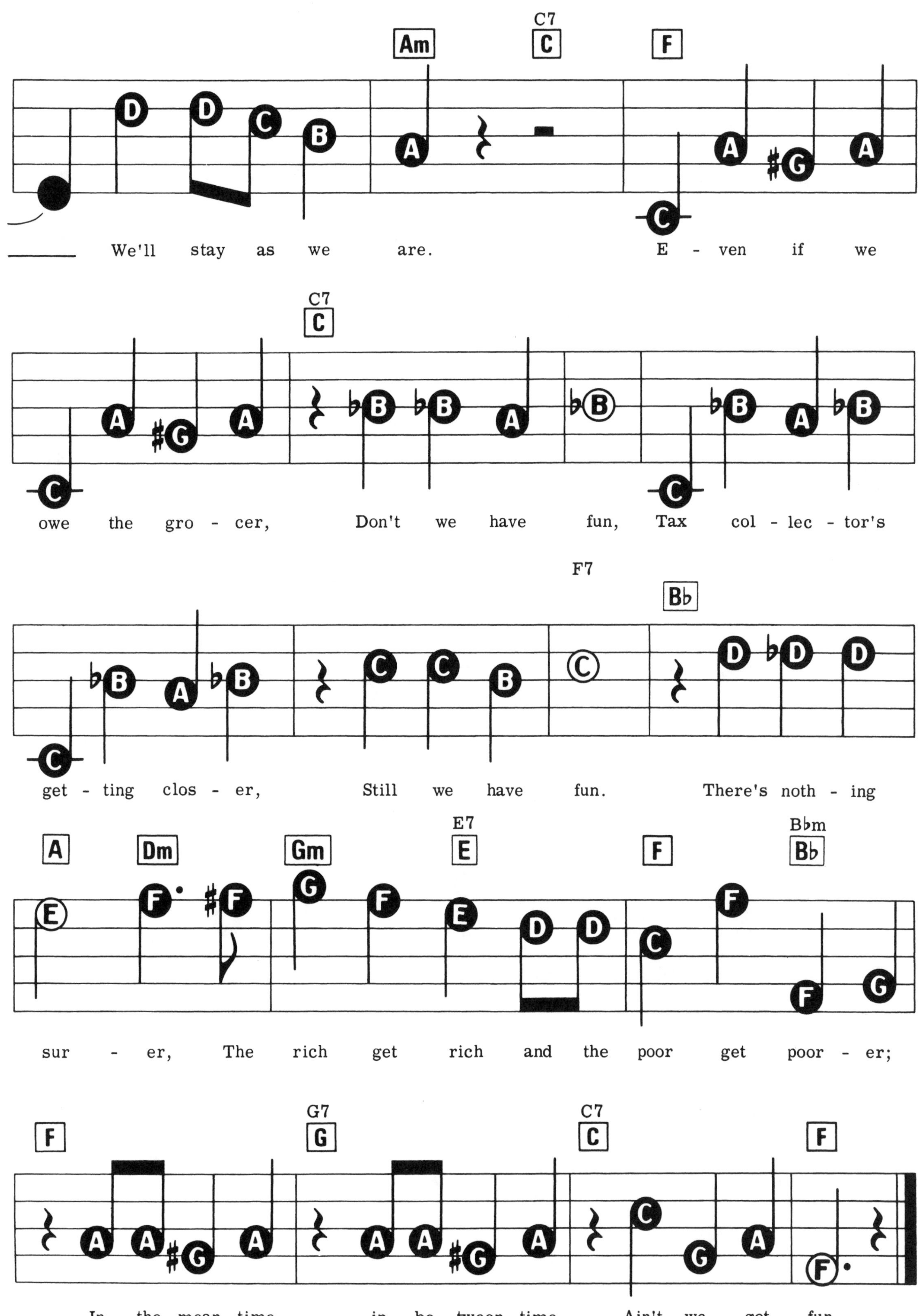
Am C7 C F
We'll stay as we are. E - ven if we
C7 C
owe the gro - cer, Don't we have fun, Tax col - lec - tor's
F7 Bb
get - ting clos - er, Still we have fun. There's noth - ing
A Dm Gm E7 E F Bbm Bb
sur - er, The rich get rich and the poor get poor - er;
F G7 G C7 C F
In the mean - time, in be - tween time, Ain't we got fun.

Alexander's Ragtime Band

from ALEXANDER'S RAGTIME BAND

Registration 5
Rhythm: Fox Trot or Swing

Words and Music by
Irving Berlin

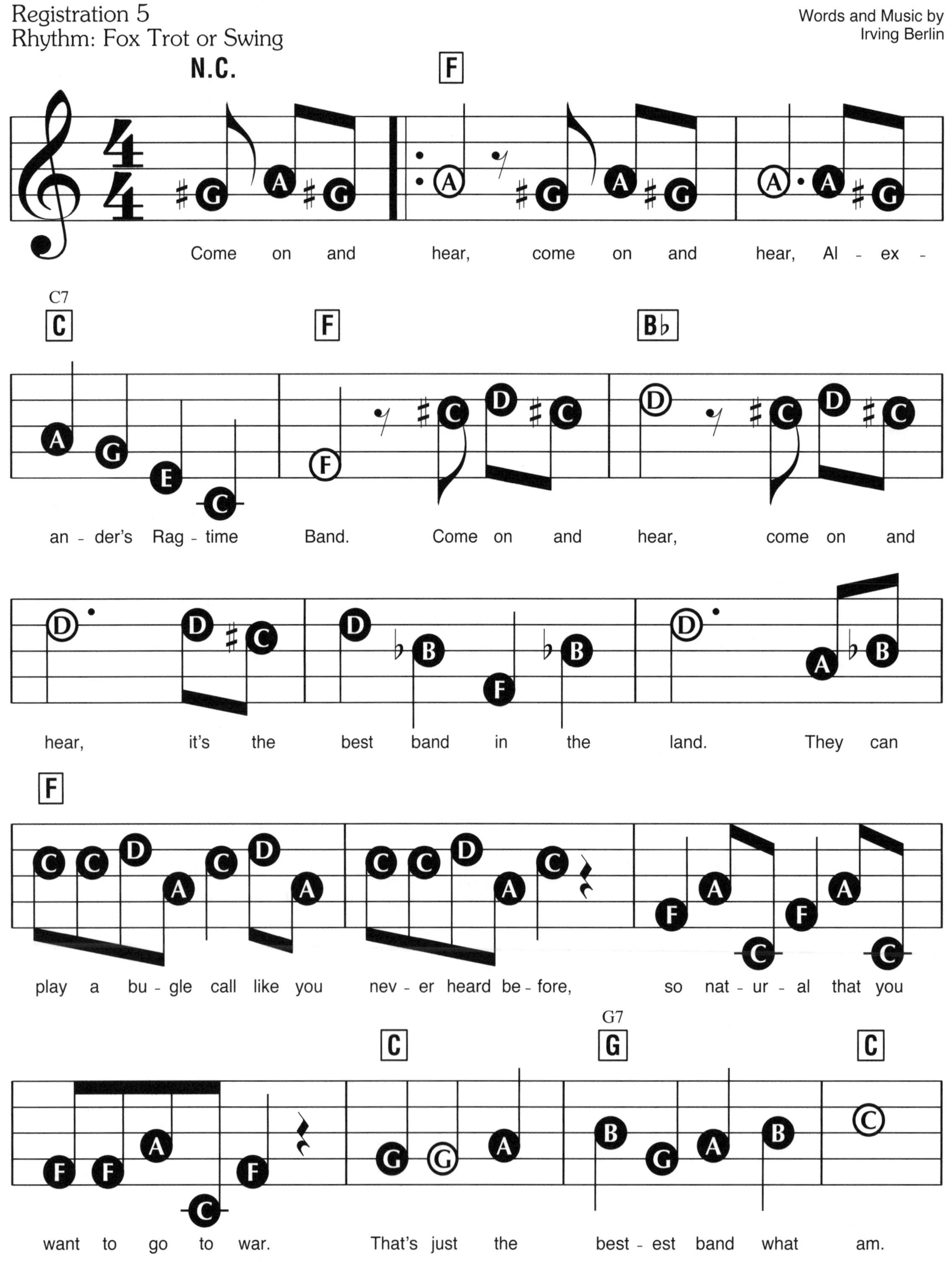

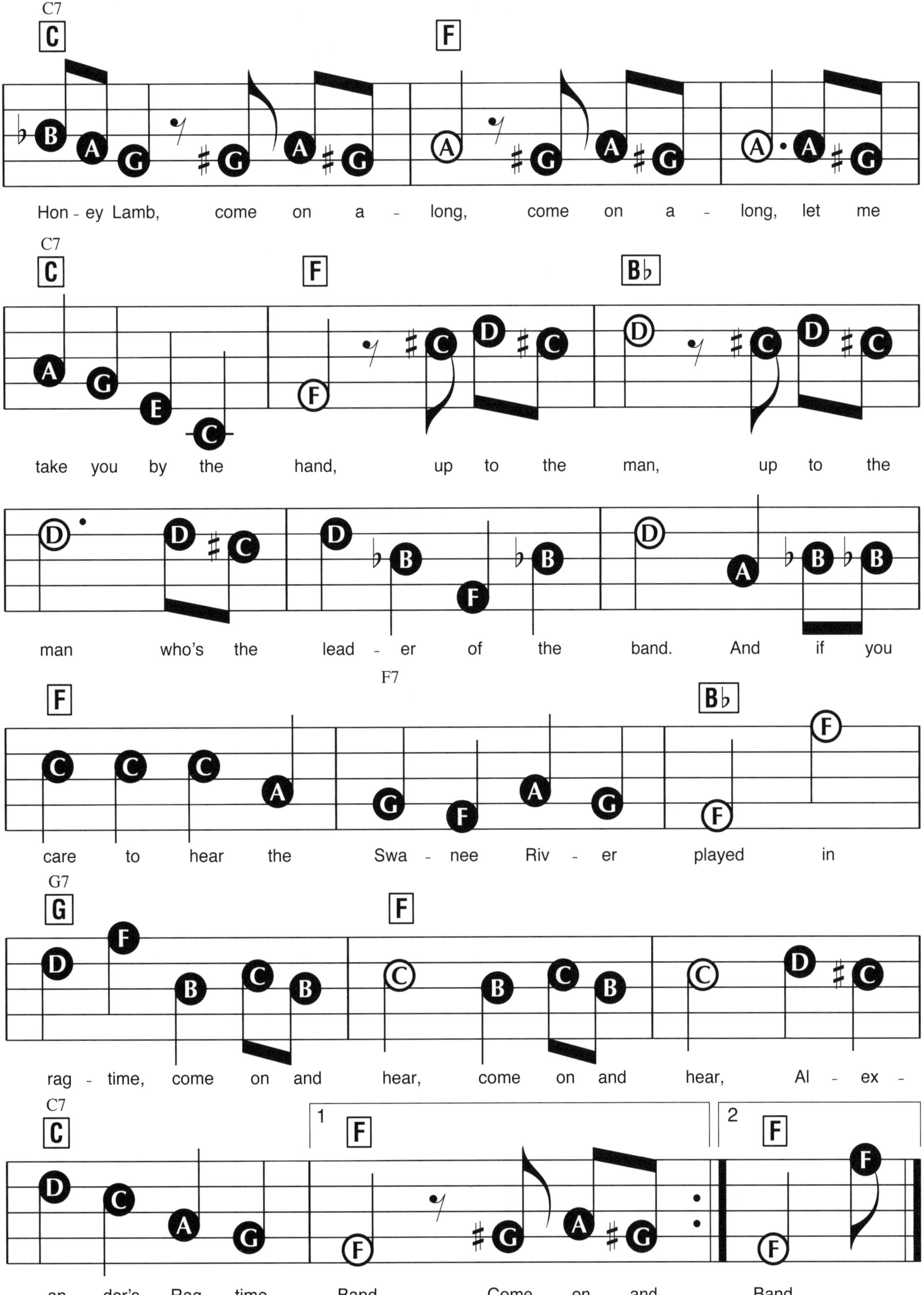
C7
C
F
Hon - ey Lamb, come on a - long, come on a - long, let me
C7
C
F
B♭
take you by the hand, up to the man, up to the
man who's the lead - er of the band. And if you
F
F7
B♭
care to hear the Swa - nee Riv - er played in
G7
G
F
rag - time, come on and hear, come on and hear, Al - ex -
C7
C
1
F
2
F
an - der's Rag - time Band. Come on and Band.

Amazing Grace

Registration 6
Rhythm: Waltz

Words by John Newton
Traditional American Melody
From Carrell and Clayton's *Virginia Harmony*

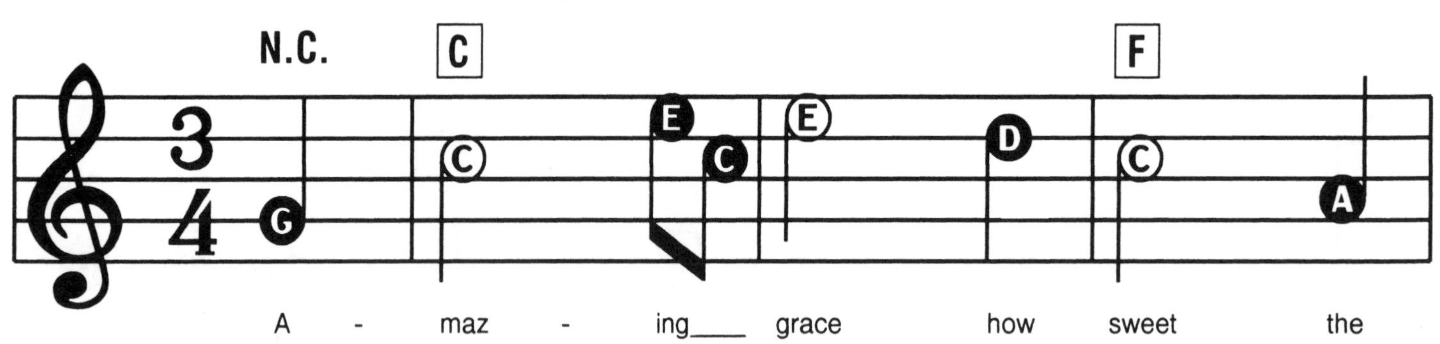

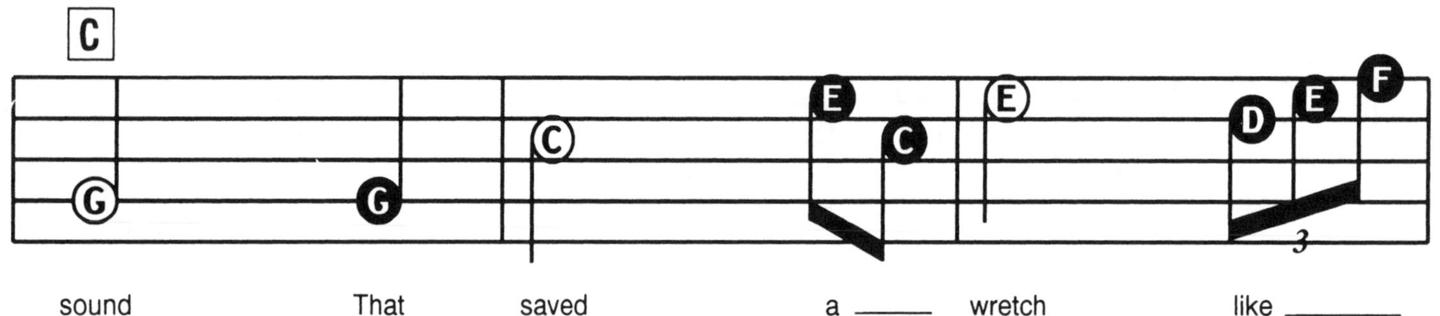

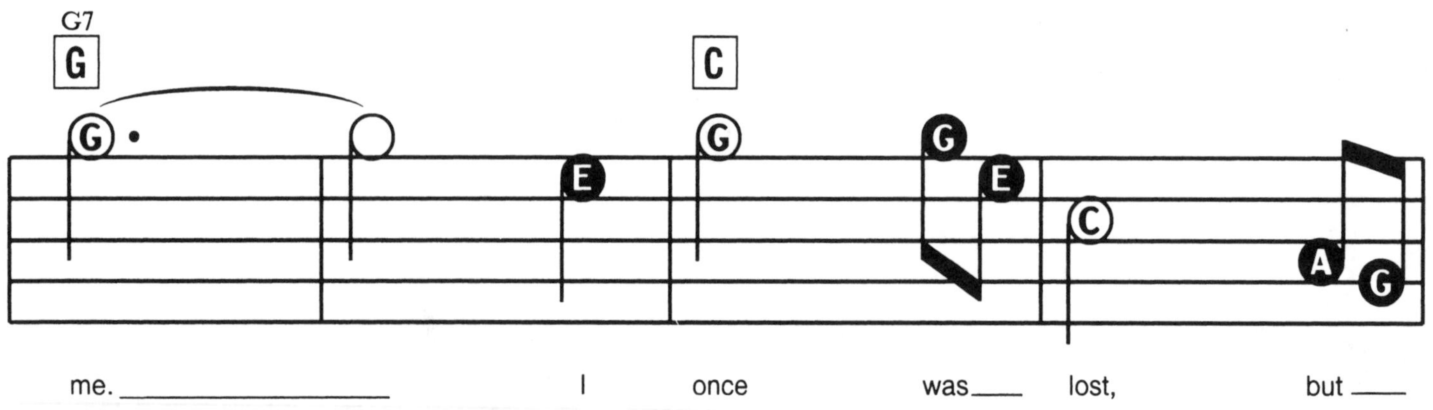

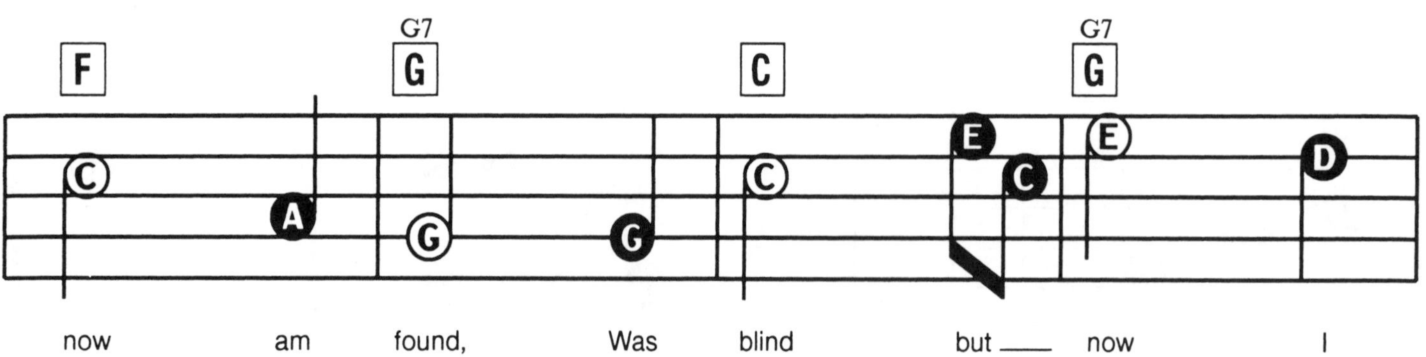

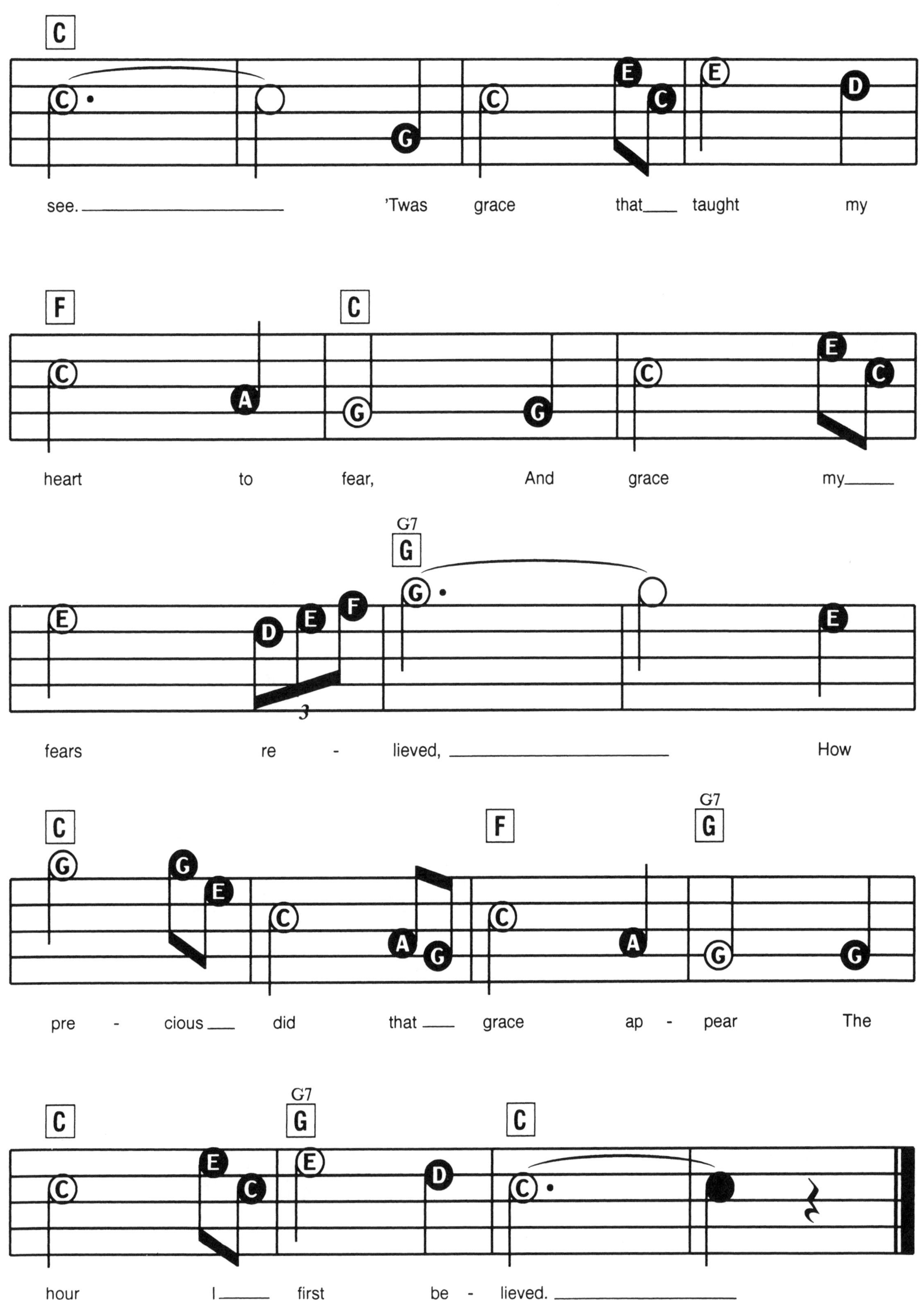
C
C
G
C
E
C
E
D
see.
'Twas
grace
that
taught
my
F
C
C
A
G
G
C
E
C
heart
to
fear,
And
grace
my
G7
G
E
D
E
F
G
E
3
fears
re
-
lieved,
How
C
F
G7
G
G
G
E
C
A
G
C
A
G
G
pre
-
cious
did
that
grace
ap
-
pear
The
C
G7
G
C
C
E
C
E
D
C
hour
I
first
be
-
lieved.

Auld Lang Syne

Registration 8
Rhythm: Fox Trot

Words by Robert Burns
Traditional Scottish Melody

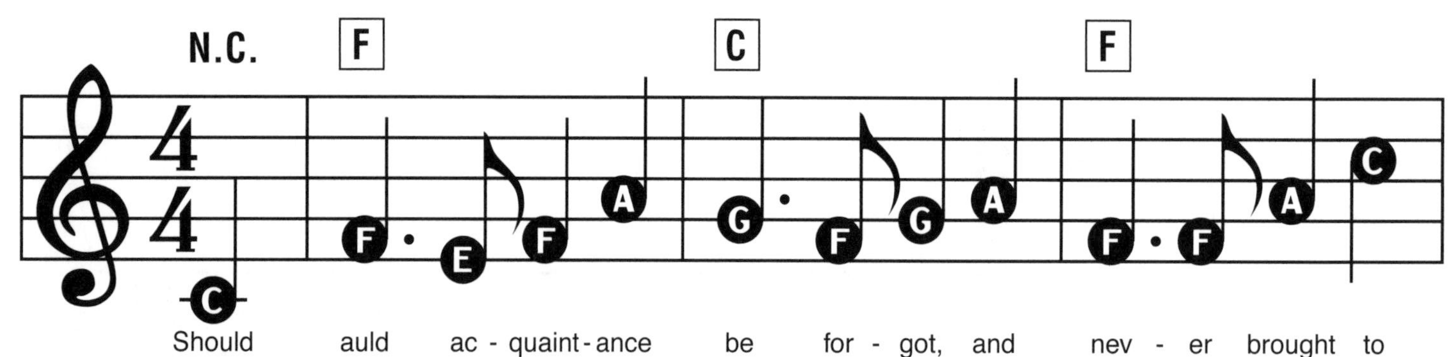

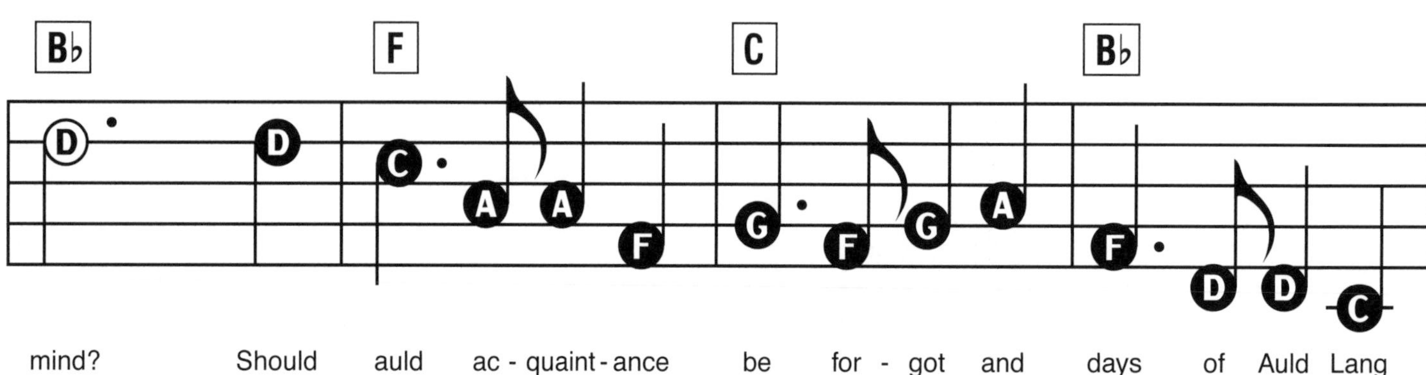

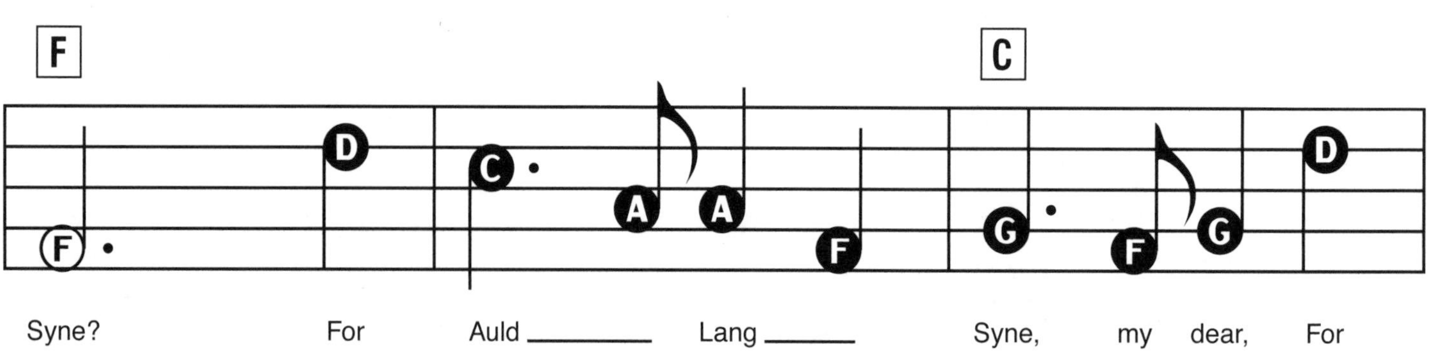

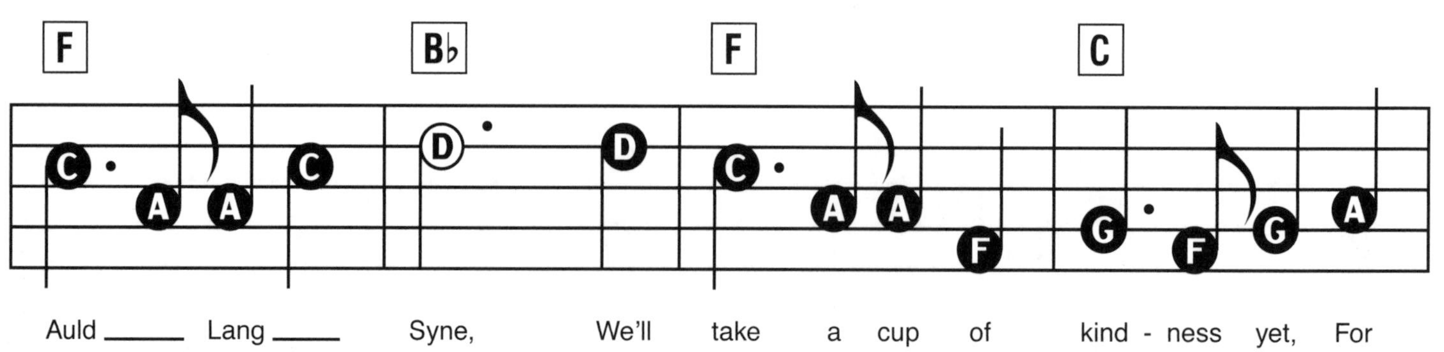

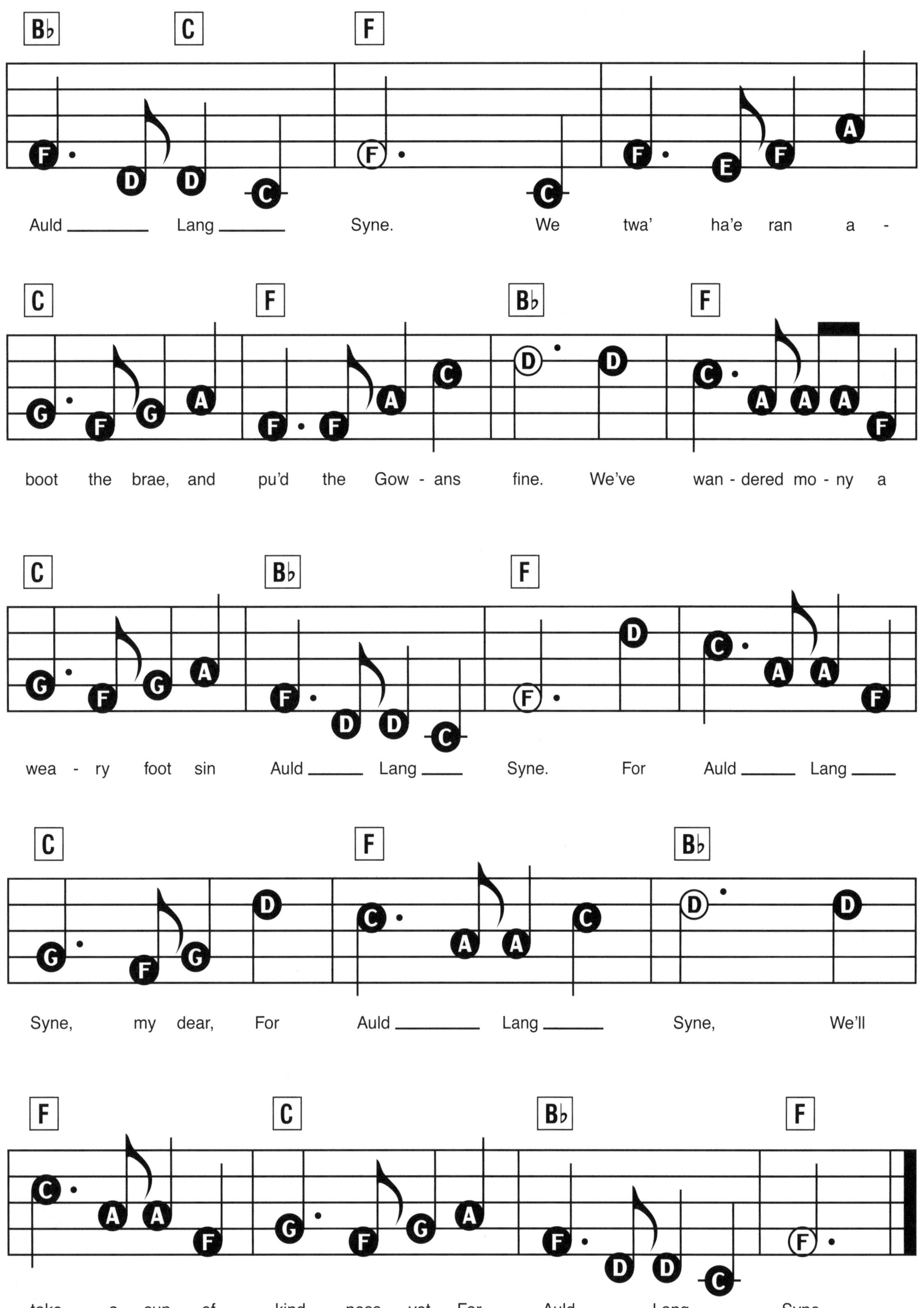
B♭ C F
Auld Lang Syne. We twa' ha'e ran a -
C F B♭ F
boot the brae, and pu'd the Gow - ans fine. We've wan - dered mo - ny a
C B♭ F
wea - ry foot sin Auld Lang Syne. For Auld Lang
C F B♭
Syne, my dear, For Auld Lang Syne, We'll
F C B♭ F
take a cup of kind - ness yet, For Auld Lang Syne.

Baby, Won't You Please Come Home

Registration 7
Rhythm: Fox Trot or Swing

Words and Music by Charles Warfield
and Clarence Williams

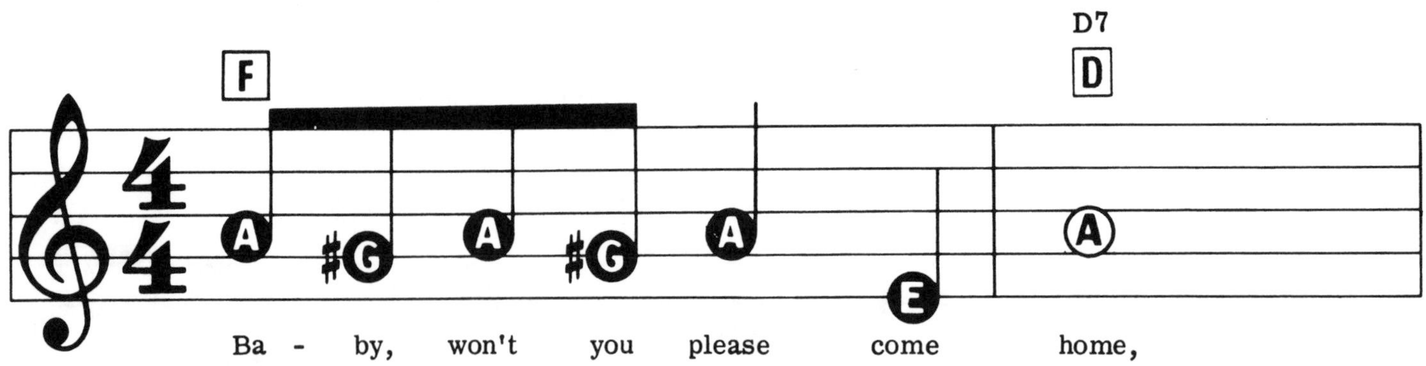

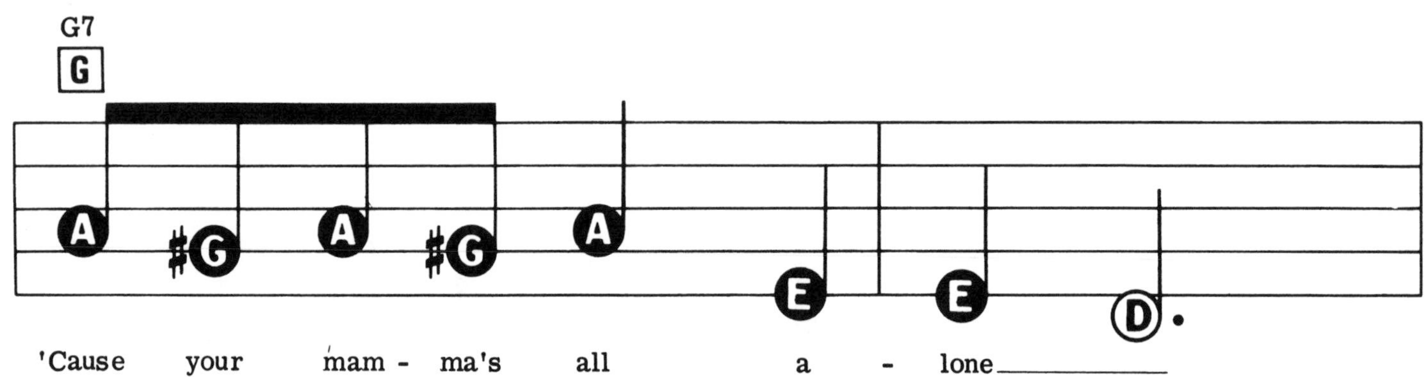

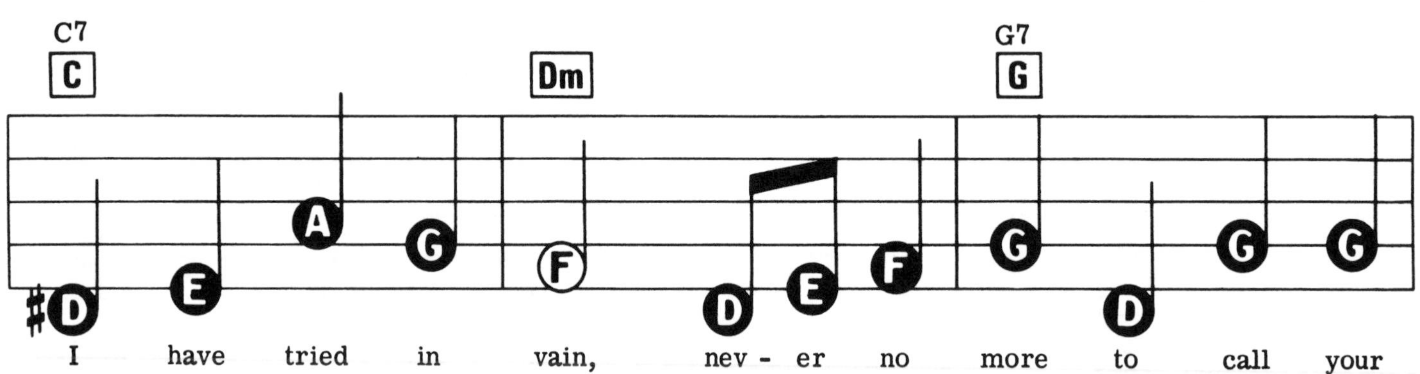

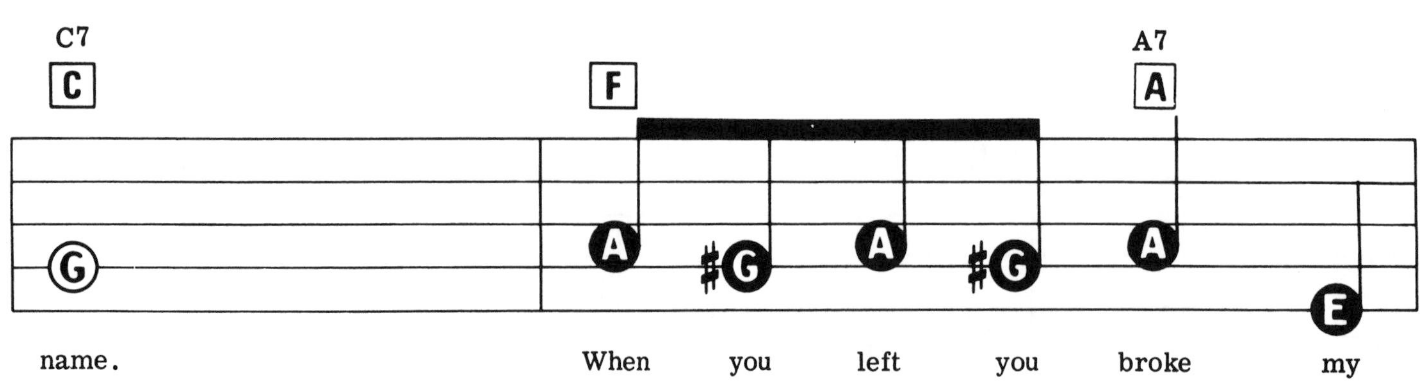

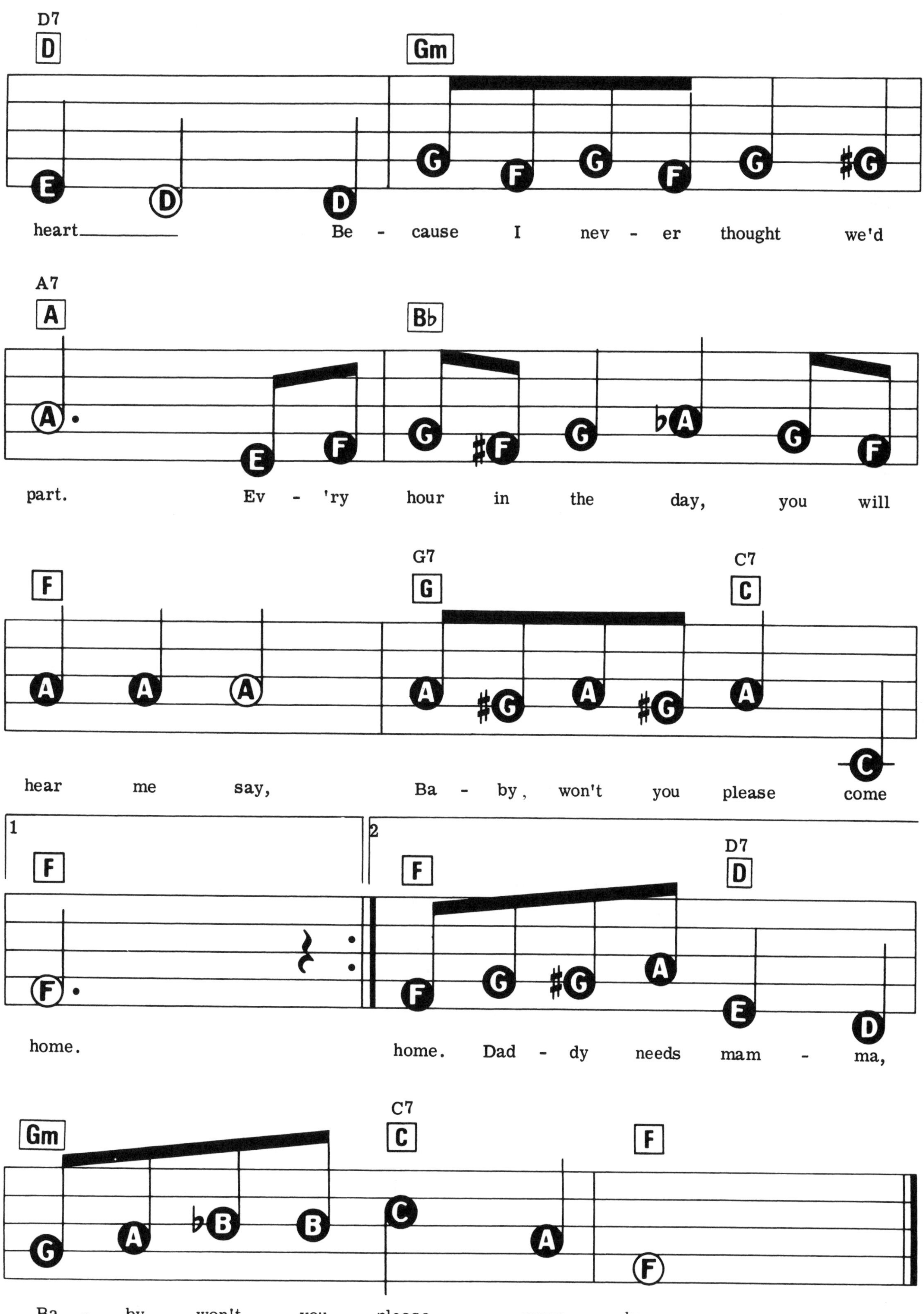
D7
D
Gm
E D D G F G F G #G
heart Be - cause I nev - er thought we'd
A7
A
Bb
A E F G #F G bA G F
part. Ev - 'ry hour in the day, you will
F
G7
G
C7
C
A A A A #G A #G A C
hear me say, Ba - by, won't you please come
1
F
2
F
D7
D
F F G #G A E D
home. home. Dad - dy needs mam - ma,
Gm
C7
C
F
G A bB B C A F
Ba - by, won't you please come home.

Beautiful Dreamer

Registration 5
Rhythm: Waltz

Words and Music by
Stephen C. Foster

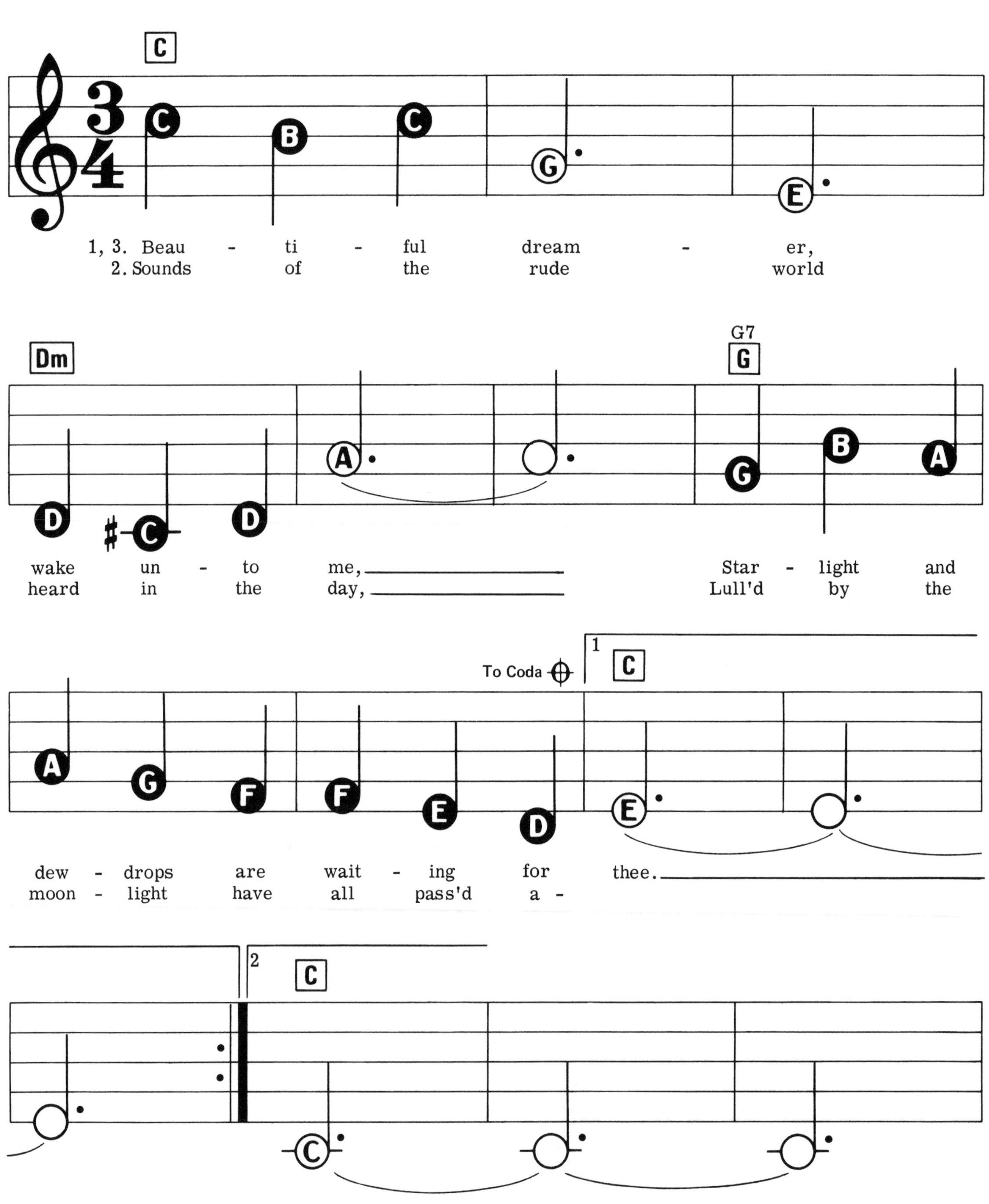

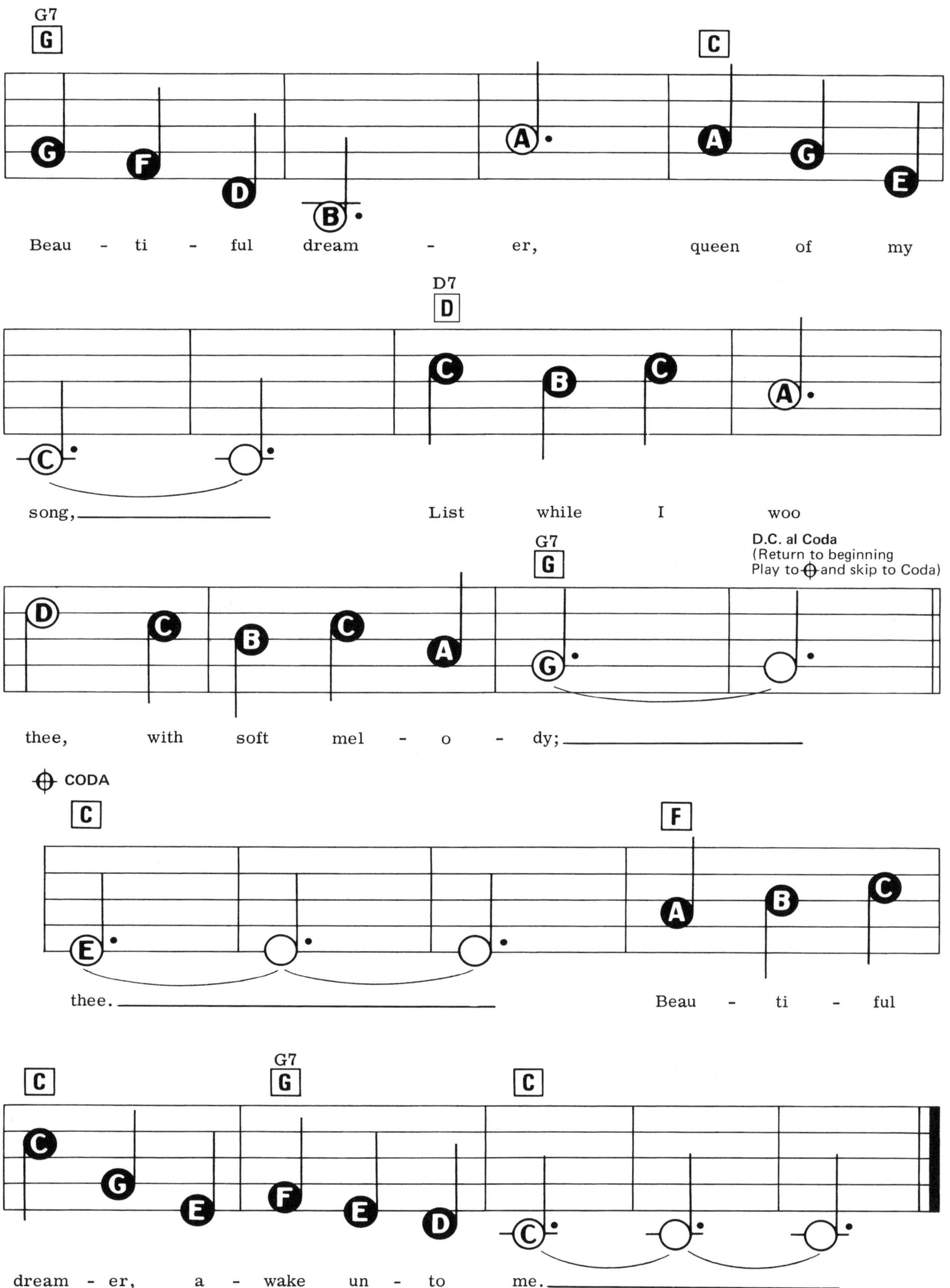
G7
G
C
Beau - ti - ful dream - er, queen of my
D7
D
song, List while I woo
G7
G
D.C. al Coda
(Return to beginning
Play to ⊕ and skip to Coda)
thee, with soft mel - o - dy;
⊕ CODA
C
F
thee. Beau - ti - ful
C
G7
G
C
dream - er, a - wake un - to me.

A Bicycle Built for Two

(Daisy Bell)

Registration 2
Rhythm: Waltz

Words and Music by
Harry Dacre

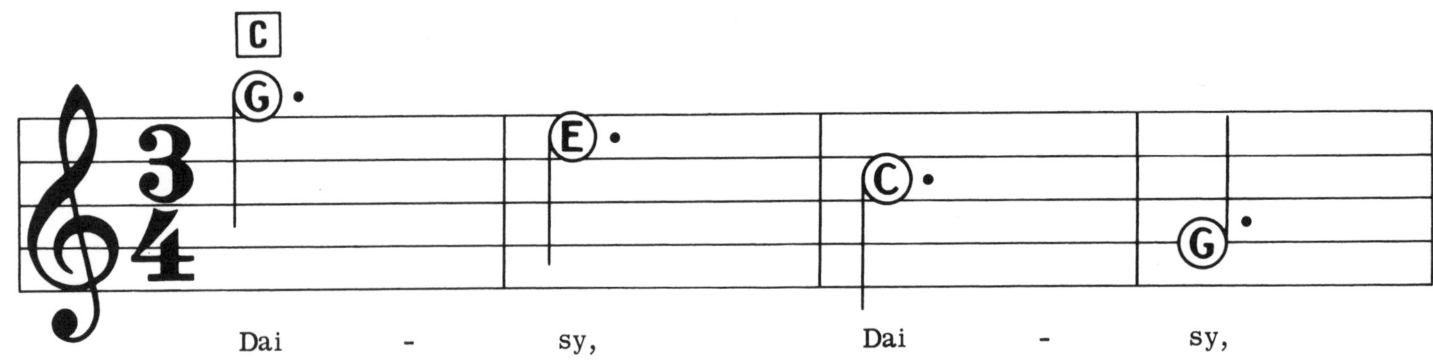

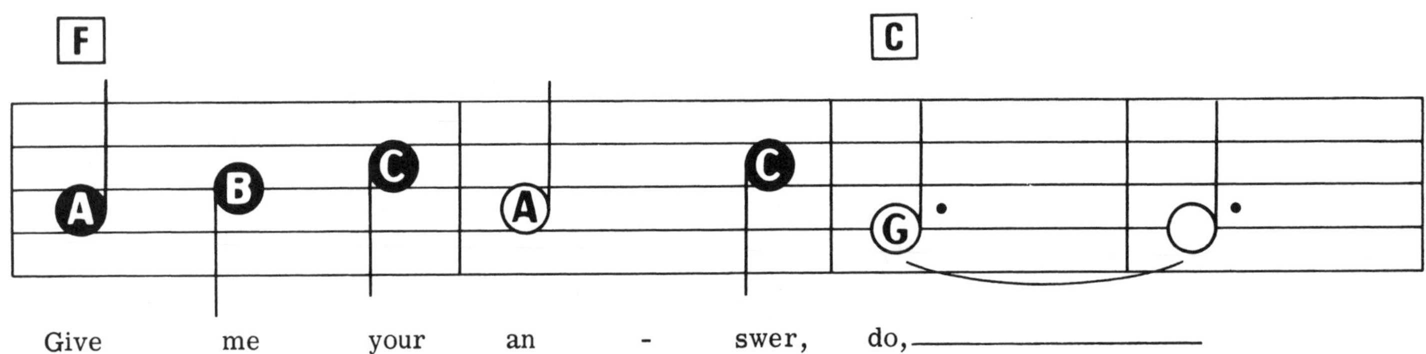

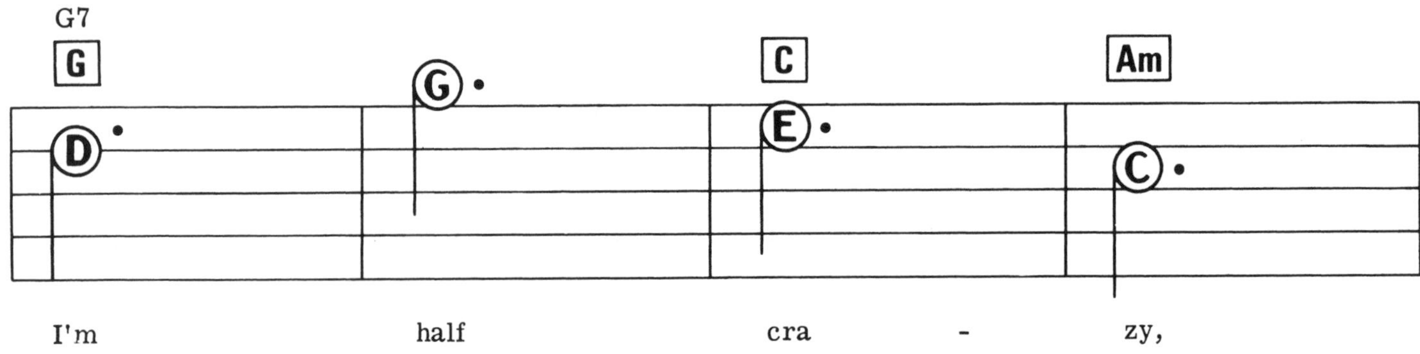

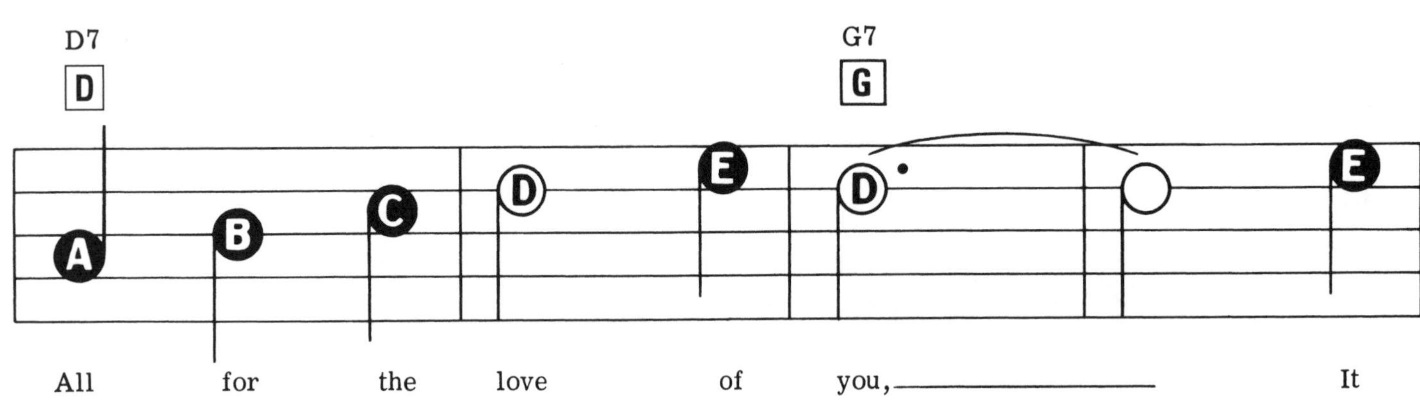

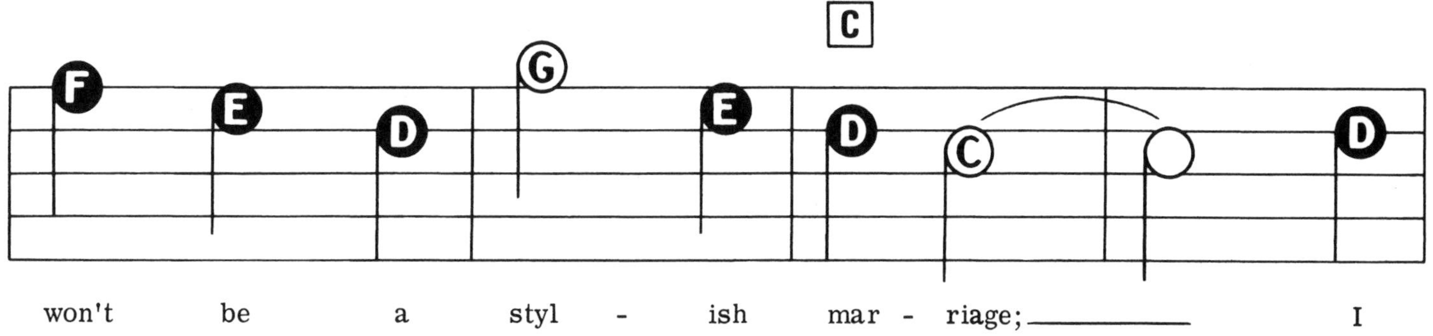
C
F
E
D
G
E
D
C
D
won't be a styl - ish mar - riage;
I

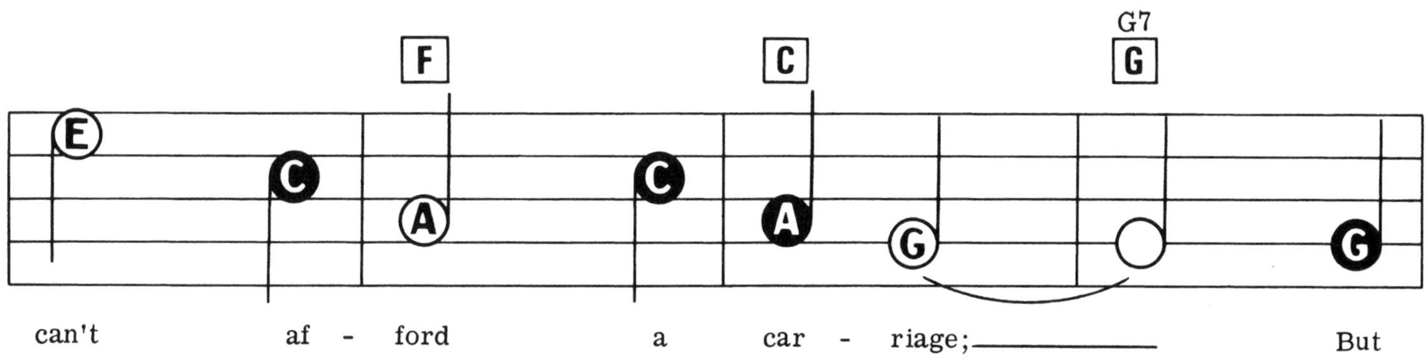
F
C
G7
G
E
C
A
C
A
G
G
can't af - ford a car - riage;
But

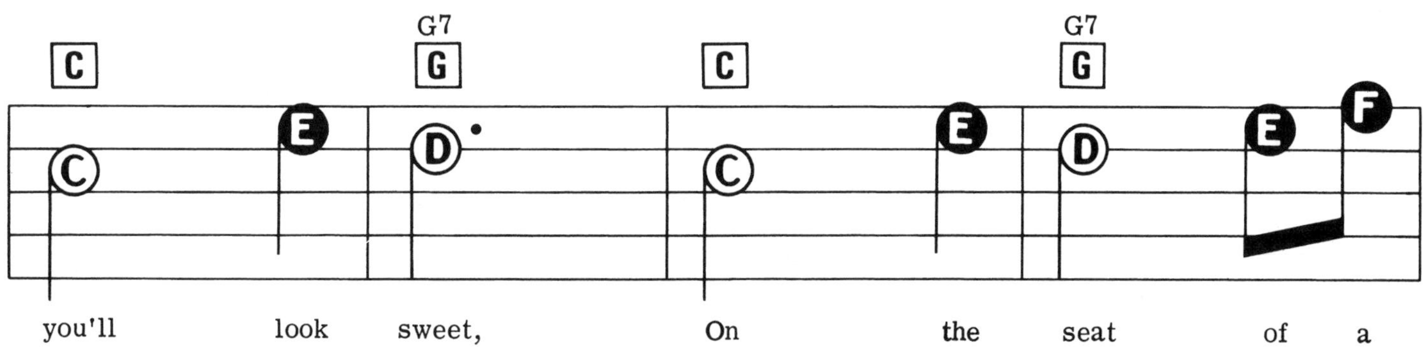
C
G7
G
C
G7
G
C
E
D
C
E
D
E
F
you'll look sweet, On the seat of a

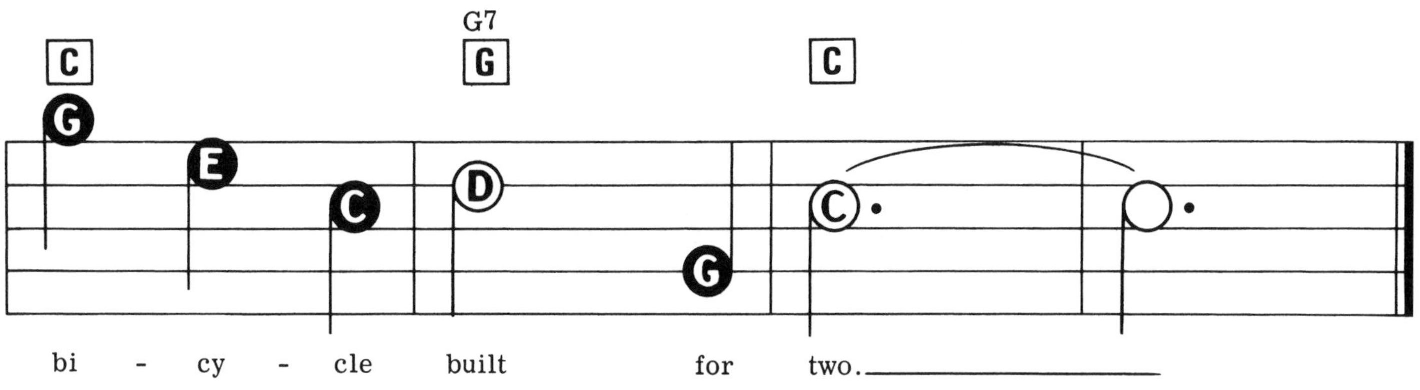
C
G7
G
C
G
E
C
D
G
C
bi - cy - cle built for two.

Bill Bailey, Won't You Please Come Home

Registration 7
Rhythm: Swing

Words and Music by
Hughie Cannon

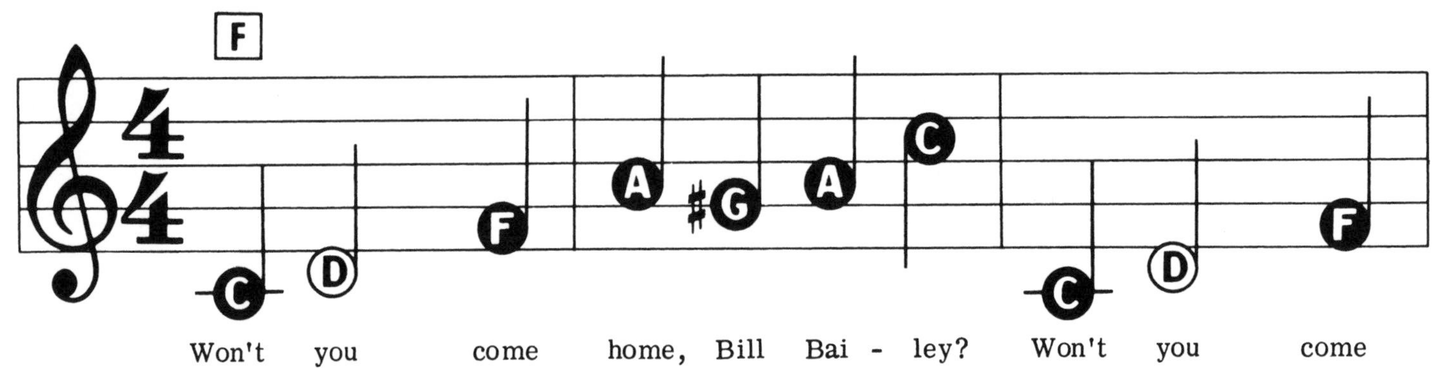

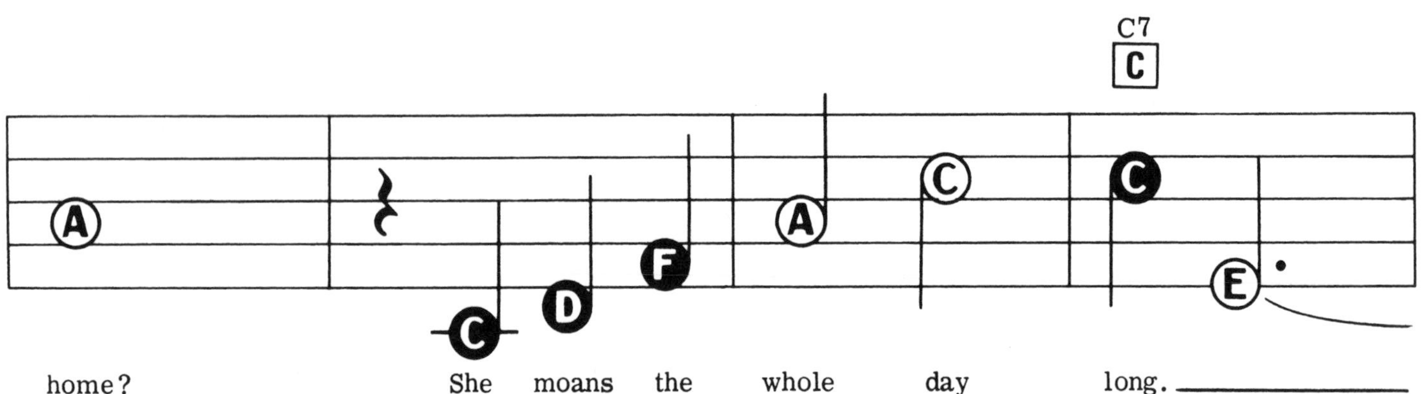

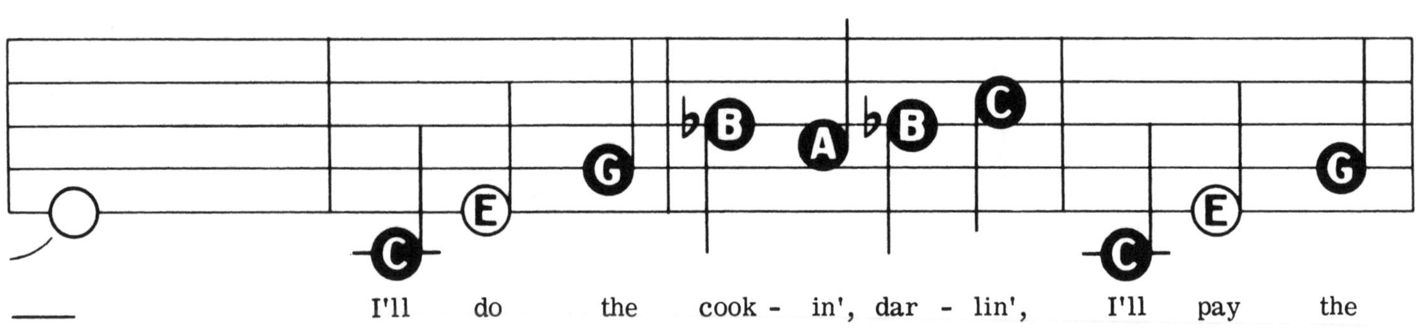

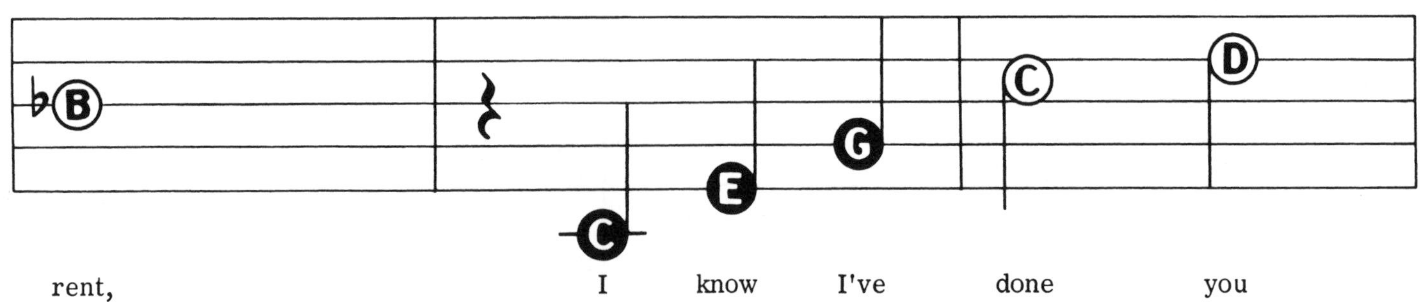

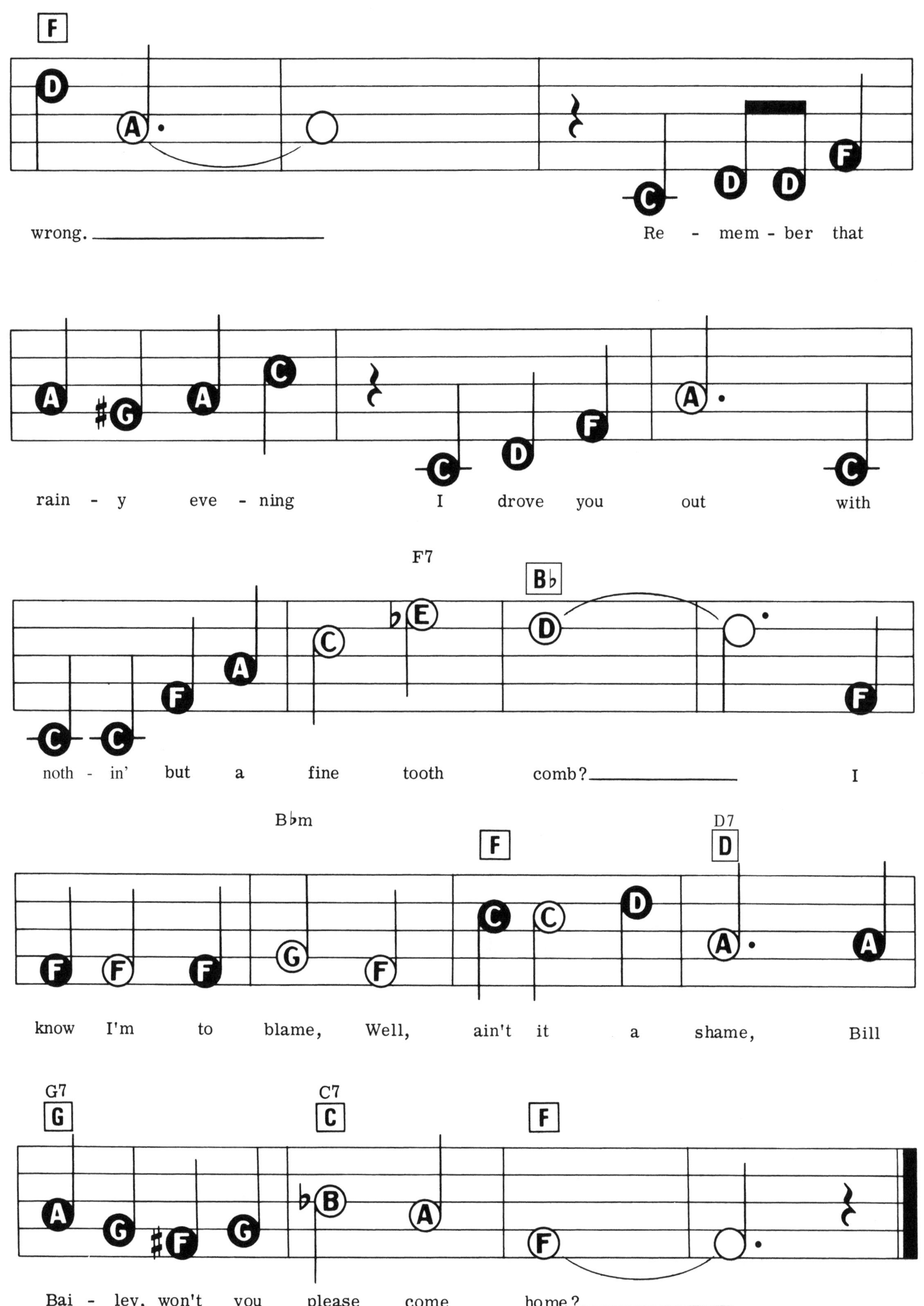
F
D A A C D D F
wrong. Re - mem - ber that
A G A C C D F A C
rain - y eve - ning I drove you out with
F7
B♭
C C F A C E D F
noth - in' but a fine tooth comb? I
B♭m
F
D7
D
F F F G F C C D A A
know I'm to blame, Well, ain't it a shame, Bill
G7
G
C7
C
F
A G F G B A F
Bai - ley, won't you please come home?

By the Light of the Silvery Moon

Registration 2
Rhythm: Swing

Lyric by Ed Madden
Music by Gus Edwards

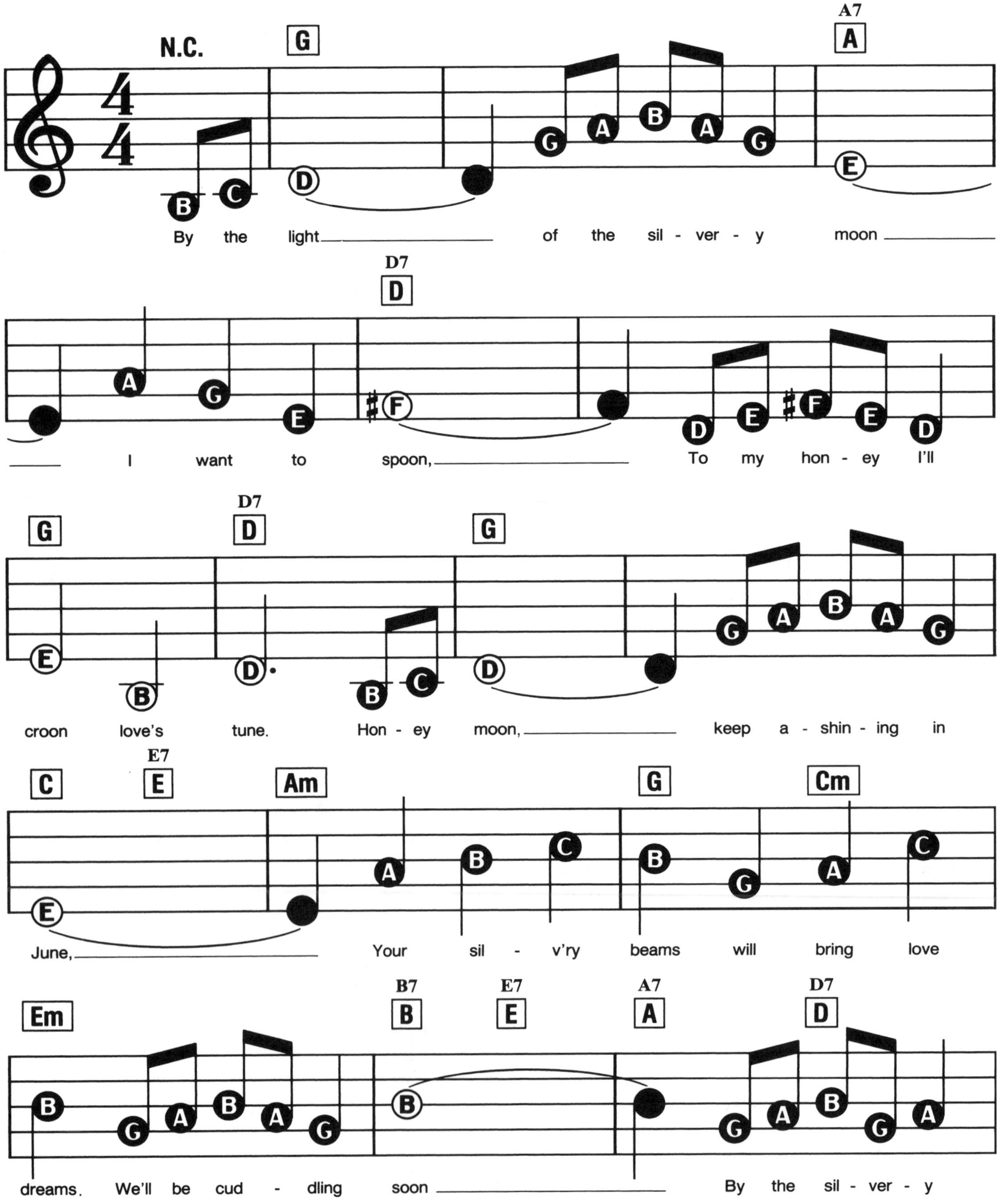

N.C. G A7 A

By the light of the sil - ver - y moon

D7 D

I want to spoon, To my hon - ey I'll

G D7 D G

croon love's tune. Hon - ey moon, keep a - shin - ing in

C E7 E Am G Cm

June, Your sil - v'ry beams will bring love

Em B7 B E7 E A7 A D7 D

dreams. We'll be cud - dling soon By the sil - ver - y

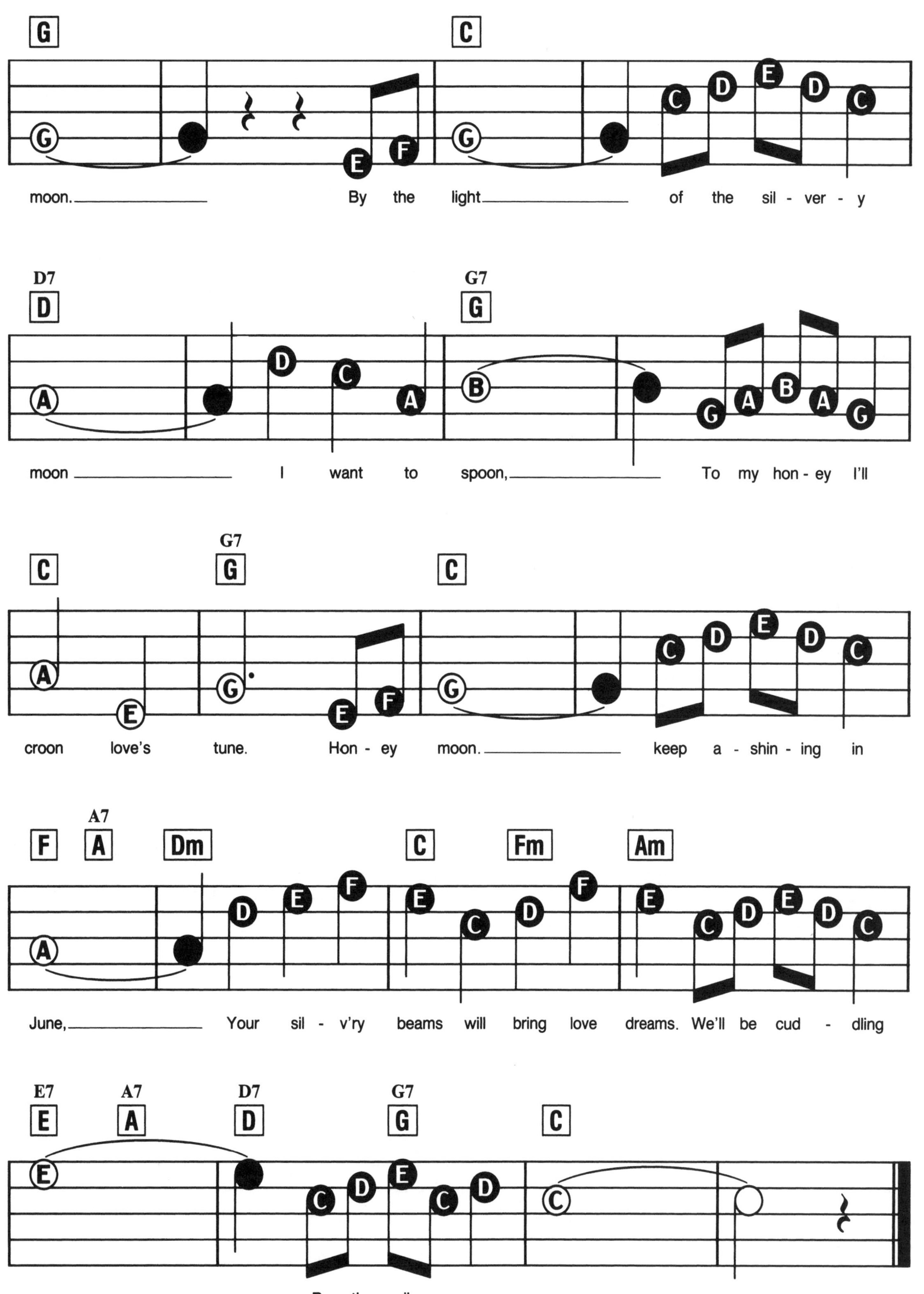
G C
moon. By the light of the sil - ver - y
D7 G7
D G
moon I want to spoon, To my hon - ey I'll
G7
C G C
croon love's tune. Hon - ey moon. keep a - shin - ing in
A7
F A Dm C Fm Am
June, Your sil - v'ry beams will bring love dreams. We'll be cud - dling
E7 A7 D7 G7
E A D G C
soon By the sil - ver - y moon.

Careless Love

Registration 8
Rhythm: Fox Trot or Swing

Anonymous

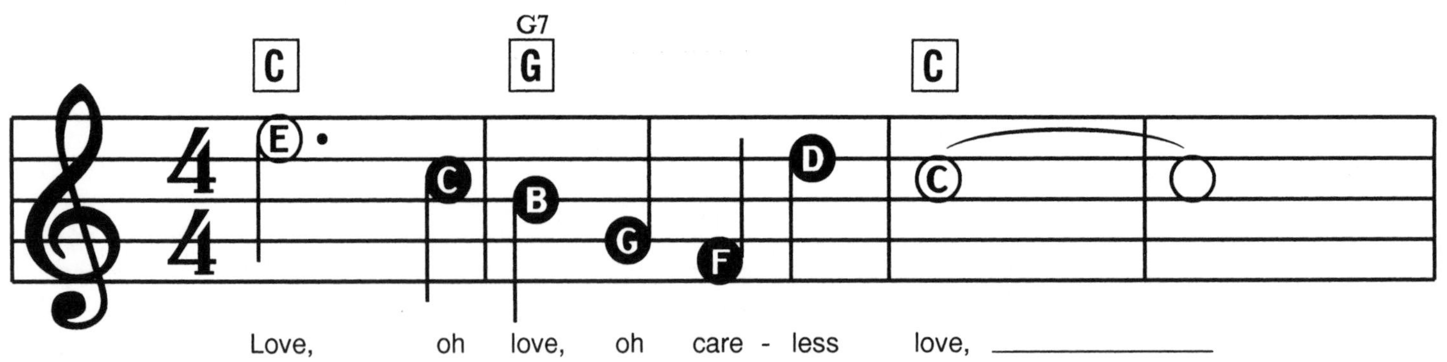

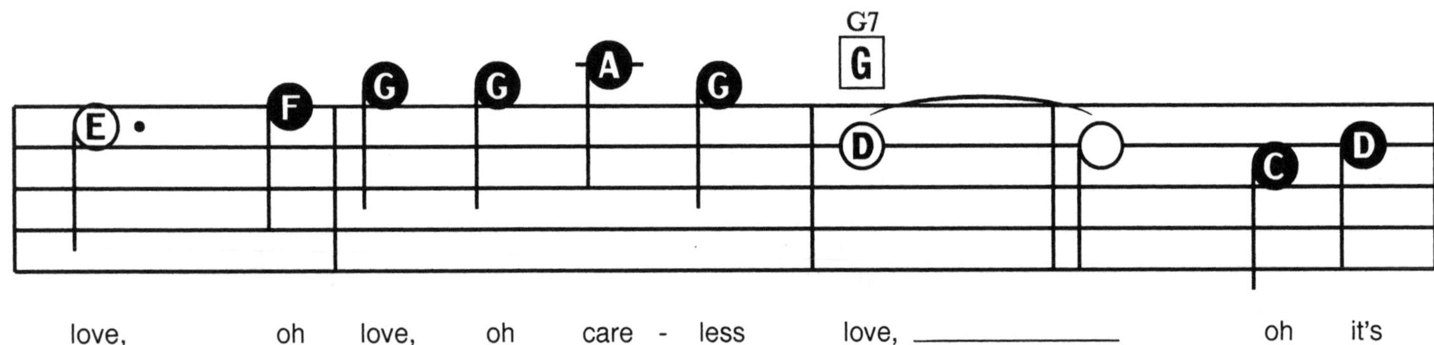

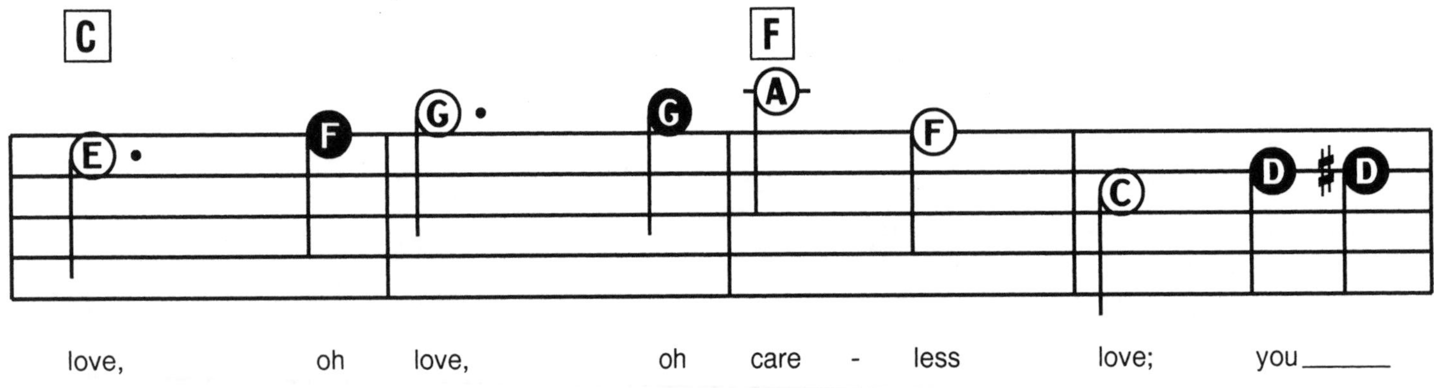

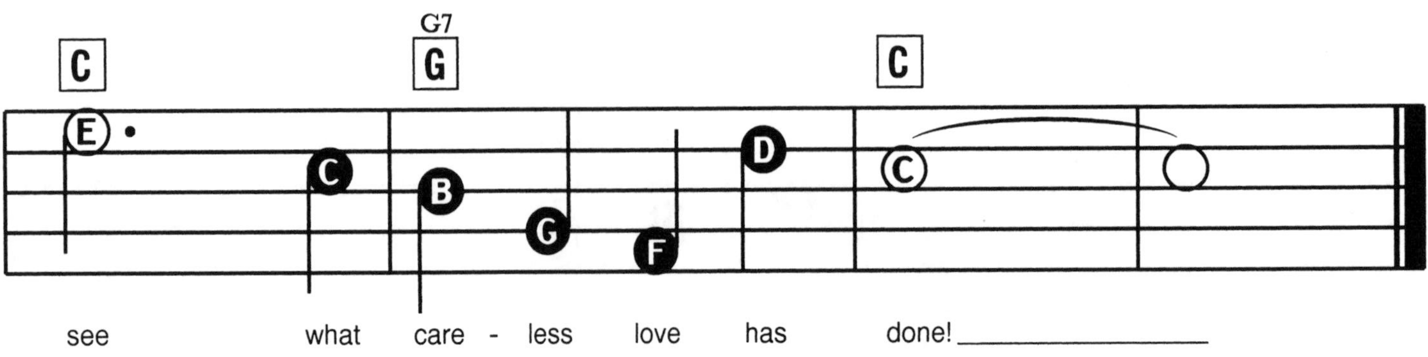

Carolina in the Morning

Registration 5
Rhythm: Swing or Jazz

Lyrics by Gus Kahn
Music by Walter Donaldson

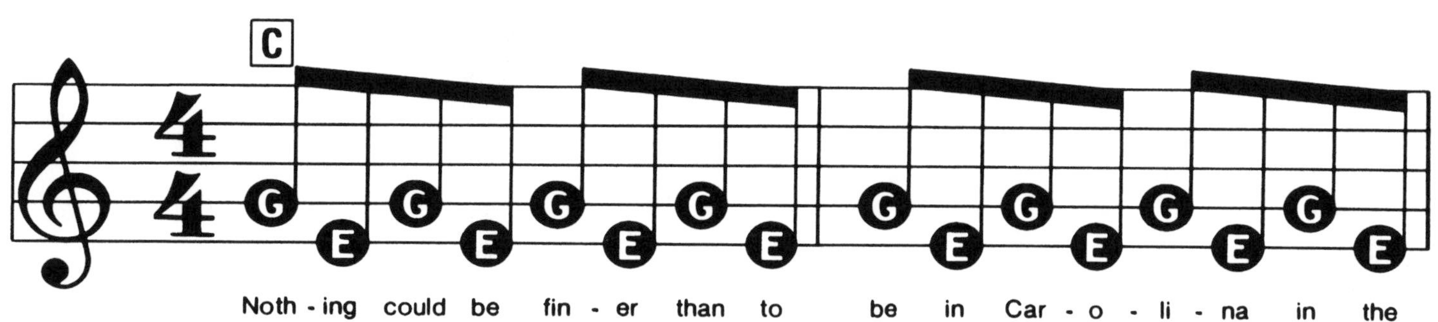

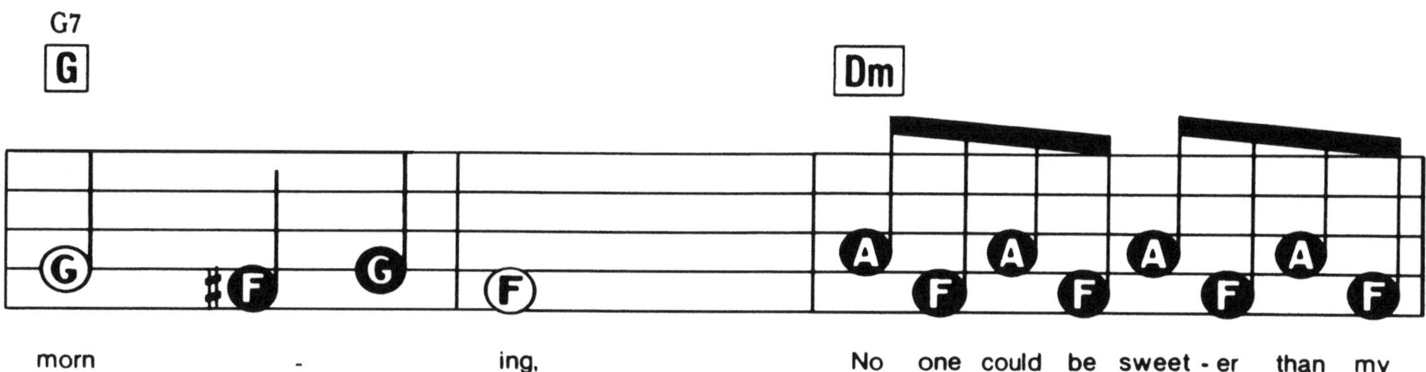

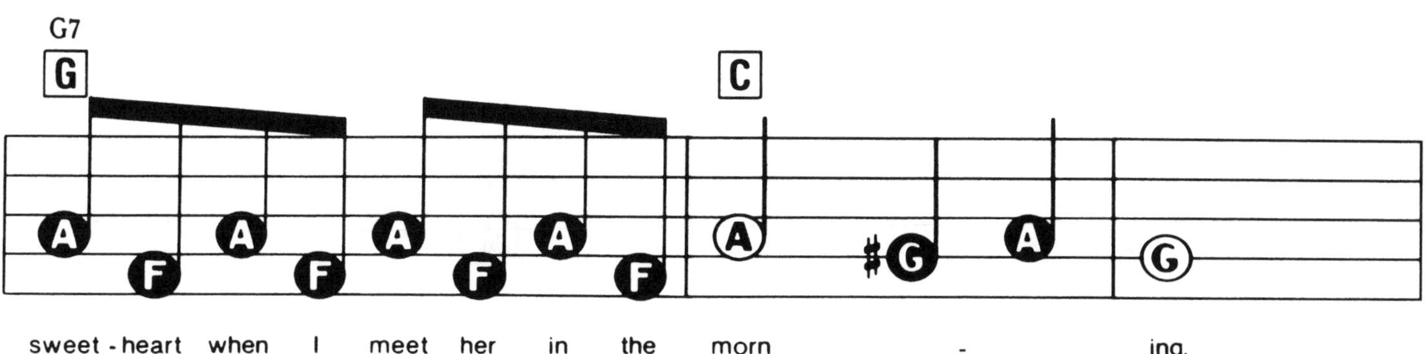

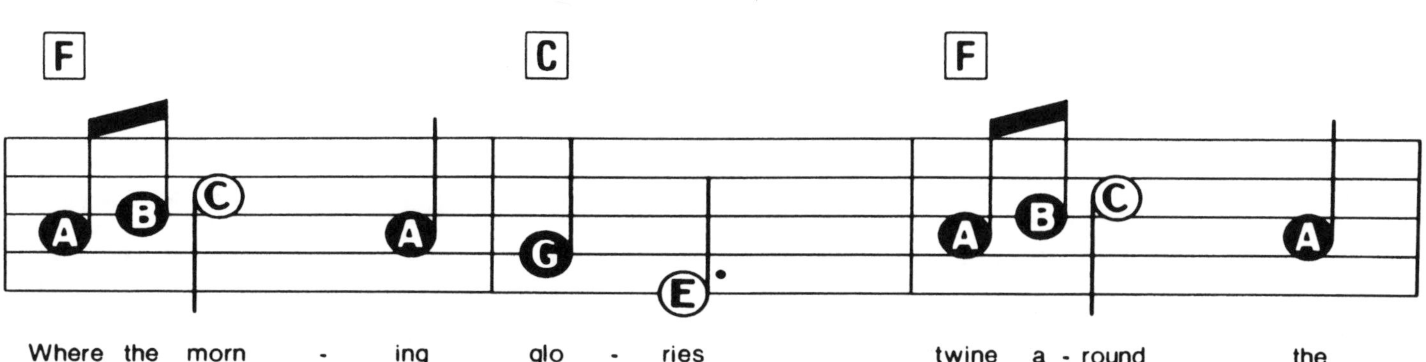

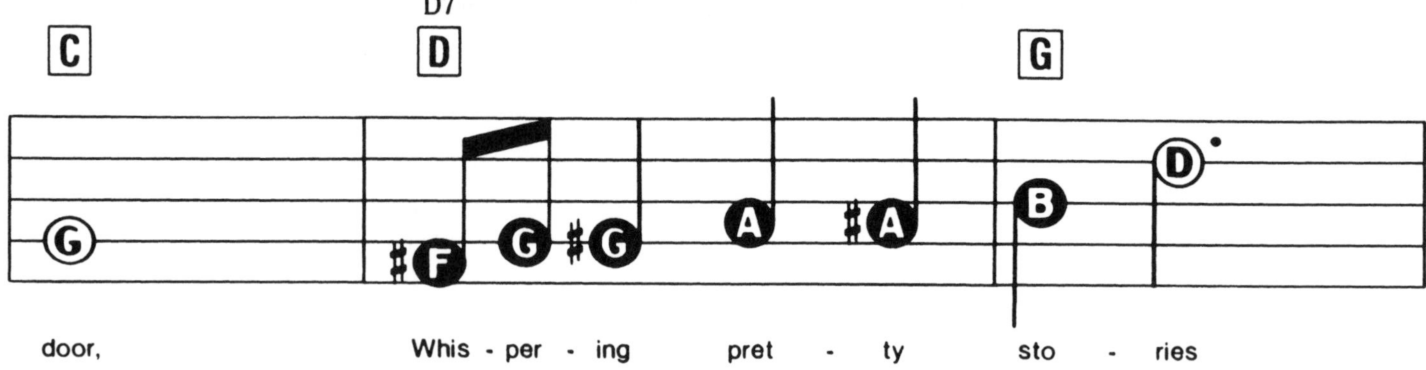
D7
C
D
G
G
F
G
G
A
A
B
D
door,
Whis - per - ing
pret - ty
sto - ries

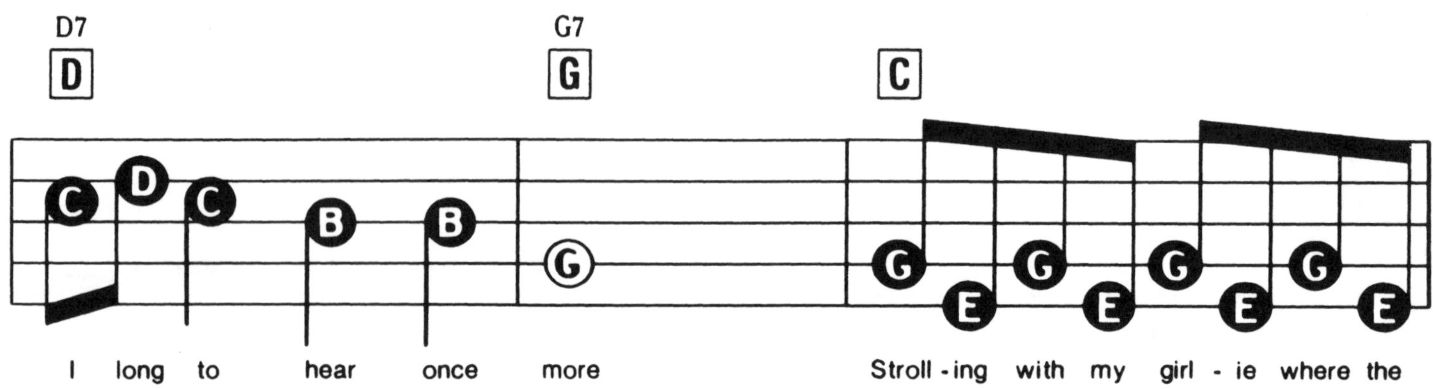
D7
G7
D
G
C
C
D
C
B
B
G
G
E
G
E
G
E
G
E
I long to
hear
once
more
Stroll - ing with my girl - ie where the

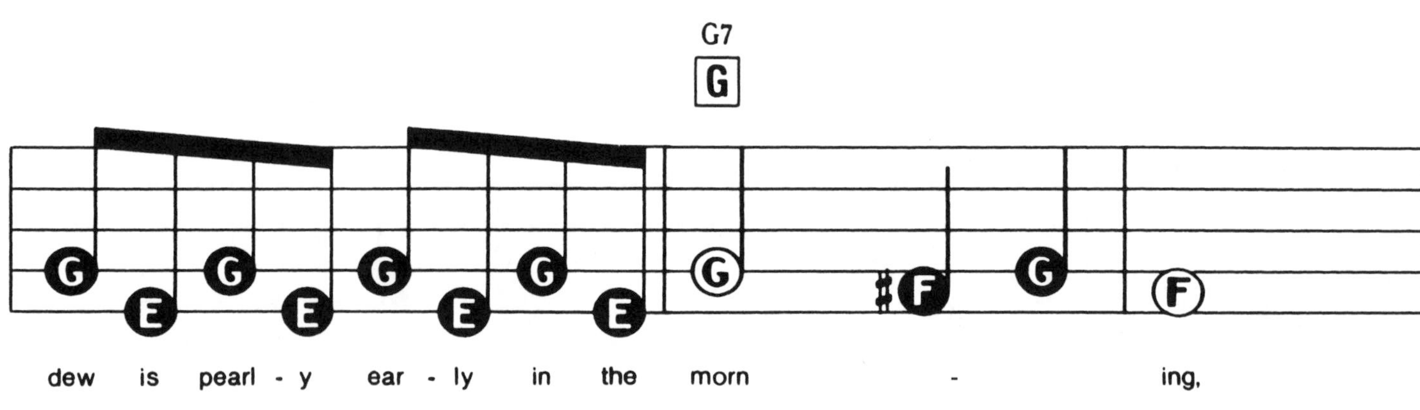
G7
G
G
E
G
E
G
E
G
E
G
F
G
F
dew is pearl - y ear - ly in the morn - ing,

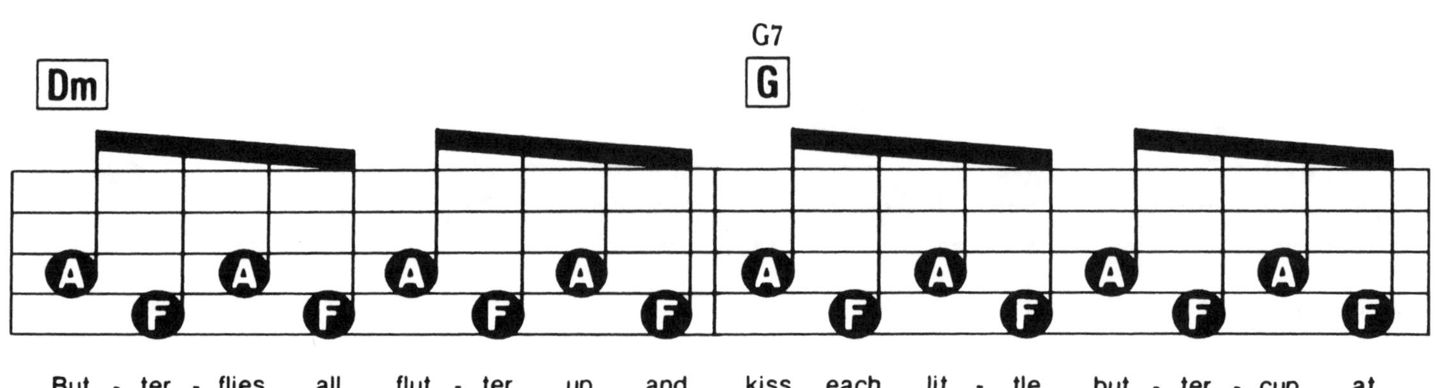
Dm
G7
G
A
F
A
F
A
F
A
F
A
F
A
F
A
F
A
F
But - ter - flies all flut - ter up and kiss each lit - tle but - ter - cup at

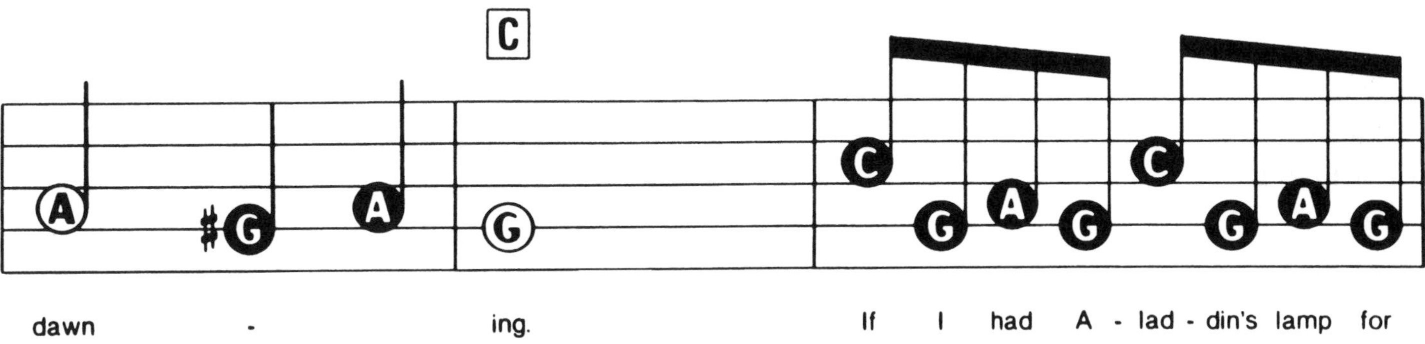
C
A
G
A
G
C
G
A
G
C
G
A
G
dawn - ing. If I had A - lad - din's lamp for

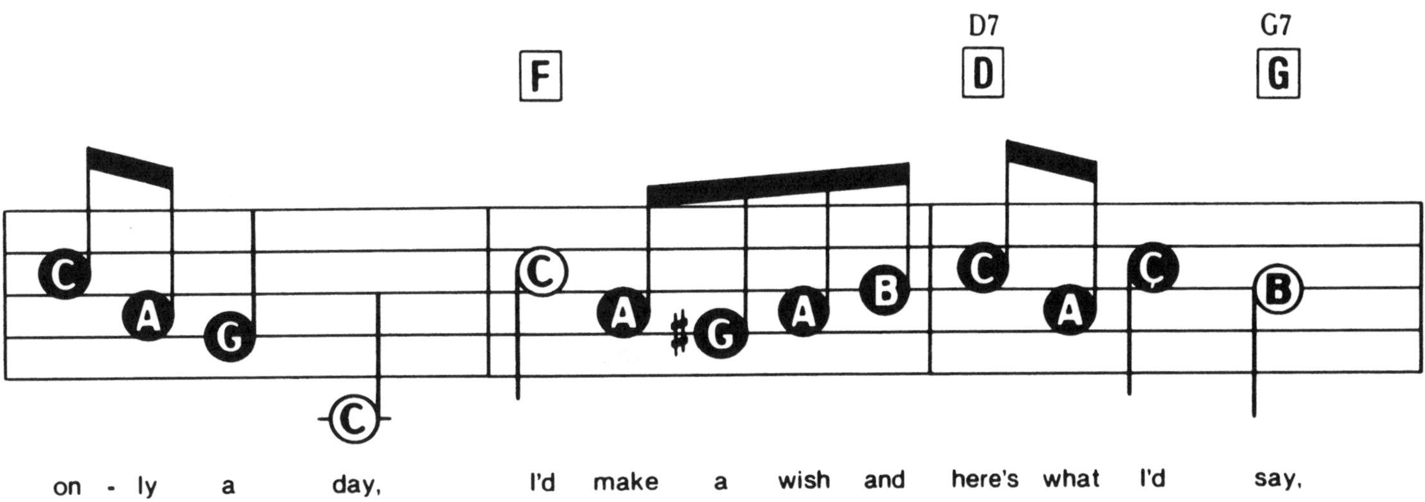
F
D7
D
G7
G
C
A
G
C
C
A
G
A
B
C
A
C
B
on - ly a day, I'd make a wish and here's what I'd say,

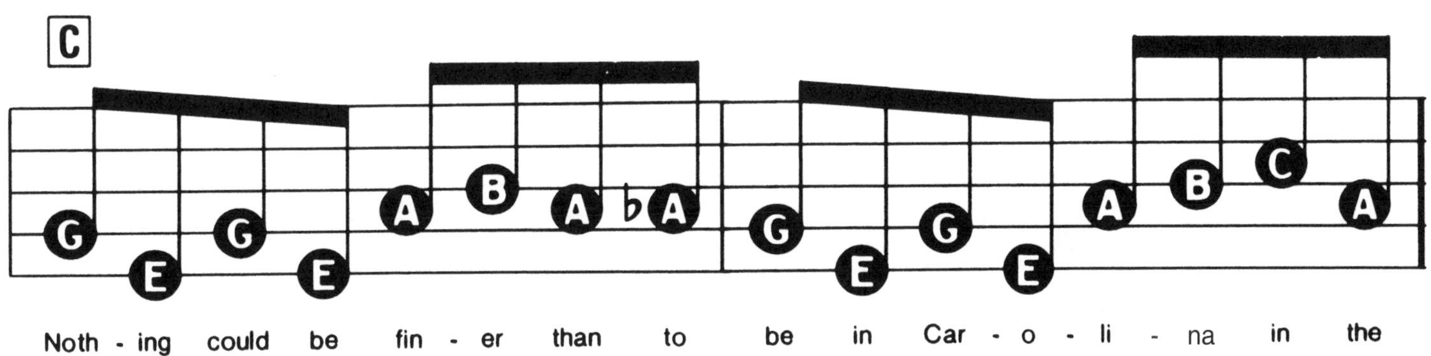
C
G
E
G
E
A
B
A
A
G
E
G
E
A
B
C
A
Noth - ing could be fin - er than to be in Car - o - li - na in the

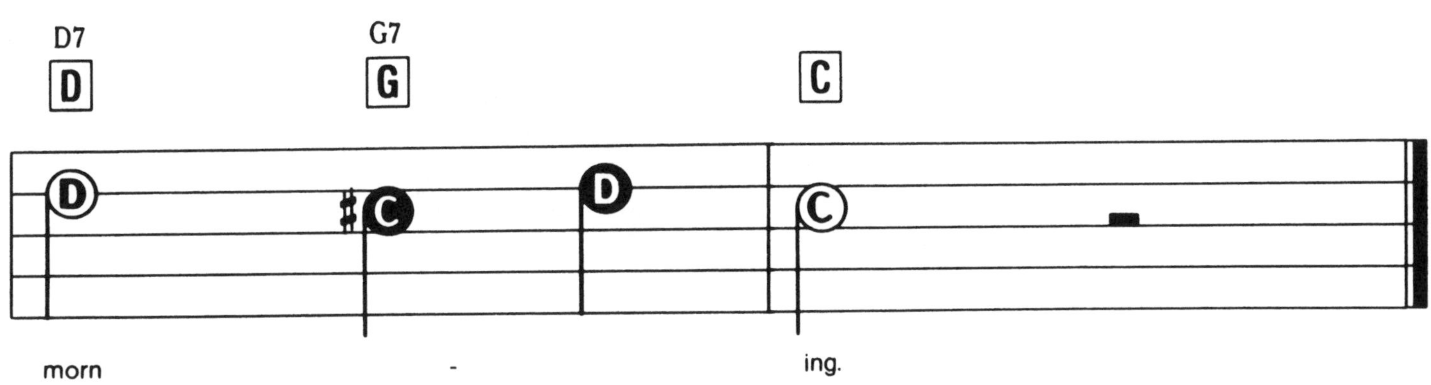
D7
D
G7
G
C
D
C
D
C
morn - ing.

Chicago
(That Toddlin' Town)

Registration 7
Rhythm: Swing

Words and Music by
Fred Fisher

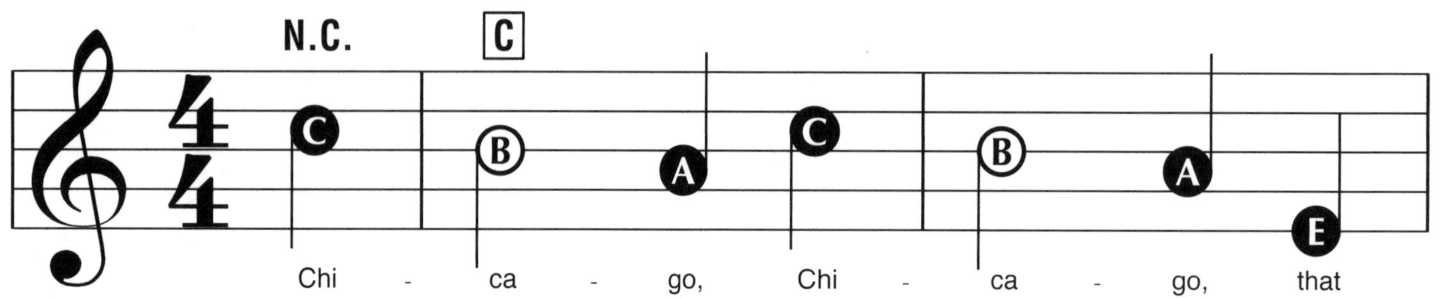

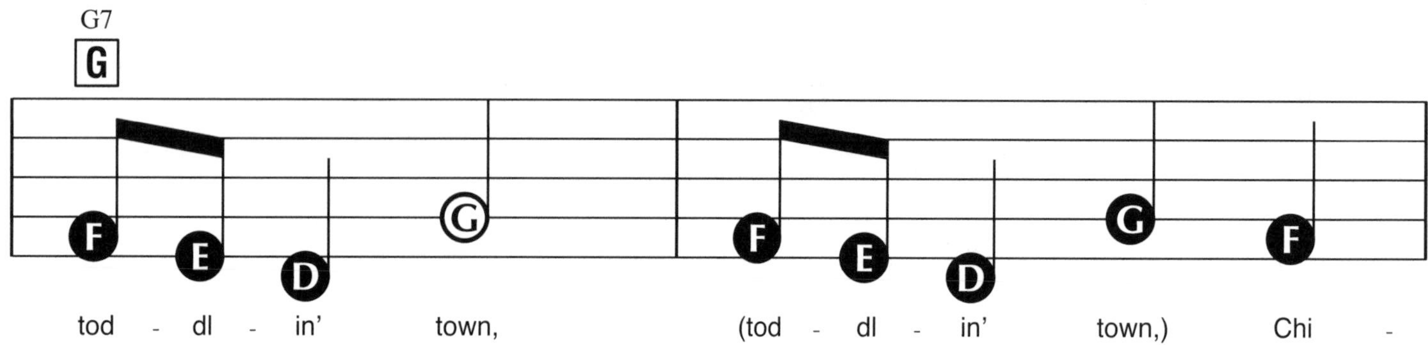

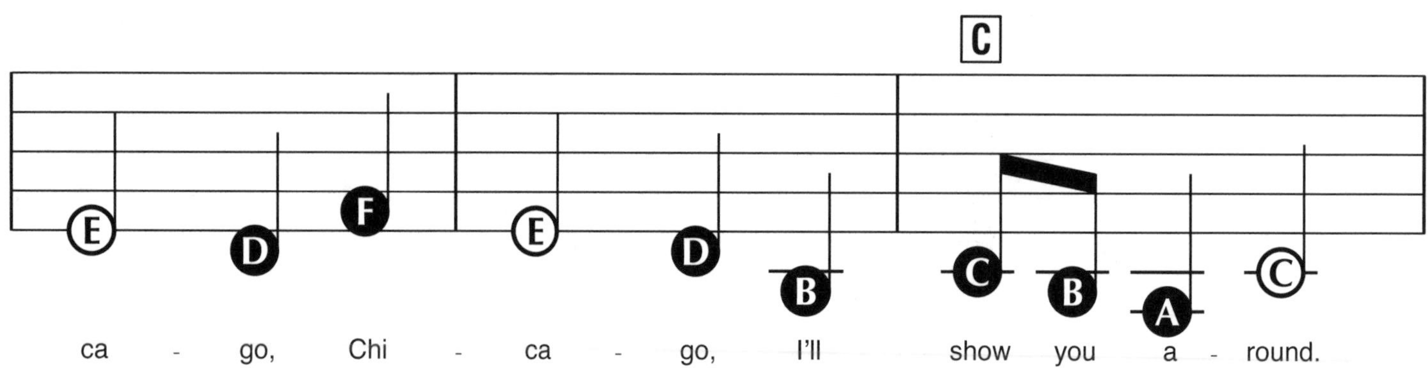

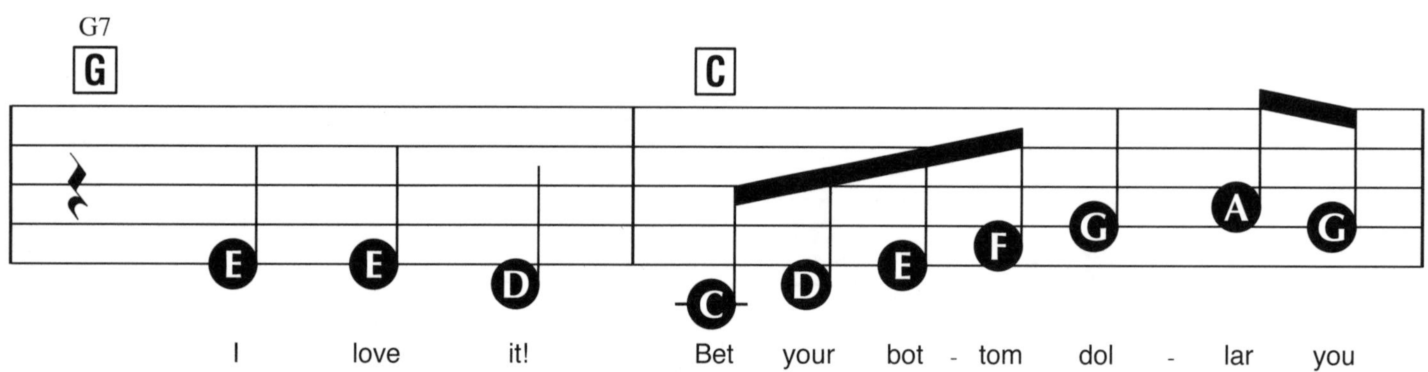

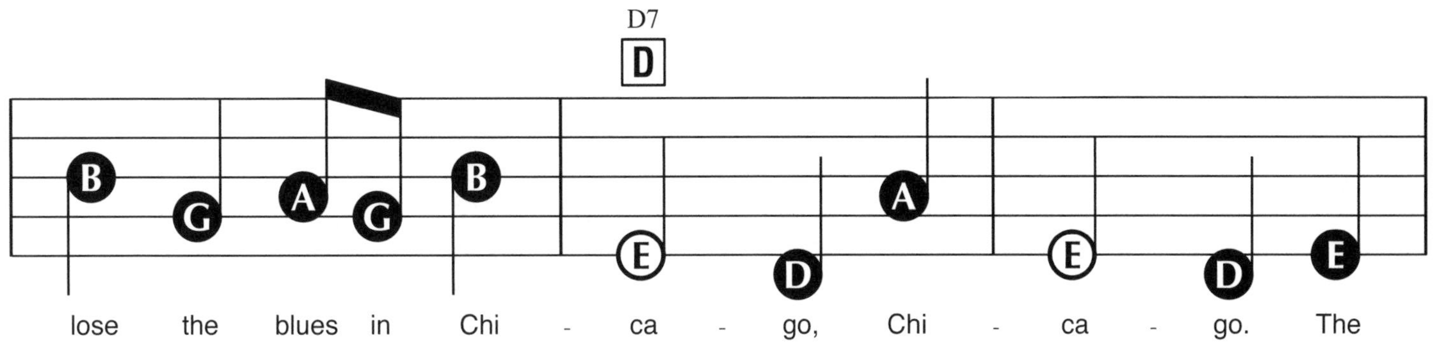
D7
D
B
G
A
G
B
E
D
A
E
D
E
lose the blues in Chi - ca - go, Chi - ca - go. The

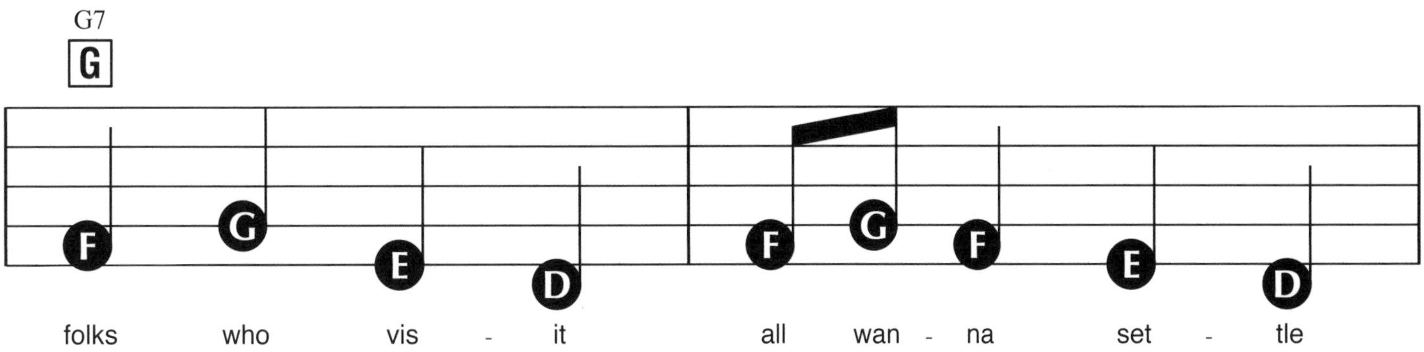
G7
G
F
G
E
D
F
G
F
E
D
folks who vis - it all wan - na set - tle

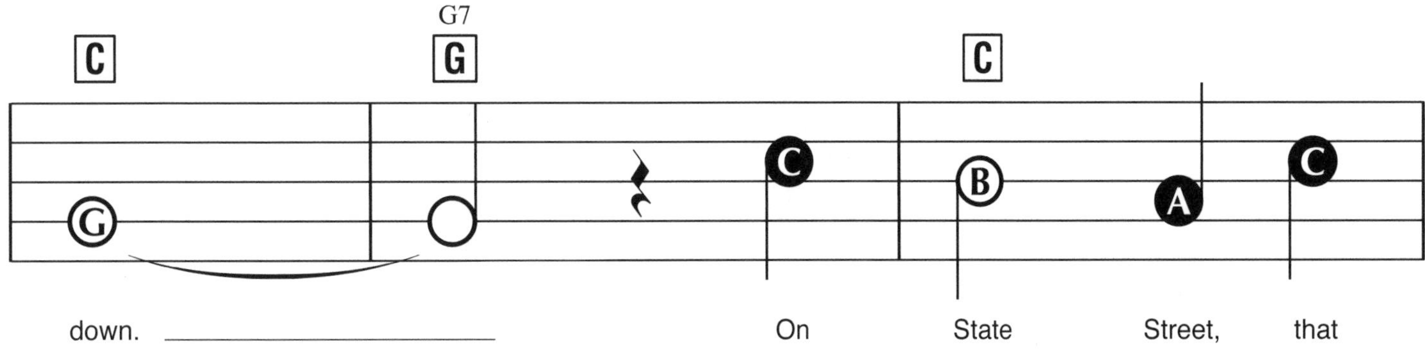
C
G7
G
C
G
G
C
B
A
C
down. On State Street, that

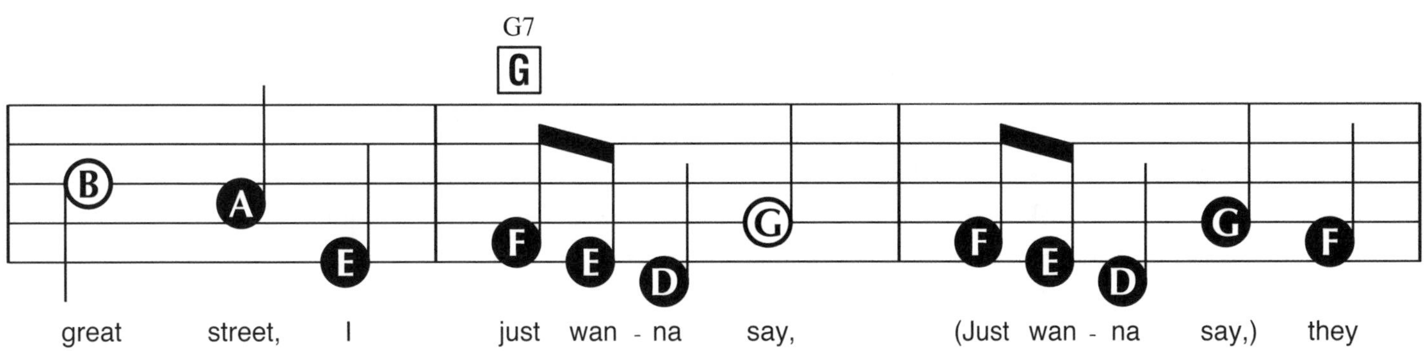
G7
G
B
A
E
F
E
D
G
F
E
D
G
F
great street, I just wan - na say, (Just wan - na say,) they

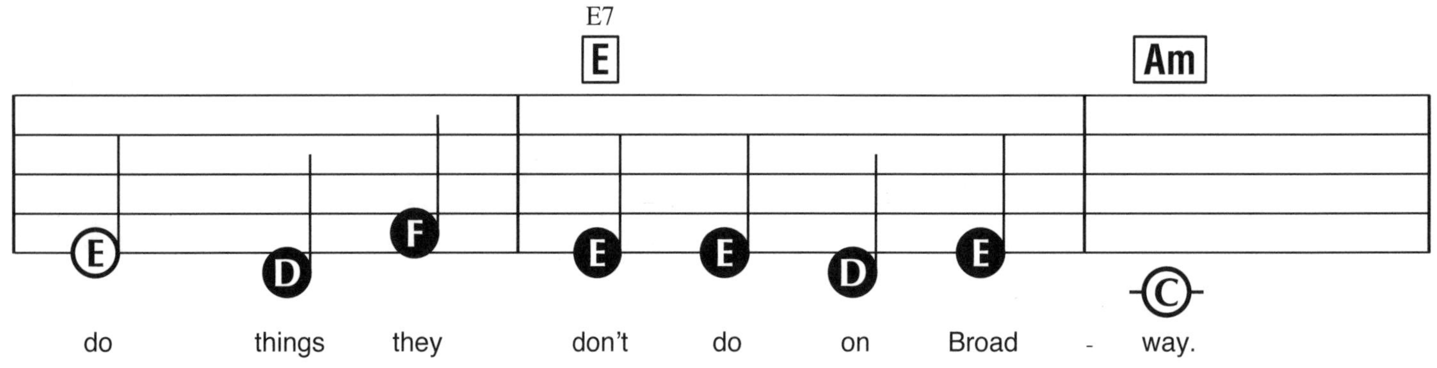
E7
E
Am
E D F E E D E C
do things they don't do on Broad - way.

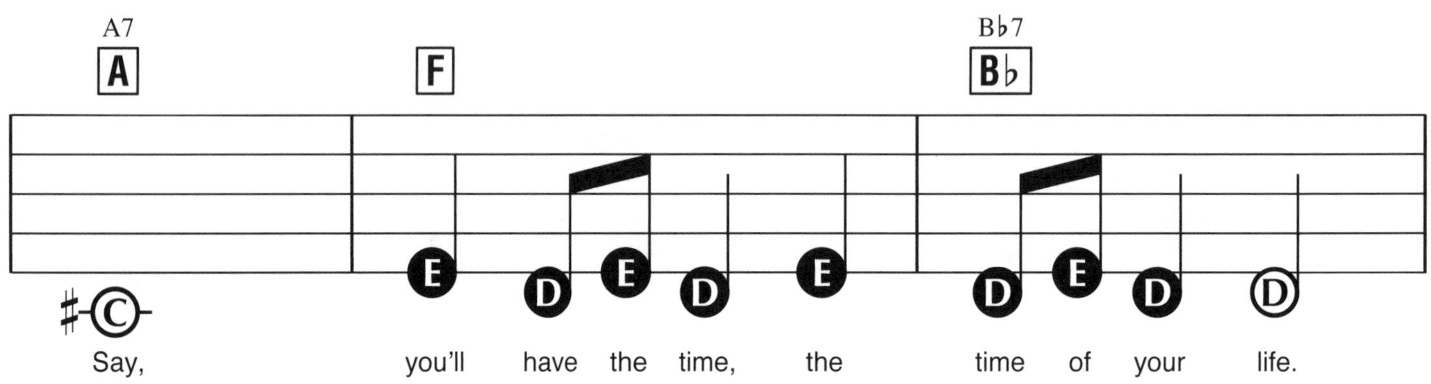
A7
A
F
B♭7
B♭
♯C E D E D E D E D D
Say, you'll have the time, the time of your life.

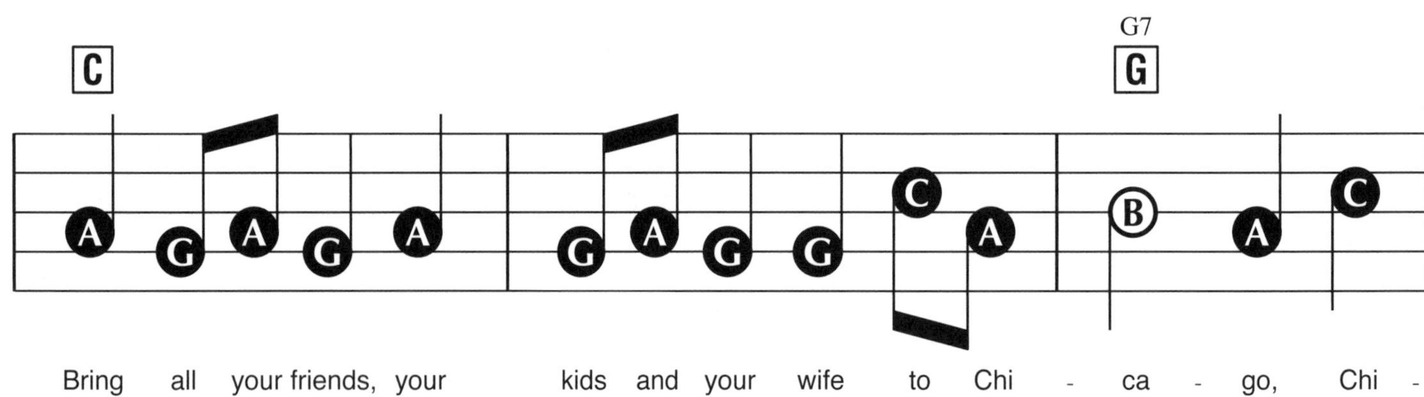
C
G7
G
A G A G A G A G G C A B A C
Bring all your friends, your kids and your wife to Chi - ca - go, Chi -

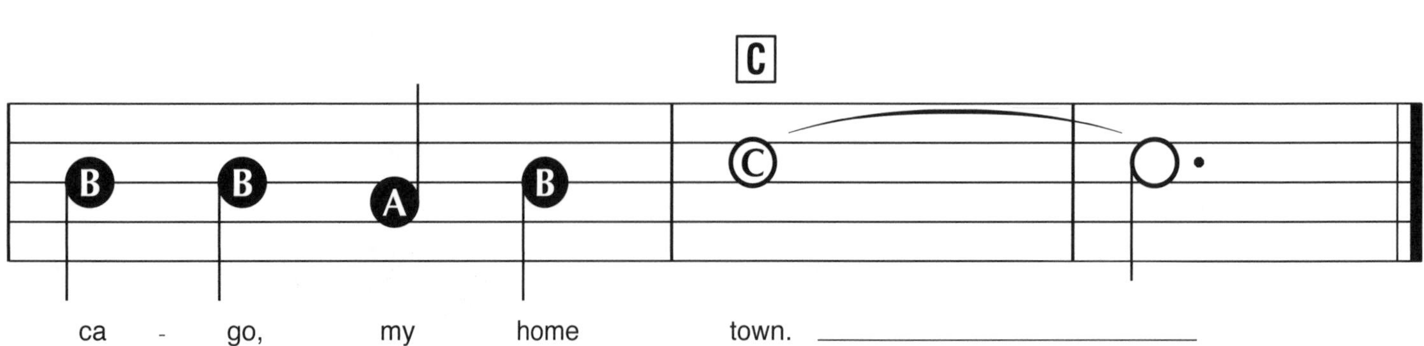
C
B B A B C
ca - go, my home town.

Good Night, Ladies

Registration 3
Rhythm: Fox Trot

Words by E.P. Christy
Traditional Music

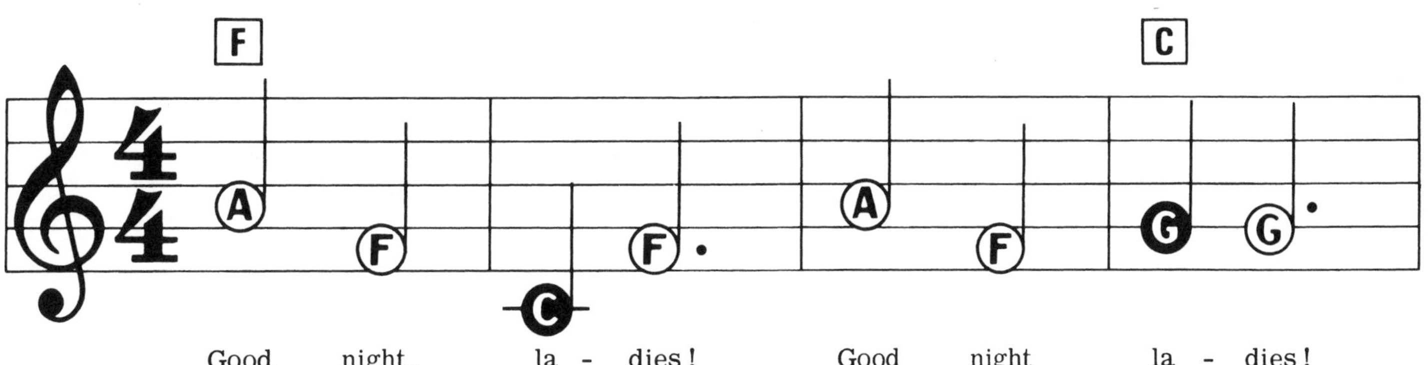

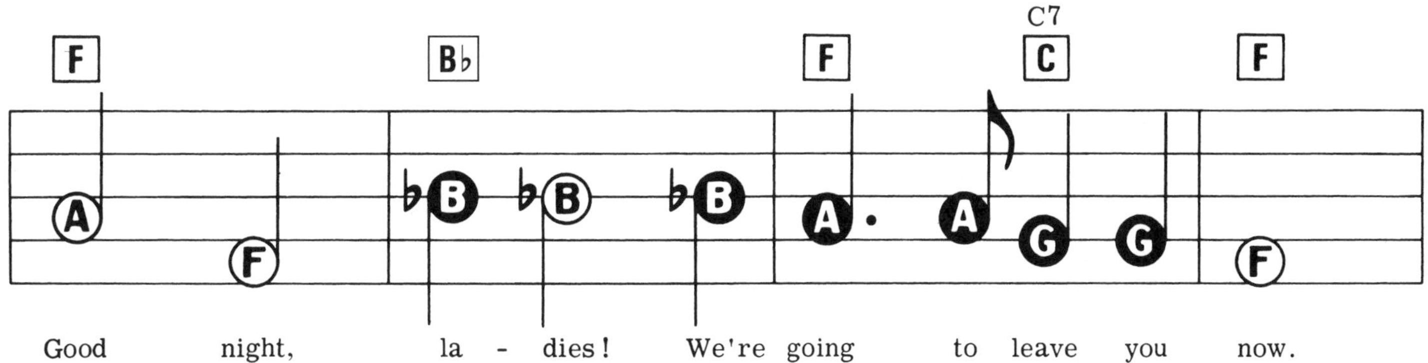

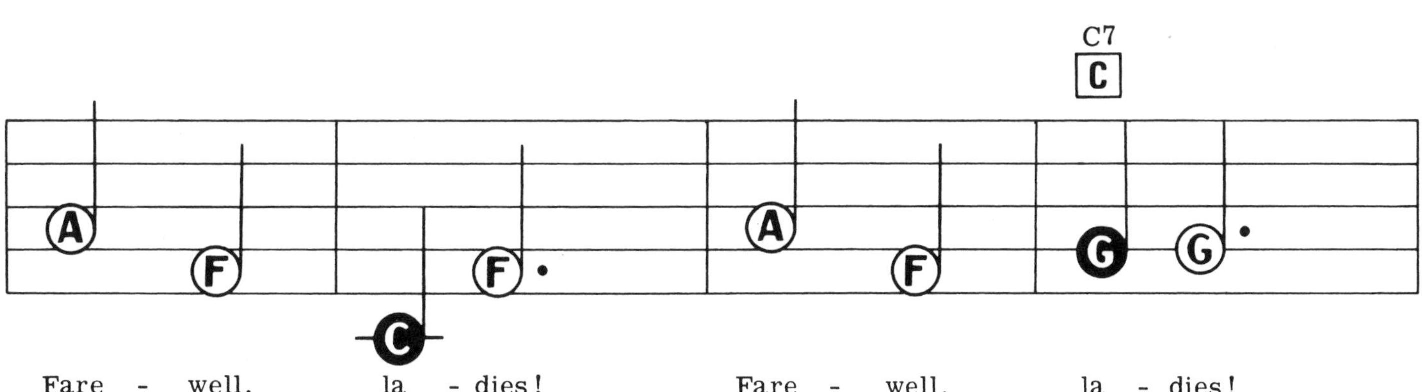

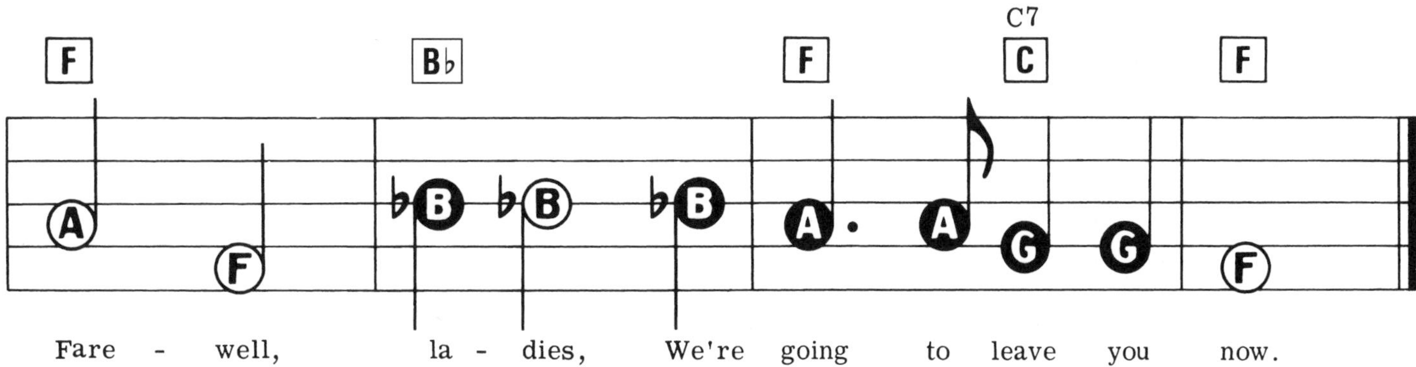

Chinatown, My Chinatown

Registration 4
Rhythm: Swing

Words by William Jerome
Music by Jean Schwartz

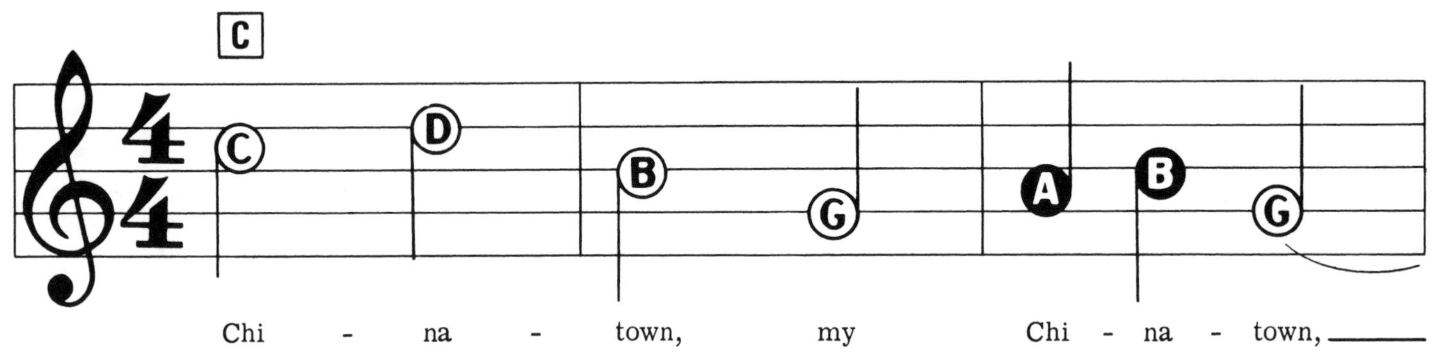

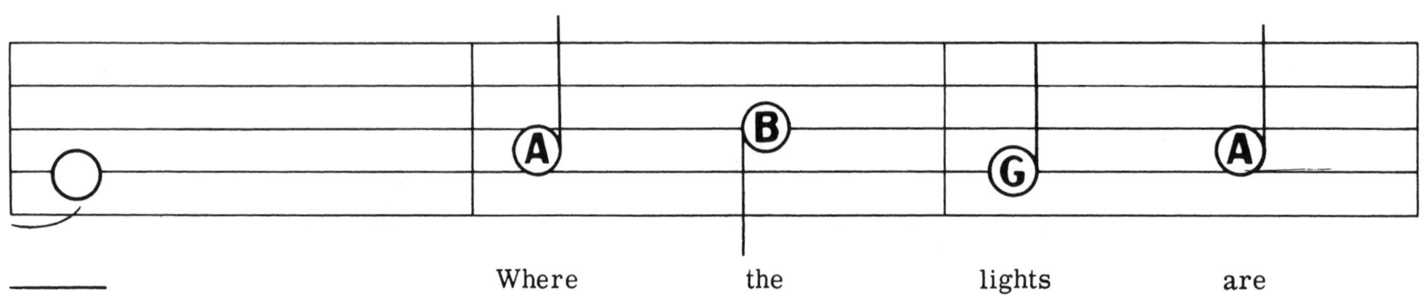

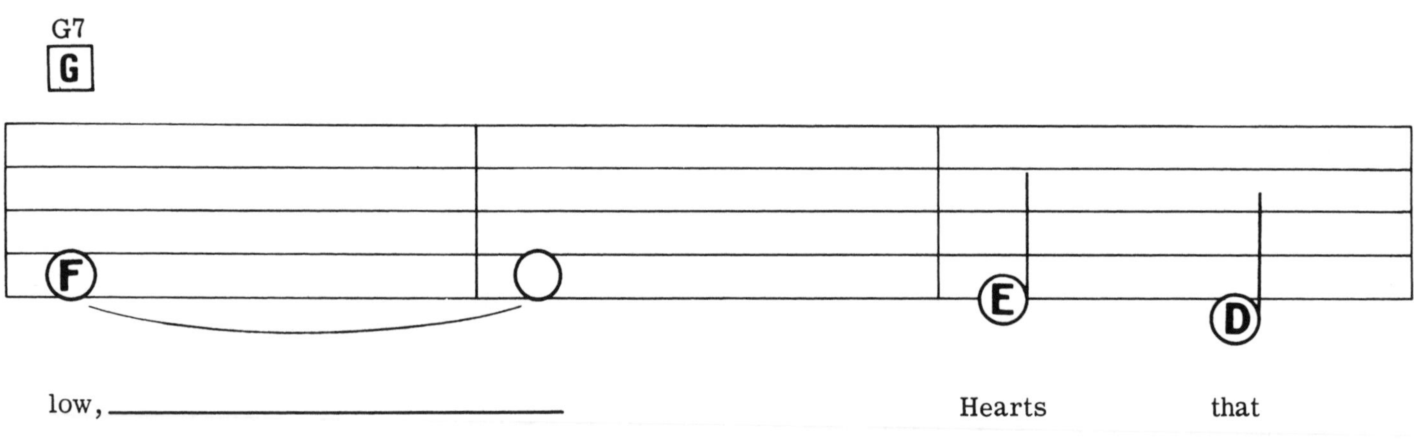

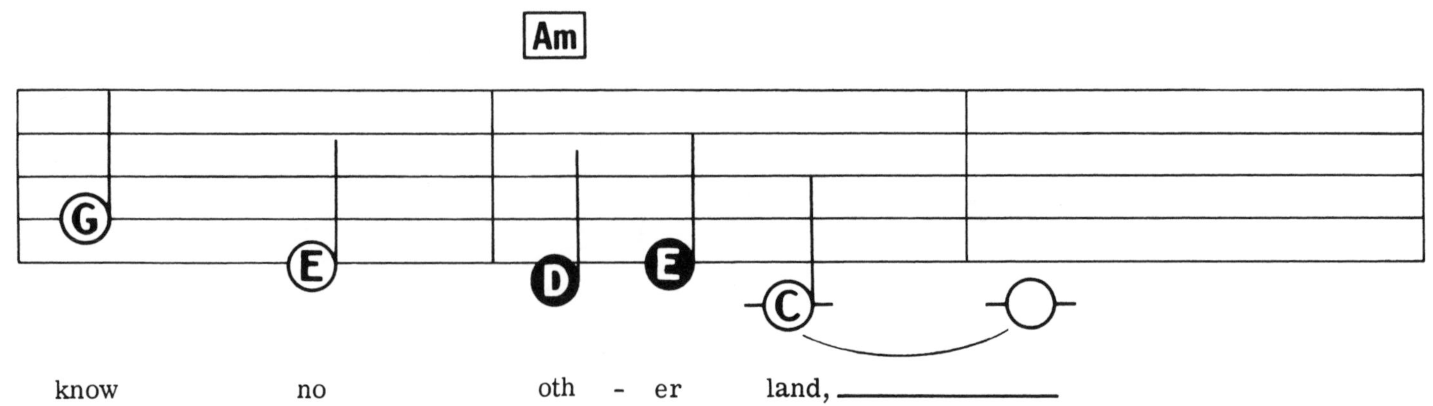

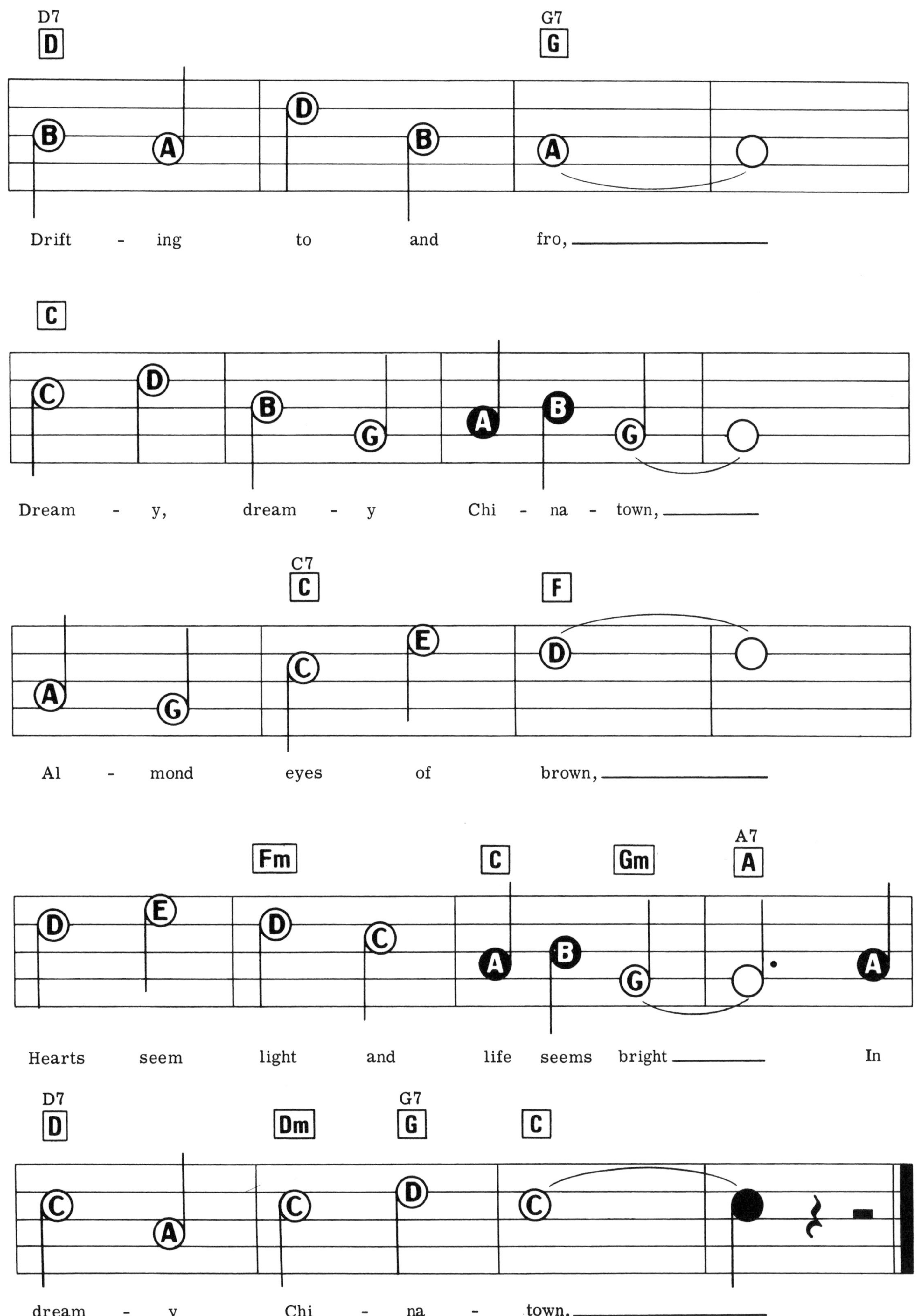
D7 D
G7 G
B A D B A
Drift - ing to and fro,
C
C D B G A B G
Dream - y, dream - y Chi - na - town,
C7 C
F
A G C E D
Al - mond eyes of brown,
Fm
C
Gm
A7 A
D E D C A B G A
Hearts seem light and life seems bright In
D7 D
Dm
G7 G
C
C A C D C
dream - y Chi - na - town.

(Oh, My Darling)
Clementine

Registration 5
Rhythm: Waltz

Words and Music by
Percy Montrose

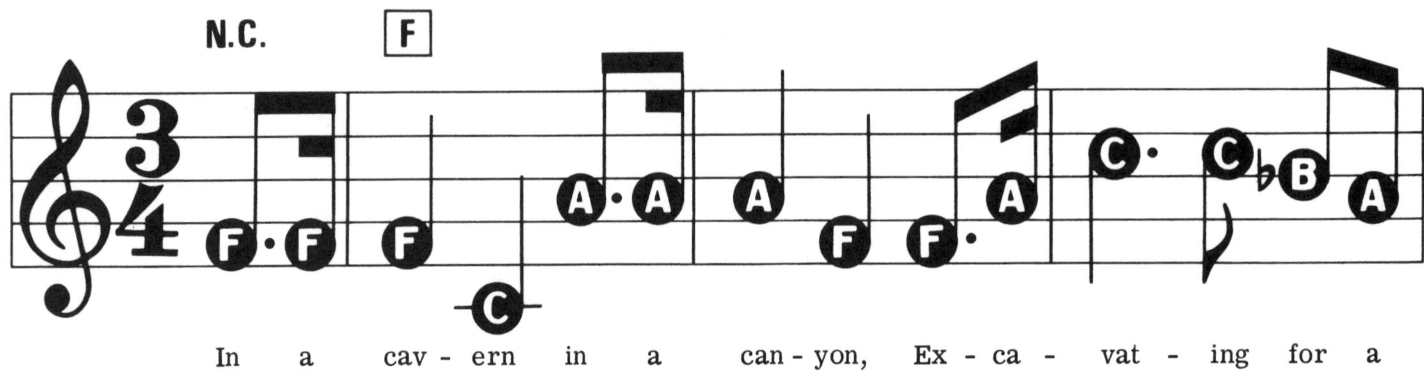

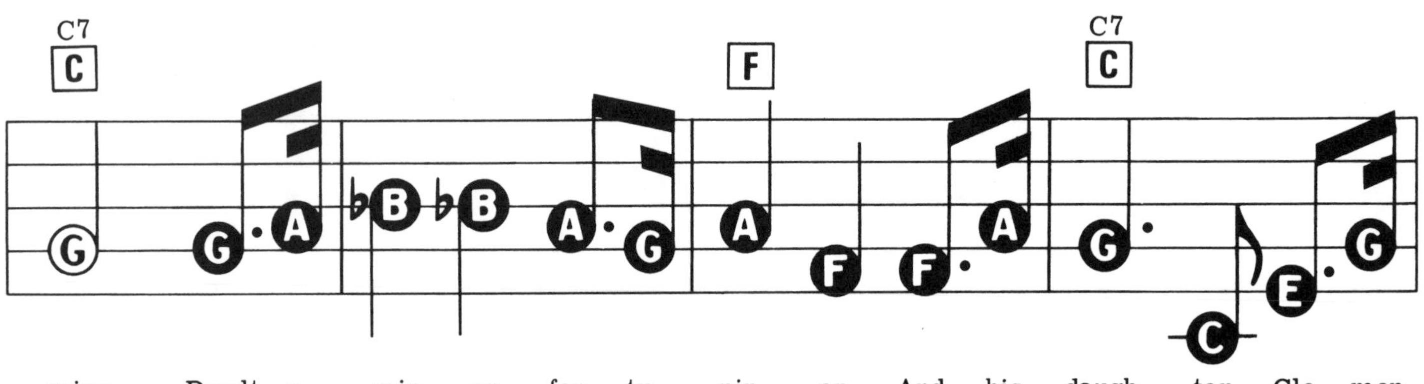

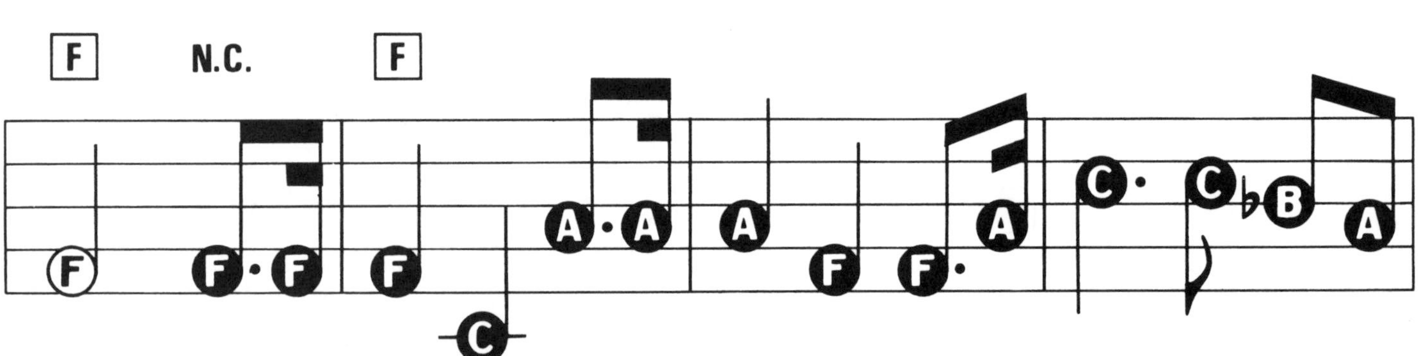

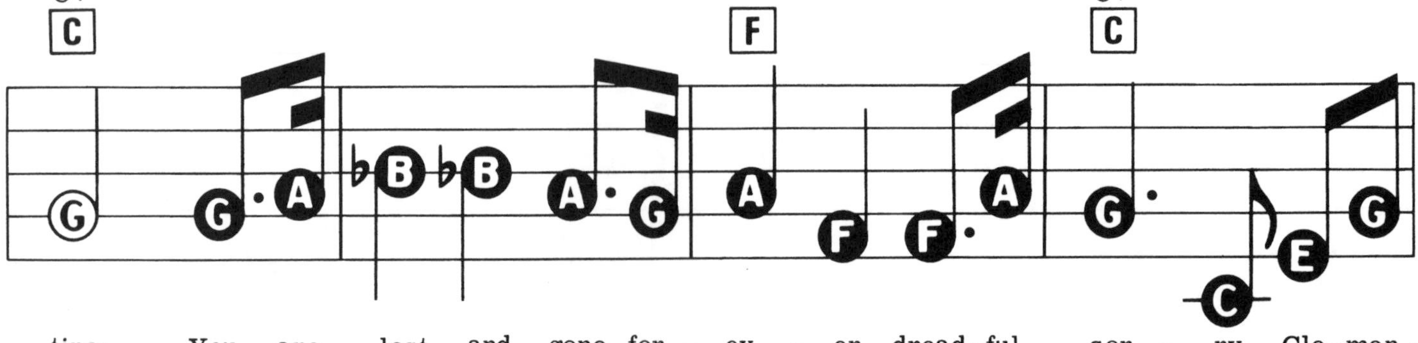

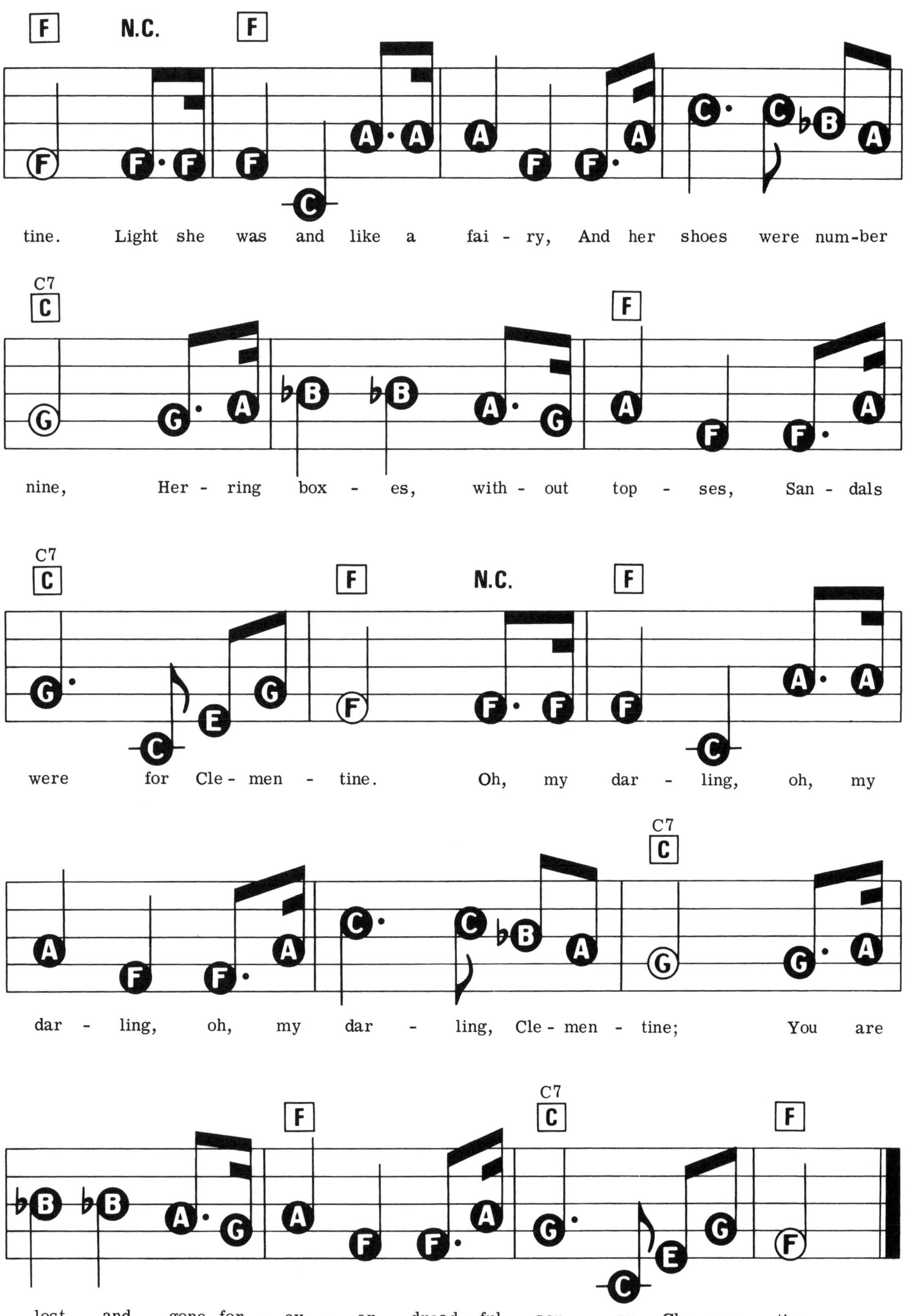
F N.C. F
tine. Light she was and like a fai - ry, And her shoes were num-ber
C7 C F
nine, Her - ring box - es, with - out top - ses, San - dals
C7 C F N.C. F
were for Cle - men - tine. Oh, my dar - ling, oh, my
C7 C
dar - ling, oh, my dar - ling, Cle - men - tine; You are
F C7 C F
lost and gone for - ev - er dread - ful sor - ry Cle - men - tine.

Cuddle Up a Little Closer, Lovey Mine

from THE THREE TWINS

Registration 3
Rhythm: Swing

Words by Otto Harbach
Music by Karl Hoshna

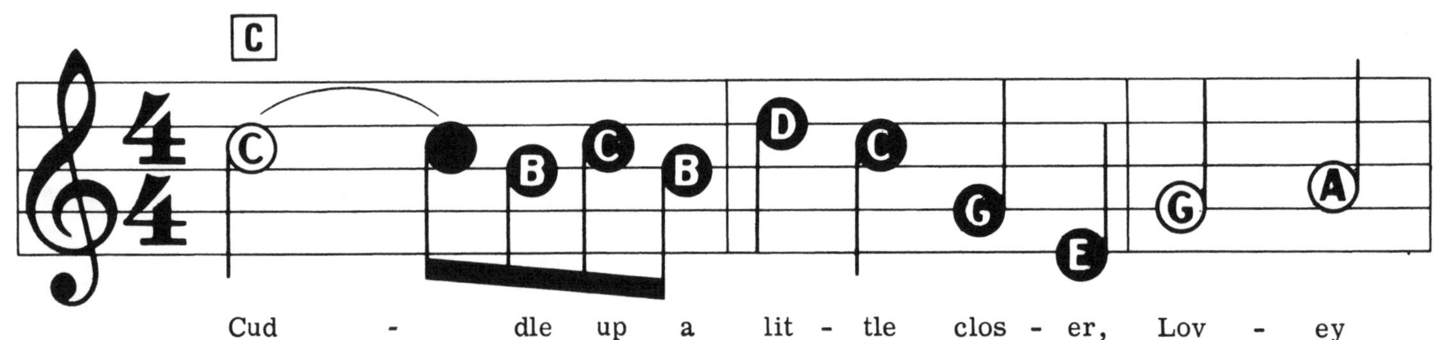

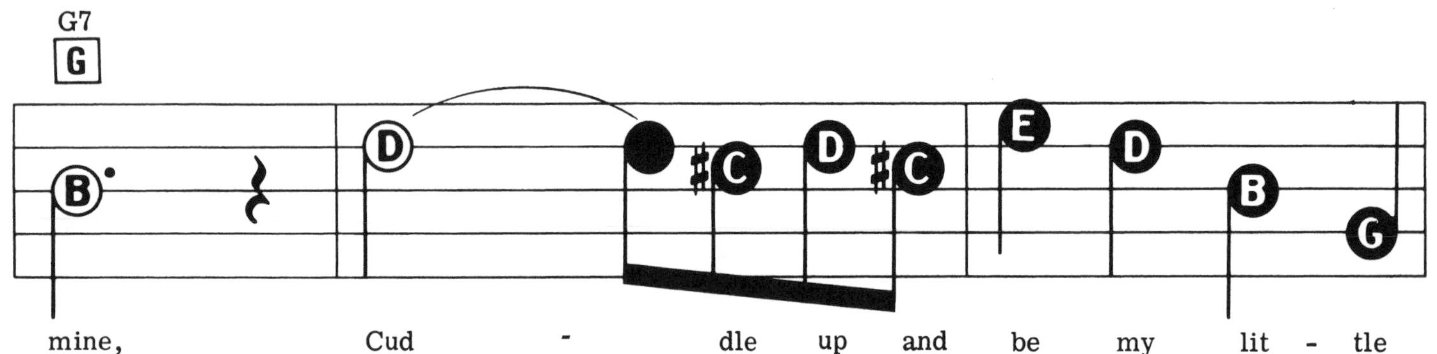

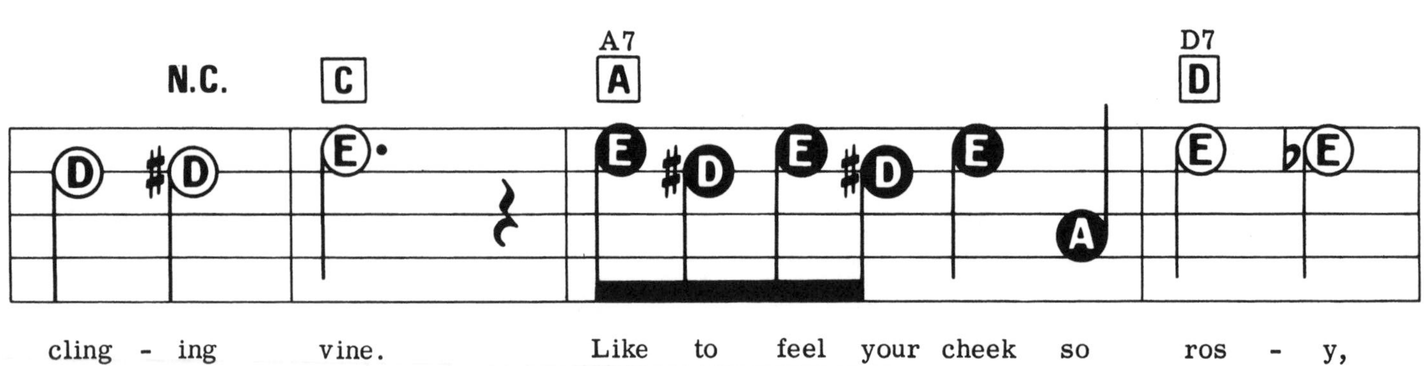

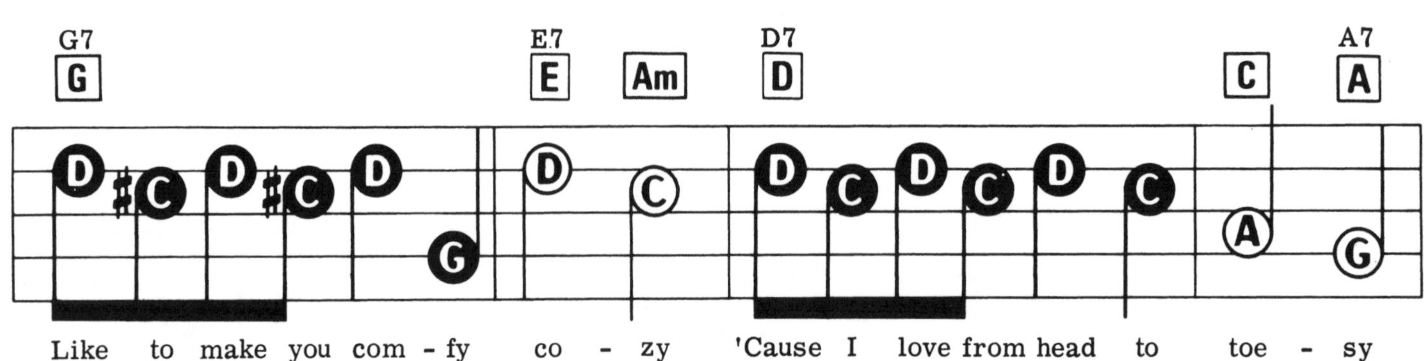

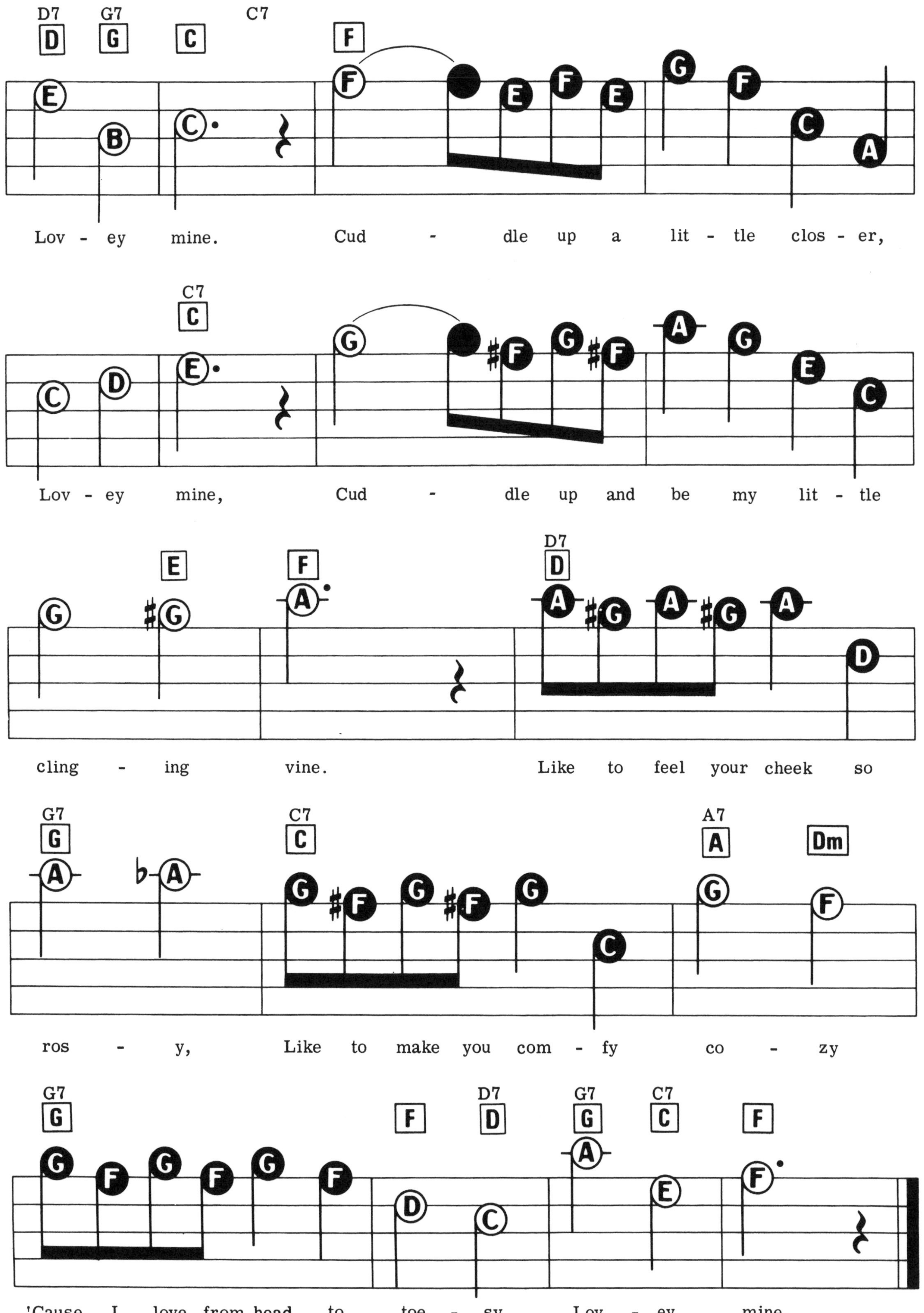
D7 G7 C7
Lov - ey mine. Cud - dle up a lit - tle clos - er,
C7
Lov - ey mine, Cud - dle up and be my lit - tle
D7
cling - ing vine. Like to feel your cheek so
G7 C7 A7 Dm
ros - y, Like to make you com - fy co - zy
G7 D7 G7 C7
'Cause I love from head to toe - sy Lov - ey mine.

The Darktown Strutters' Ball
from THE STORY OF VERNON AND IRENE CASTLE

Registration 8
Rhythm: Polka, Fox Trot or Dixie

Words and Music by
Shelton Brooks

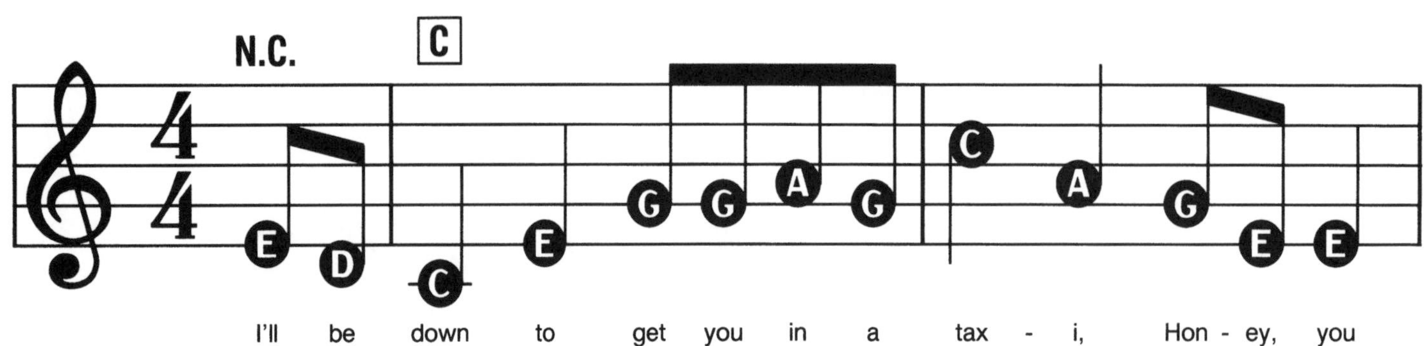

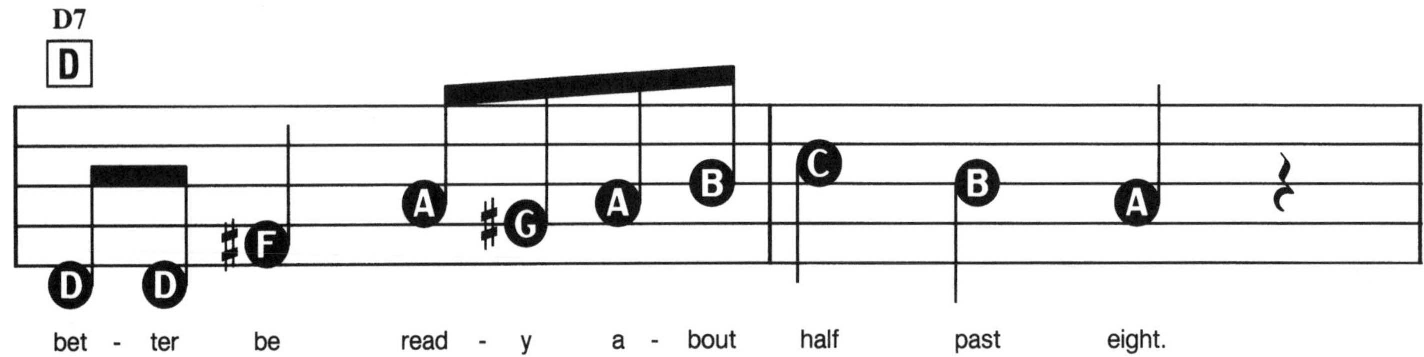

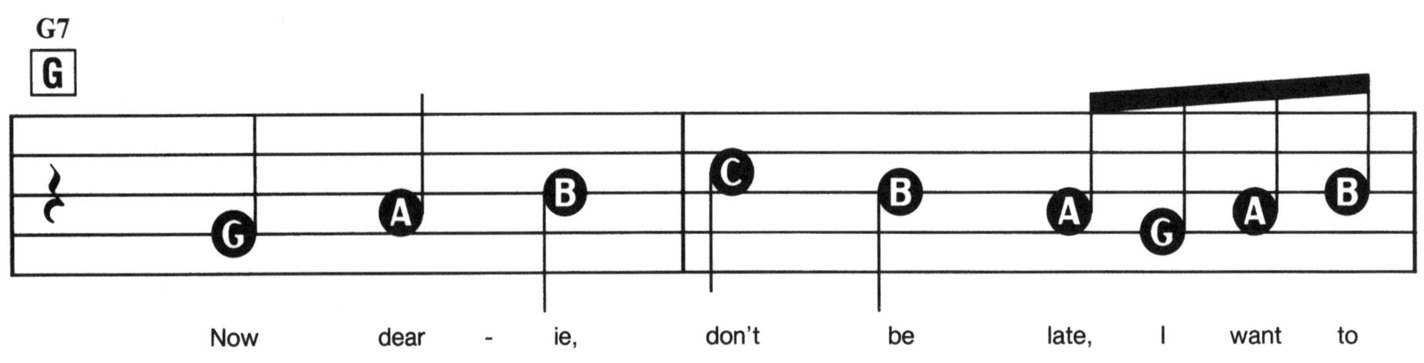

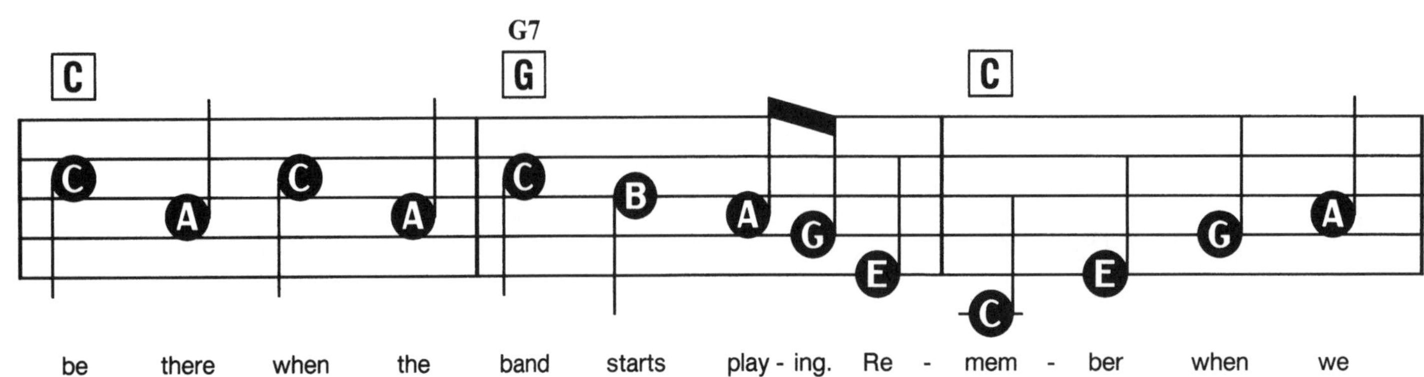

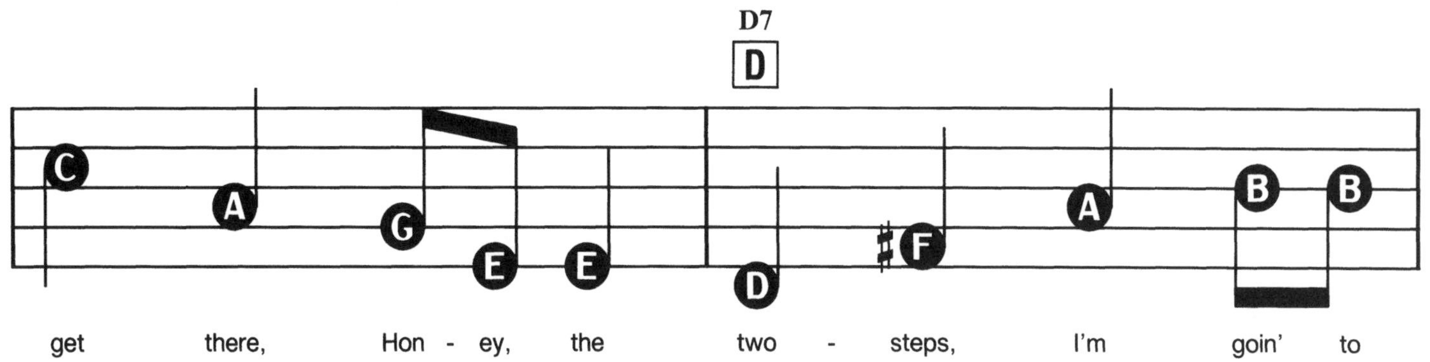
D7
D
C A G E E D F A B B
get there, Hon - ey, the two - steps, I'm goin' to

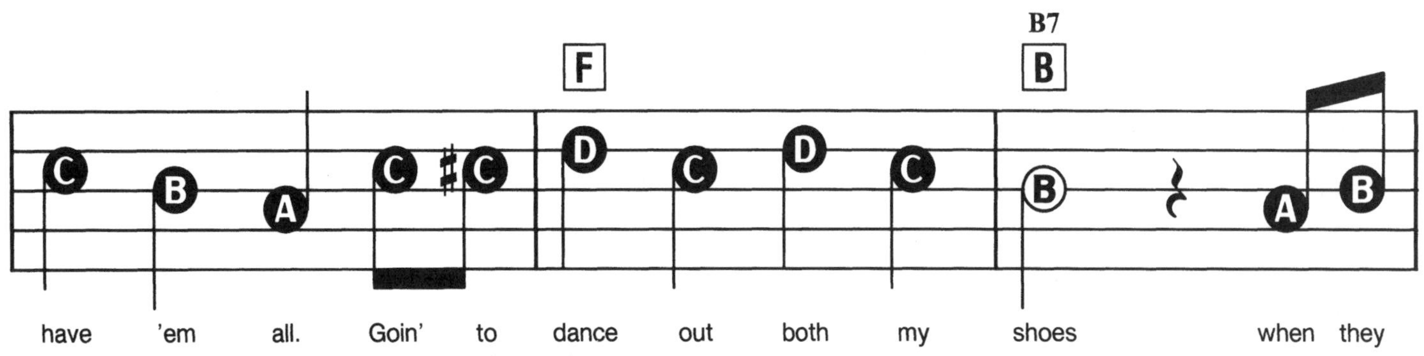
F
B7
B
C B A C C D C D C B A B
have 'em all. Goin' to dance out both my shoes when they

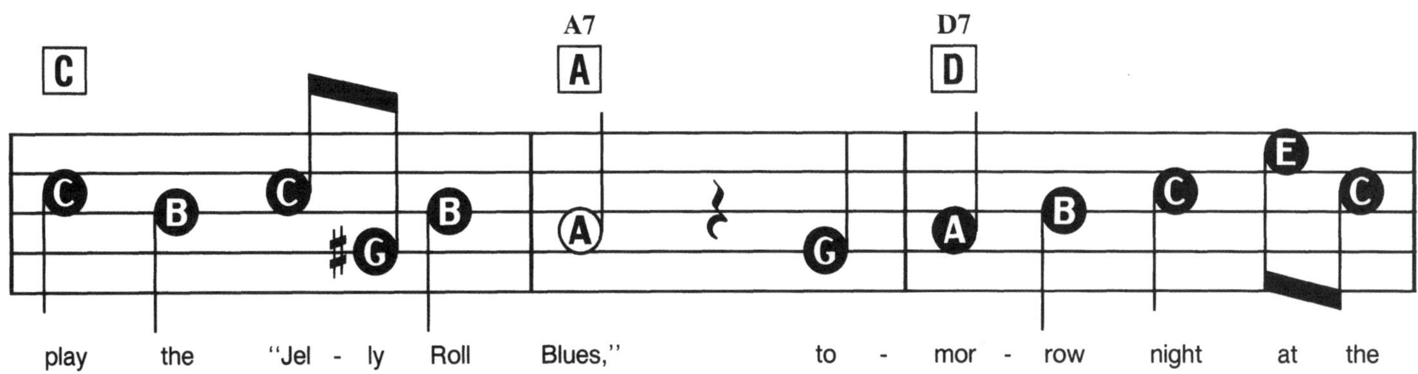
C
A7
A
D7
D
C B C G B A G A B C E C
play the "Jel - ly Roll Blues," to - mor - row night at the

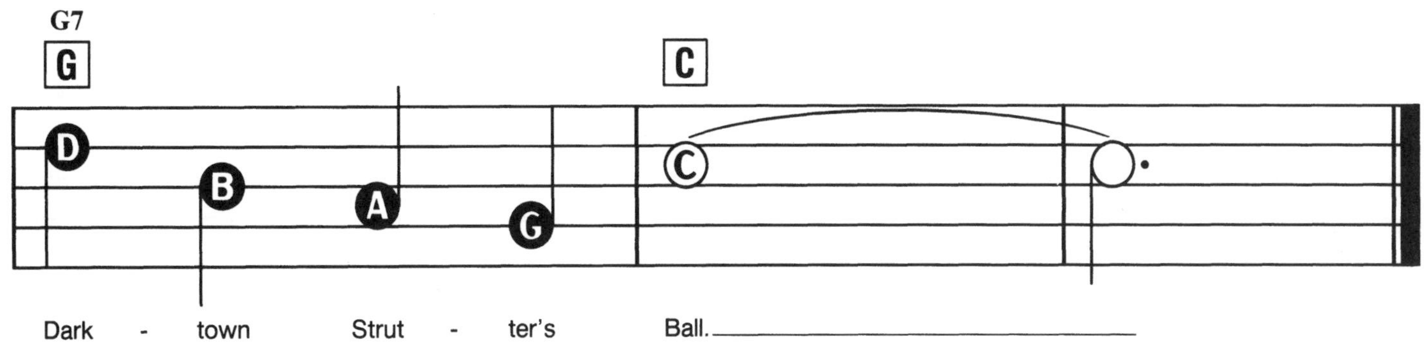
G7
G
C
D B A G C
Dark - town Strut - ter's Ball.

Down by the Old Mill Stream

Registration 3
Rhythm: Waltz

Words and Music by
Tell Taylor

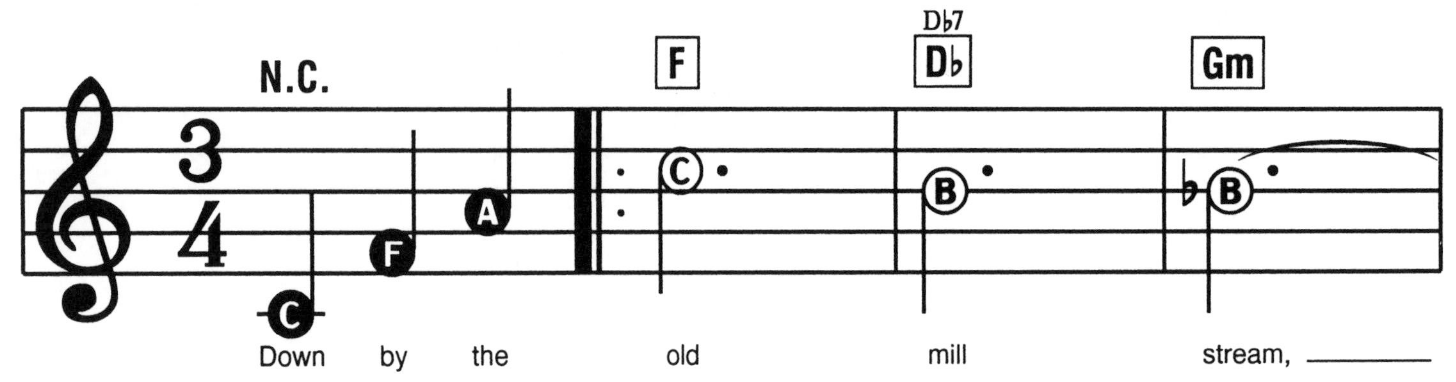

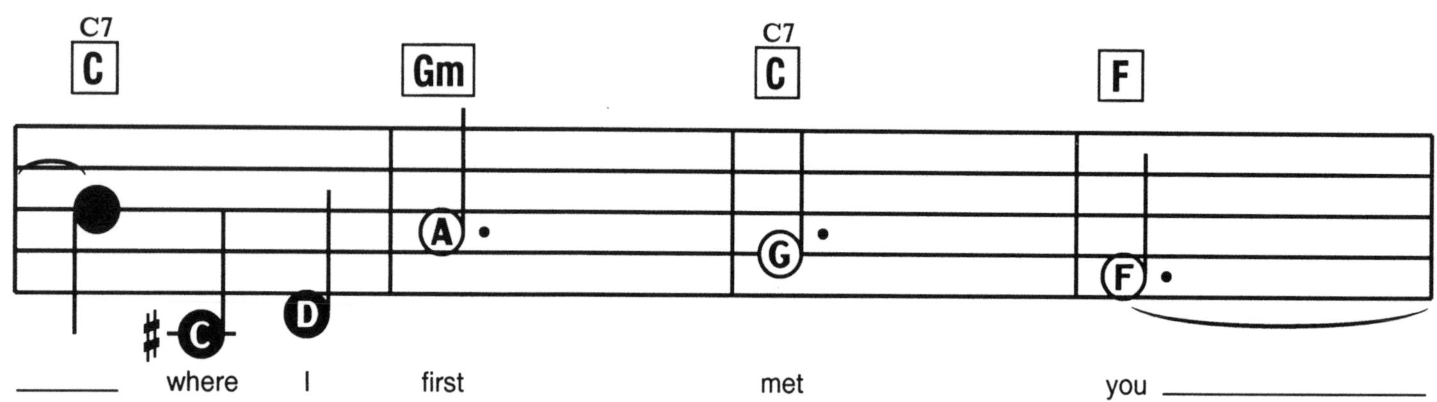

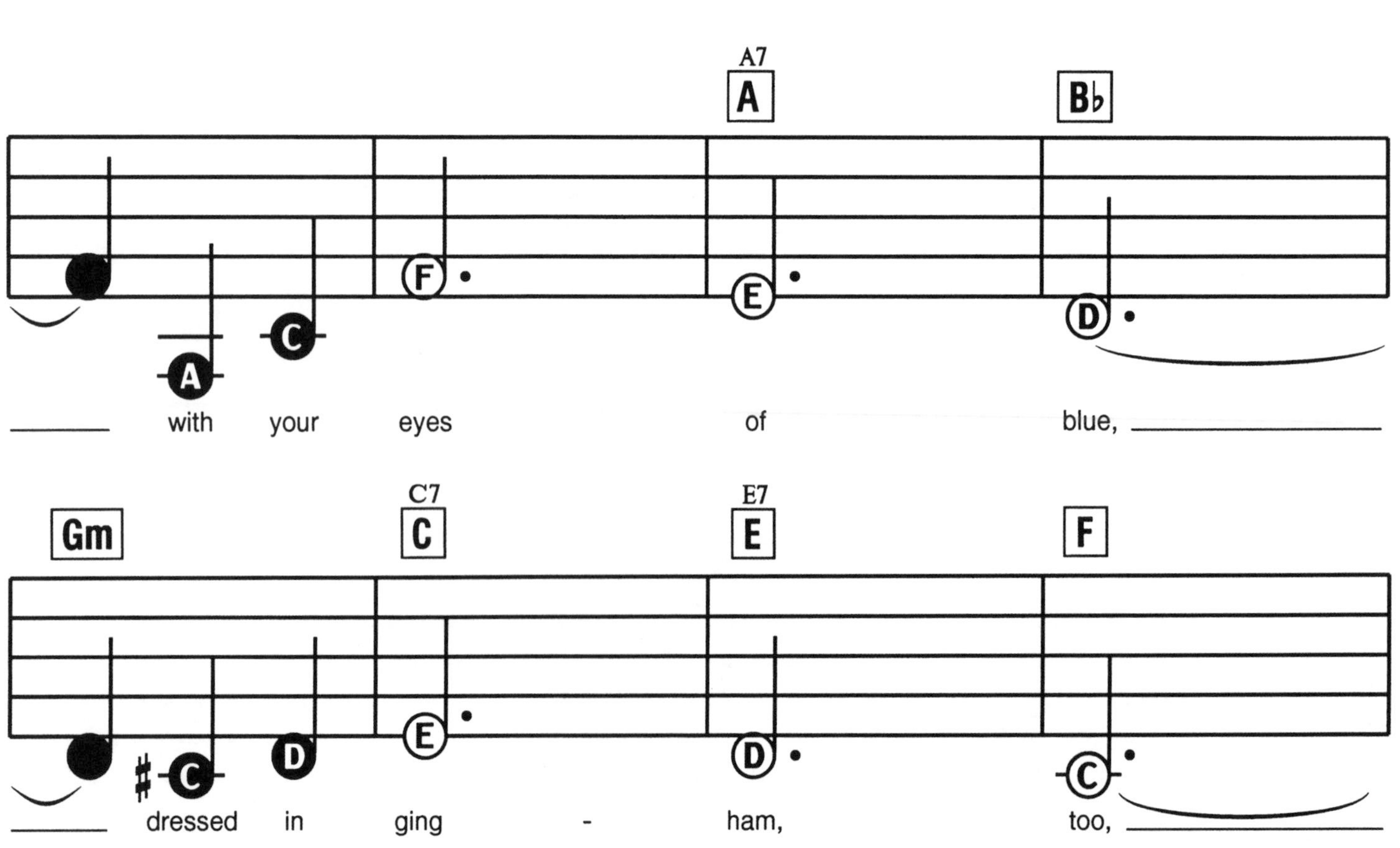

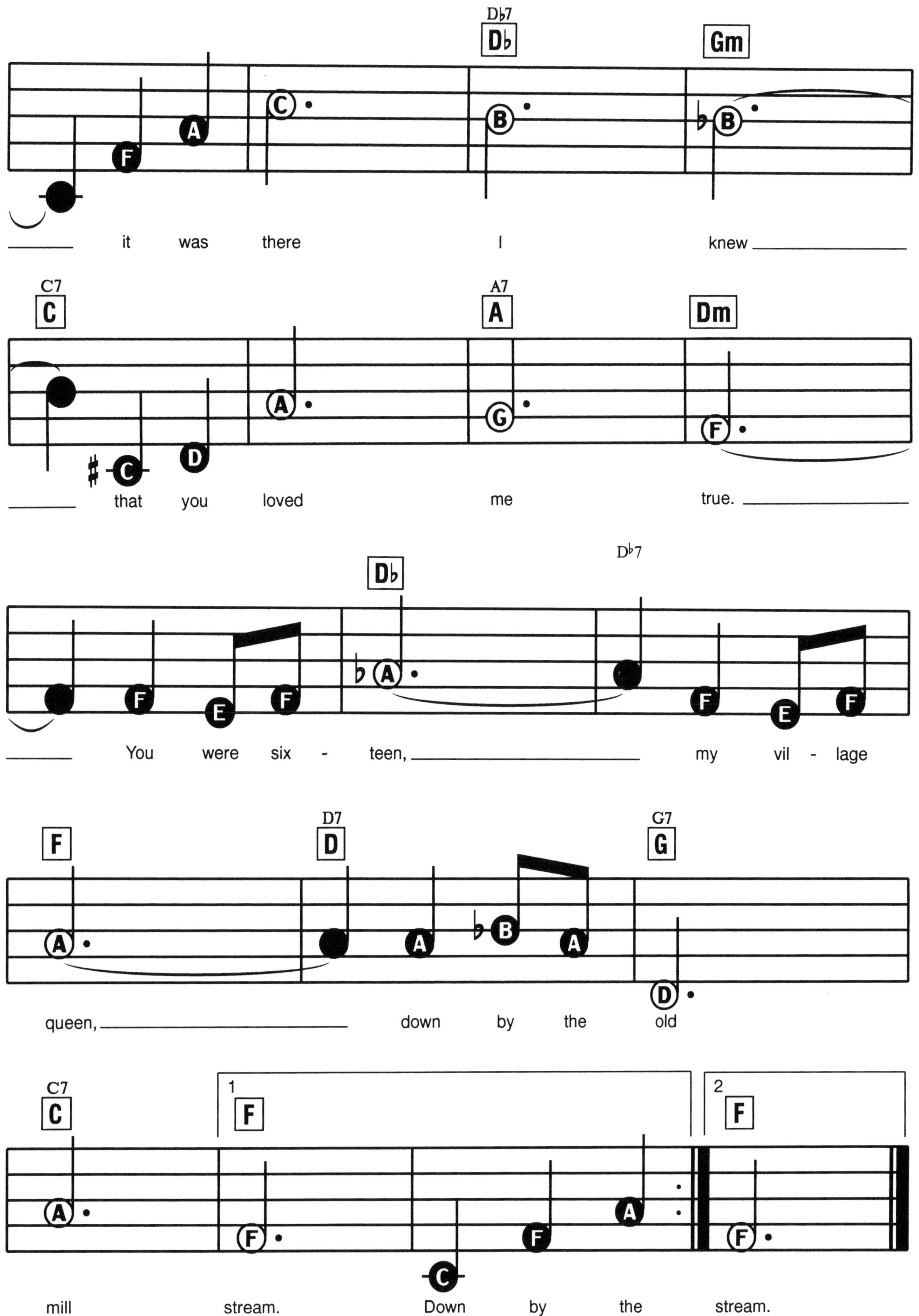

D♭7
D♭
Gm
it was there I knew
C7
C
A7
A
Dm
that you loved me true.
D♭
D♭7
You were six - teen, my vil - lage
F
D7
D
G7
G
queen, down by the old
C7
C
1
F
2
F
mill stream. Down by the stream.

Down in the Valley

Registration 8
Rhythm: Waltz

Words and Music by
F. Luther

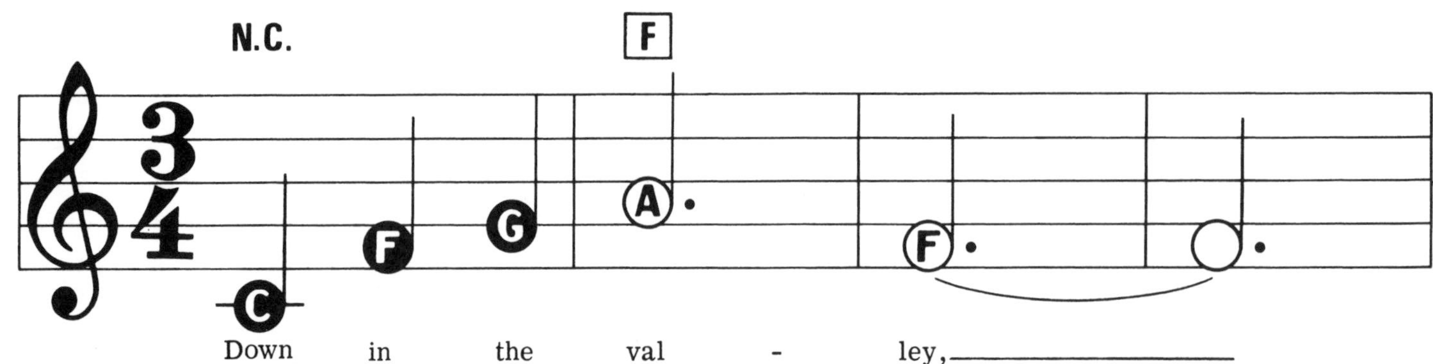

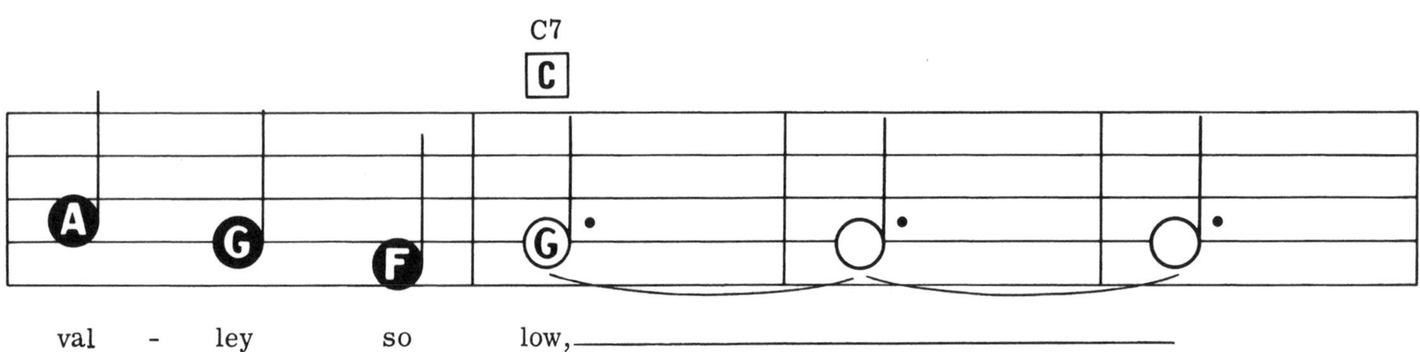

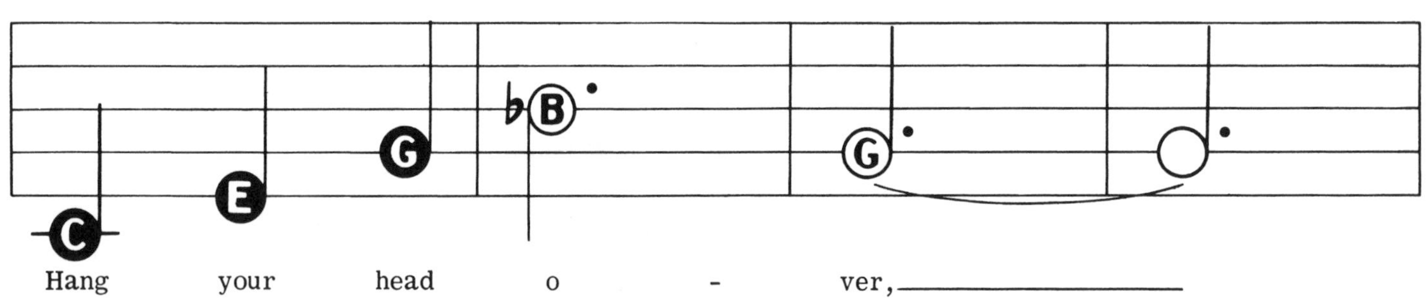

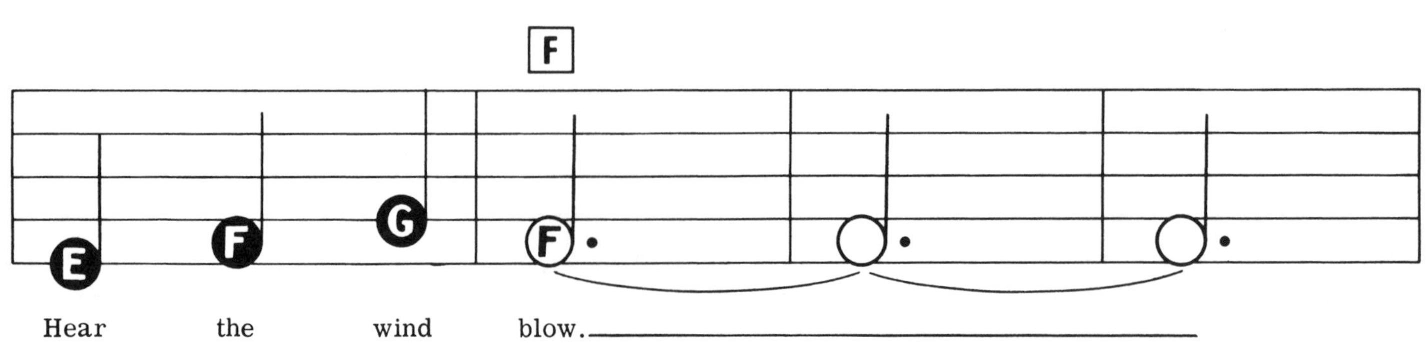

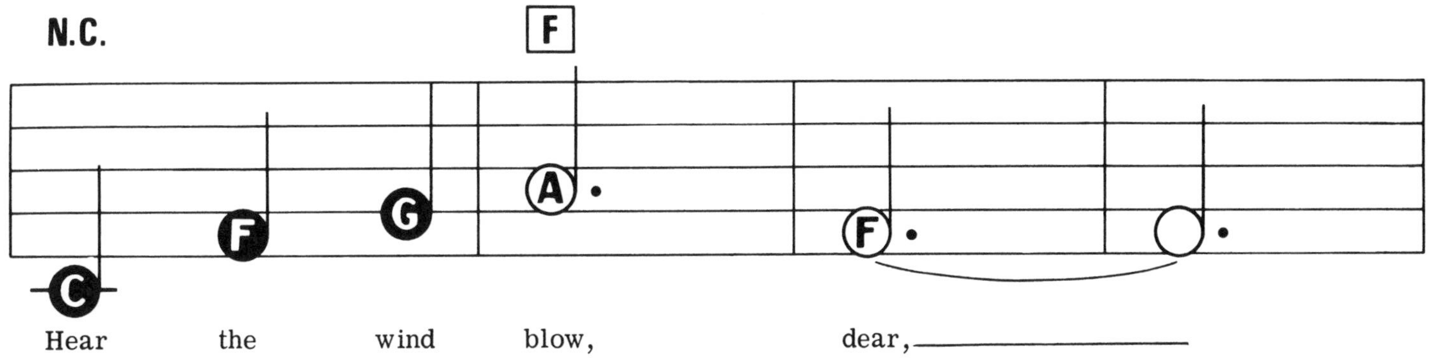
N.C.
F
C
F
G
A
F
Hear the wind blow, dear,

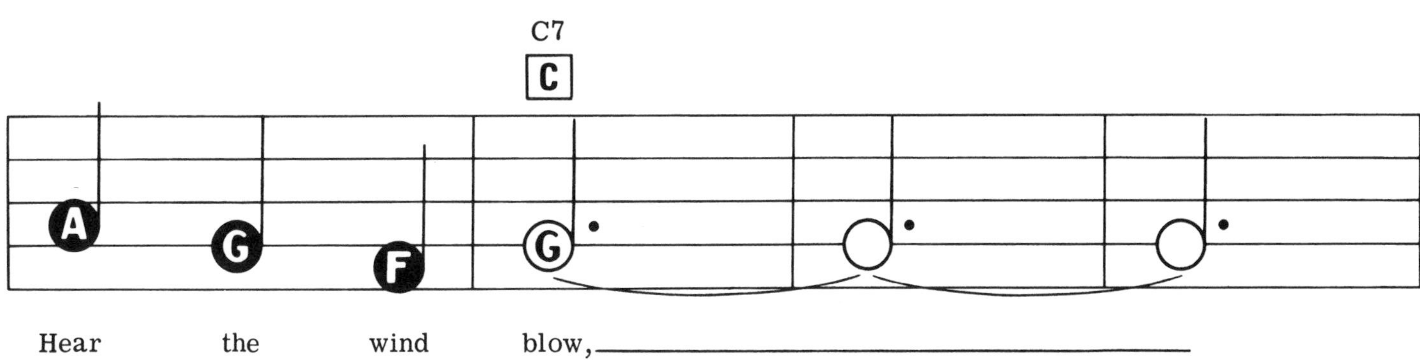
C7
C
A
G
F
G
Hear the wind blow,

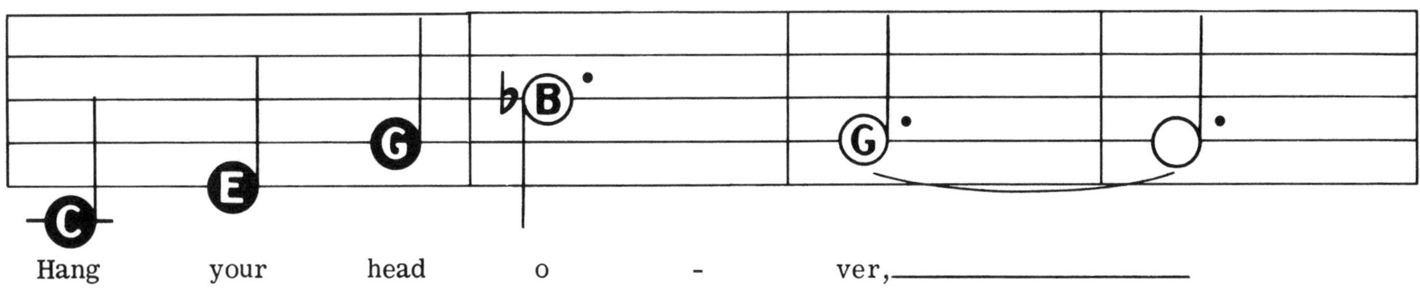
C
E
G
B
G
Hang your head o - ver,

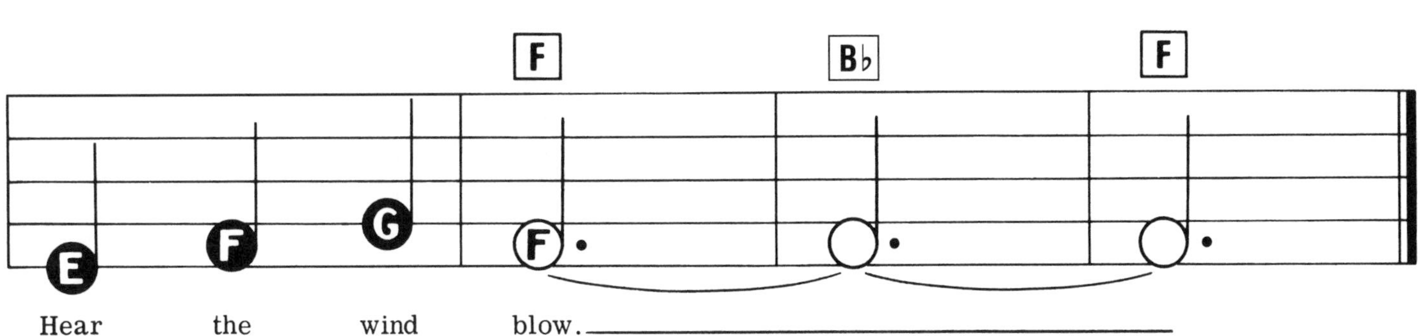
F
B♭
F
E
F
G
F
Hear the wind blow.

For He's a Jolly Good Fellow

Registration 4
Rhythm: Waltz

Traditional

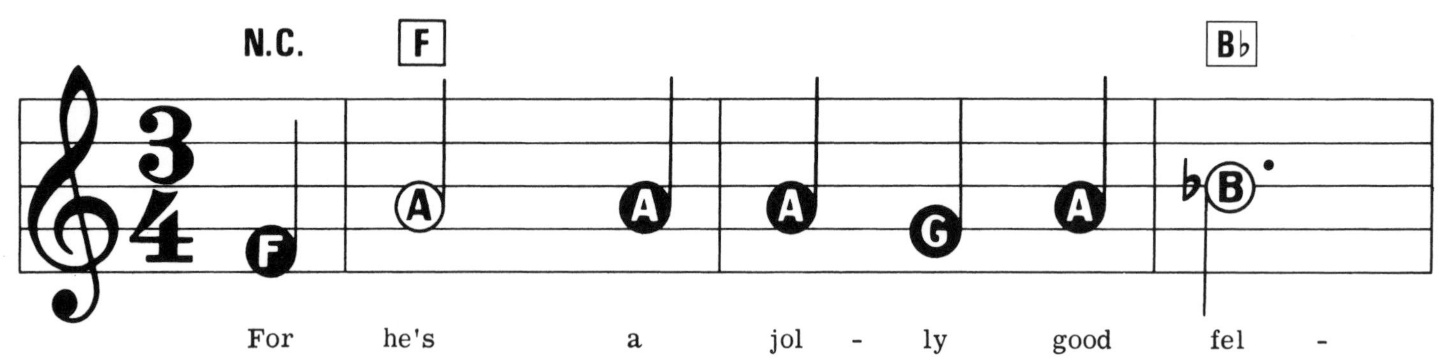

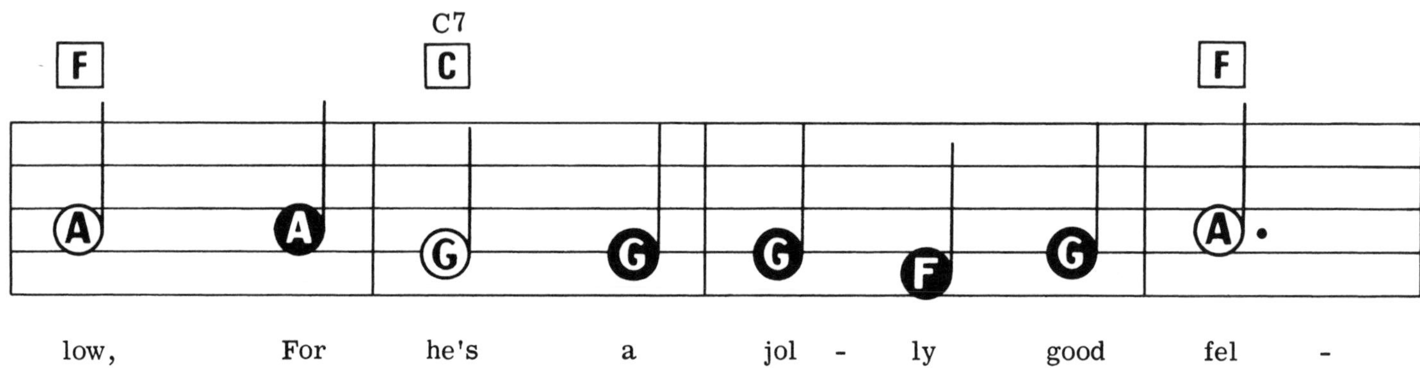

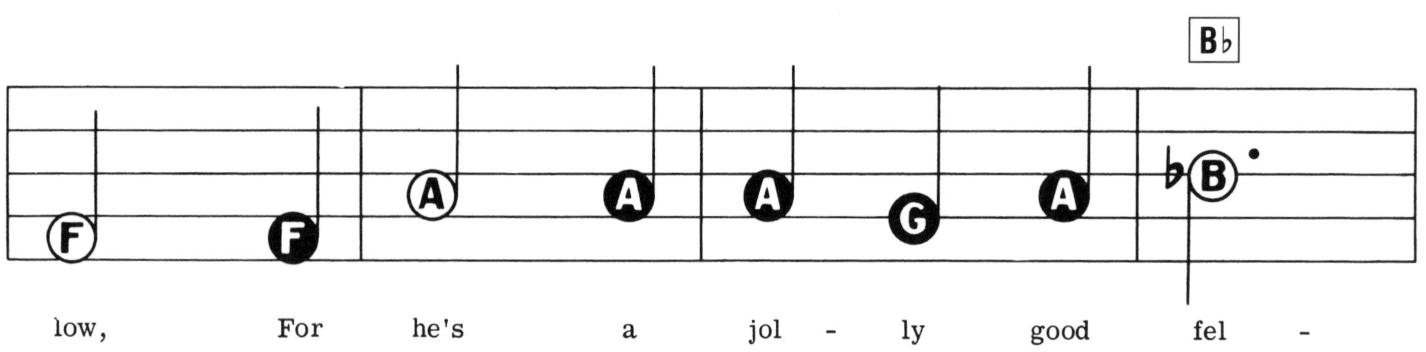

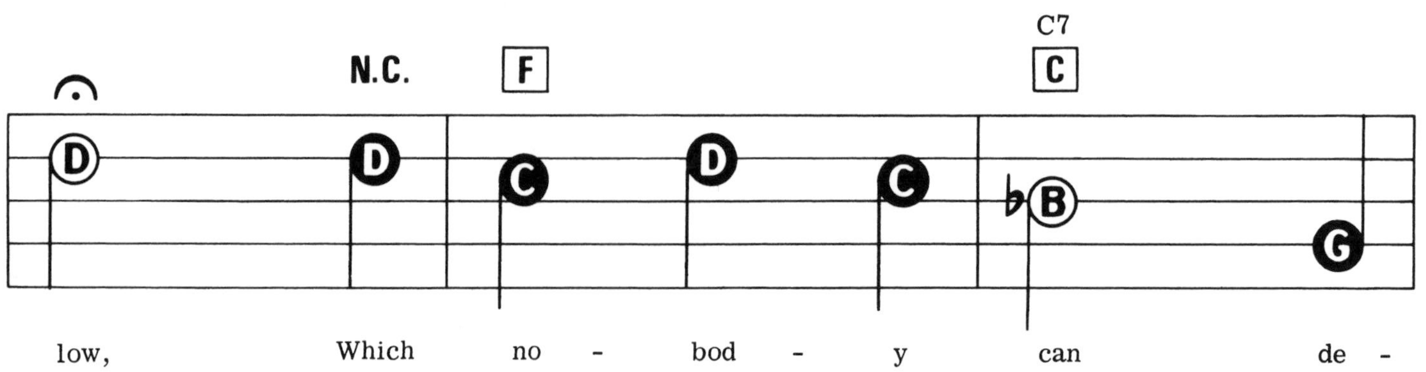

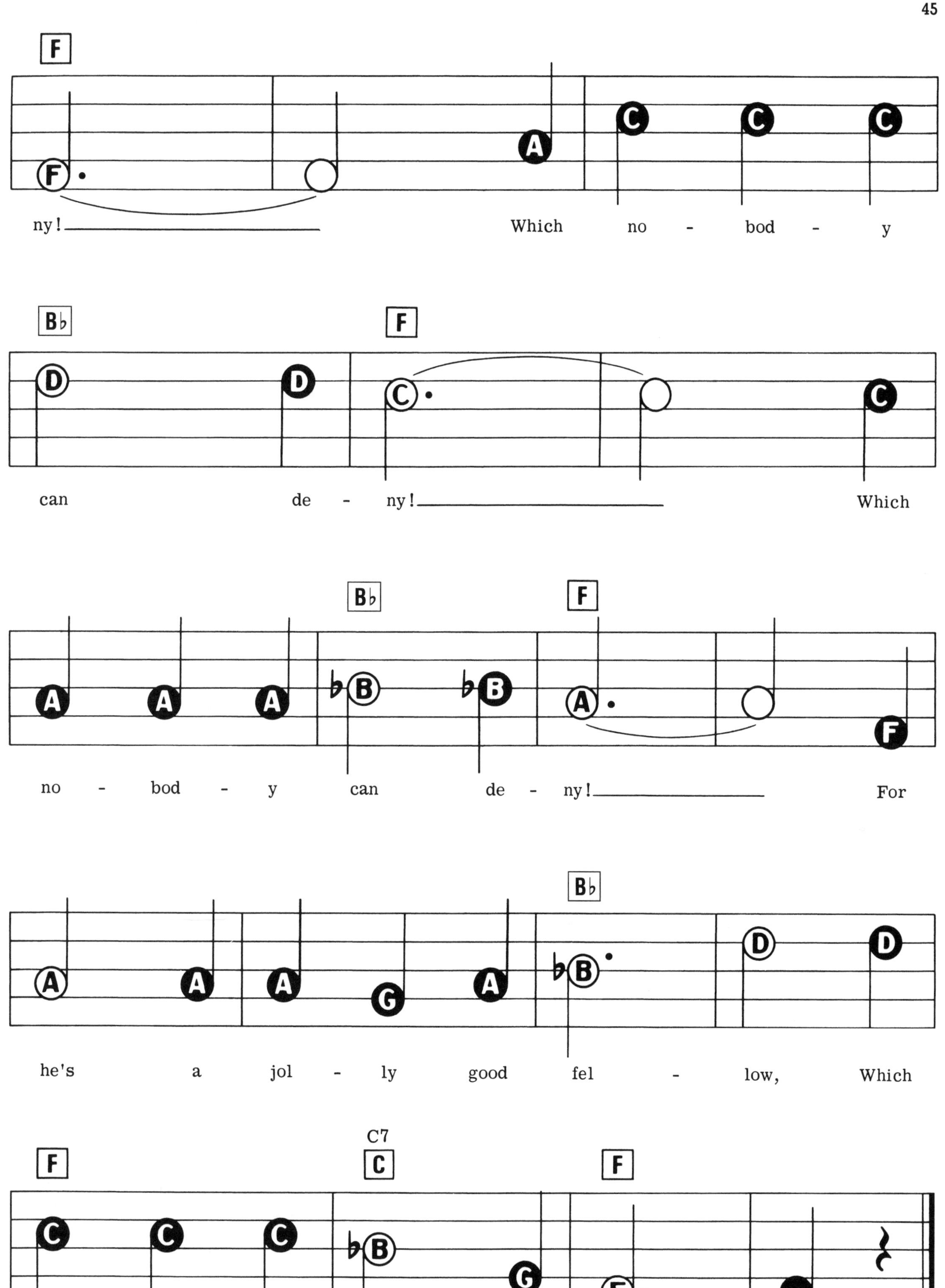
F
F
A
C
C
C
ny!
Which
no - bod - y
B♭
F
D
D
C
C
can
de - ny!
Which
B♭
F
A
A
A
B
B
A
F
no - bod - y
can
de - ny!
For
B♭
A
A
A
G
A
B
D
D
he's
a
jol - ly
good
fel - low,
Which
F
C7
C
F
C
C
C
B
G
F
no - bod - y
can
de - ny!

For Me and My Gal
from FOR ME AND MY GAL

Registration 3
Rhythm: Swing

Words by Edgar Leslie and E. Ray Goetz
Music by George W. Meyer

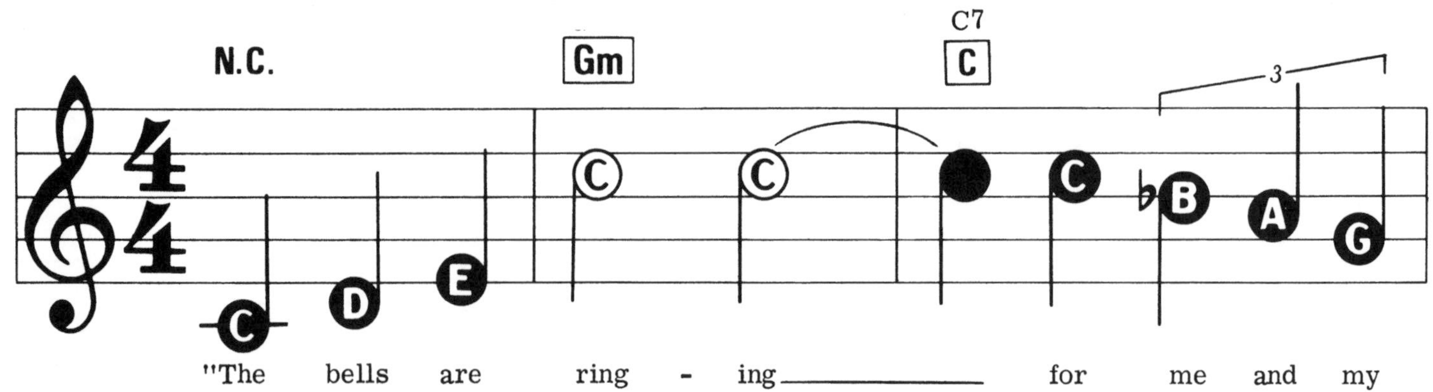

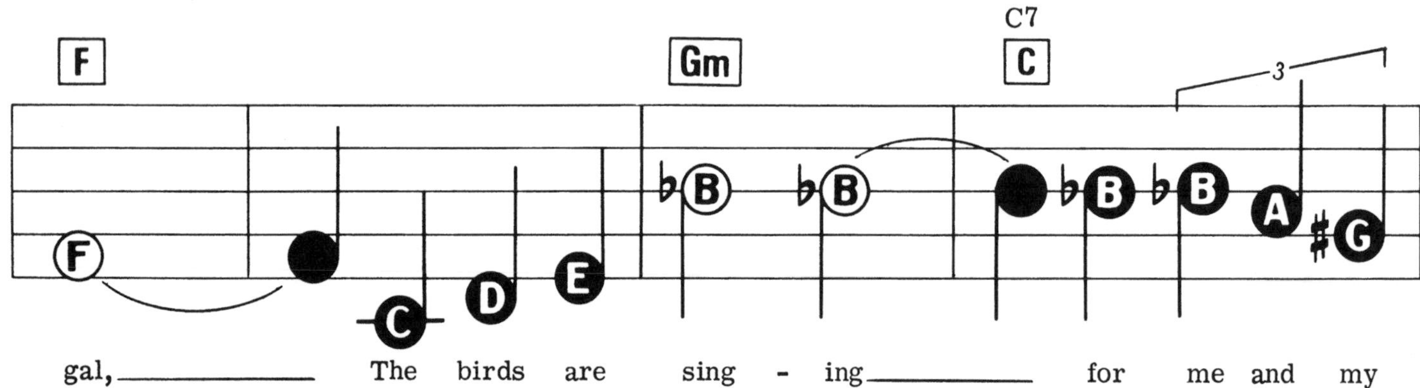

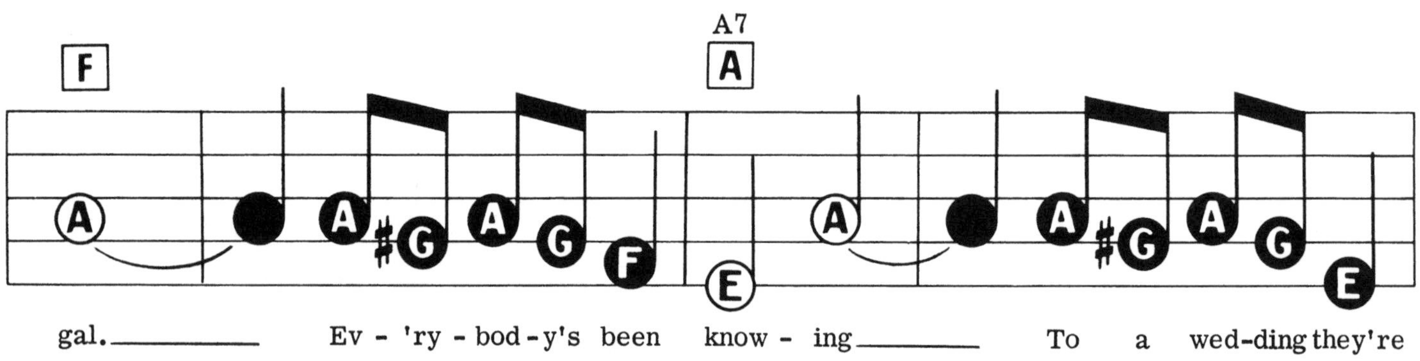

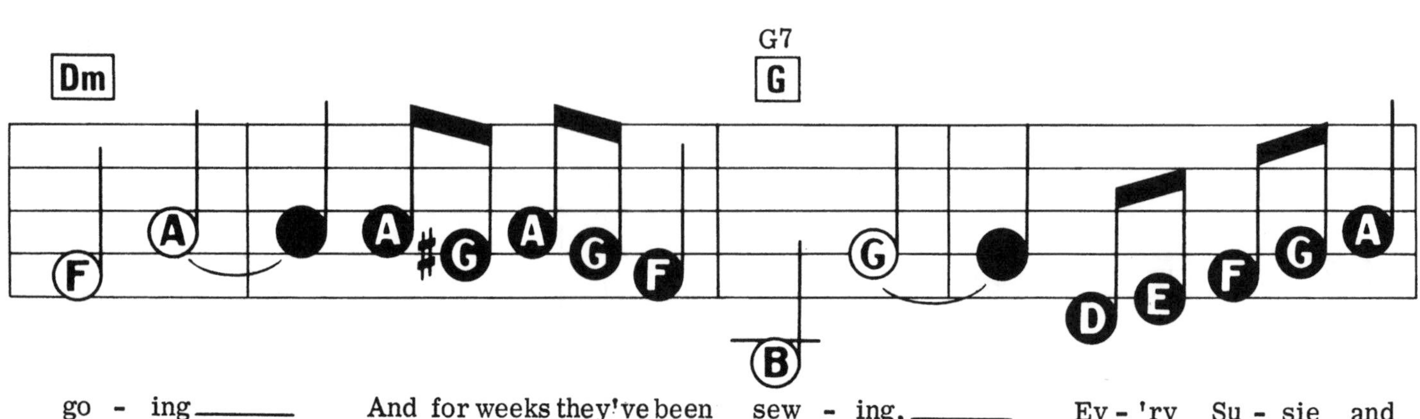

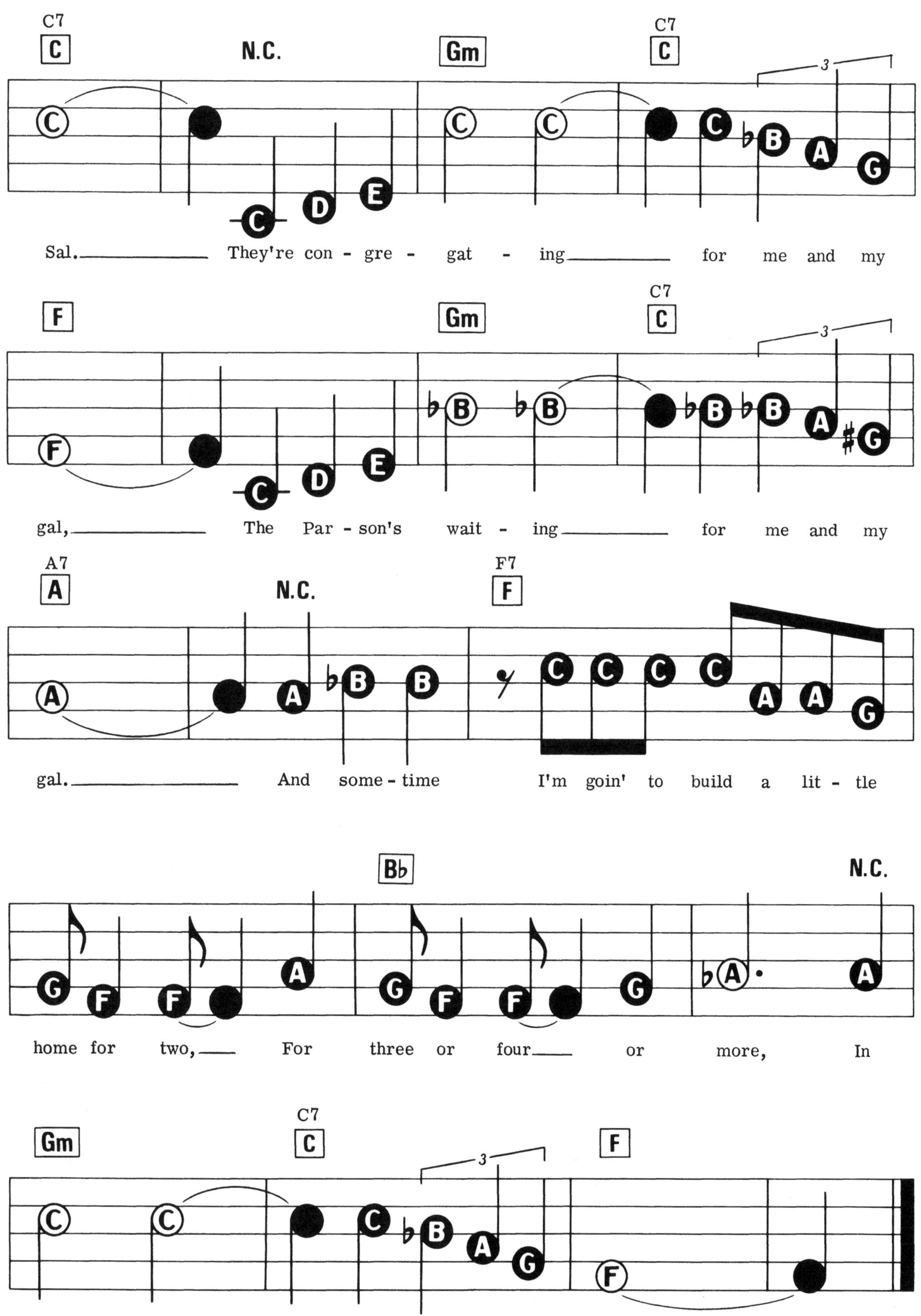
C7 C N.C. Gm C7 C
Sal. They're con - gre - gat - ing for me and my
F Gm C7 C
gal, The Par - son's wait - ing for me and my
A7 A N.C. F7 F
gal. And some - time I'm goin' to build a lit - tle
B♭ N.C.
home for two, For three or four or more, In
Gm C7 C F
Love - land for me and my gal."

Give My Regards to Broadway
from YANKEE DOODLE DANDY

Registration 2
Rhythm: Fox Trot

Words and Music by
George M. Cohan

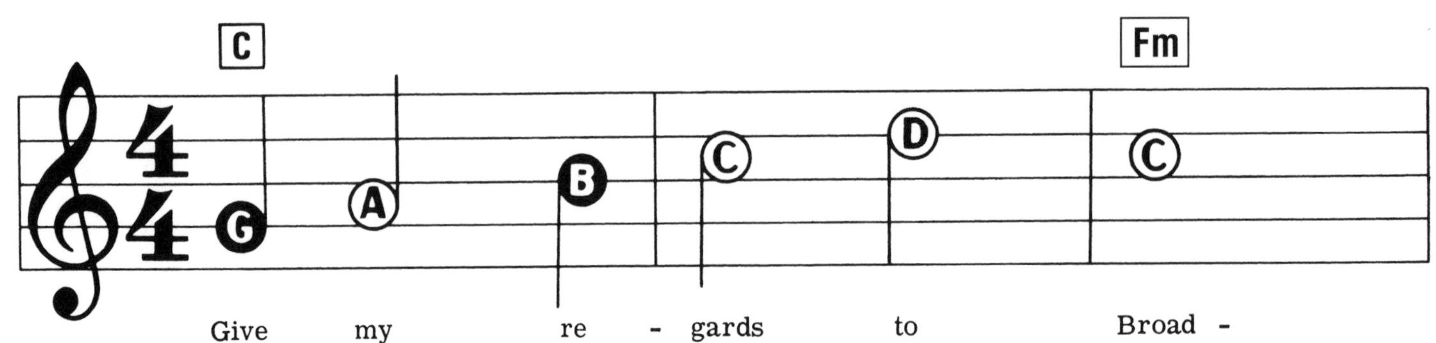

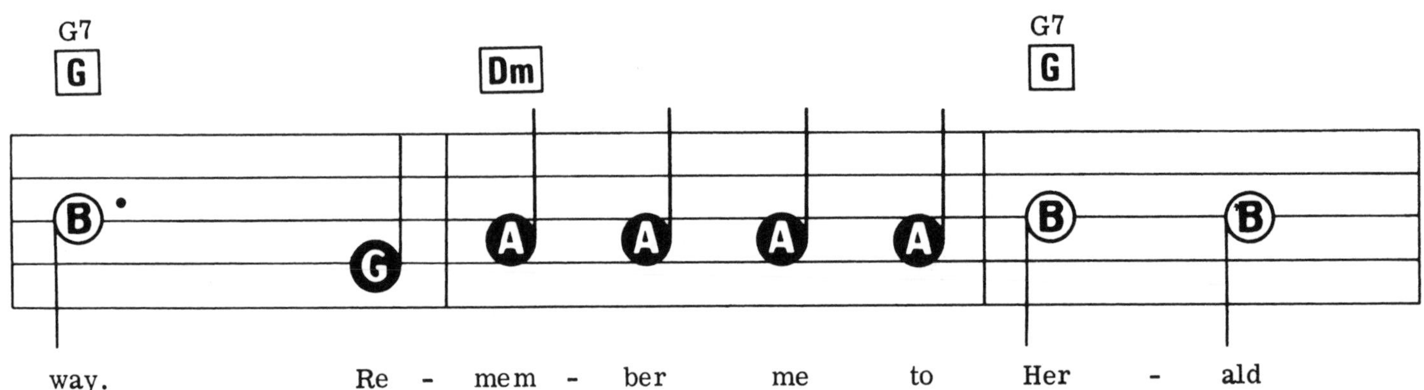

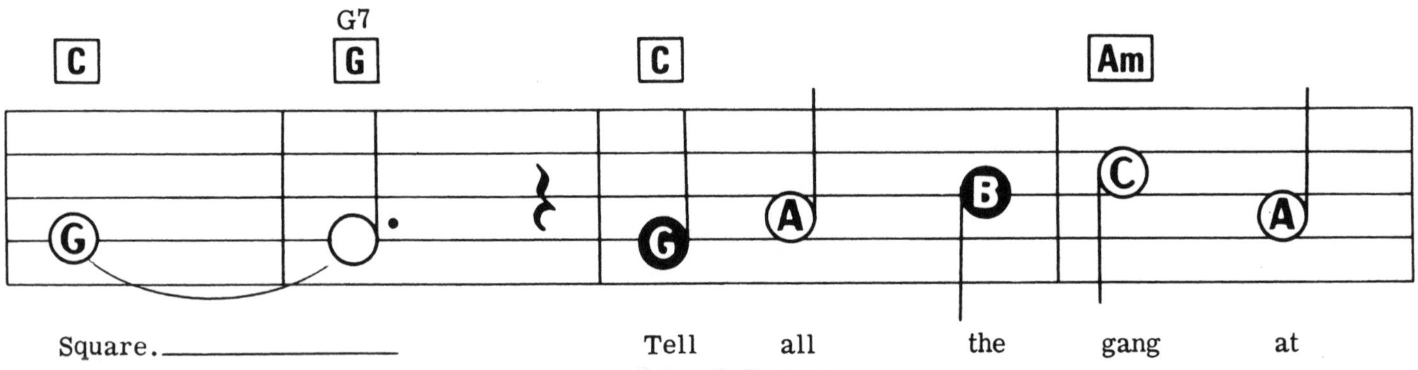

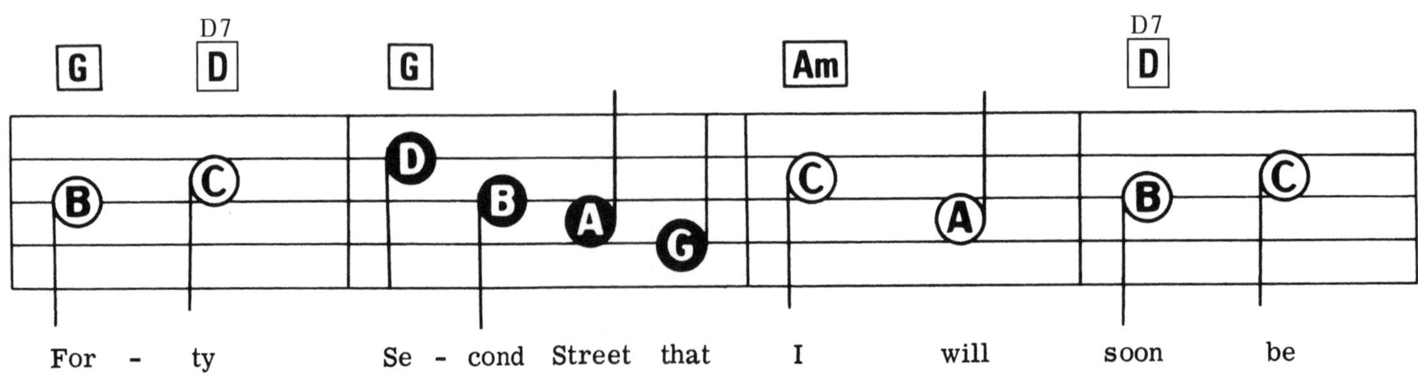

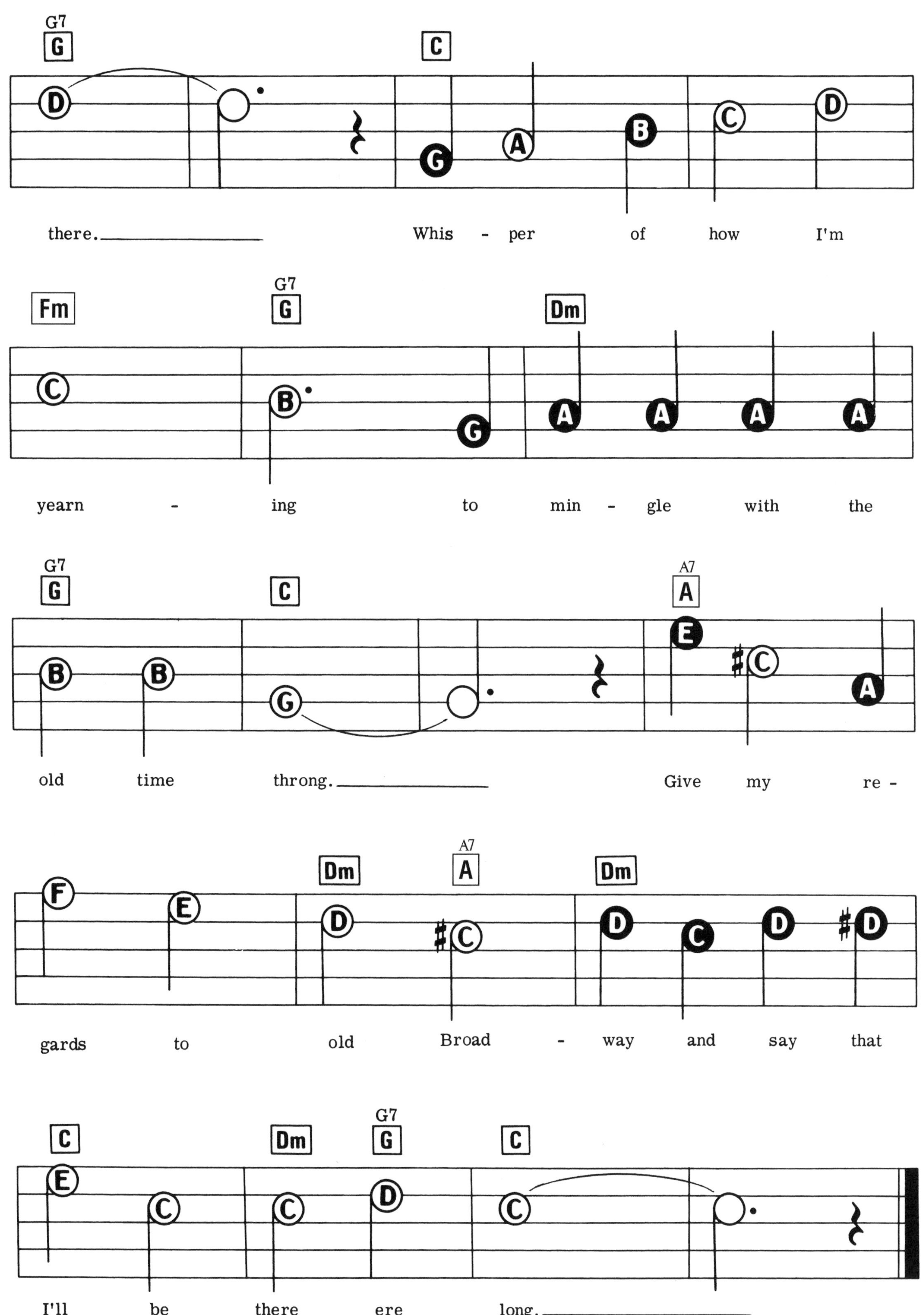
G7
G
C
D
G
A
B
C
D
there.
Whis - per of how I'm
Fm
G7
G
Dm
C
B
G
A A A A
yearn - ing to min - gle with the
G7
G
C
A7
A
B B
G
E
C
A
old time throng.
Give my re -
Dm
A7
A
Dm
F E D C D C D D
gards to old Broad - way and say that
C
Dm
G7
G
C
E C C D C
I'll be there ere long.

The Glow Worm

Registration
Rhythm: Fox Trot or Cha-Cha

English Words and Music by Lilla Cayley Robinson
German Words and Music by Paul Lincke

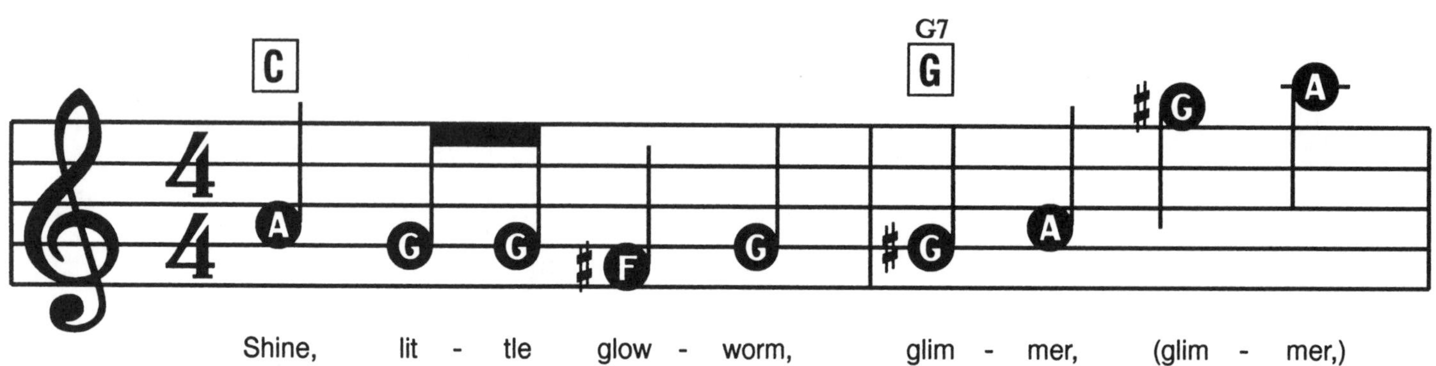

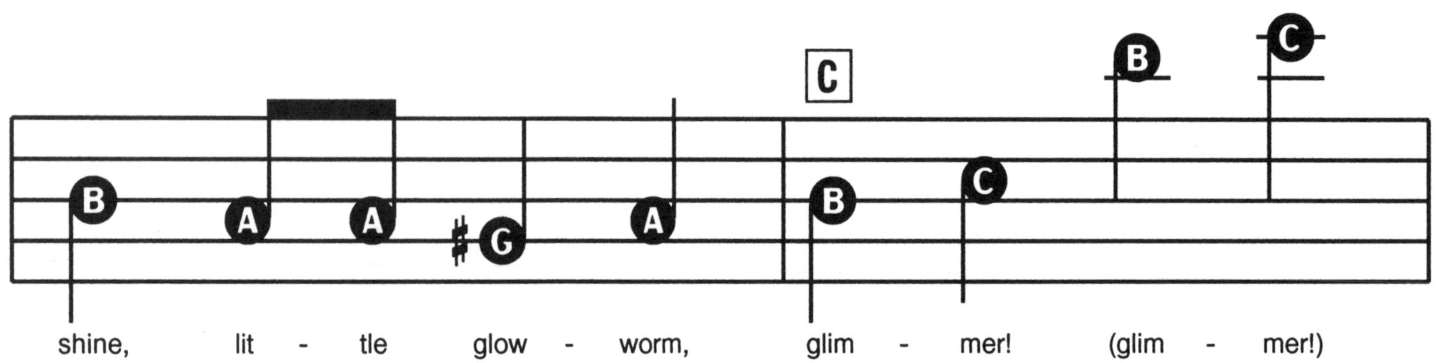

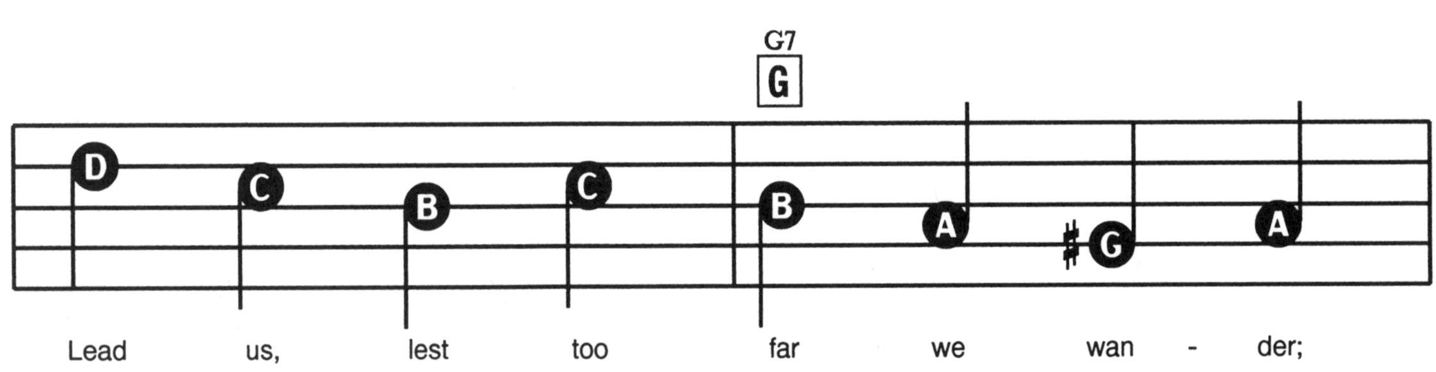

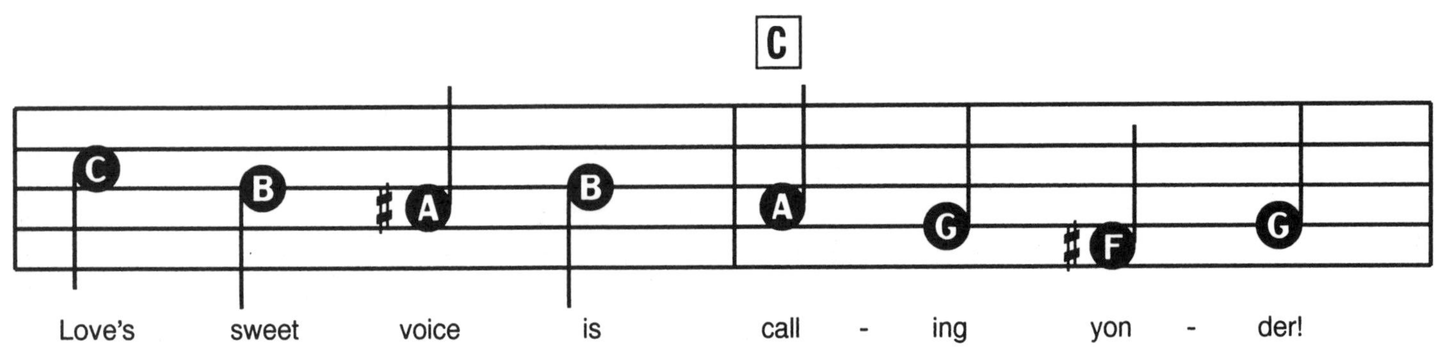

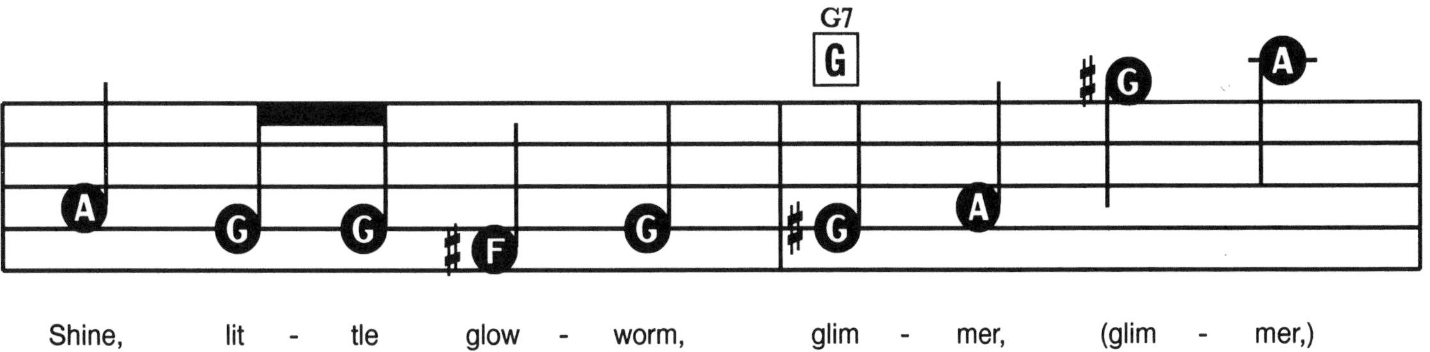
G7
G
A
G
G
F
G
G
A
G
A
Shine, lit - tle glow - worm, glim - mer, (glim - mer,)

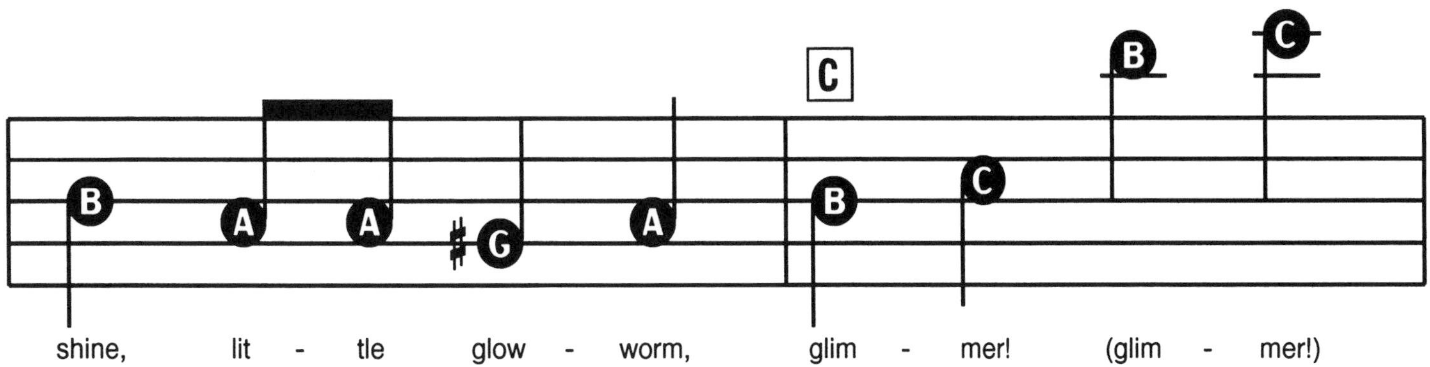
C
B
A
A
G
A
B
C
B
C
shine, lit - tle glow - worm, glim - mer! (glim - mer!)

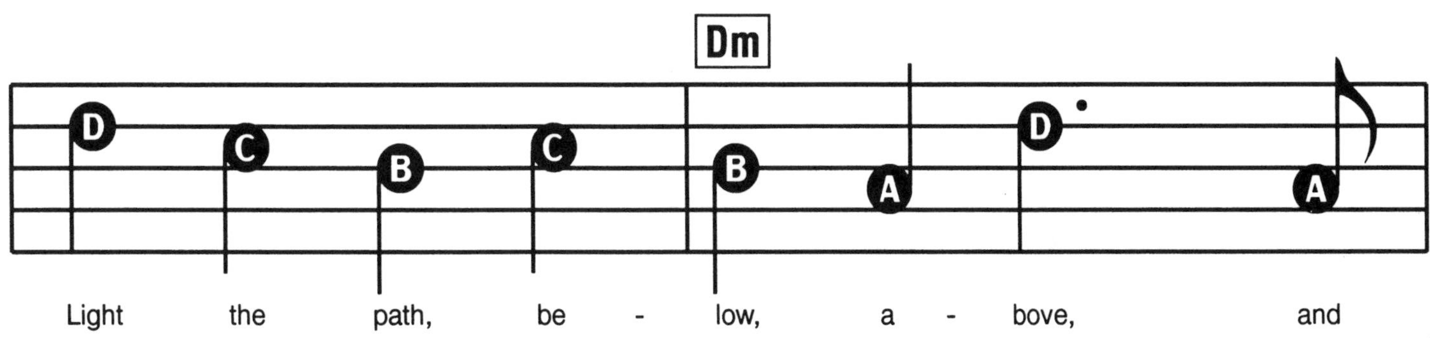
Dm
D
C
B
C
B
A
D
A
Light the path, be - low, a - bove, and

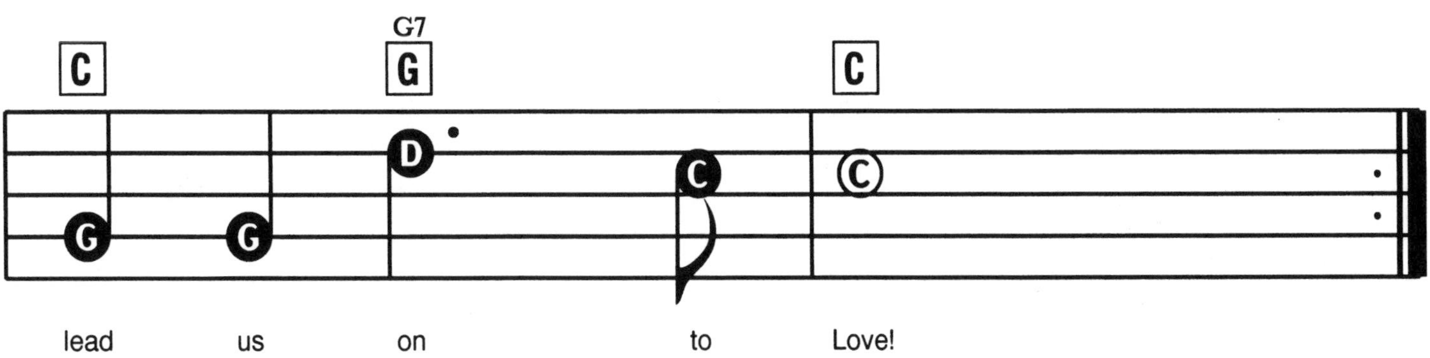
C
G7
G
C
G
G
D
C
C
lead us on to Love!

Hail, Hail, the Gang's All Here

Registration 5
Rhythm: 6/8 March

Words by D.A. Esrom
Music by Theodore F. Morse and Arthur Sullivan

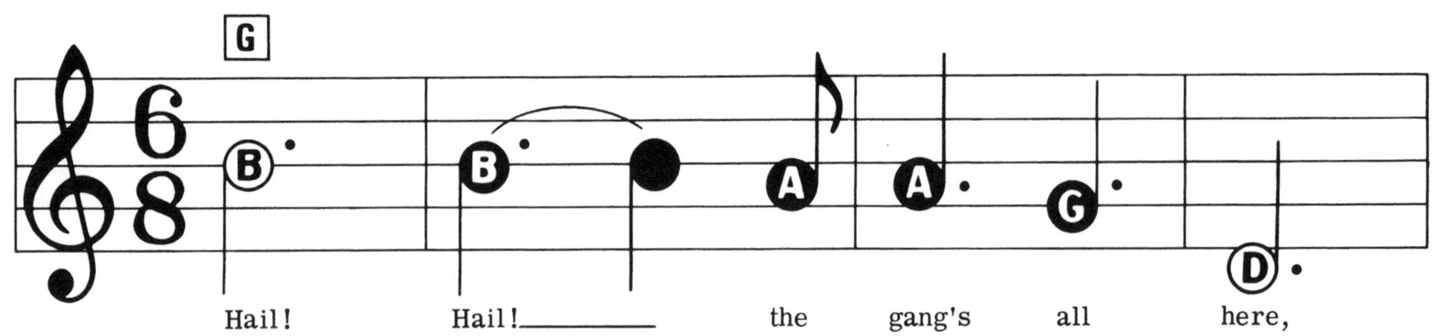

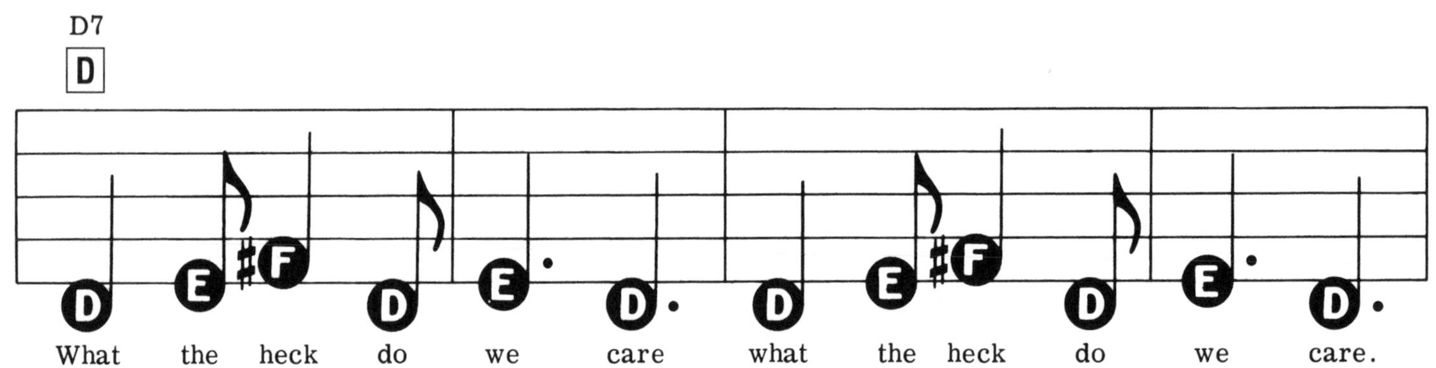

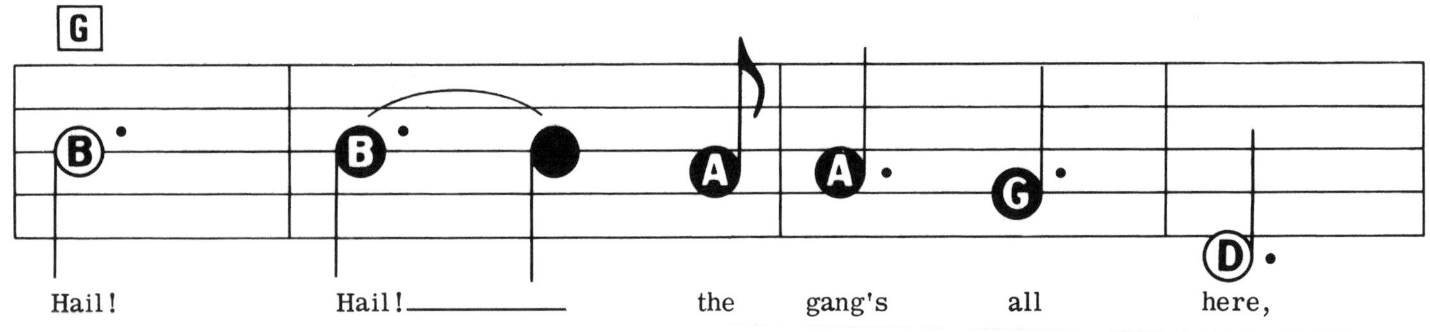

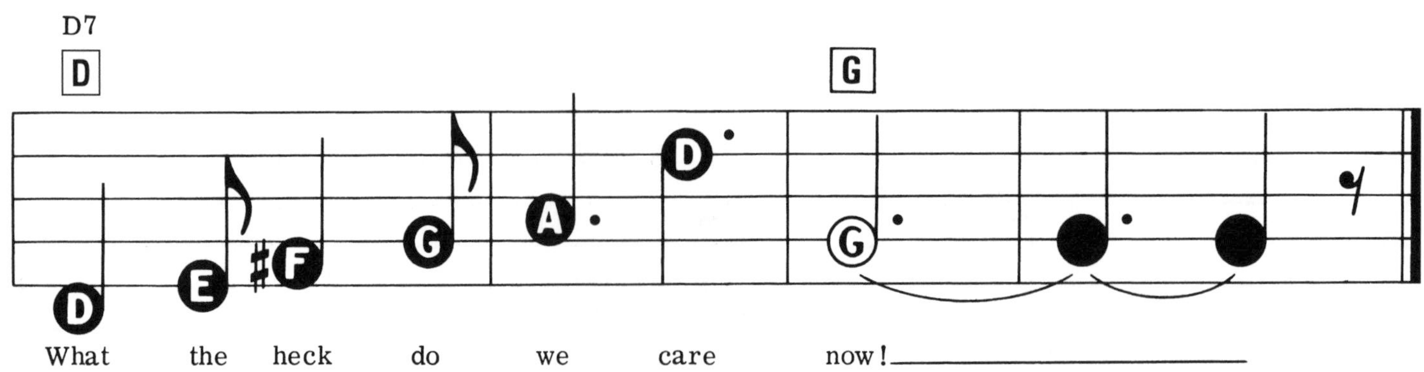

(There'll Be)
A Hot Time in the Old Town Tonight

Registration 7
Rhythm: Fox Trot

Words by Joe Hayden
Music by Theodore M. Metz

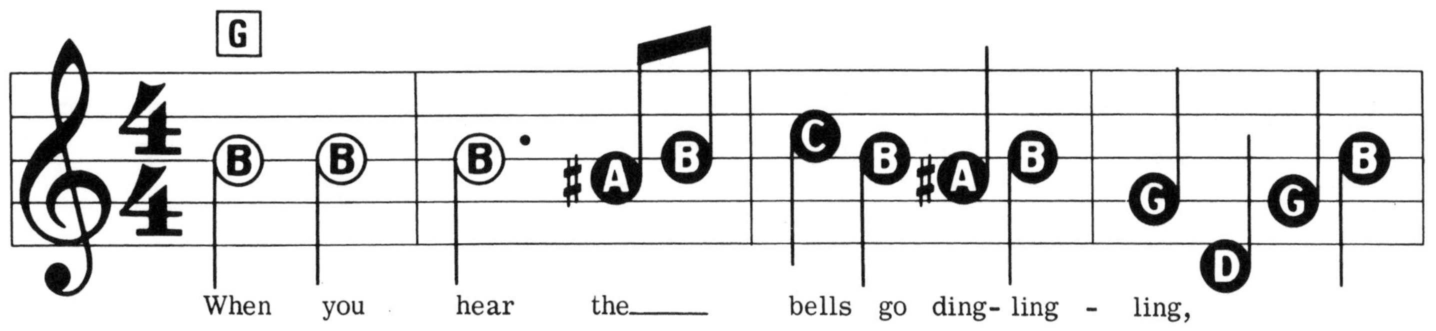

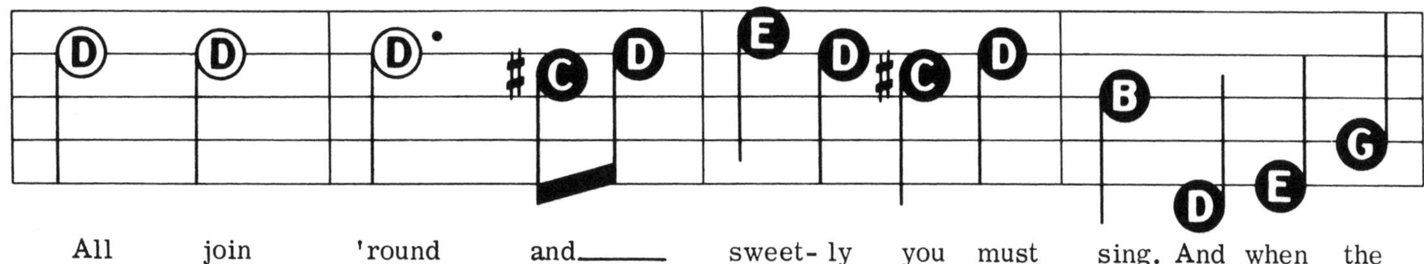

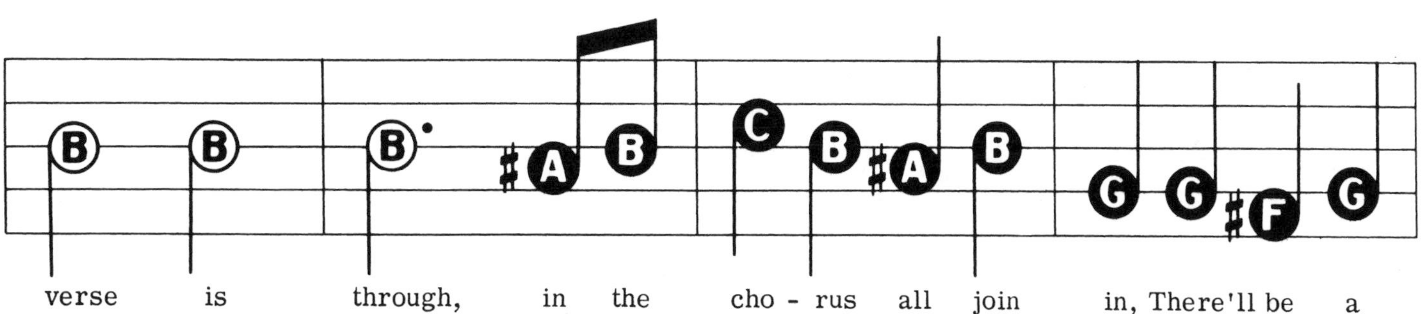

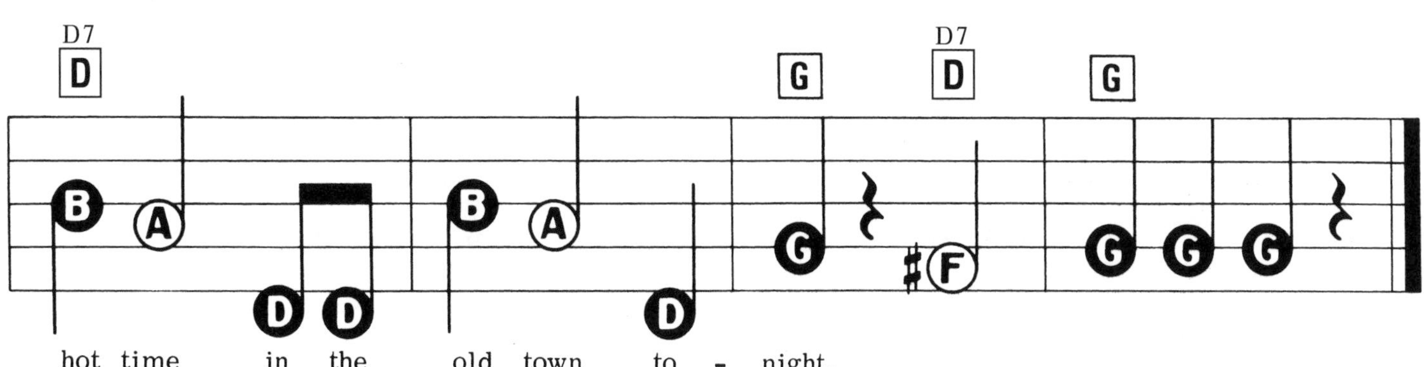

He's Got the Whole World in His Hands

Registration 6
Rhythm: Swing or Rock

Traditional Spiritual

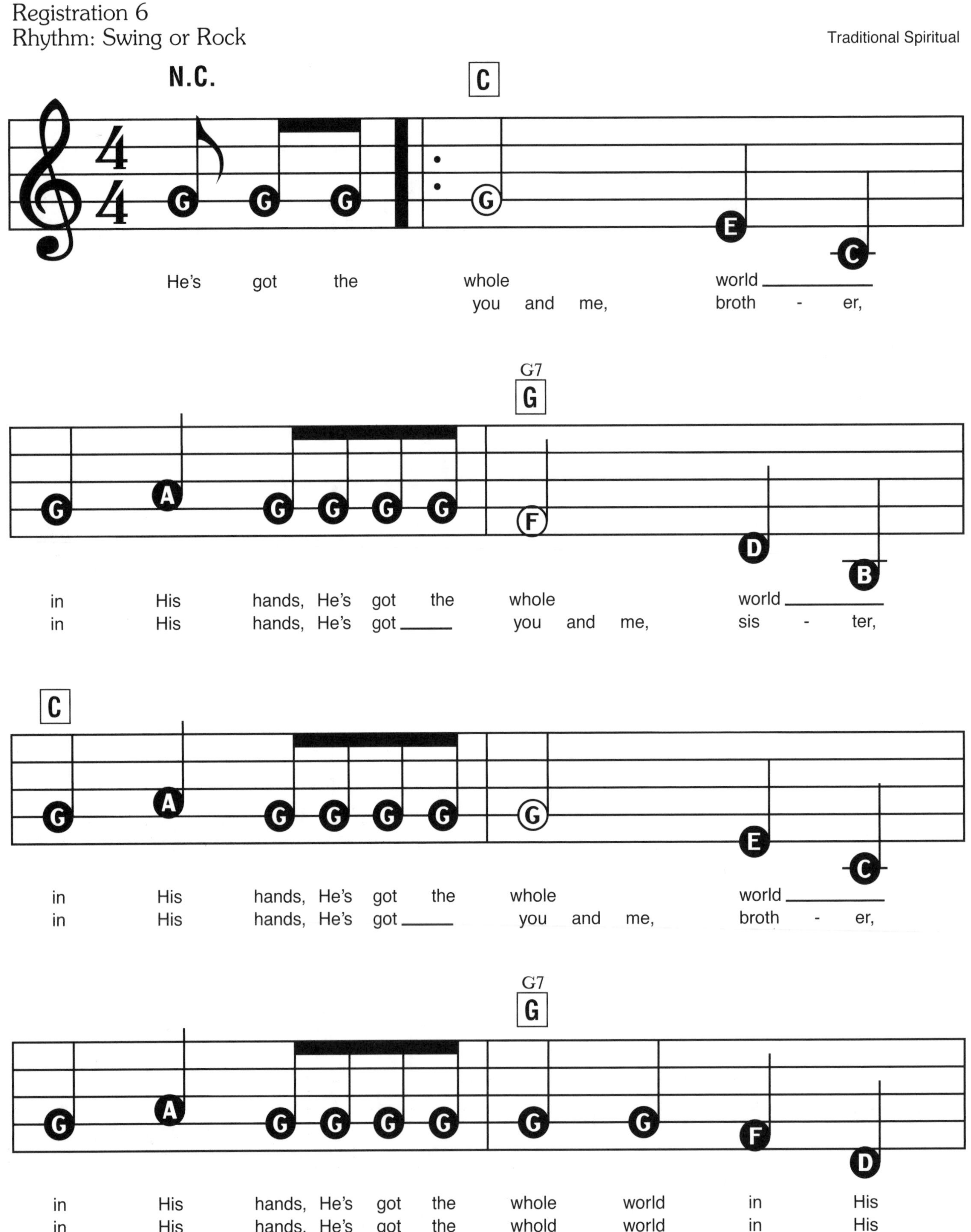

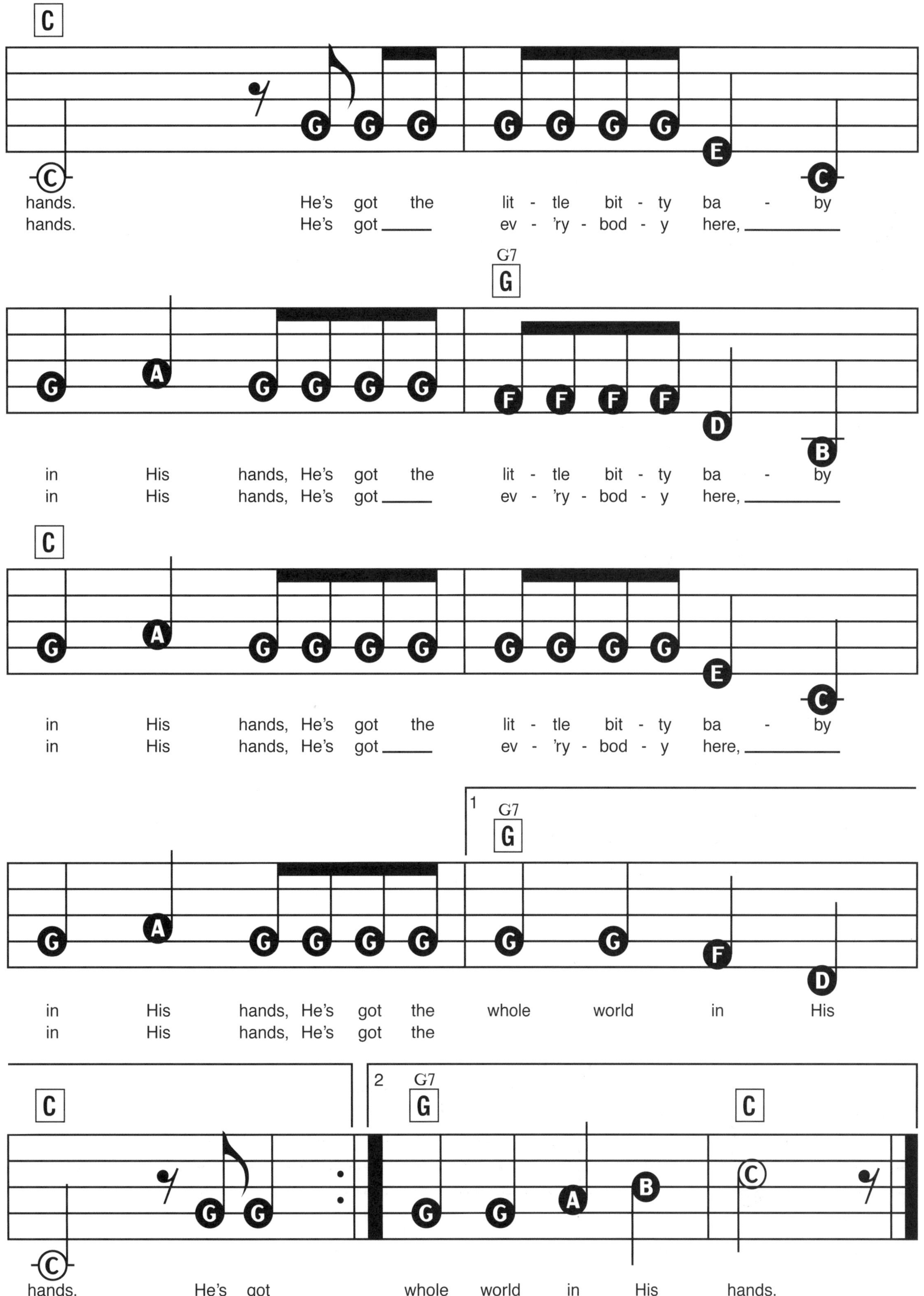
C
G G G G G G G E C
hands. He's got the lit - tle bit - ty ba - by
hands. He's got ev - 'ry - bod - y here,
G7
G
G A G G G G F F F F D B
in His hands, He's got the lit - tle bit - ty ba - by
in His hands, He's got ev - 'ry - bod - y here,
C
G A G G G G G G G G E C
in His hands, He's got the lit - tle bit - ty ba - by
in His hands, He's got ev - 'ry - bod - y here,
1
G7
G
G A G G G G G G F D
in His hands, He's got the whole world in His
in His hands, He's got the
C
C G G
hands. He's got
2
G7
G
C
G G A B C
whole world in His hands.

Hello! Ma Baby

Registration 7
Rhythm: Swing

Words by Ida Emerson
Music by Joseph E. Howard

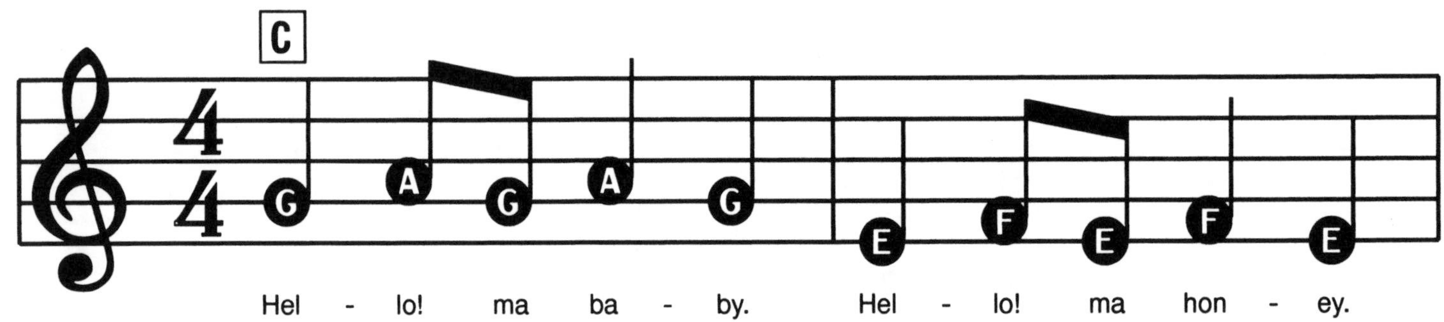

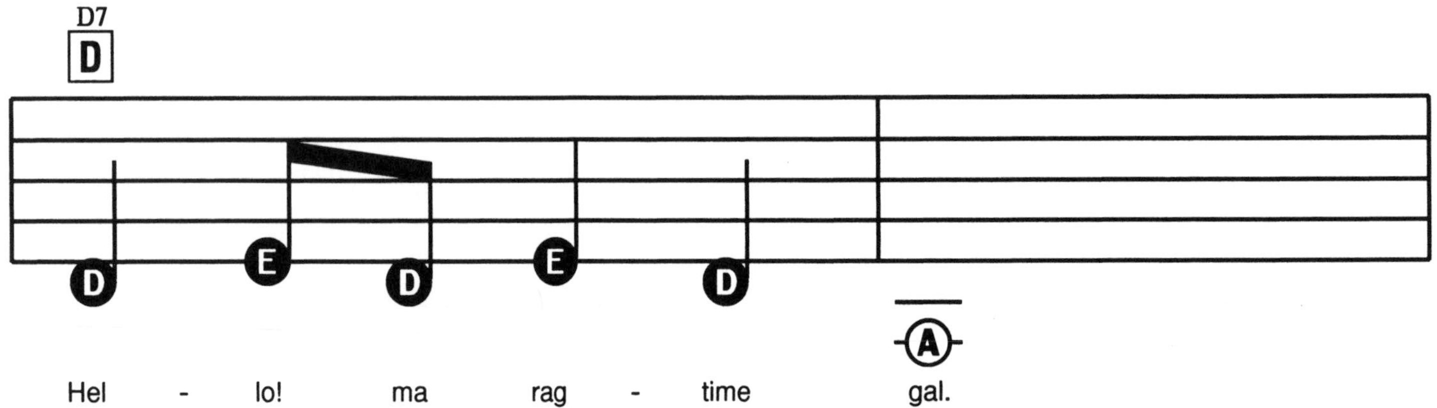

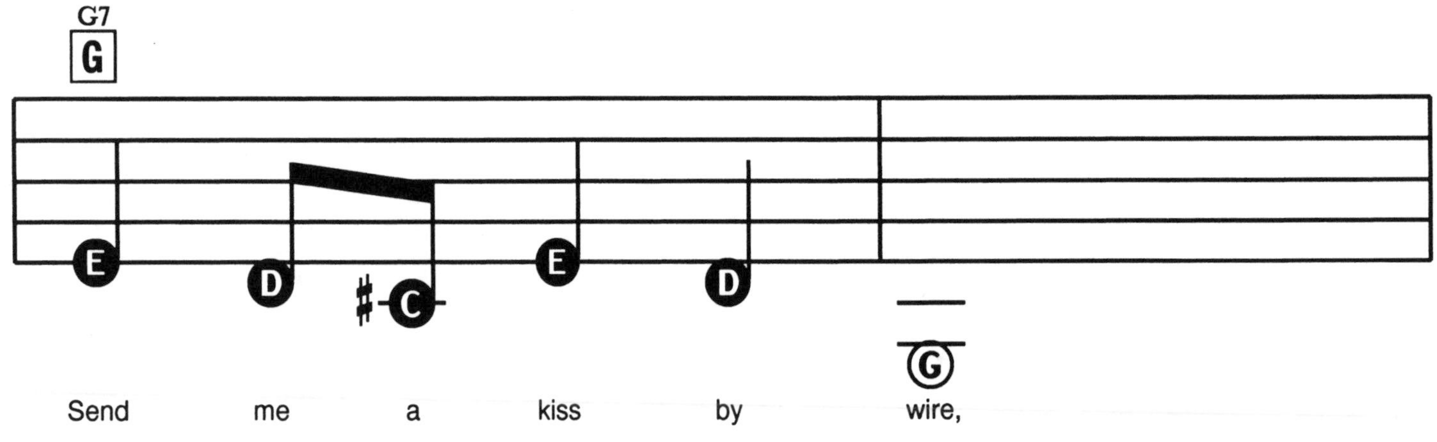

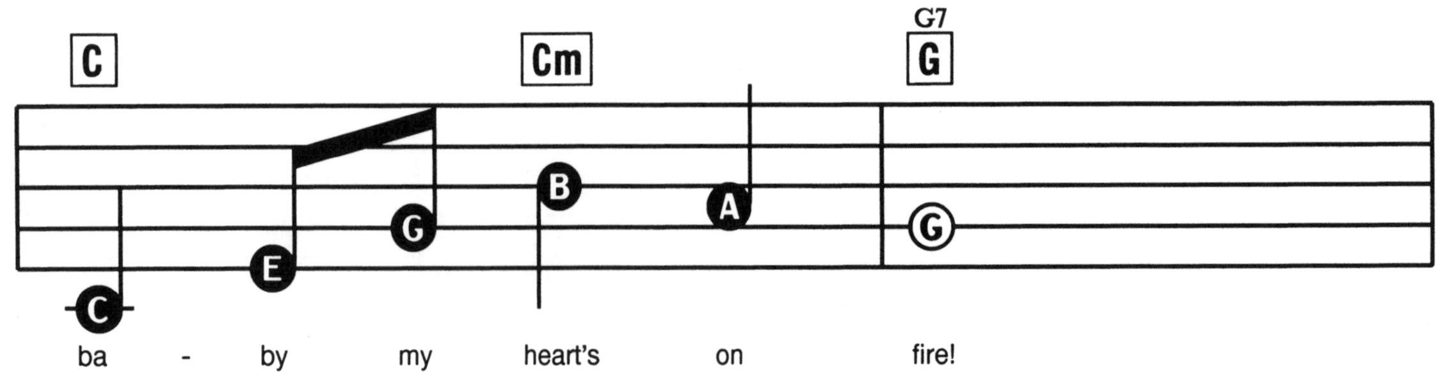

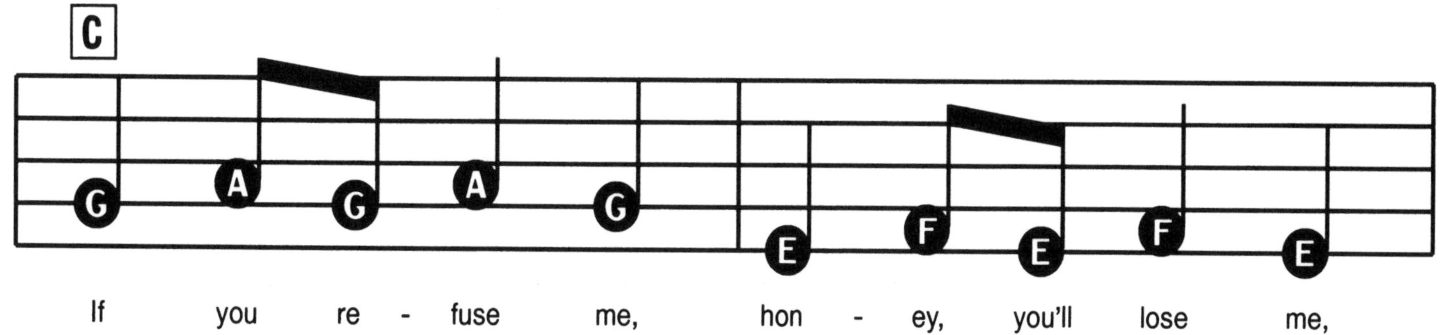
C
G
A
G
A
G
E
F
E
F
E
If you re - fuse me, hon - ey, you'll lose me,

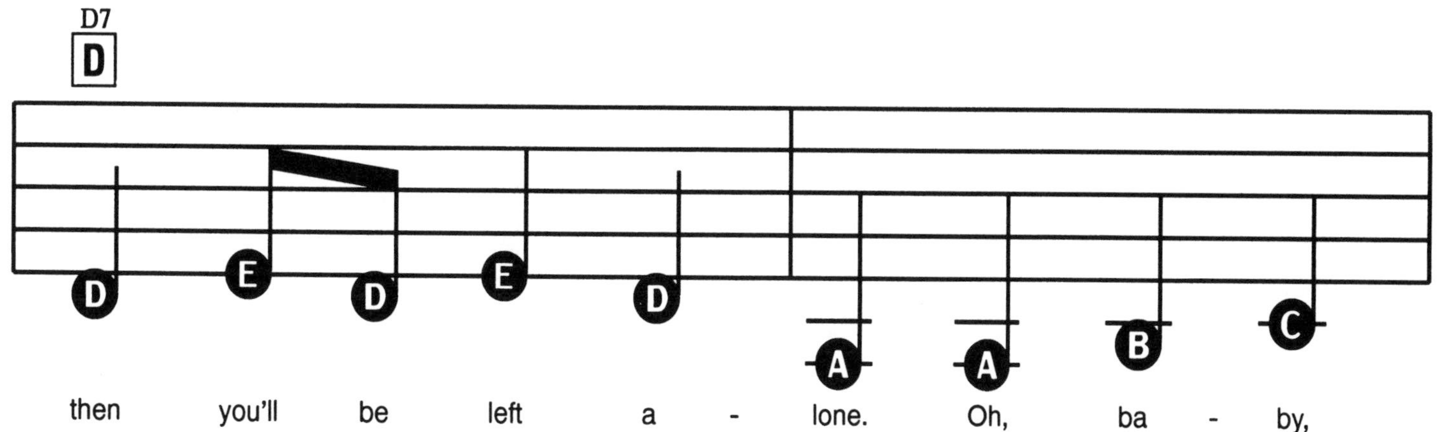
D7
D
D
E
D
E
D
A
A
B
C
then you'll be left a - lone. Oh, ba - by,

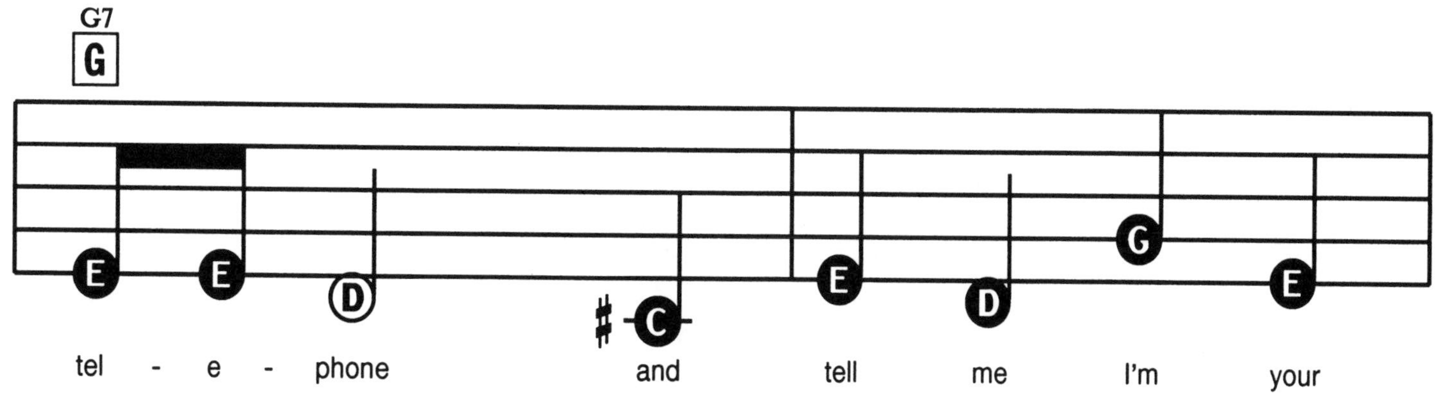
G7
G
E
E
D
C
E
D
G
E
tel - e - phone and tell me I'm your

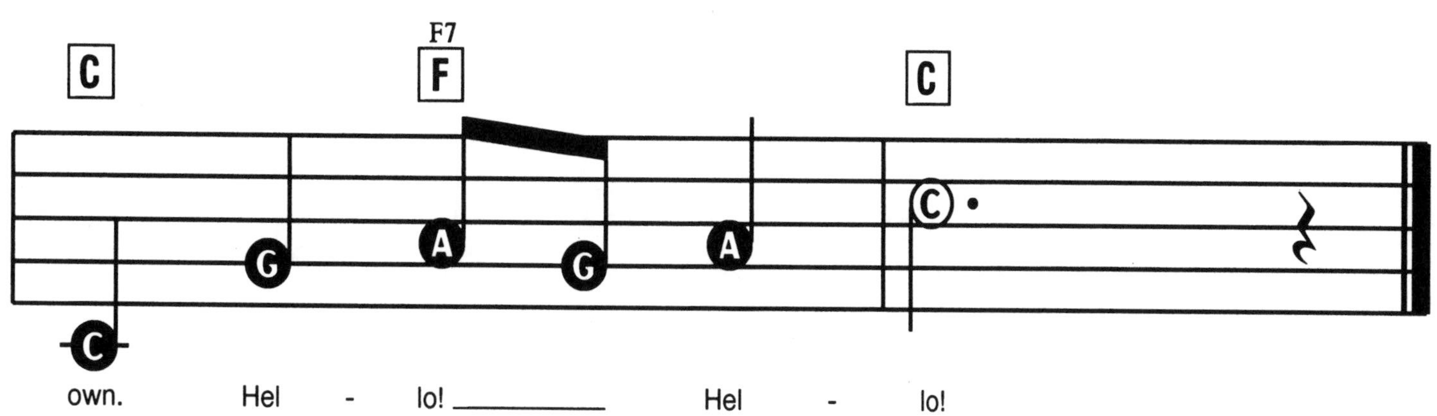
C
F7
F
C
C
G
A
G
A
C
own. Hel - lo! Hel - lo!

Home Sweet Home

Registration 1
Rhythm: Ballad

Words by John Howard Payne
Music by Henry R. Bishop

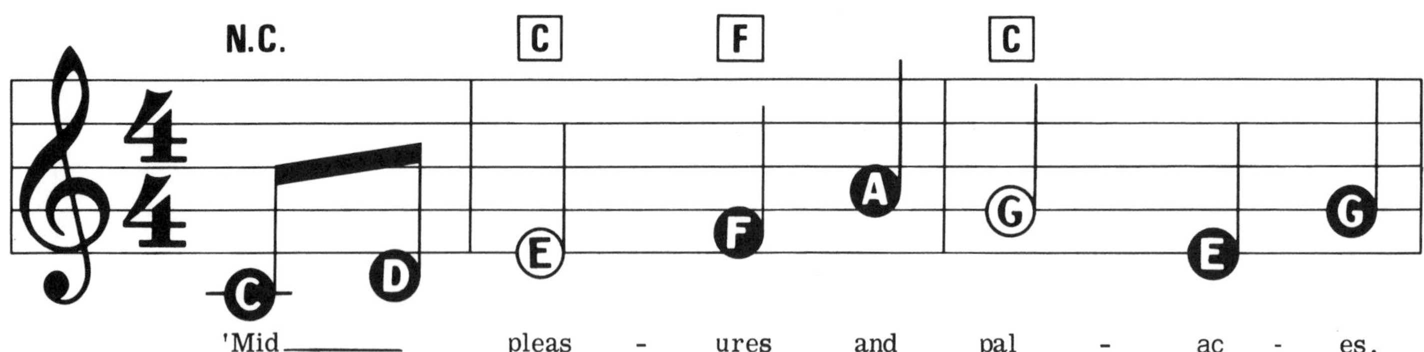

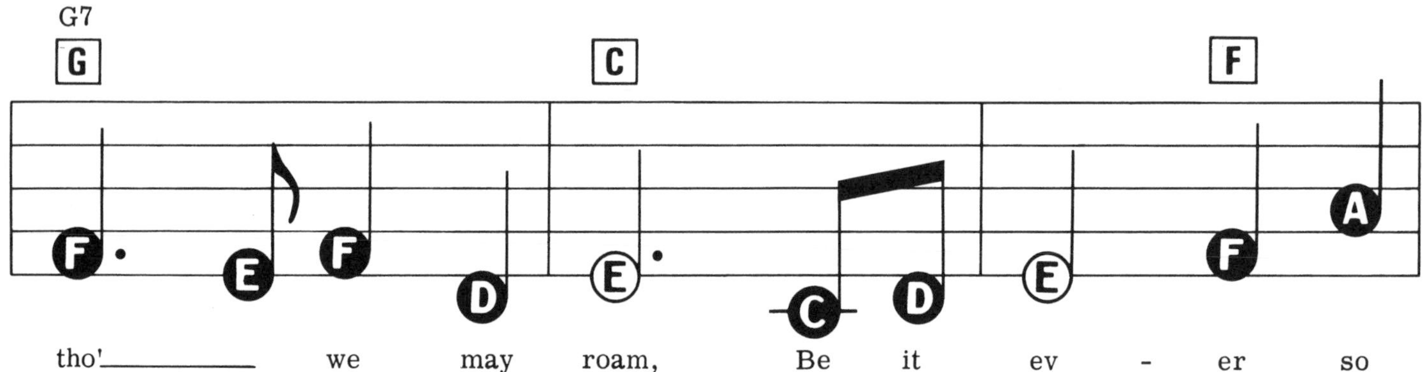

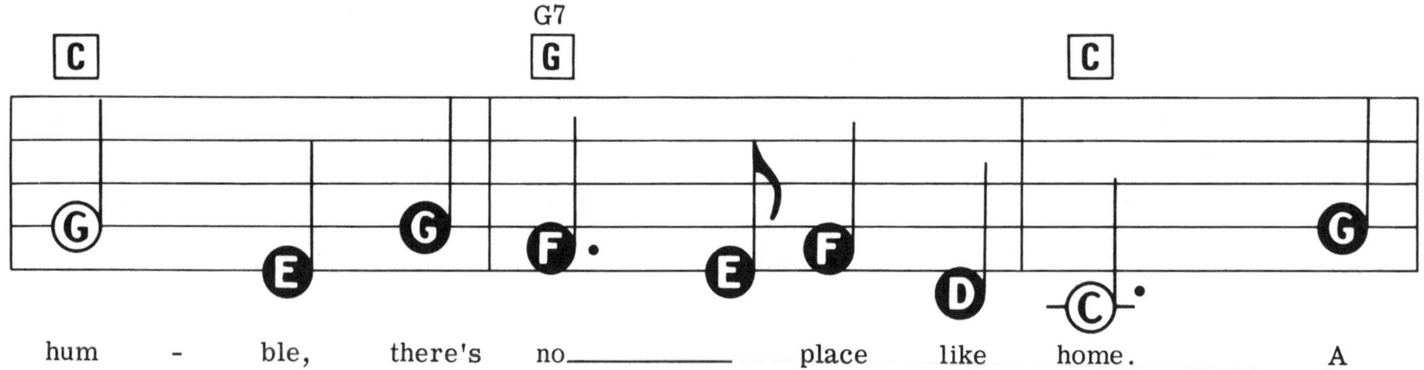

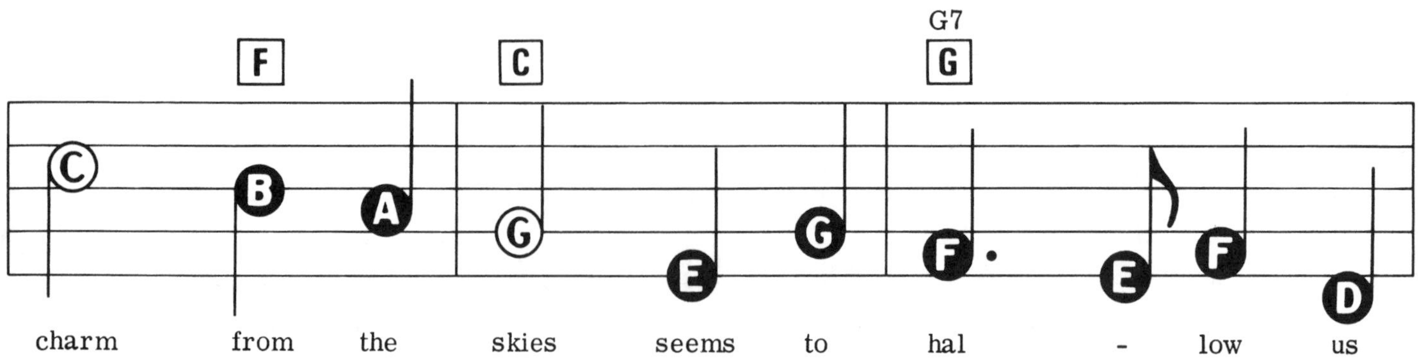

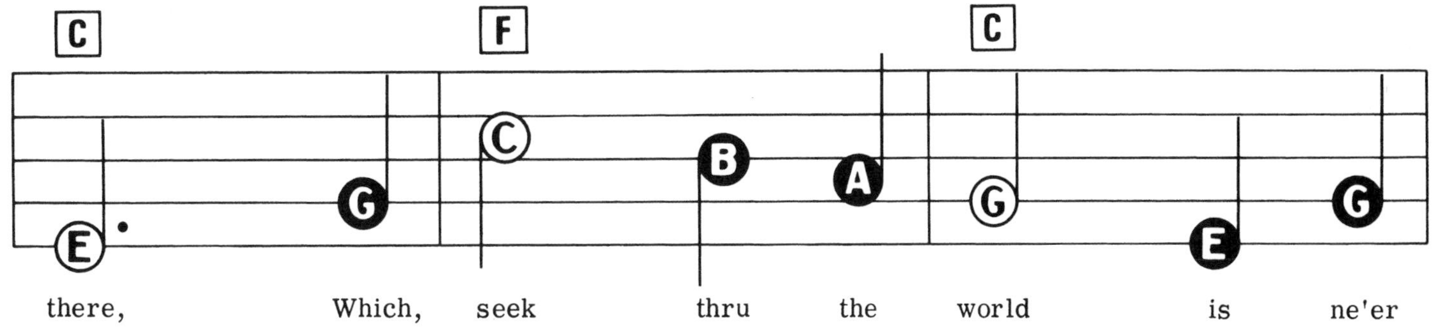
C
F
C
E
G
C
B
A
G
E
G
there,
Which,
seek
thru
the
world
is
ne'er

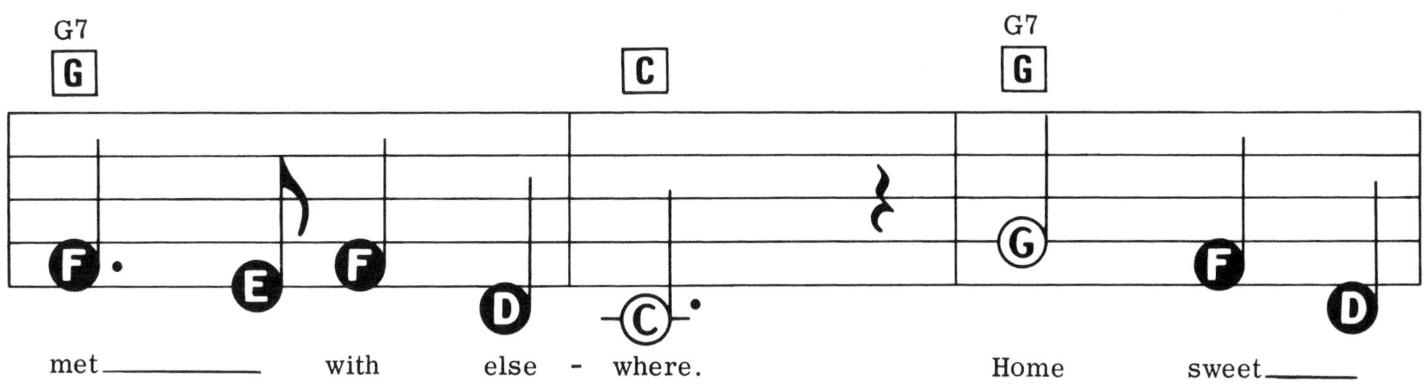
G7
G
C
G7
G
F
E
F
D
C
G
F
D
met
with
else -
where.
Home
sweet

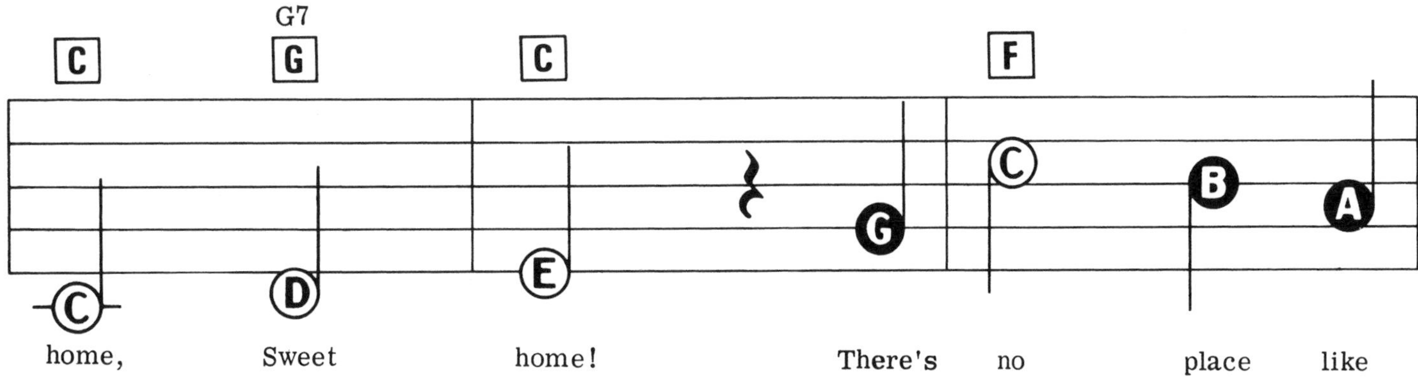
C
G7
G
C
F
C
D
E
G
C
B
A
home,
Sweet
home!
There's
no
place
like

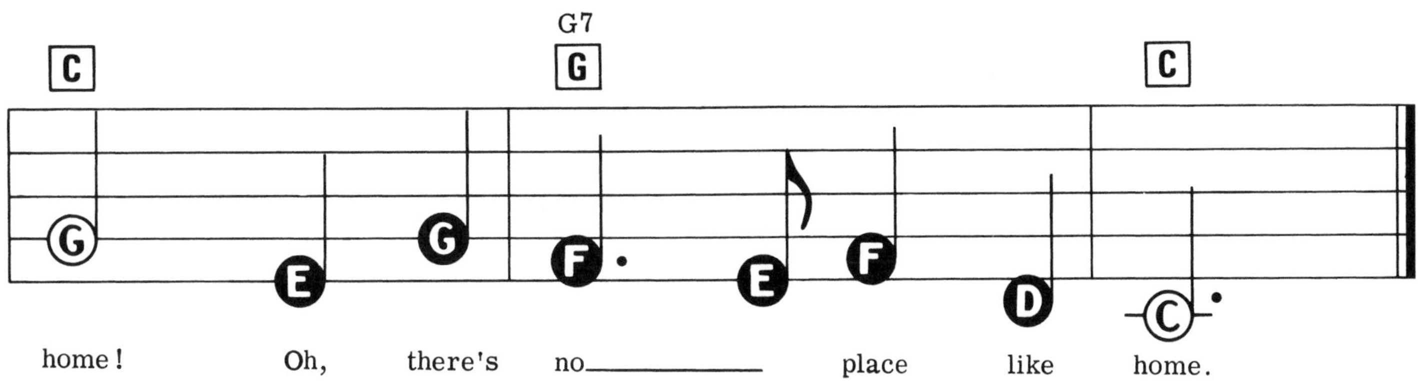
C
G7
G
C
G
E
G
F
E
F
D
C
home!
Oh,
there's
no
place
like
home.

I Love You Truly

Registration 10
Rhythm: Waltz

Words and Music by
Carrie Jacobs-Bond

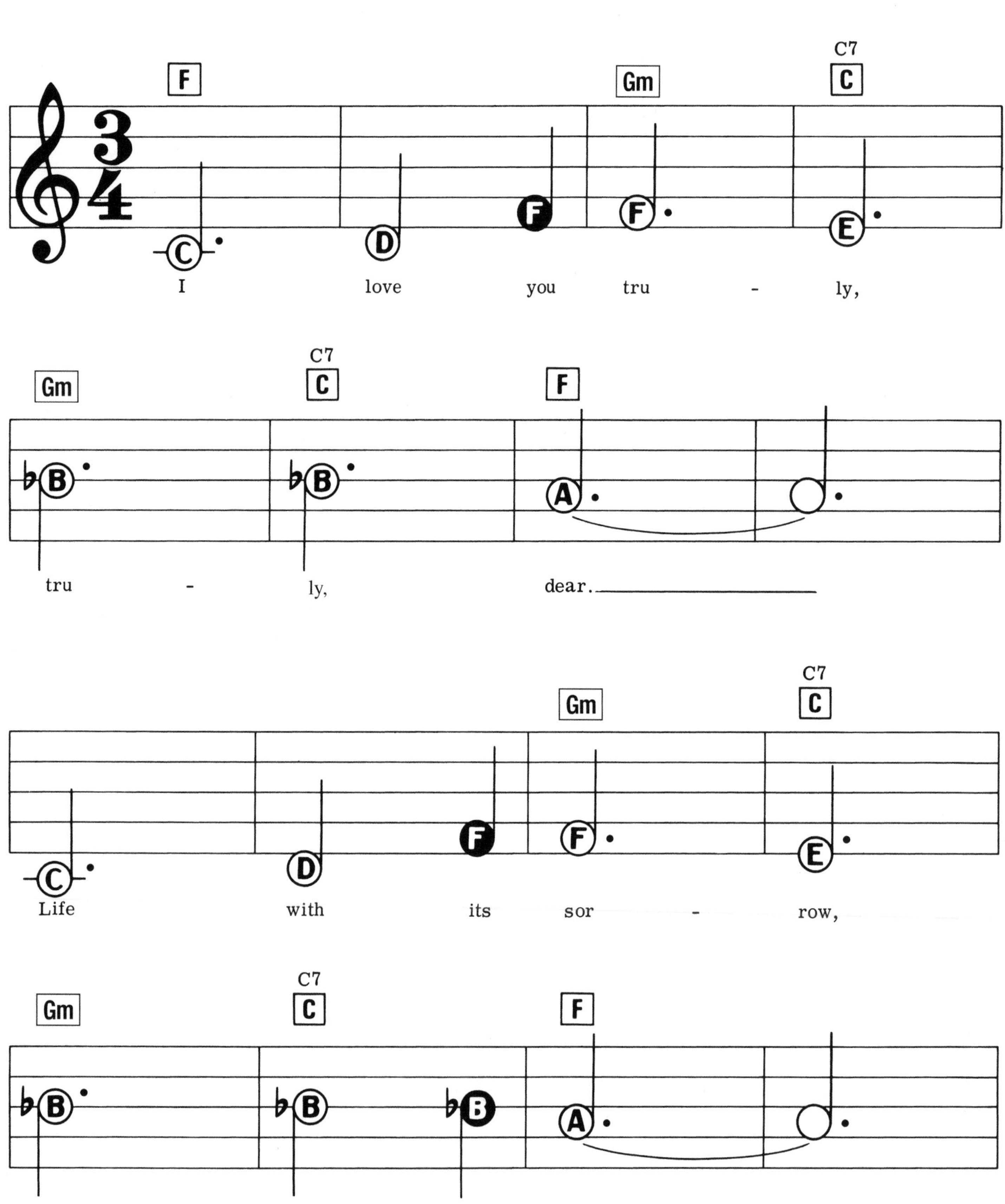

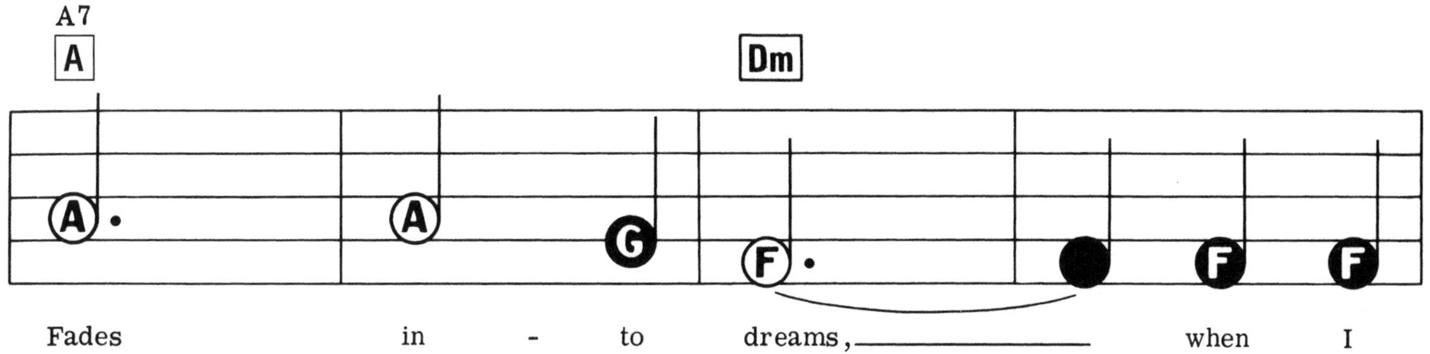
A7
A
Dm
A A G F F F
Fades in - to dreams, when I

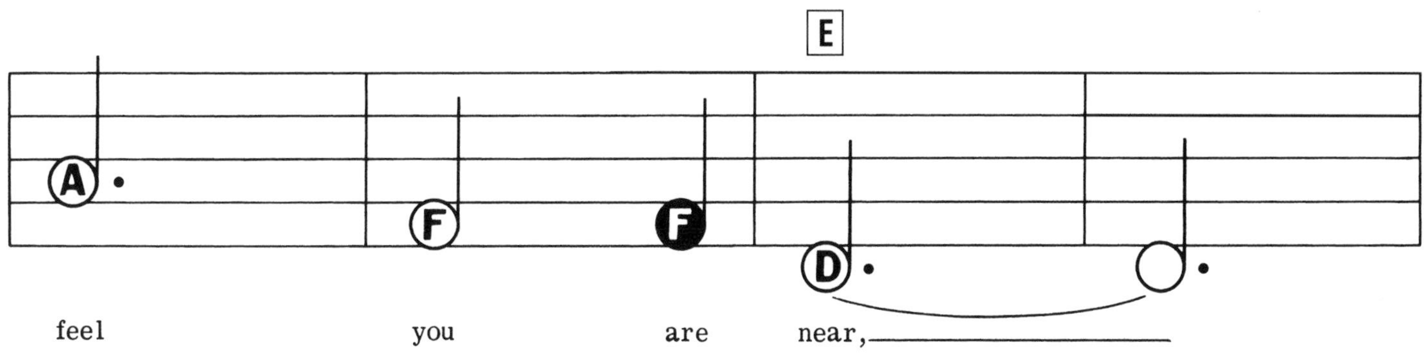
E
A F F D
feel you are near,

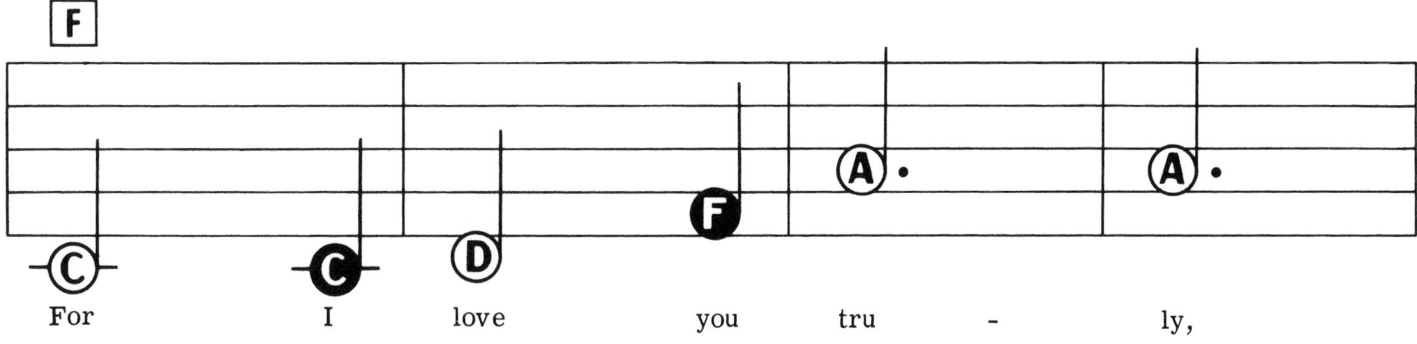
F
C C D F A A
For I love you tru - ly,

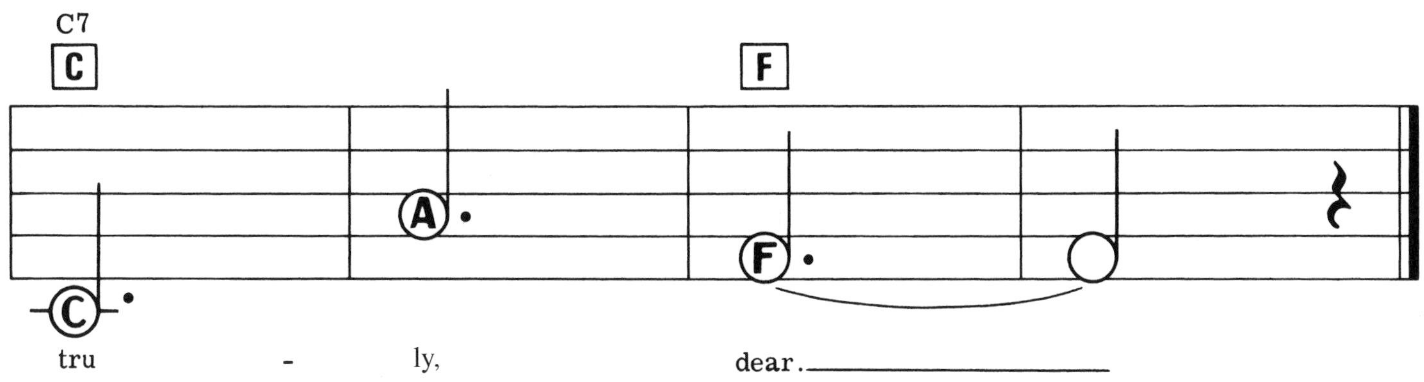
C7
C
F
C A F
tru - ly, dear.

I Wish I Were Single Again

Registration 8
Rhythm: Waltz

Words and Music by
J.C. Beckel

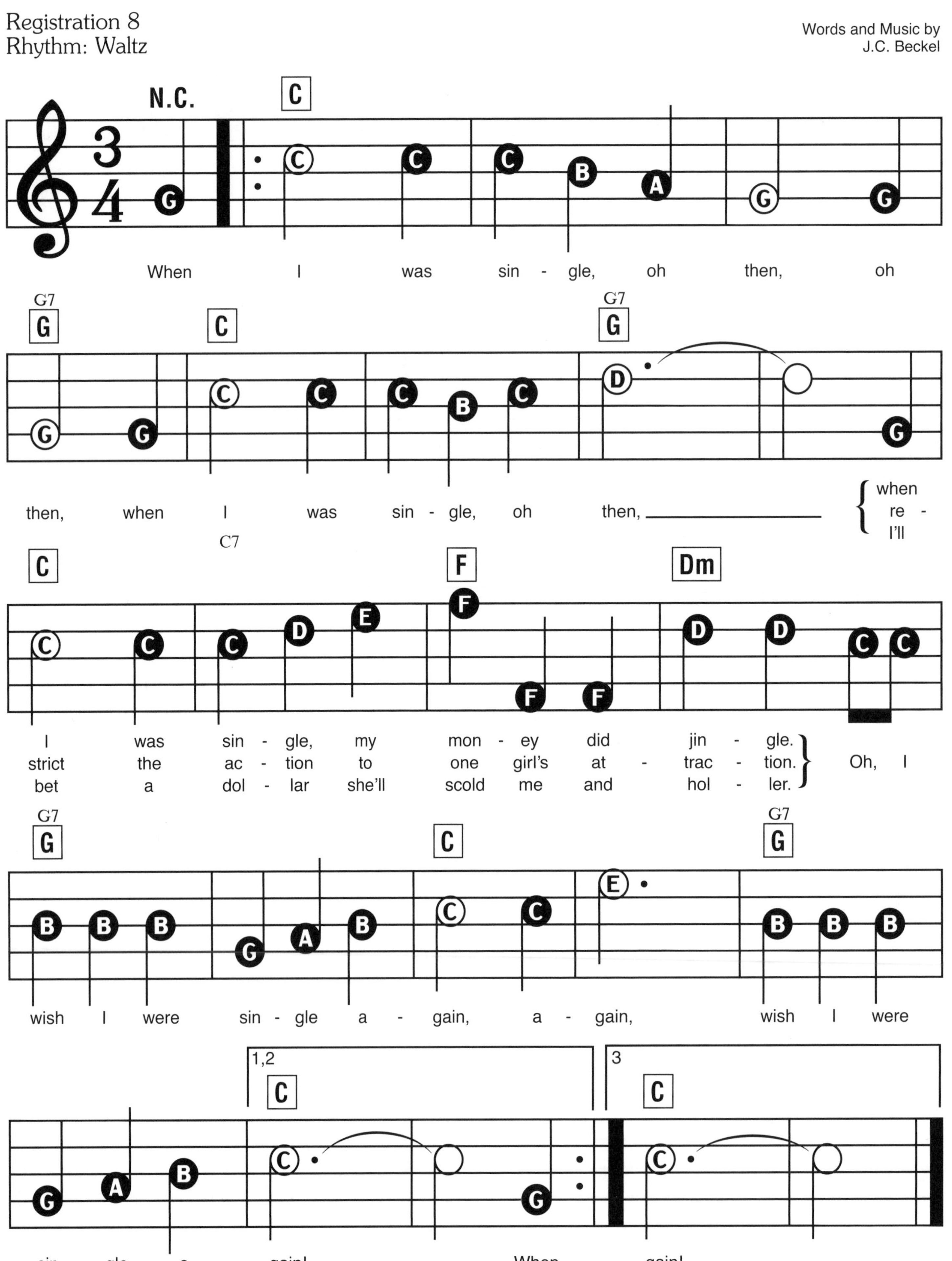

I Wonder Who's Kissing Her Now

Registration 1
Rhythm: Waltz

Lyrics by Will M. Hough and Frank R. Adams
Music by Joseph E. Howard and Harold Orlob

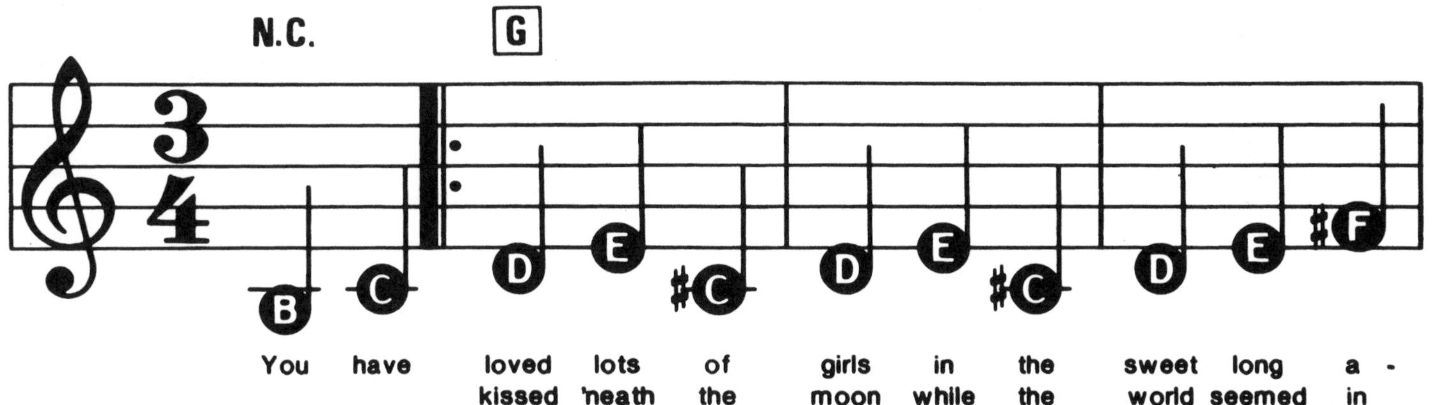

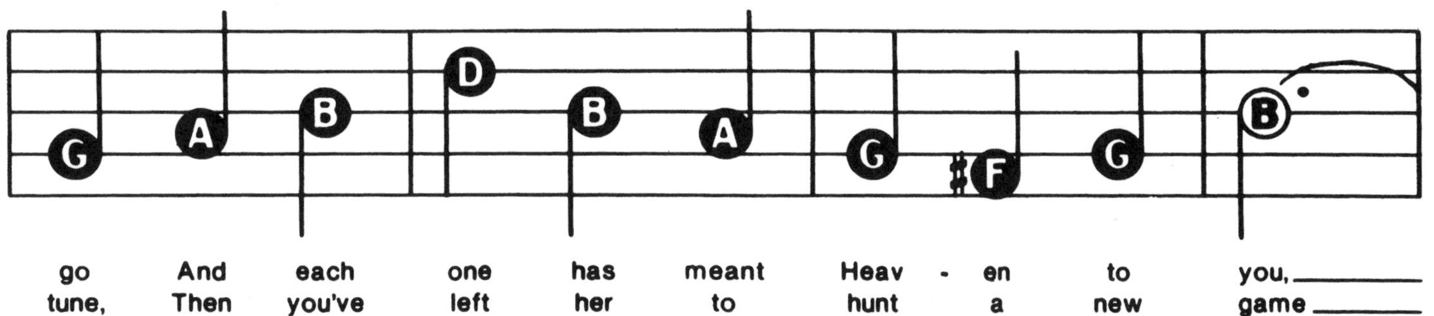

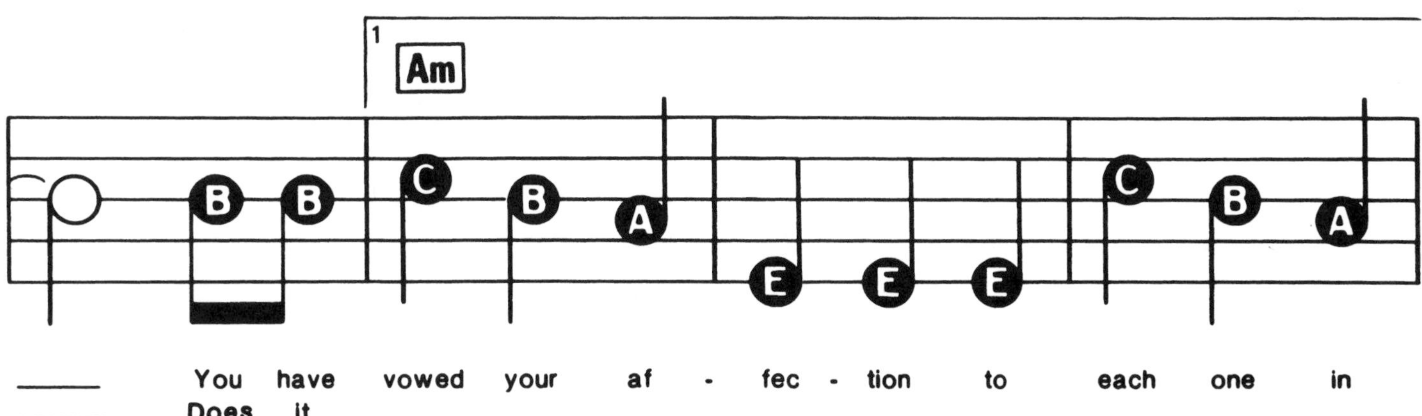

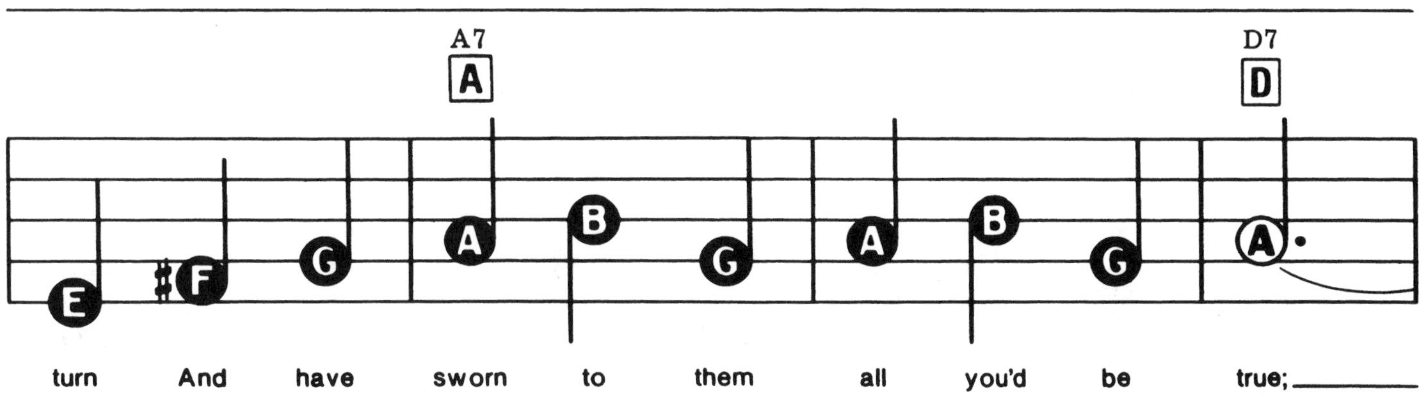

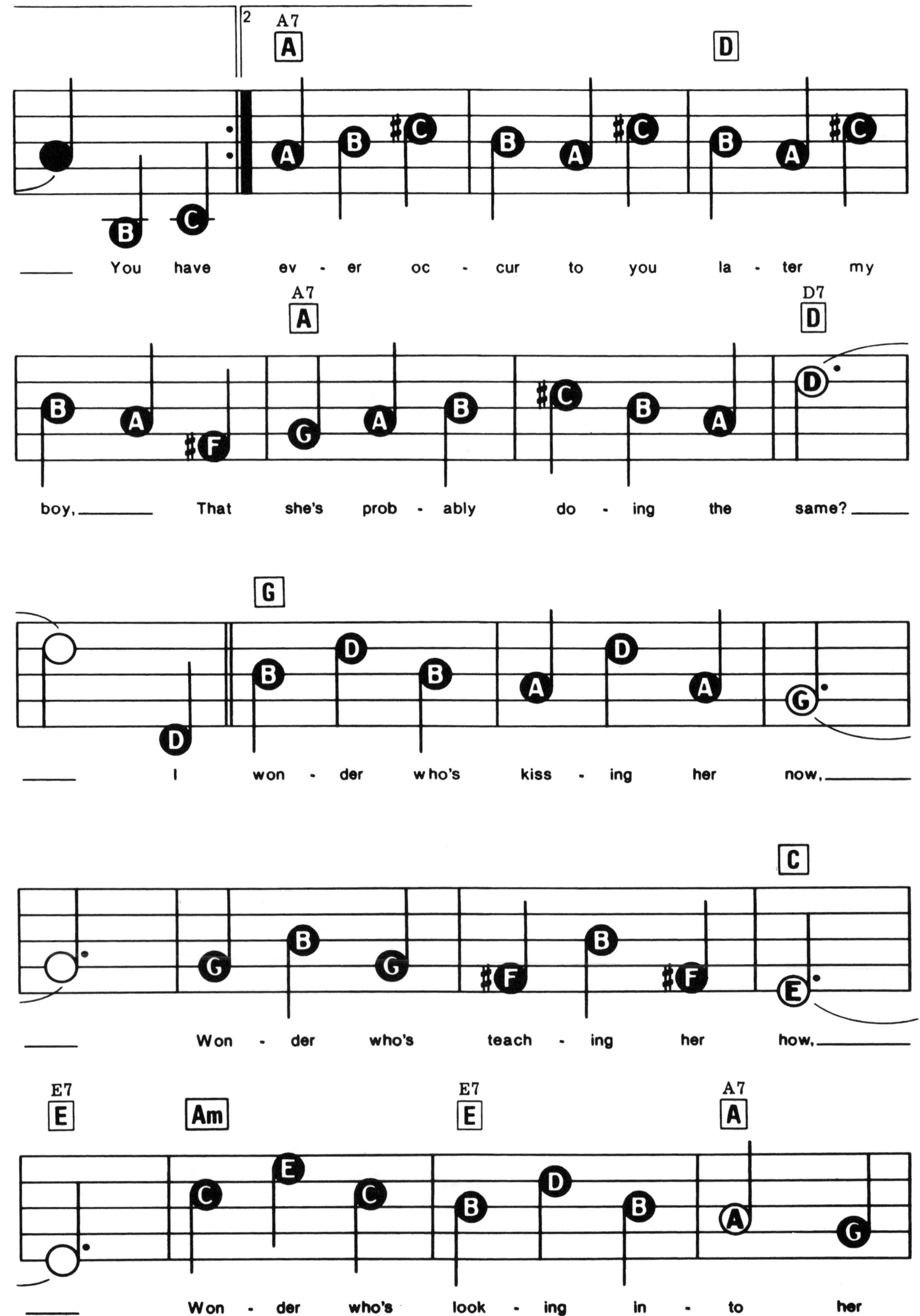
2
A7
A
D
You have ev - er oc - cur to you la - ter my
A7
A
D7
D
boy, That she's prob - ably do - ing the same?
G
I won - der who's kiss - ing her now,
C
Won - der who's teach - ing her how,
E7
E
Am
E7
E
A7
A
Won - der who's look - ing in - to her

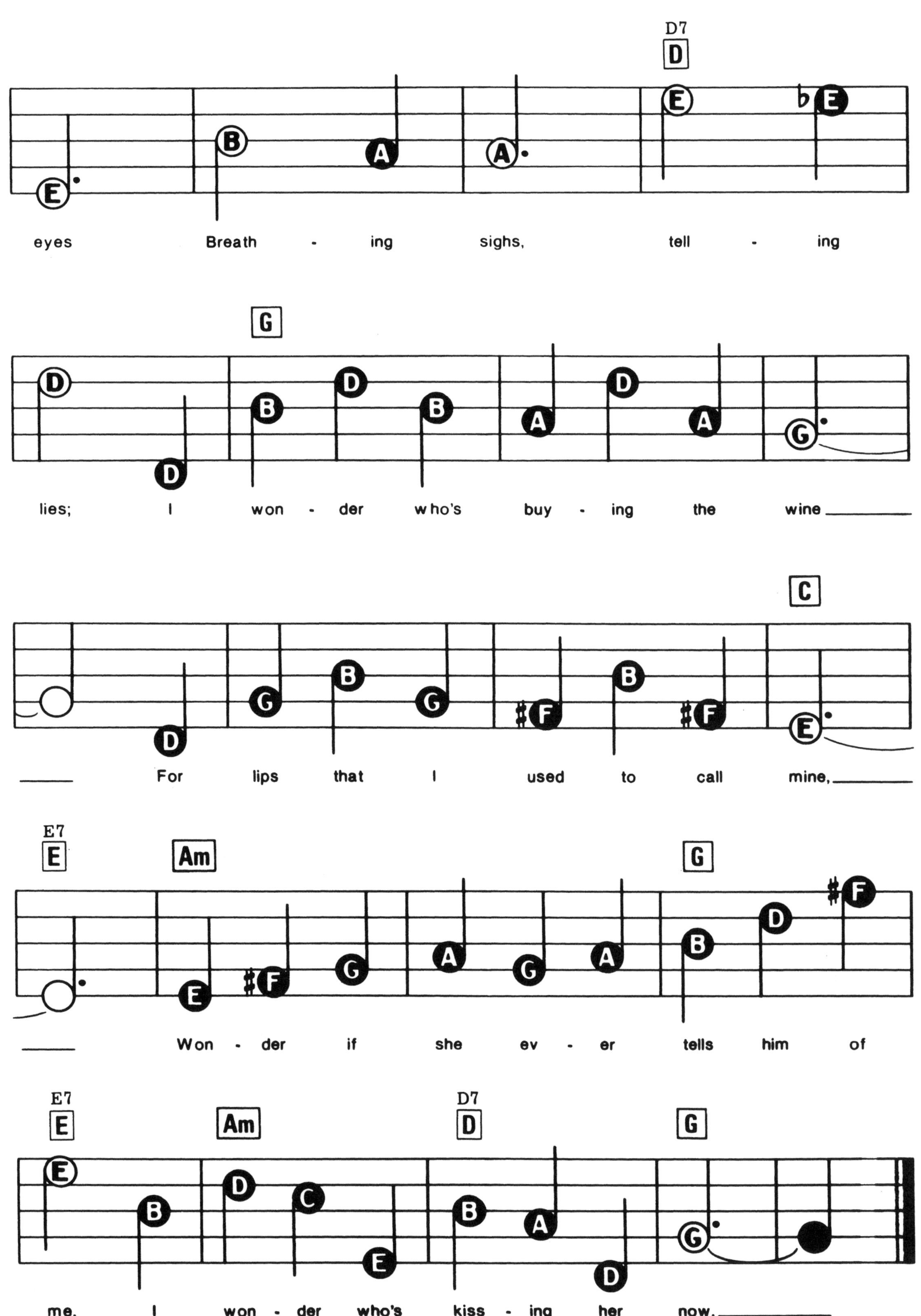
D7
D
E
A
B
E
A
A
E
E
eyes Breath - ing sighs, tell - ing
G
D
D
B
D
B
A
D
A
G
lies; I won - der who's buy - ing the wine
C
D
G
B
G
F
B
F
E
For lips that I used to call mine,
E7
E
Am
G
E
F
G
A
G
A
B
D
F
Won - der if she ev - er tells him of
E7
E
Am
D7
D
G
E
B
D
C
E
B
A
D
G
me, I won - der who's kiss - ing her now.

I'll Be with You in Apple Blossom Time

Registration 4
Rhythm: Waltz or Jazz Waltz

Words by Neville Fleeson
Music by Albert von Tilzer

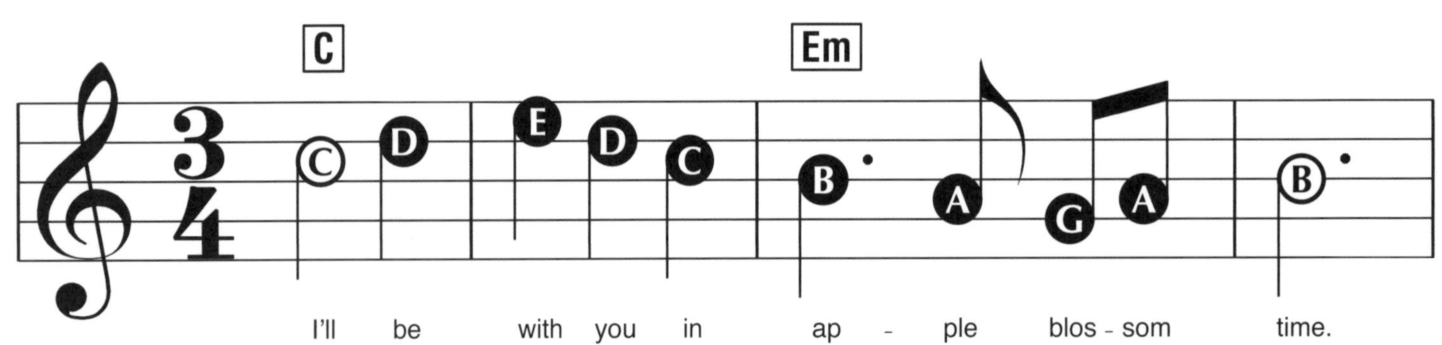

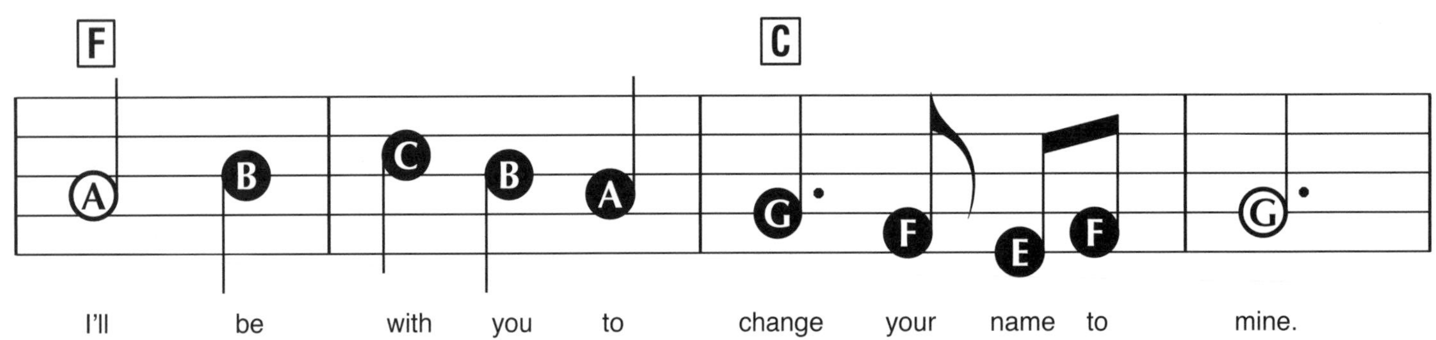

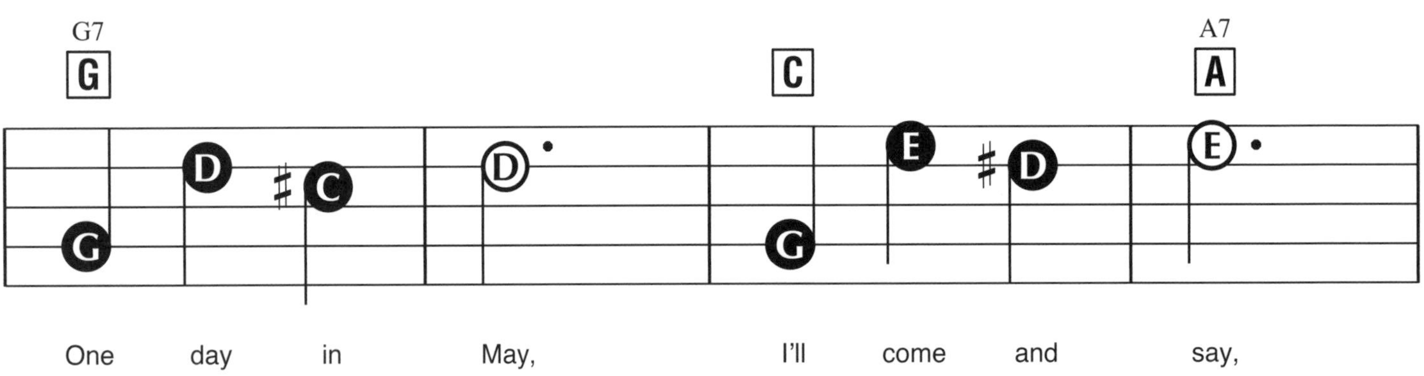

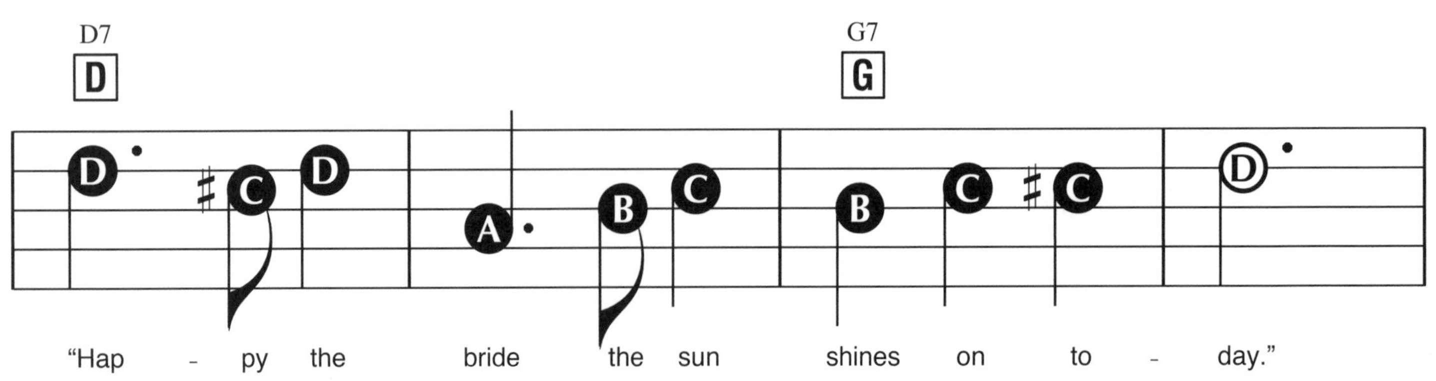

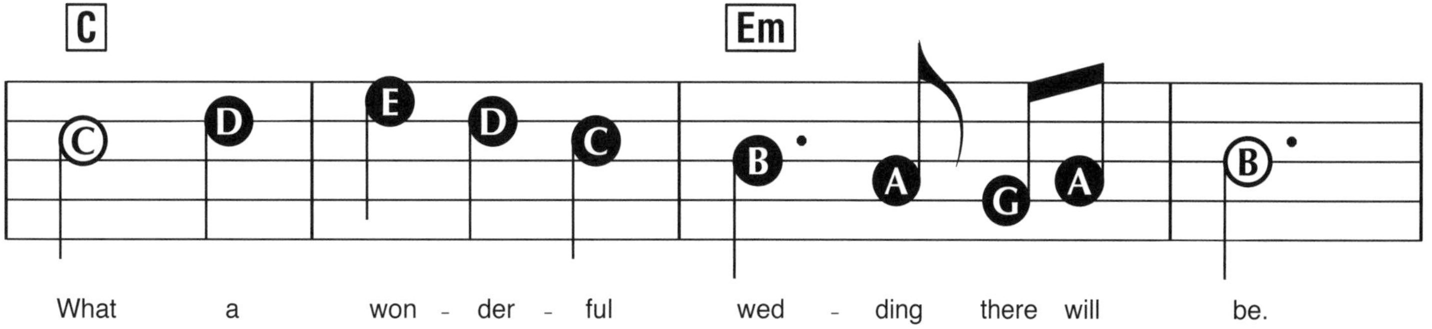
C
Em
C D E D C B A G A B
What a won - der - ful wed - ding there will be.

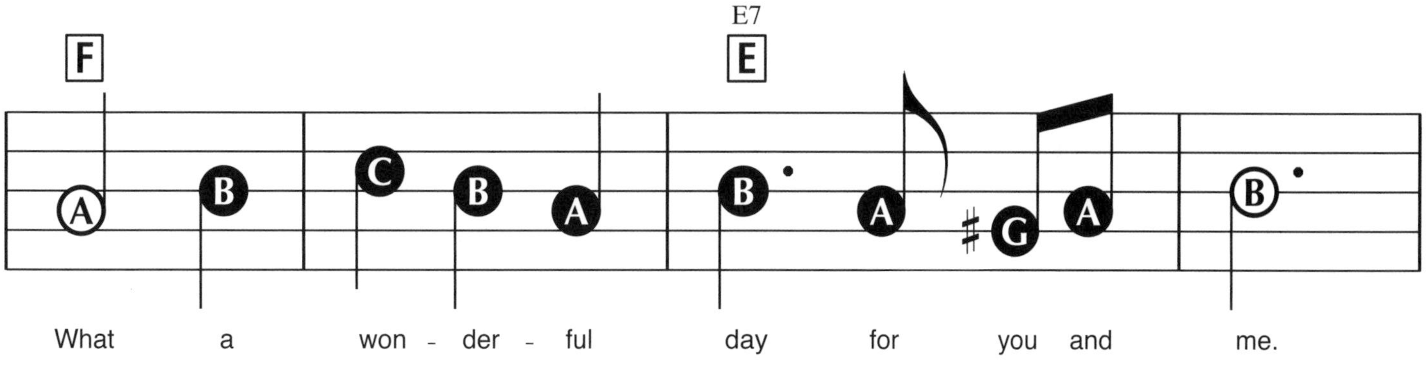
F
E7
E
A B C B A B A ♯ G A B
What a won - der - ful day for you and me.

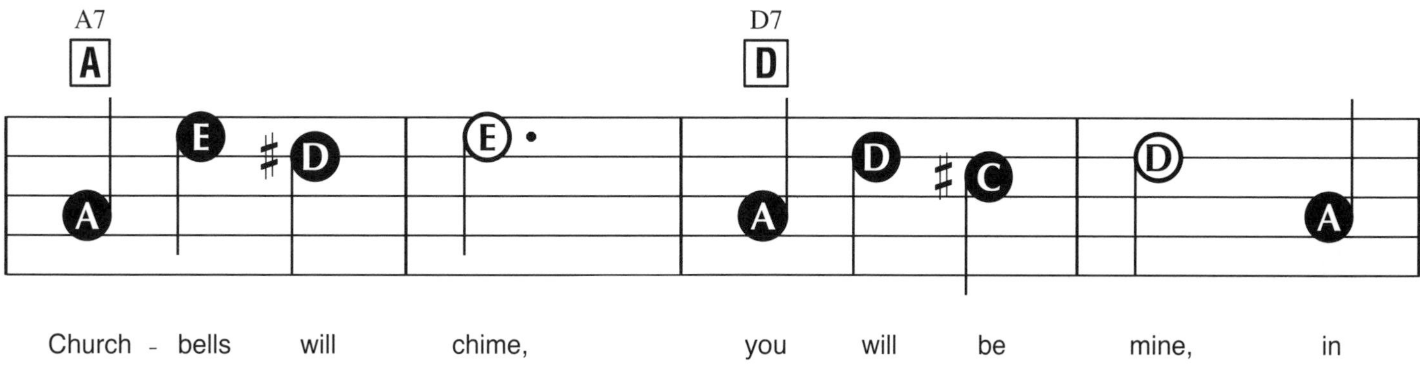
A7
A
D7
D
A E ♯ D E A D ♯ C D A
Church - bells will chime, you will be mine, in

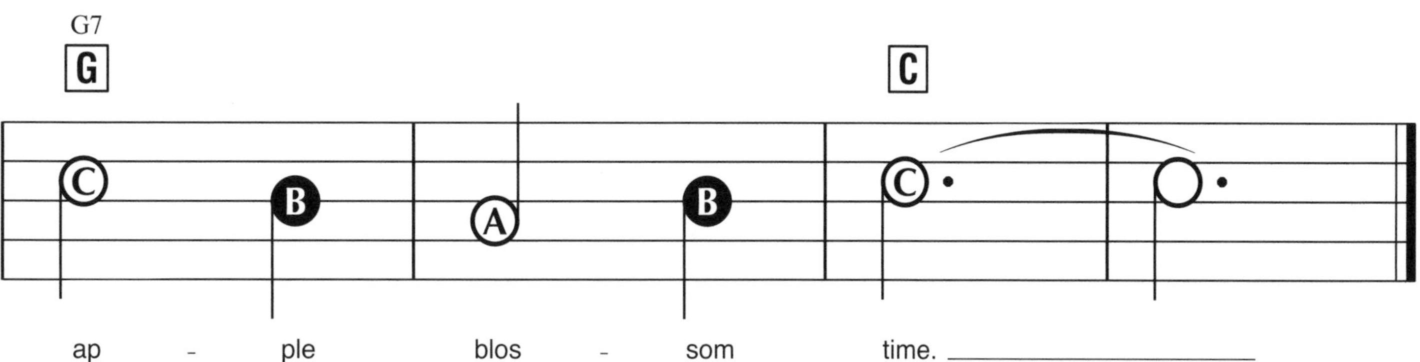
G7
G
C
C B A B C
ap - ple blos - som time.

I'm Always Chasing Rainbows

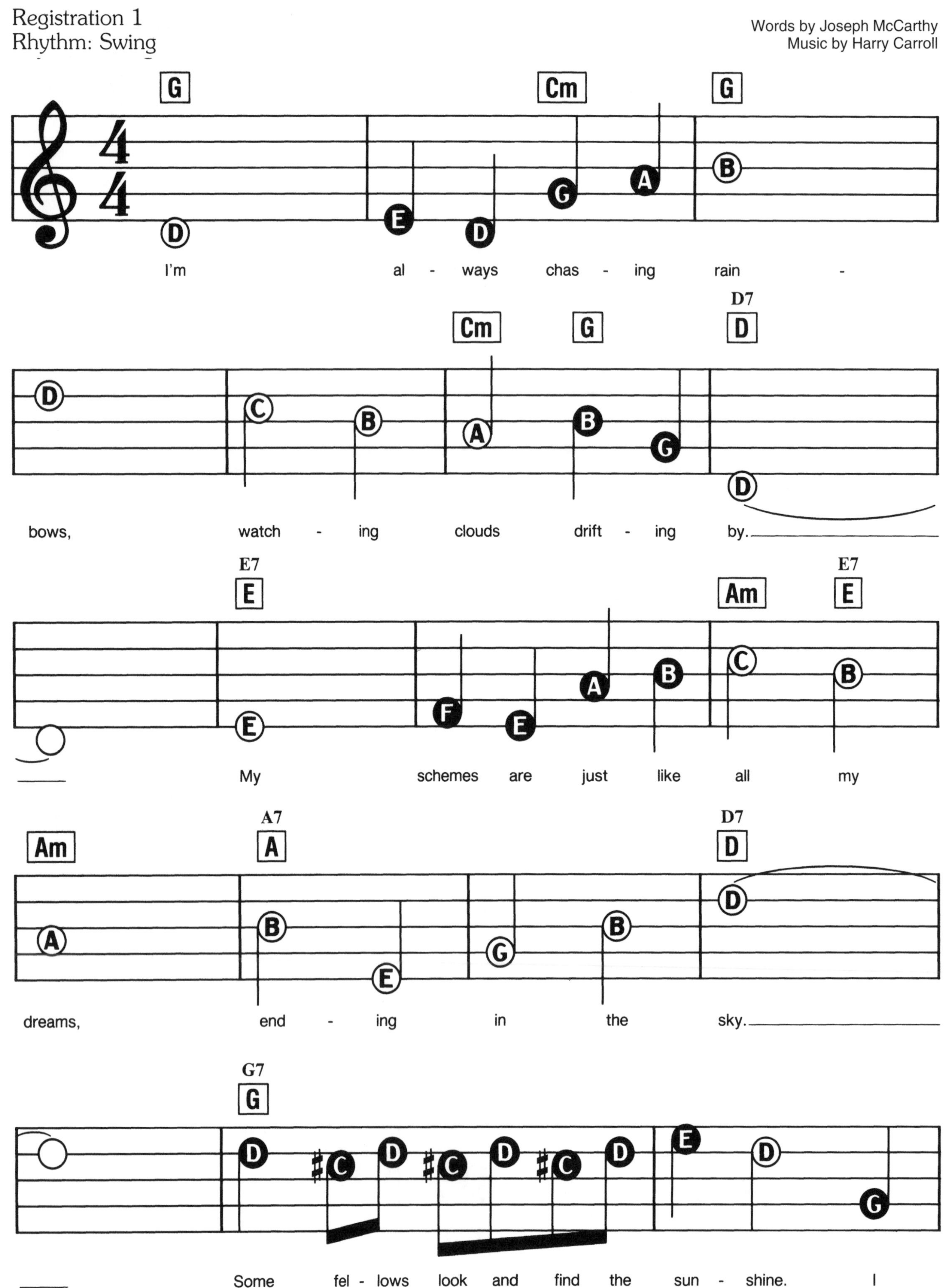

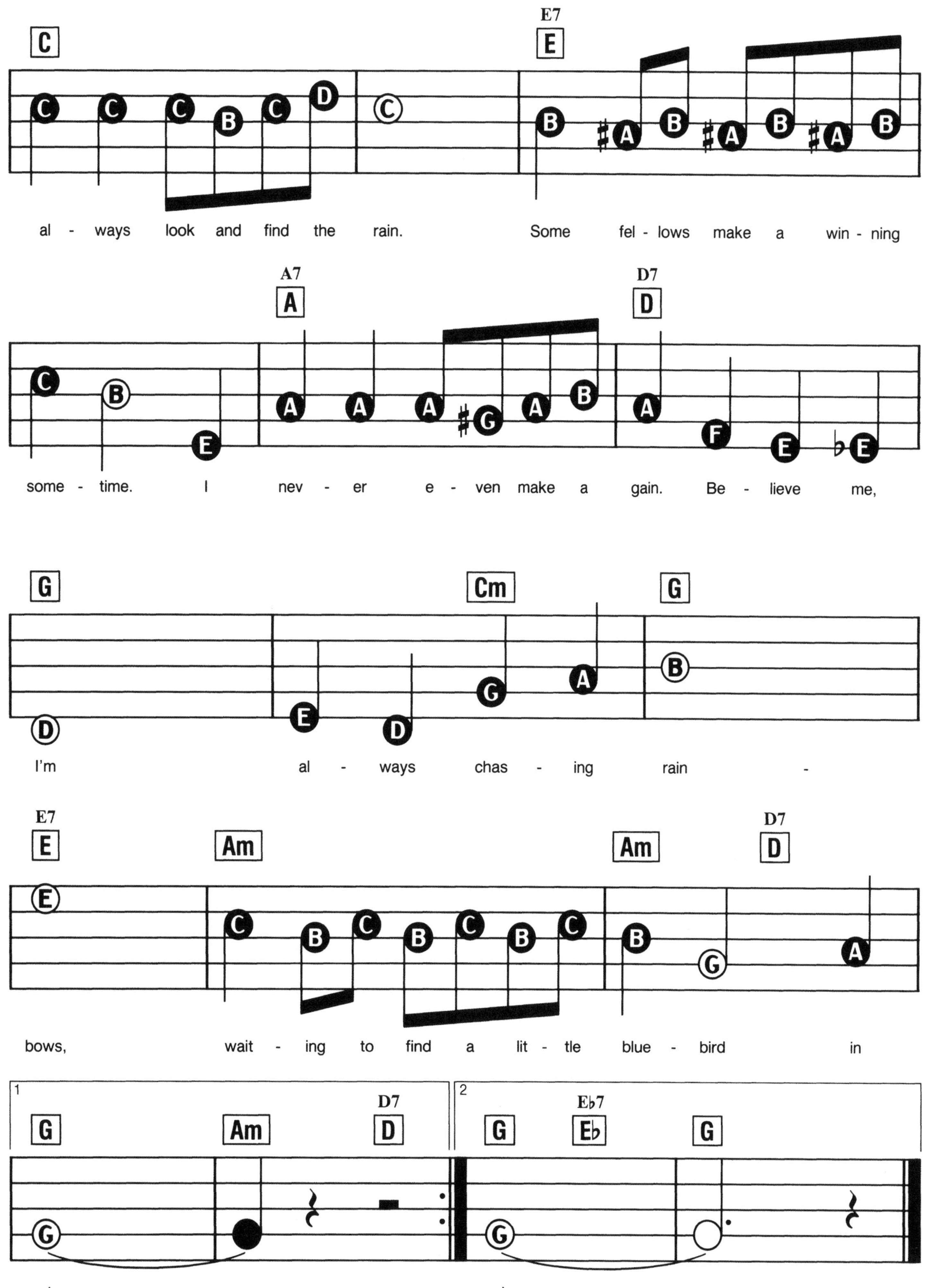
C
E7
E
al - ways look and find the rain.
Some fel - lows make a win - ning
A7
A
D7
D
some - time. I nev - er e - ven make a gain. Be - lieve me,
G
Cm
G
I'm al - ways chas - ing rain -
E7
E
Am
Am
D7
D
bows, wait - ing to find a lit - tle blue - bird in
1
G
Am
D7
D
vain.
2
G
E♭7
E♭
G
vain.

I've Been Working on the Railroad

Registration 2
Rhythm: 6/8 March

American Folksong

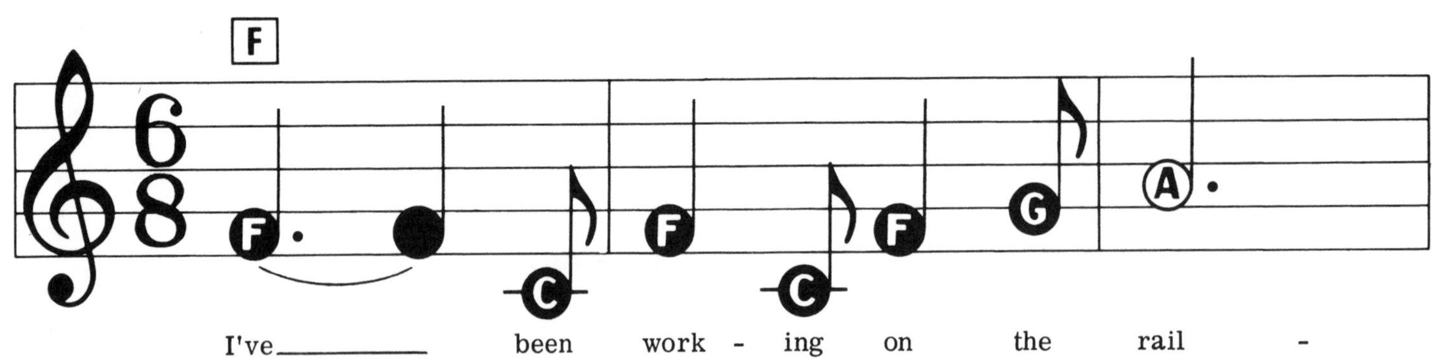

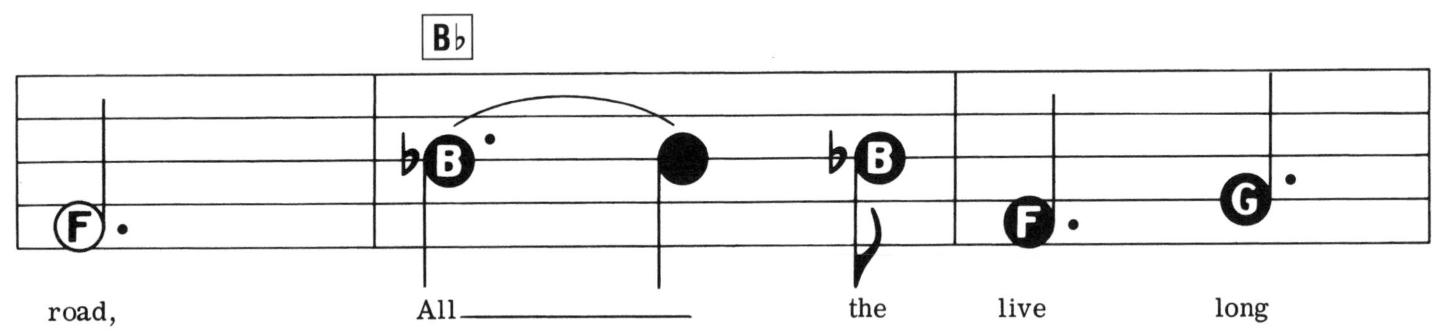

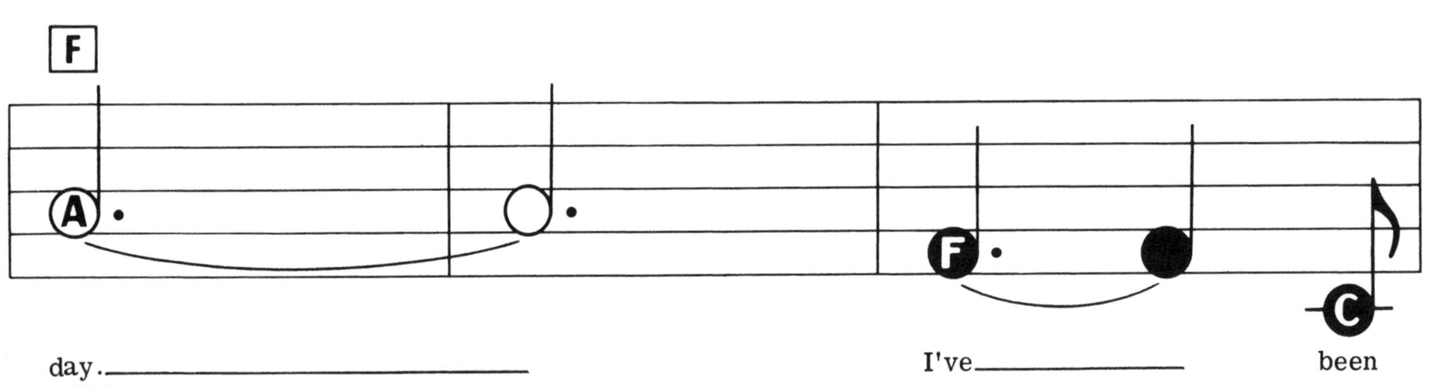

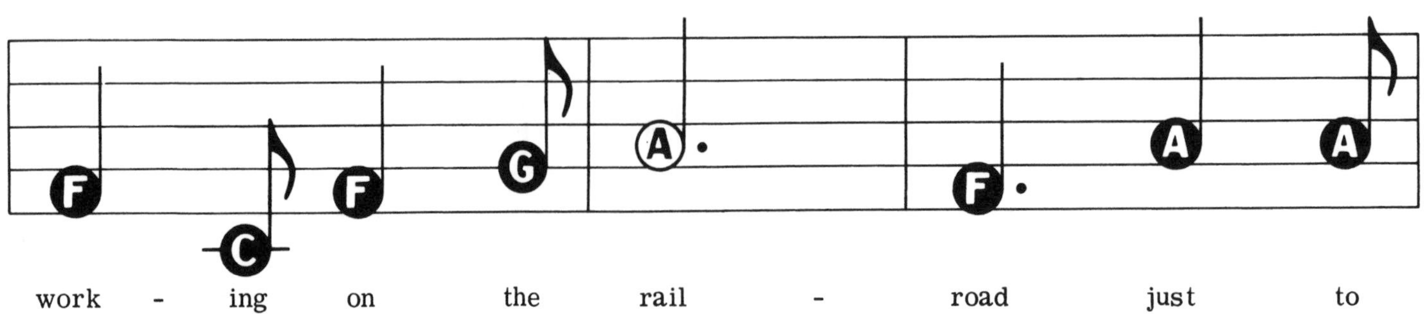

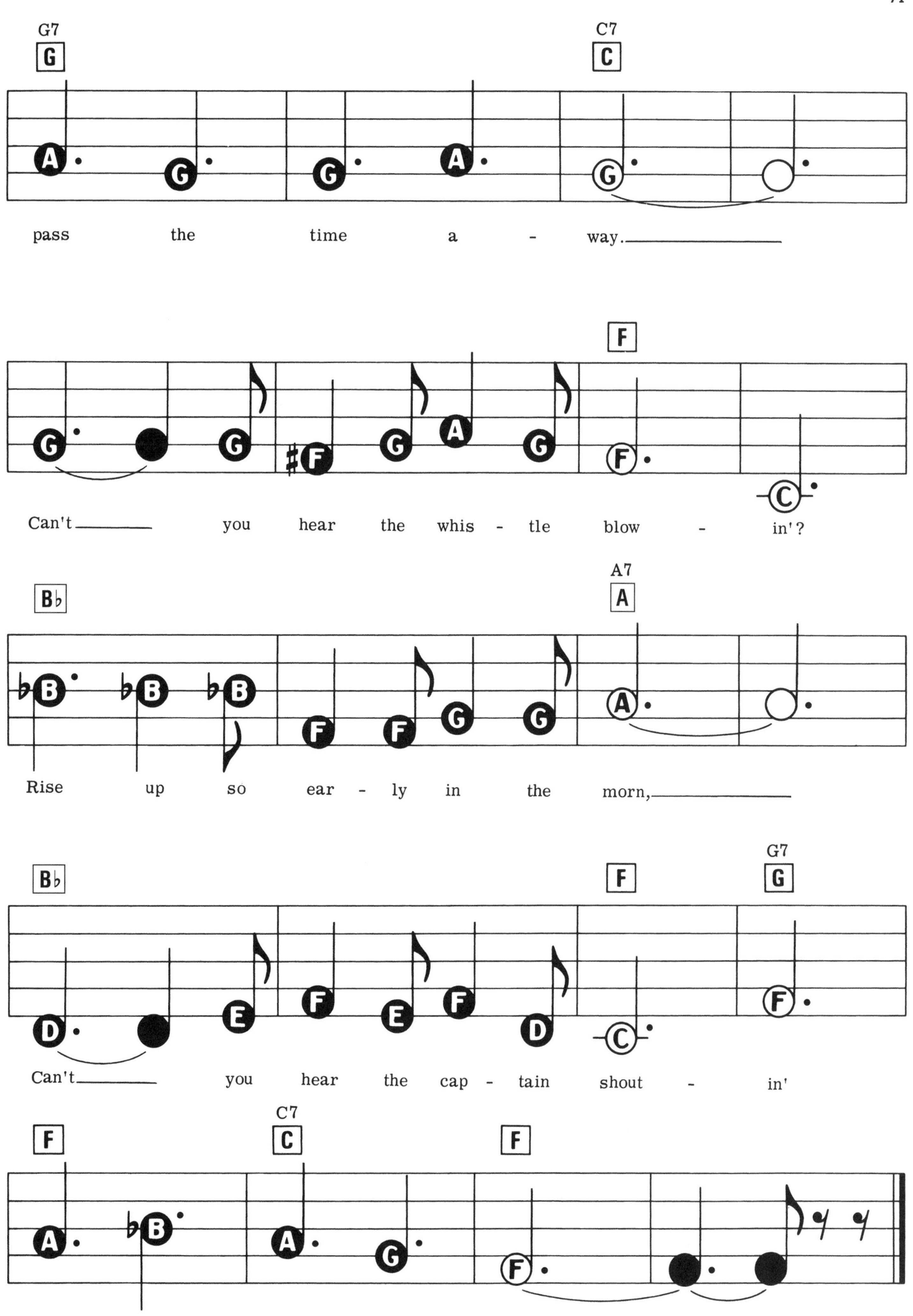
G7 G C7 C
pass the time a - way.
F
Can't you hear the whis - tle blow - in'?
B♭ A7 A
Rise up so ear - ly in the morn,
B♭ F G7 G
Can't you hear the cap - tain shout - in'
F C7 C F
"Di - nah blow your horn!"

If I Had My Way

Registration 2
Rhythm: Waltz

Words by Lou Klein
Music by James Kendis

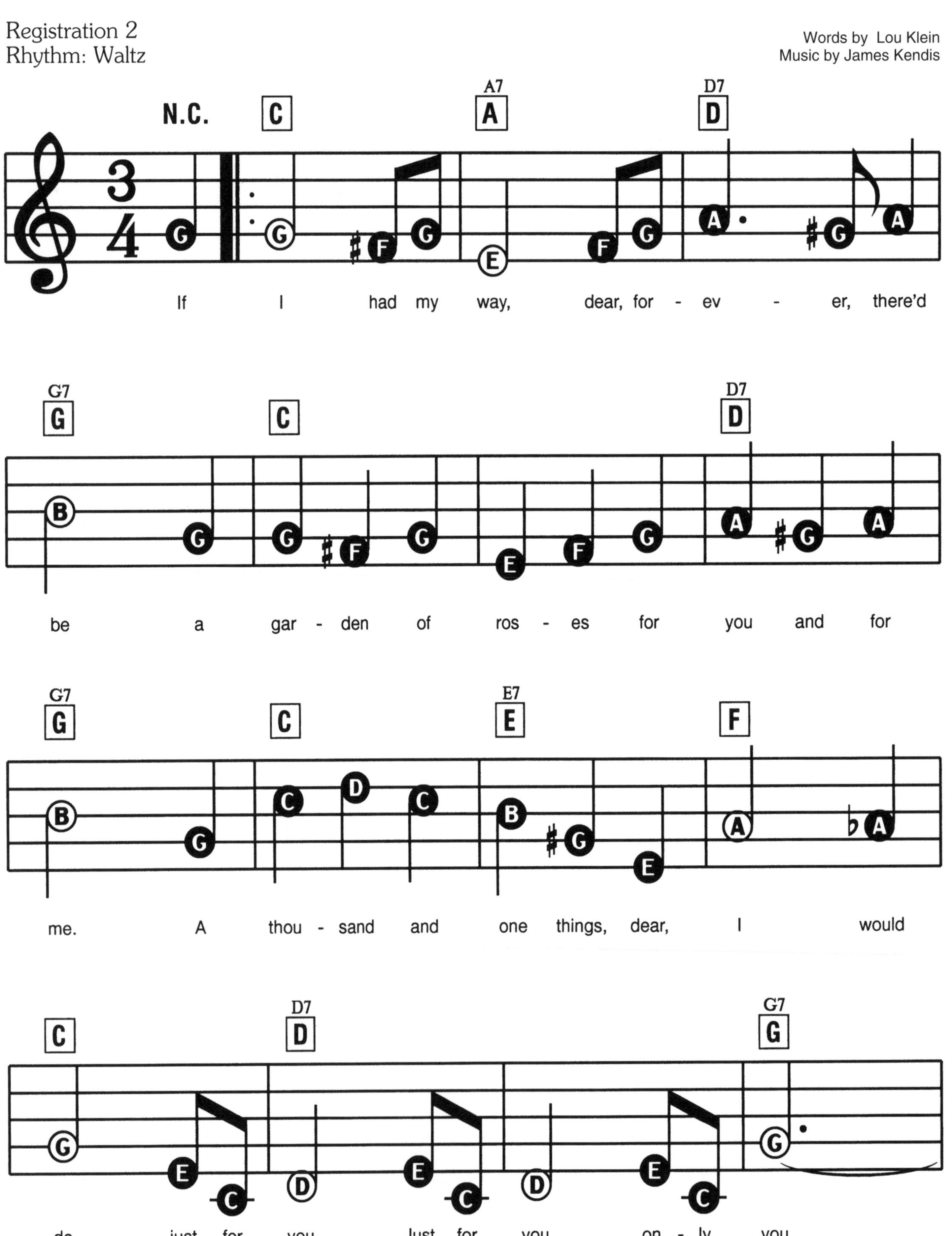

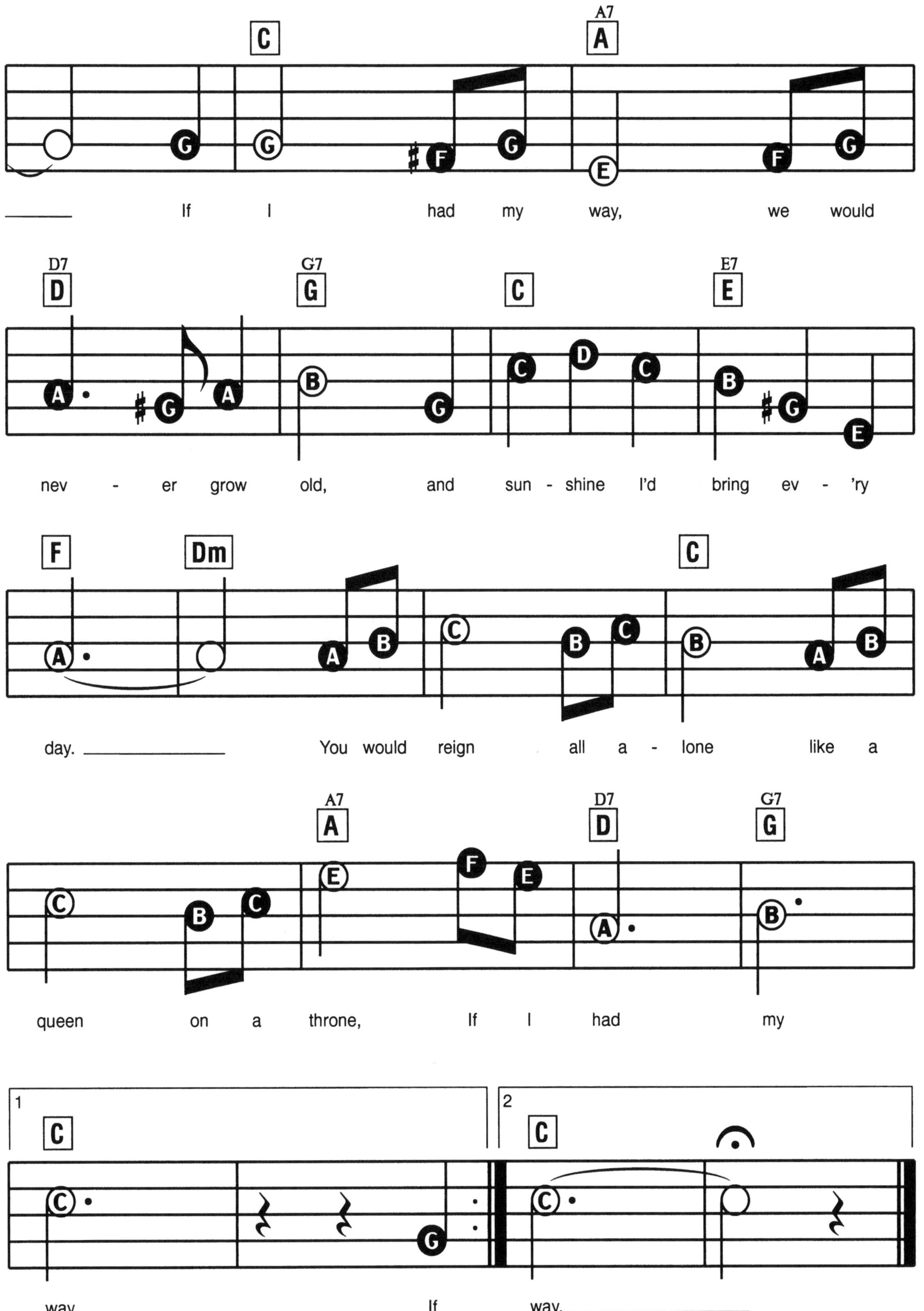
C
A7
A
G
G
F
G
E
F
G
If I had my way, we would
D7
D
G7
G
C
E7
E
A
G
A
B
G
C
D
C
B
G
E
nev - er grow old, and sun - shine I'd bring ev - 'ry
F
Dm
C
A
A
B
C
B
C
B
A
B
day. You would reign all a - lone like a
A7
A
D7
D
G7
G
C
B
C
E
F
E
A
B
queen on a throne, If I had my
1
C
C
G
2
C
C
way. If way.

If You Were the Only Girl in the World

Registration 10
Rhythm: Waltz

Words by Clifford Grey
Music by Nat D. Ayer

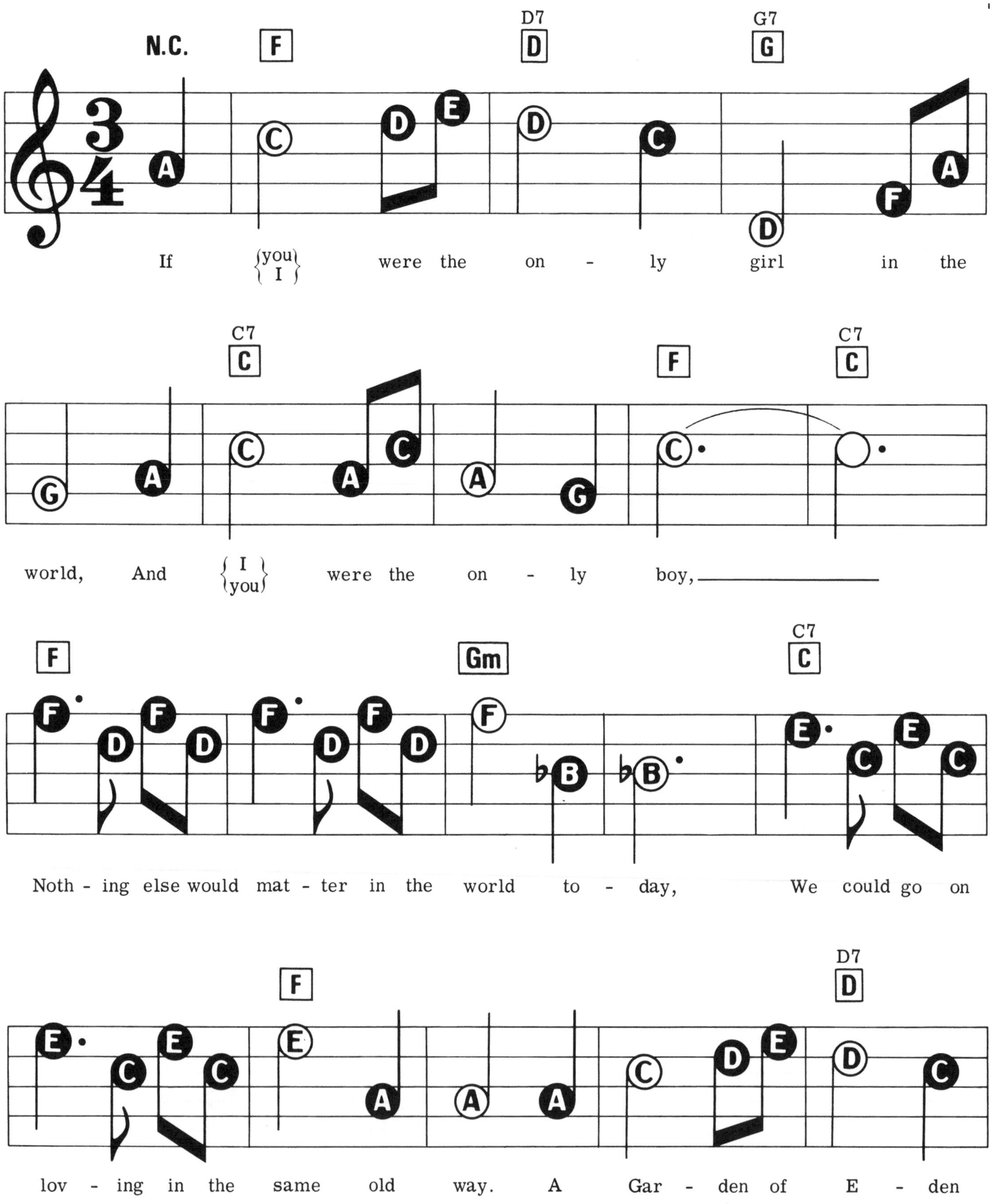

N.C. F D7 D G7 G

If {you / I} were the on - ly girl in the

C7 C F C7 C

world, And {I / you} were the on - ly boy, ___

F Gm C7 C

Noth - ing else would mat - ter in the world to - day, We could go on

F D7 D

lov - ing in the same old way. A Gar - den of E - den

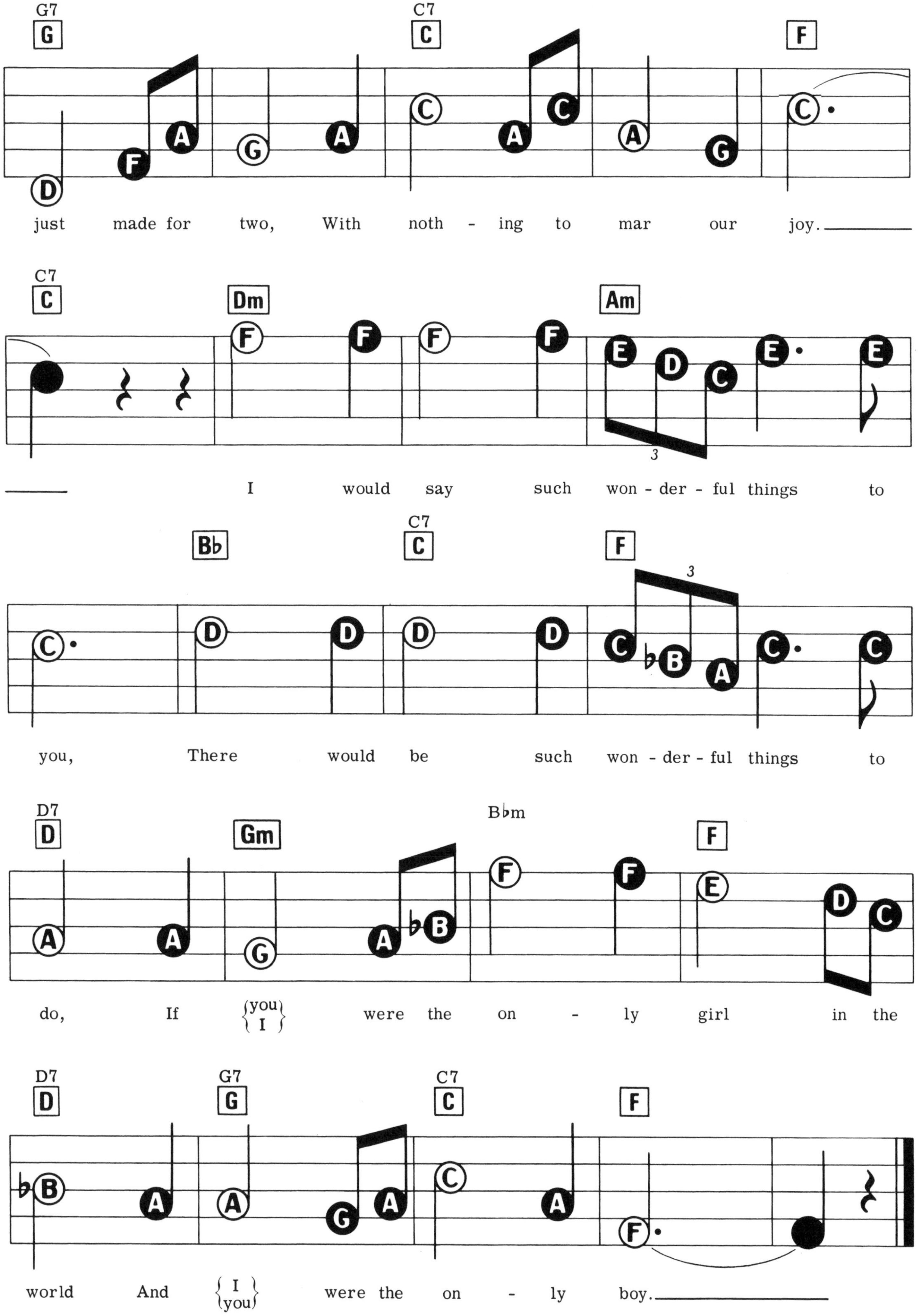
G7 G C7 C F
just made for two, With noth - ing to mar our joy.
C7 C Dm Am
I would say such won - der - ful things to
B♭ C7 C F
you, There would be such won - der - ful things to
D7 D Gm B♭m F
do, If {you / I} were the on - ly girl in the
D7 D G7 G C7 C F
world And {I / you} were the on - ly boy.

In the Good Old Summertime

from IN THE GOOD OLD SUMMERTIME

Registration 5
Rhythm: Waltz

Words by Ren Shields
Music by George Evans

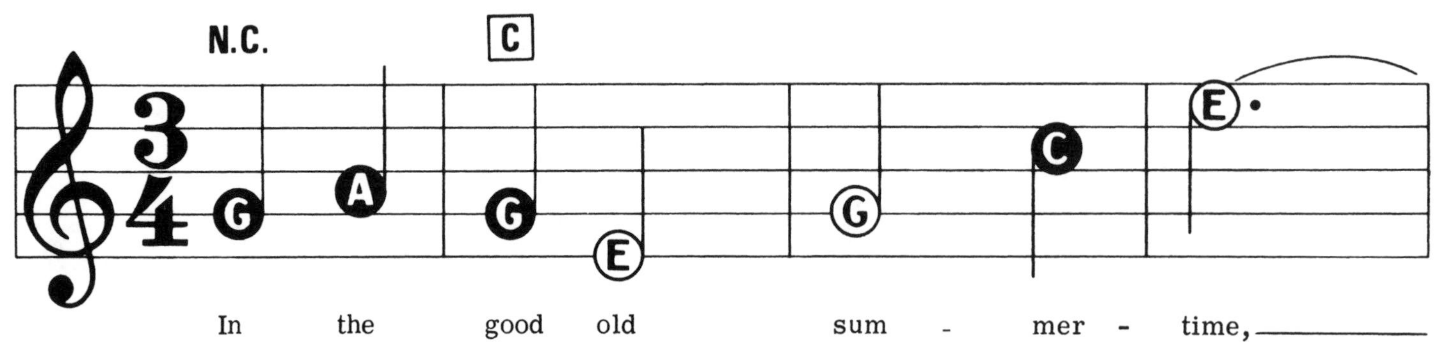

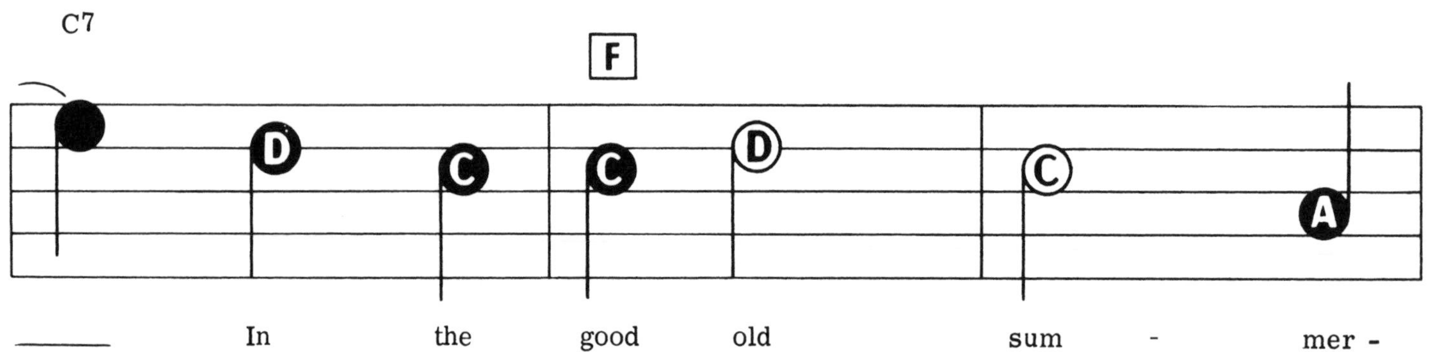

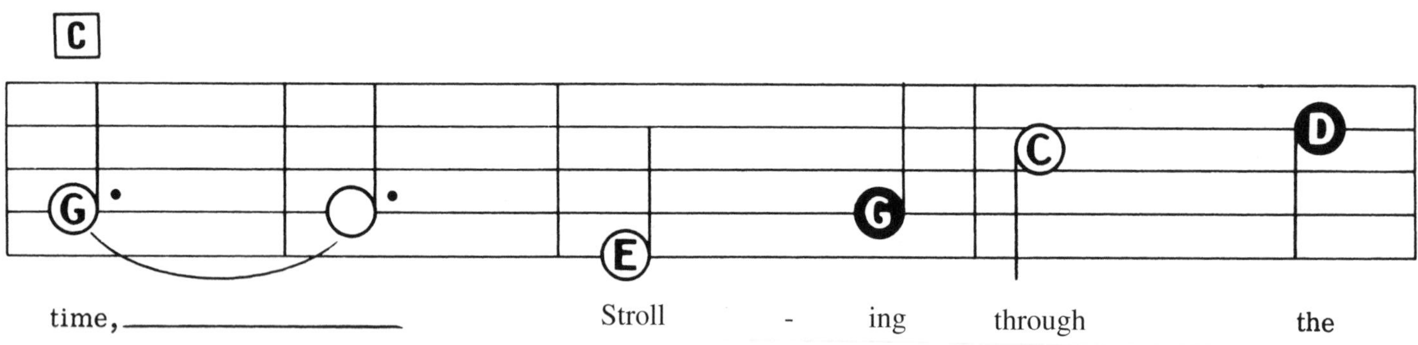

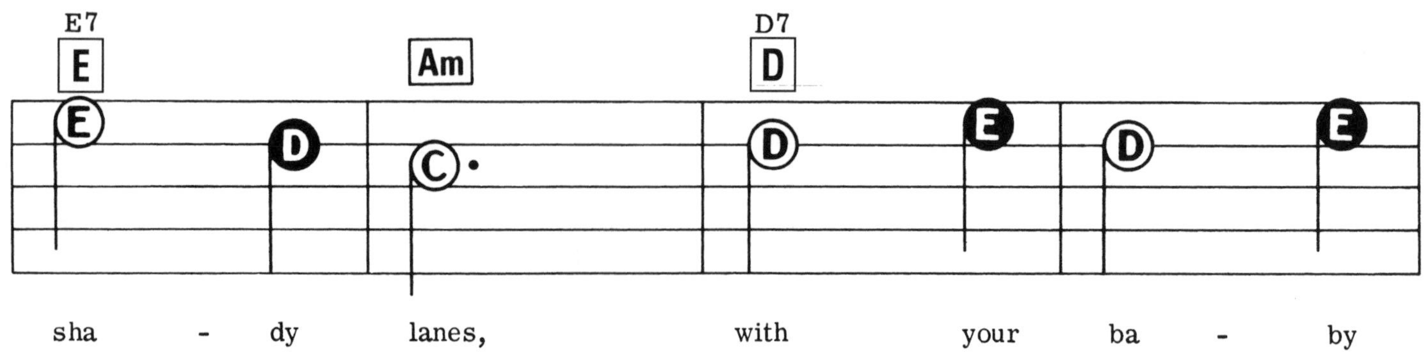

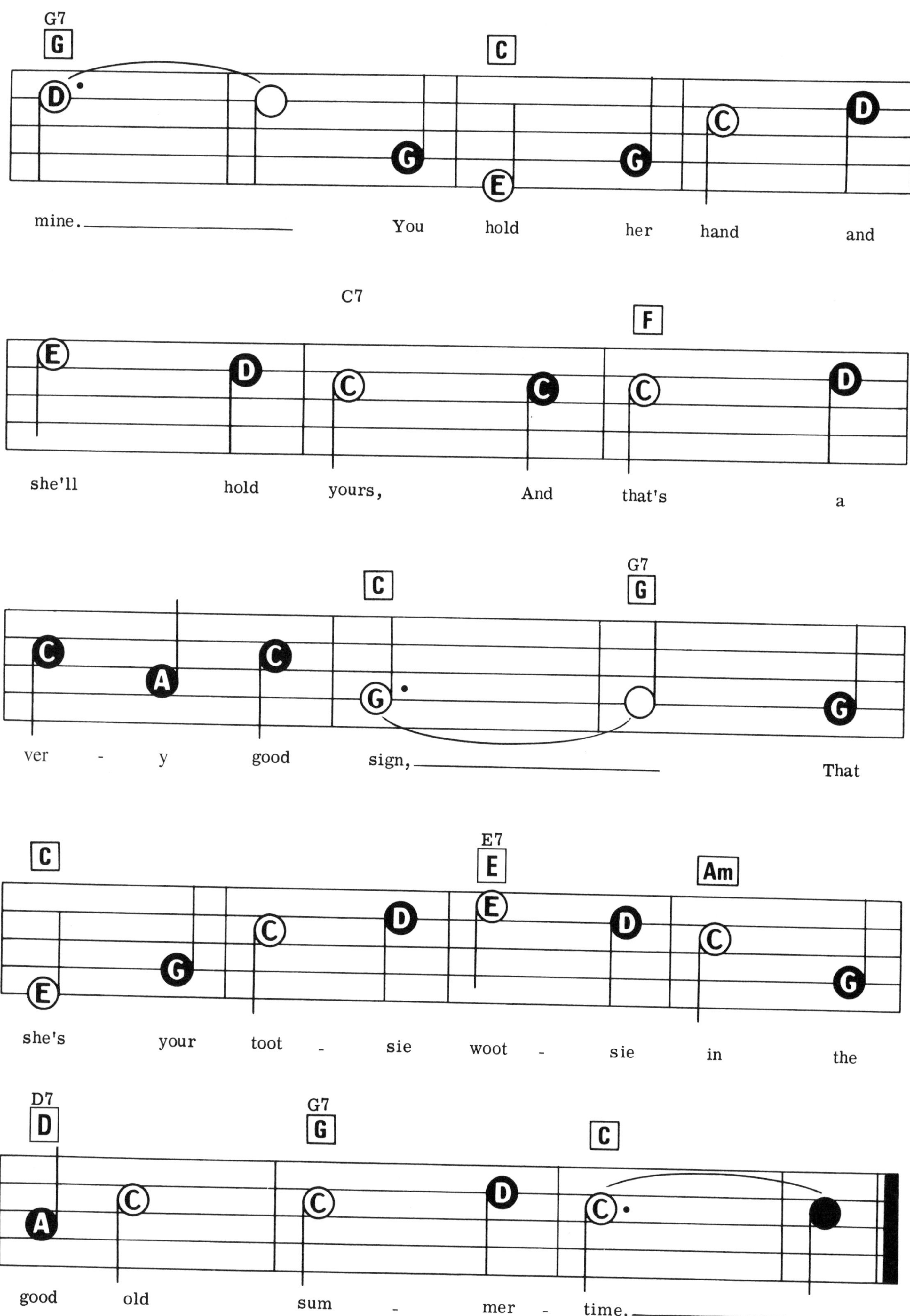
G7 G C
D G E G C D
mine. You hold her hand and
C7 F
E D C C C D
she'll hold yours, And that's a
C G7 G
C A C G G
ver - y good sign, That
C E7 E Am
E G C D E D C G
she's your toot - sie woot - sie in the
D7 D G7 G C
A C C D C
good old sum - mer - time.

In the Shade of the Old Apple Tree

Registration 3
Rhythm: Waltz

Words by Harry H. Williams
Music by Egbert Van Alstyne

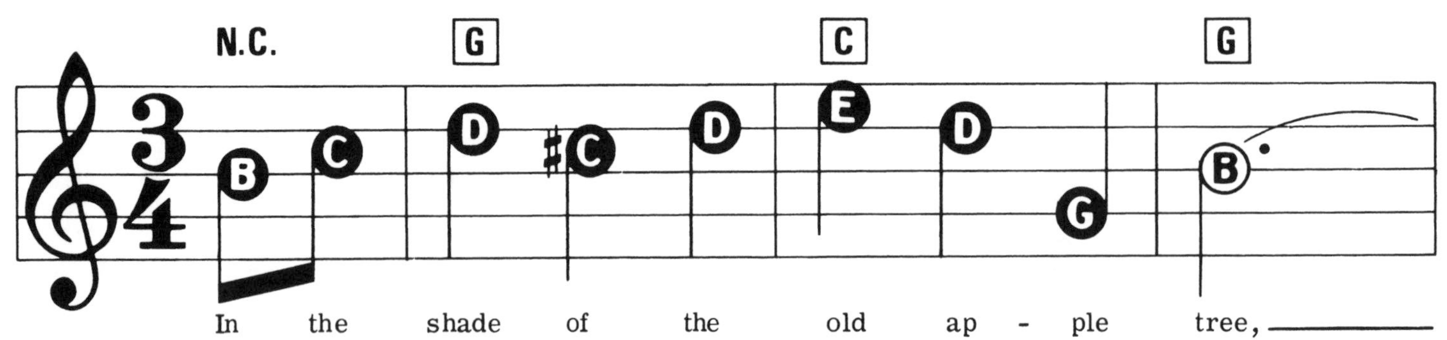

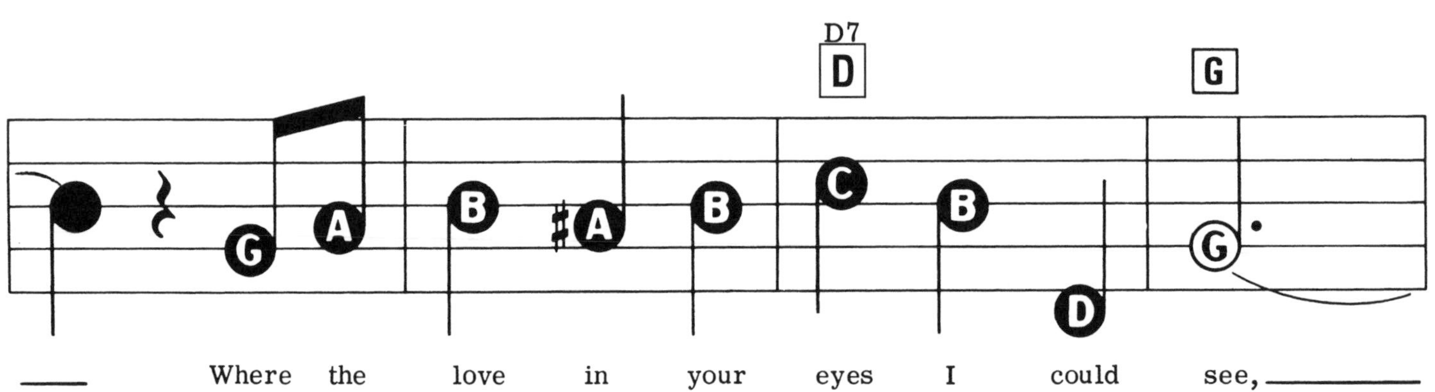

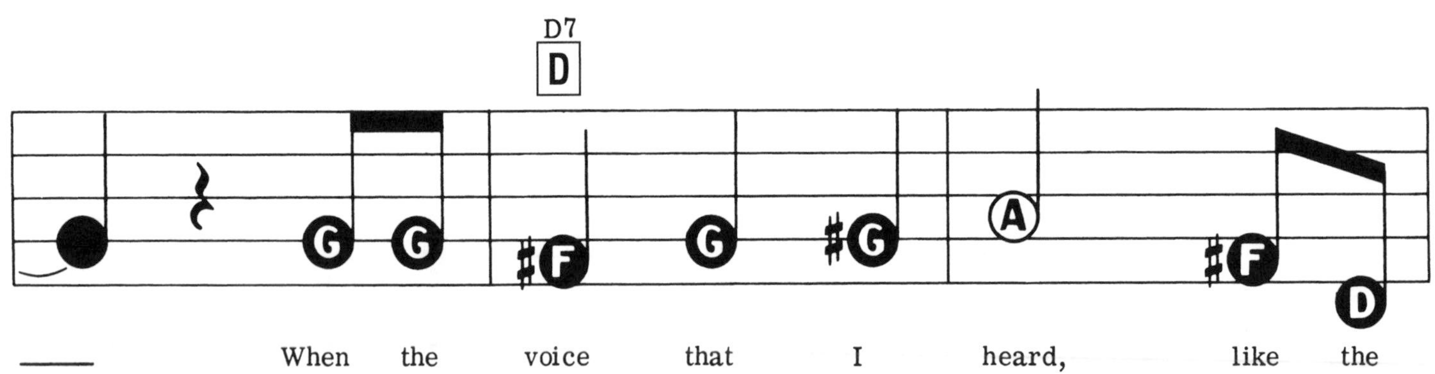

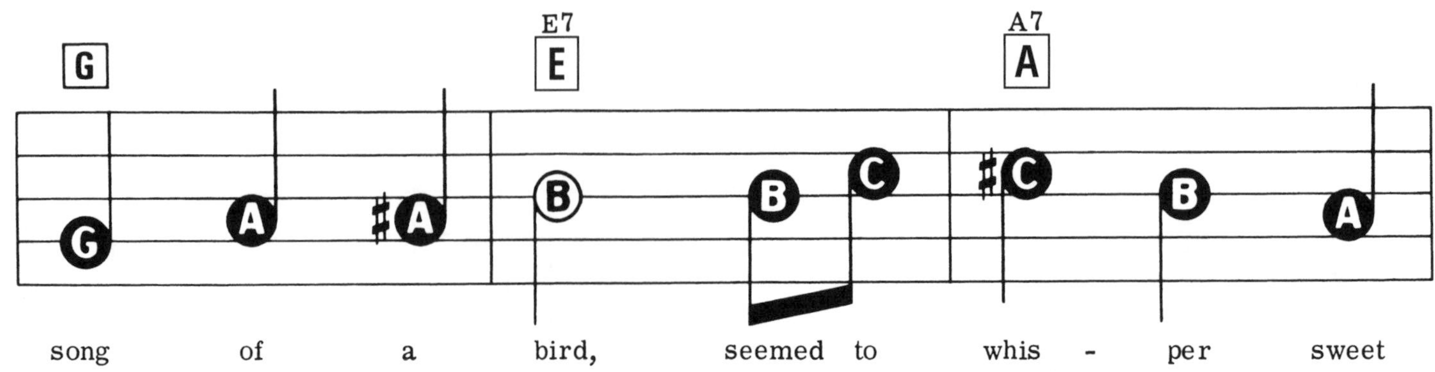

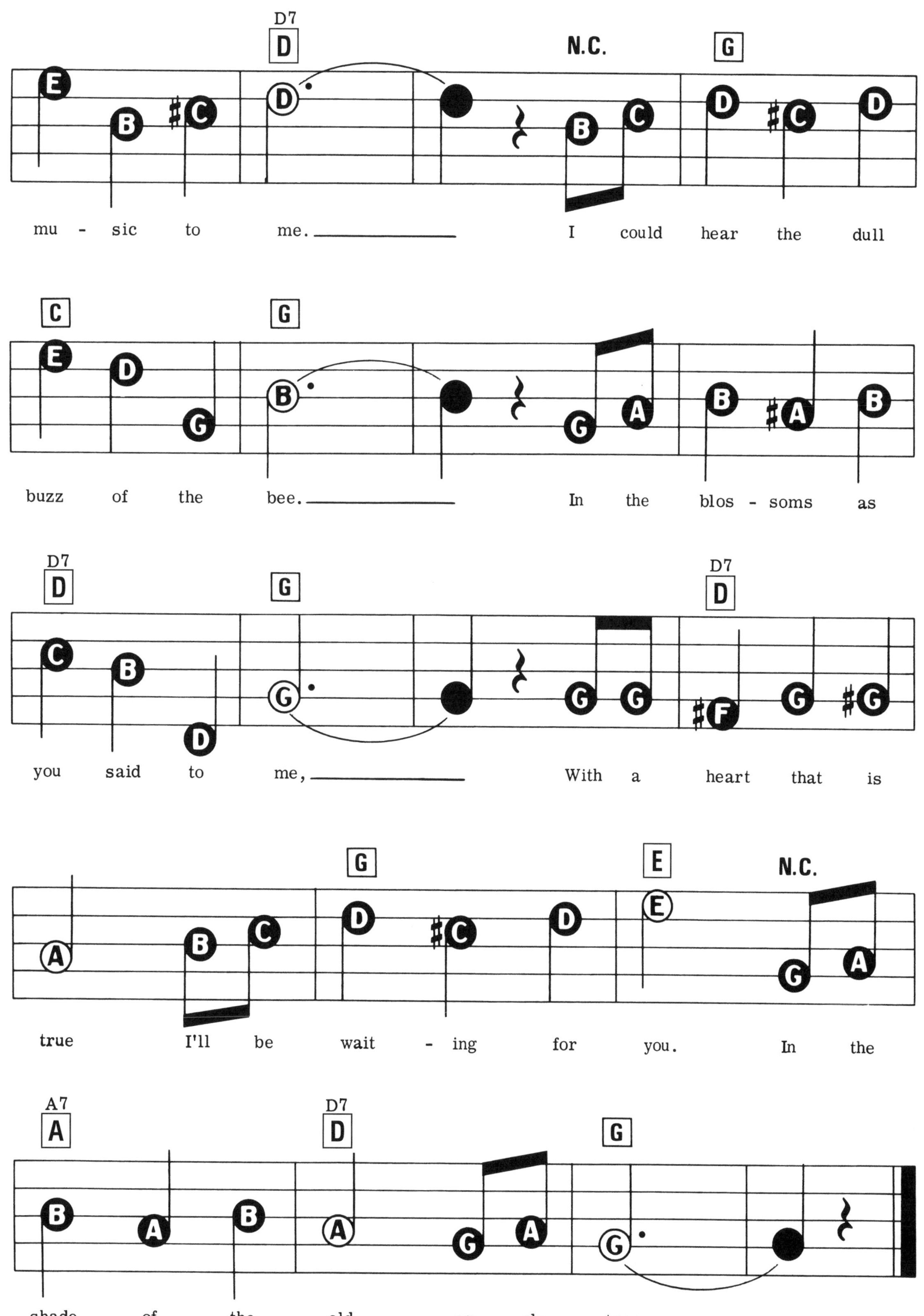
D7 D N.C. G
mu - sic to me. I could hear the dull
C G
buzz of the bee. In the blos - soms as
D7 D G D7 D
you said to me, With a heart that is
G E N.C.
true I'll be wait - ing for you. In the
A7 A D7 D G
shade of the old ap - ple tree.

Indiana
(Back Home Again in Indiana)

Registration 3
Rhythm: Swing

Words by Ballard MacDonald
Music by James F. Hanley

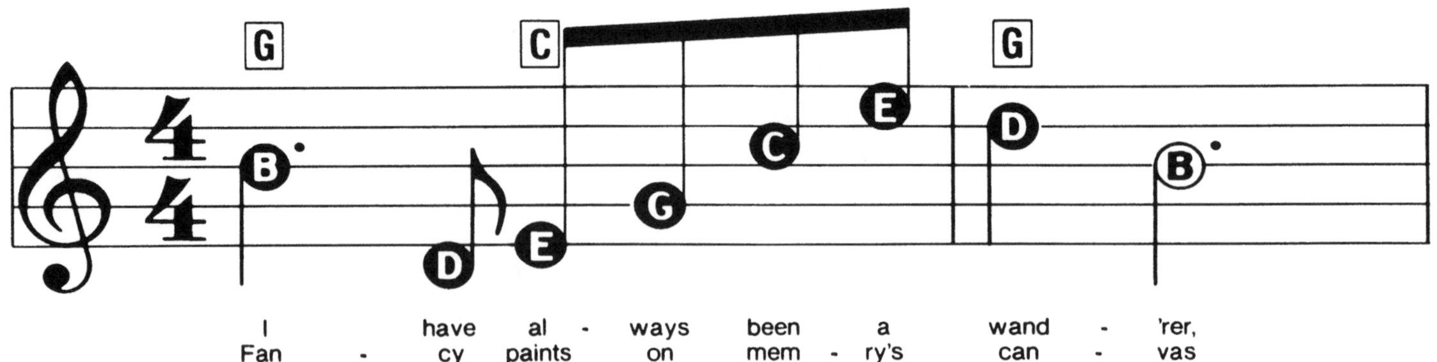

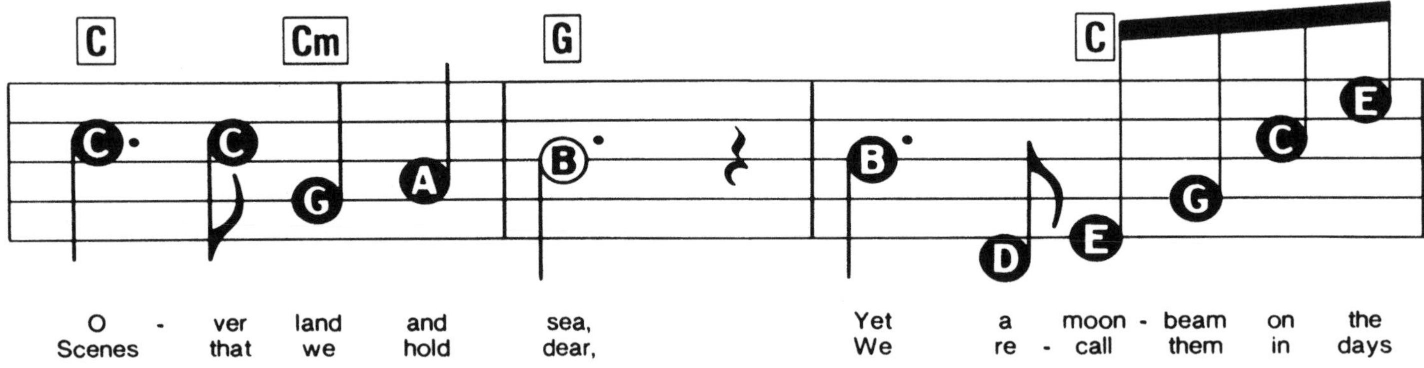

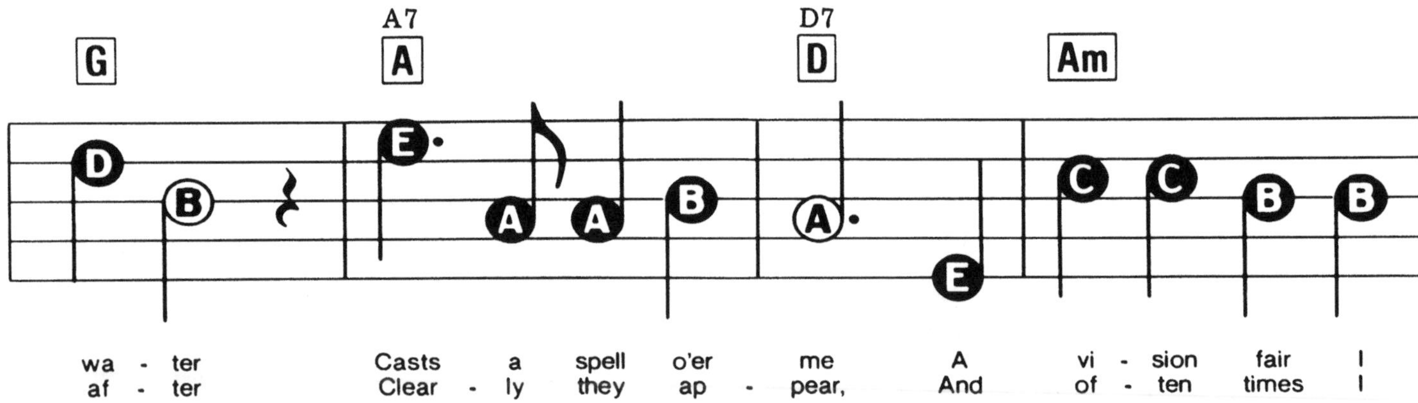

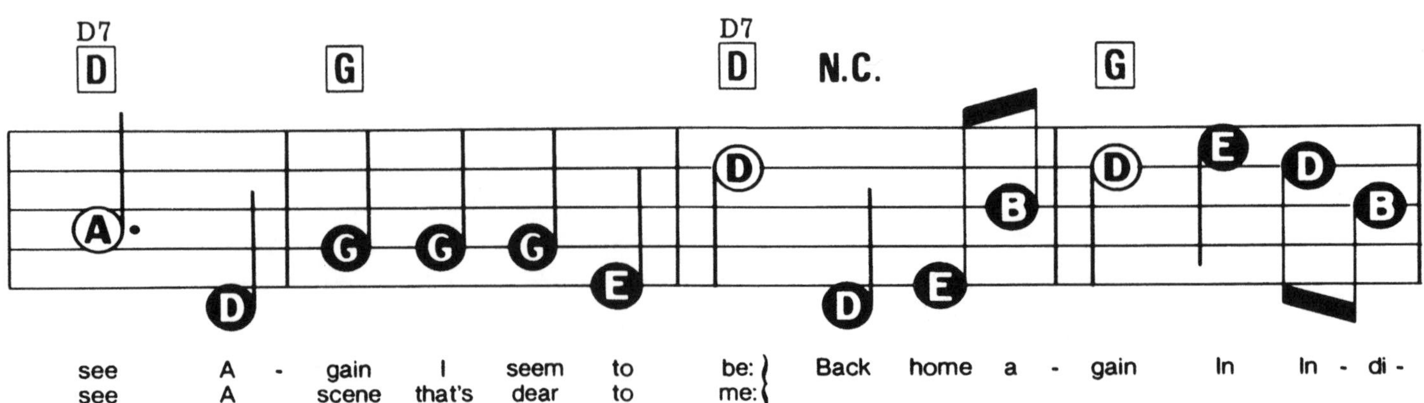

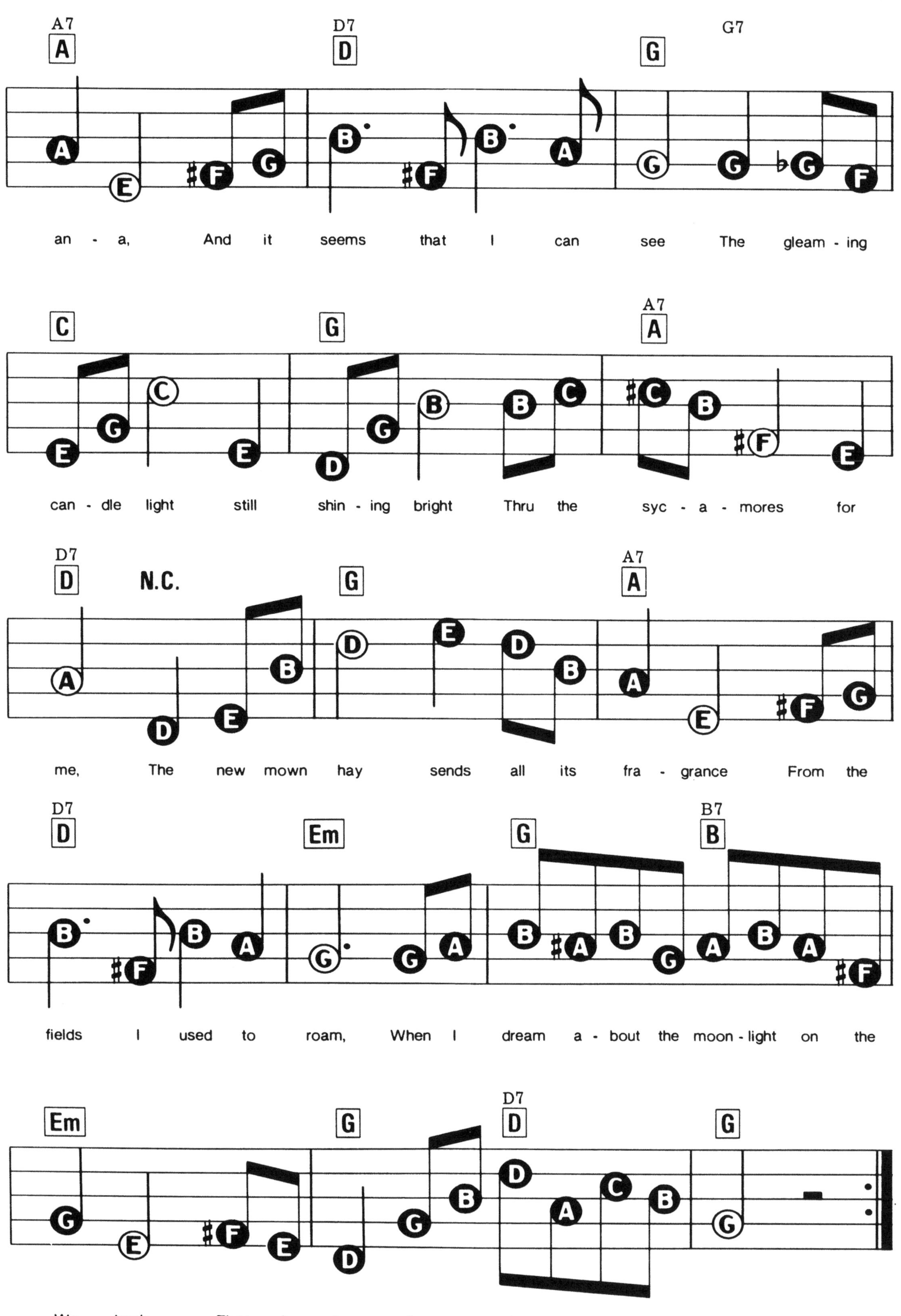
A7 A
D7 D
G
G7
A E F G
B F B A
G G G F
an - a, And it seems that I can see The gleam - ing
C
G
A7 A
E G C E
D G B B C
C B F E
can - dle light still shin - ing bright Thru the syc - a - mores for
D7 D
N.C.
G
A7 A
A D E B
D E D B
A E F G
me, The new mown hay sends all its fra - grance From the
D7 D
Em
G
B7 B
B F B A
G G A
B A B G
A B A F
fields I used to roam, When I dream a - bout the moon - light on the
Em
G
D7 D
G
G E F E
D G B
D A C B
G
Wa - bash, Then I long for my In - di - an - a home.

Kumbaya

Registration 4
Rhythm: Rhumba or Latin

Congo Folksong

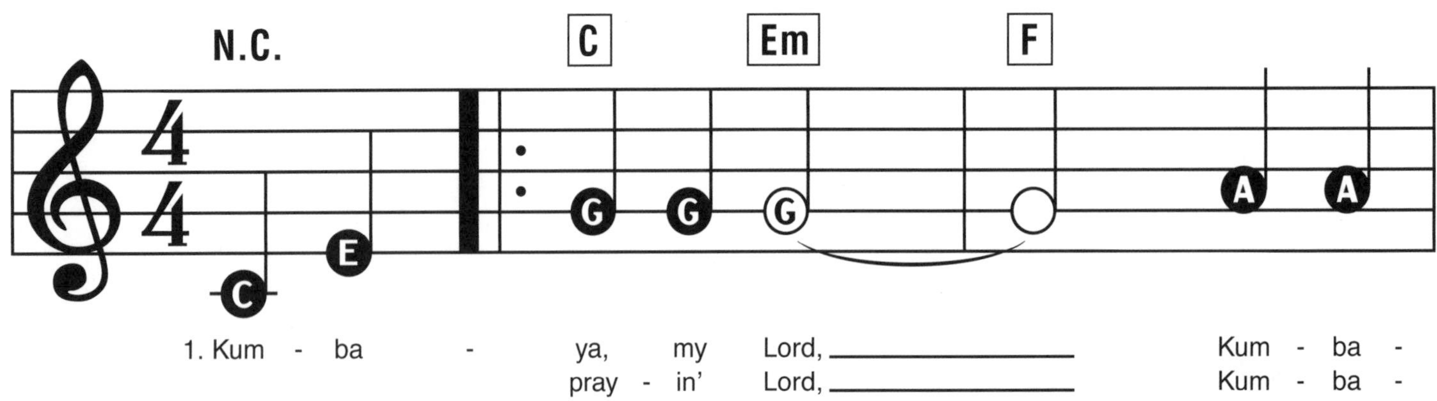

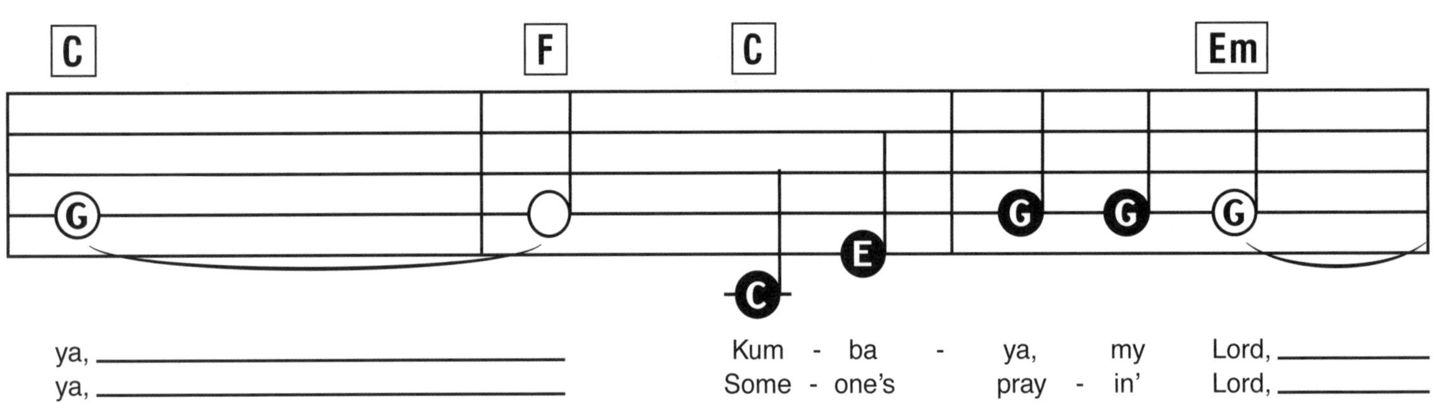

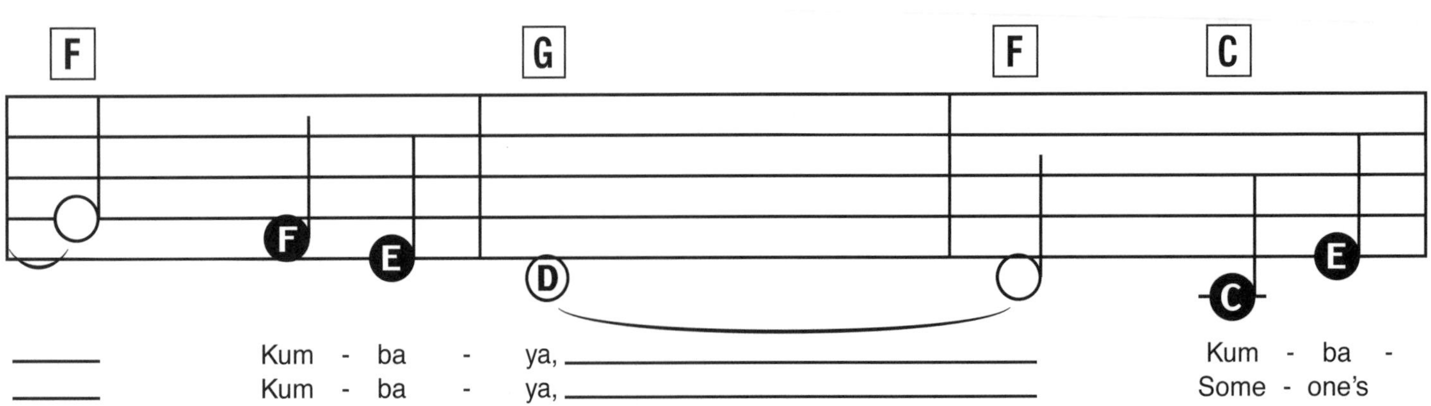

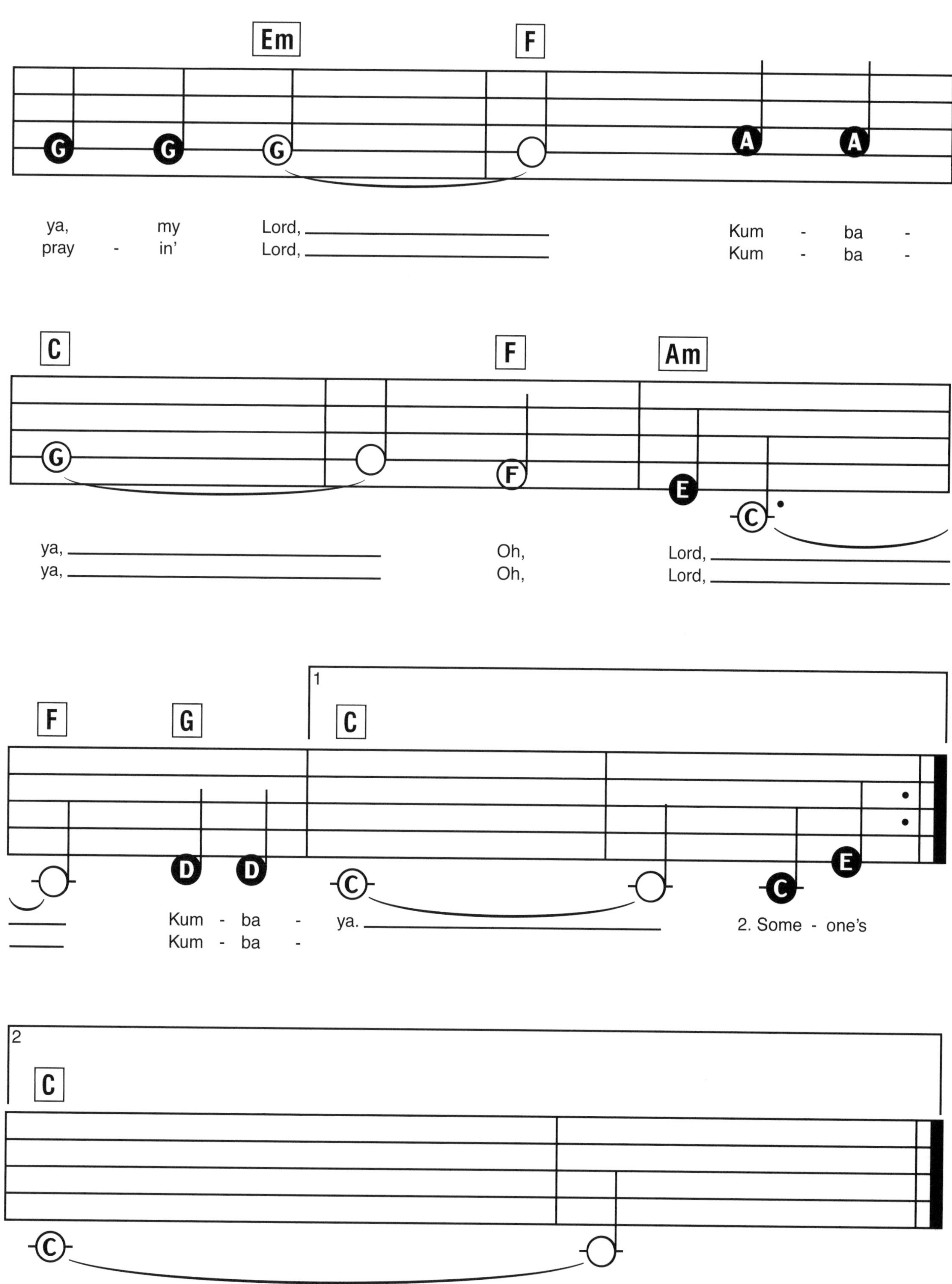
Em
F
G G G A A
ya, my Lord, Kum - ba -
pray - in' Lord, Kum - ba -
C
F
Am
G F E C
ya, Oh, Lord,
ya, Oh, Lord,
F
G
1
C
D D C C E
Kum - ba - ya. 2. Some - one's
Kum - ba -
2
C
C
ya.

Let Me Call You Sweetheart

Registration 3
Rhythm: Waltz

Words by Beth Slater Whitson
Music by Leo Friedman

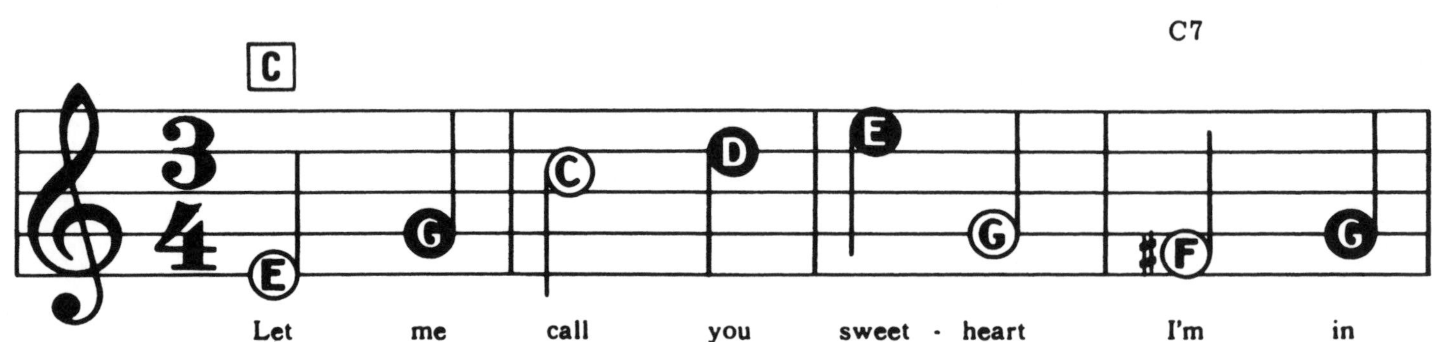

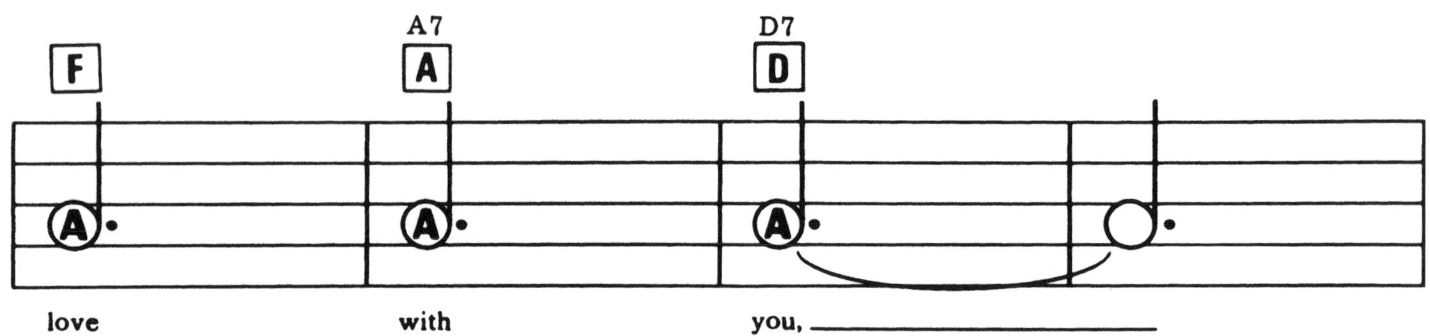

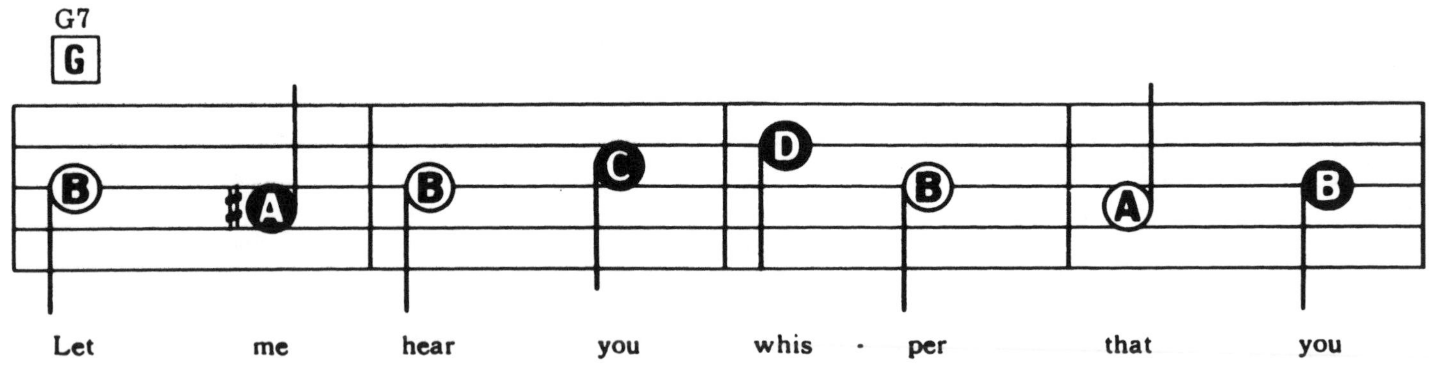

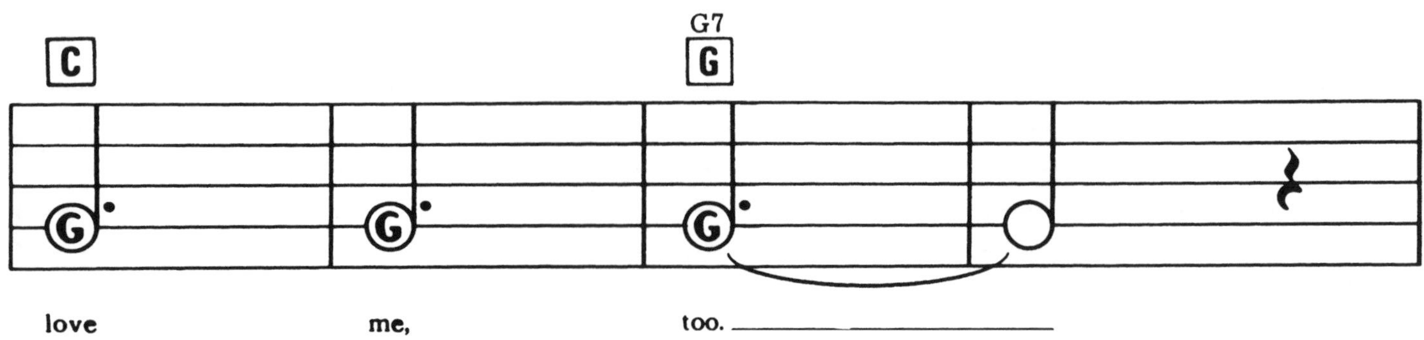

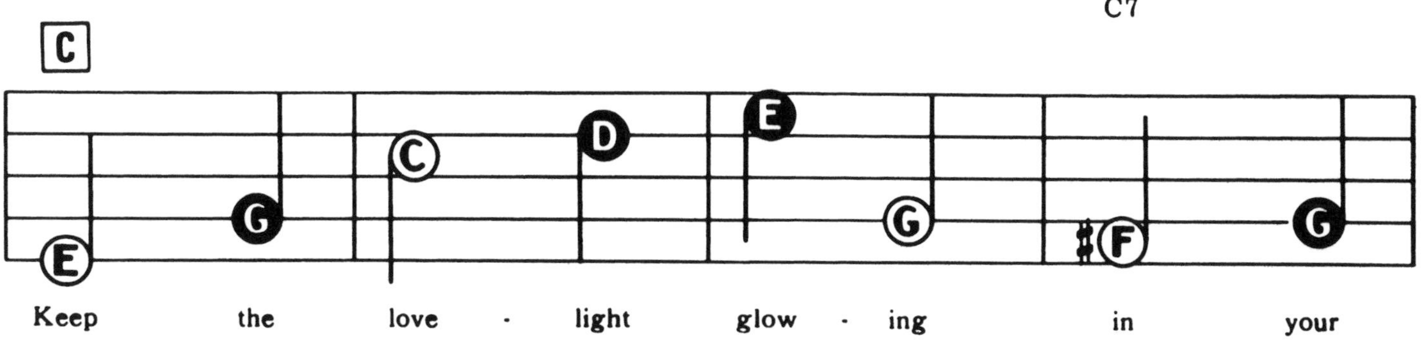
C
C7
E
G
C
D
E
G
♯F
G
Keep the love - light glow - ing in your

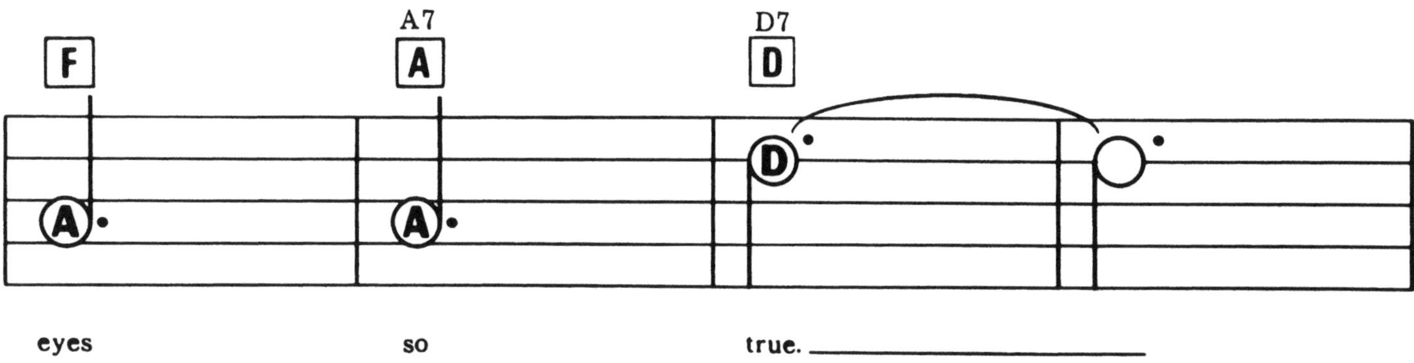
F
A7
A
D7
D
A
A
D
eyes so true.

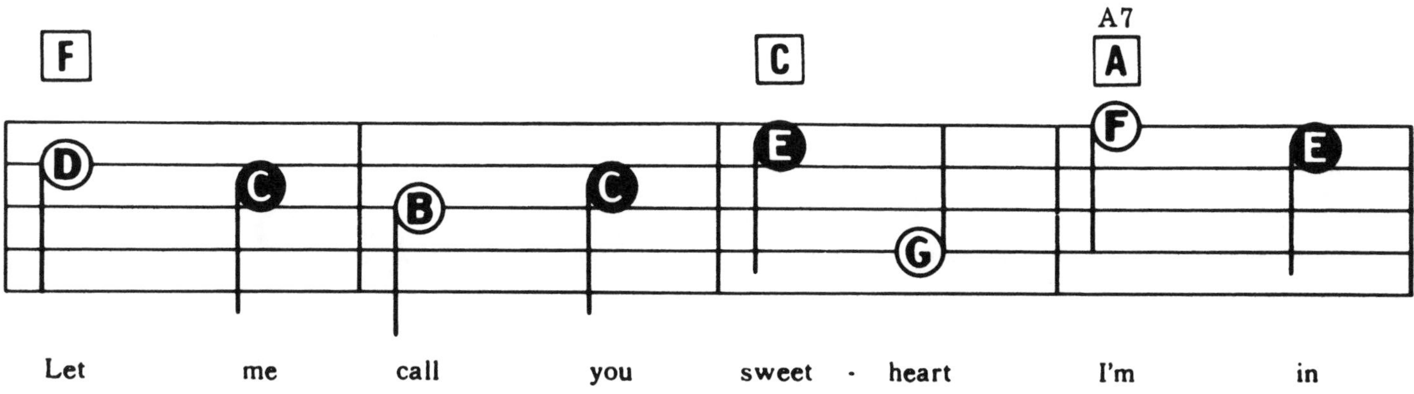
F
C
A7
A
D
C
B
C
E
G
F
E
Let me call you sweet - heart I'm in

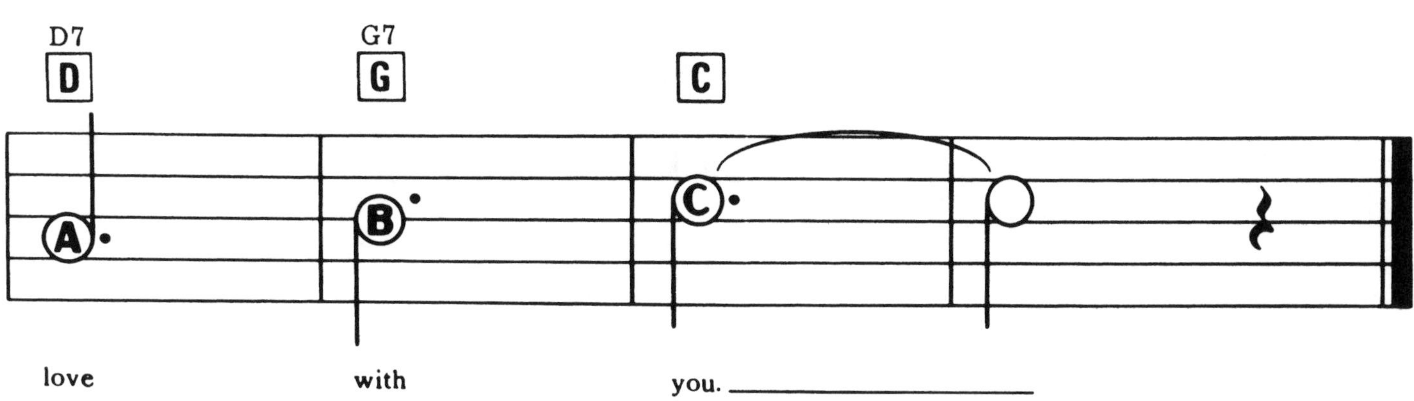
D7
D
G7
G
C
A
B
C
love with you.

Little Brown Jug

Registration 7
Rhythm: Swing

Words and Music by
Joseph E. Winner

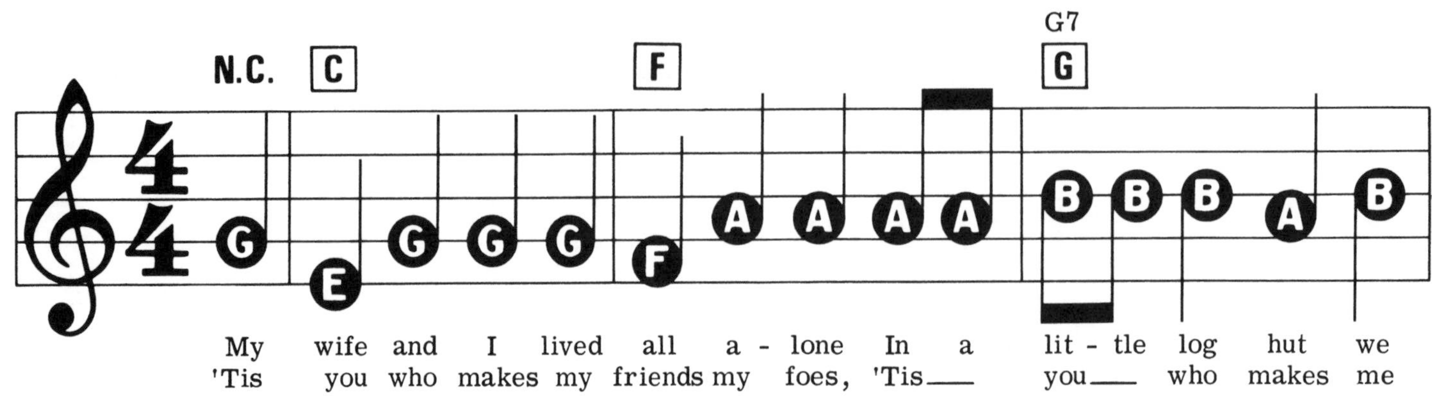

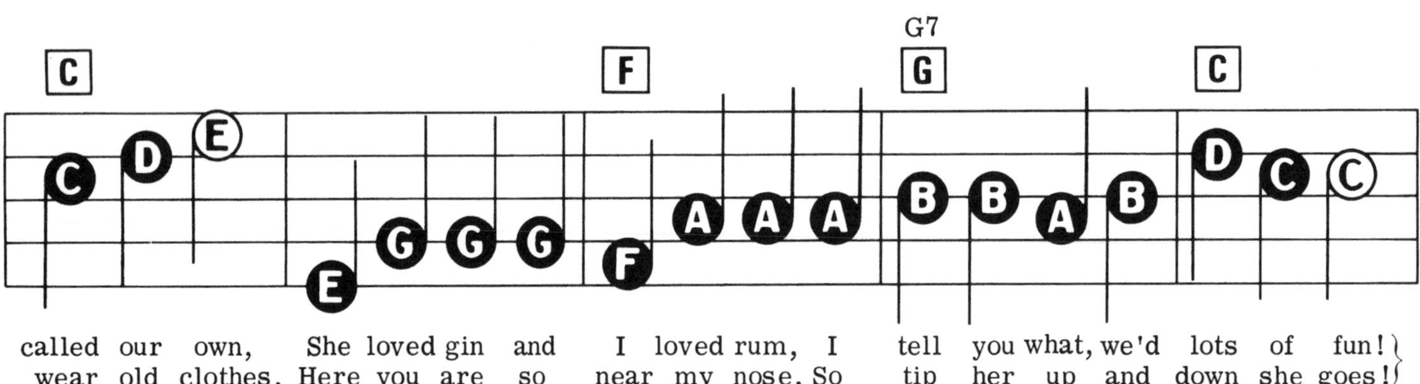

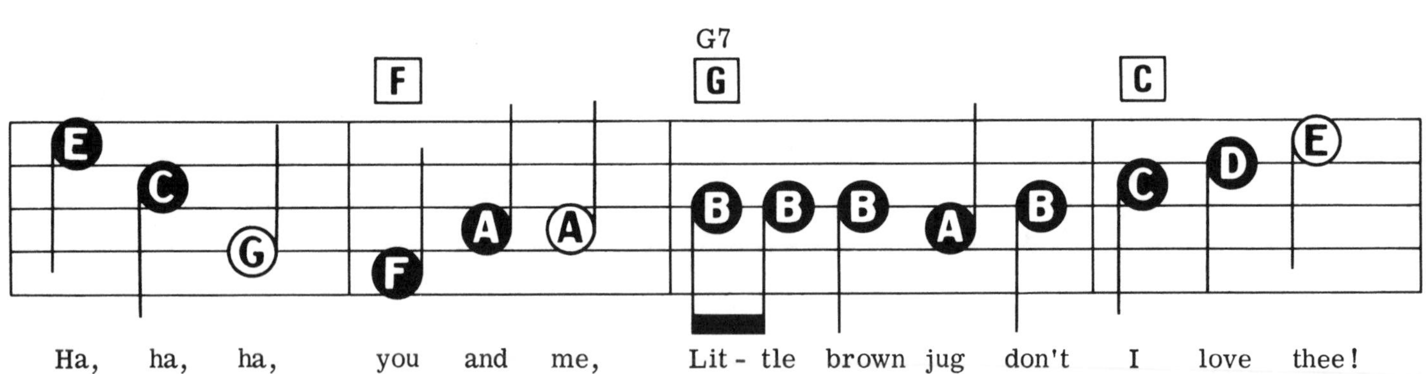

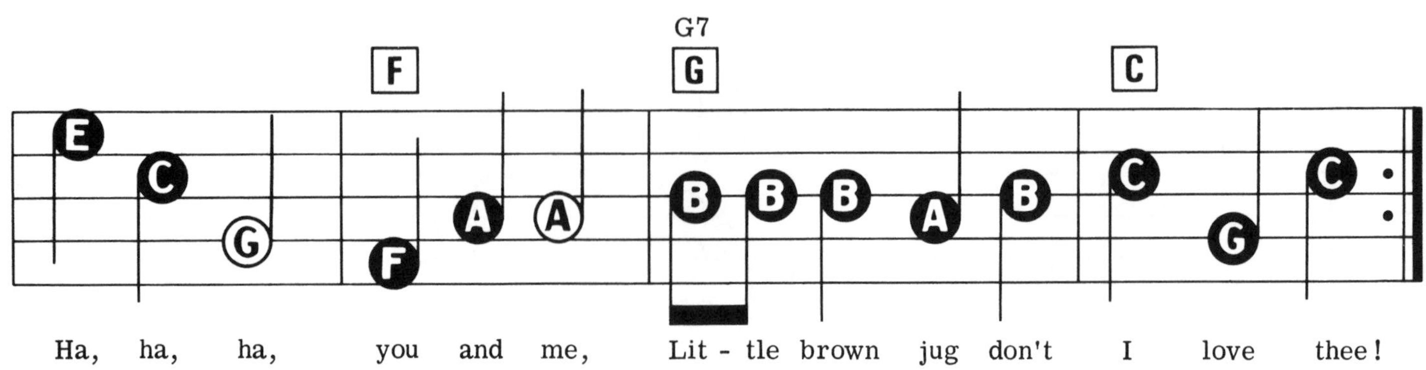

Play a Simple Melody

from the Stage Production WATCH YOUR STEP

Registration 1
Rhythm: Swing

Words and Music by
Irving Berlin

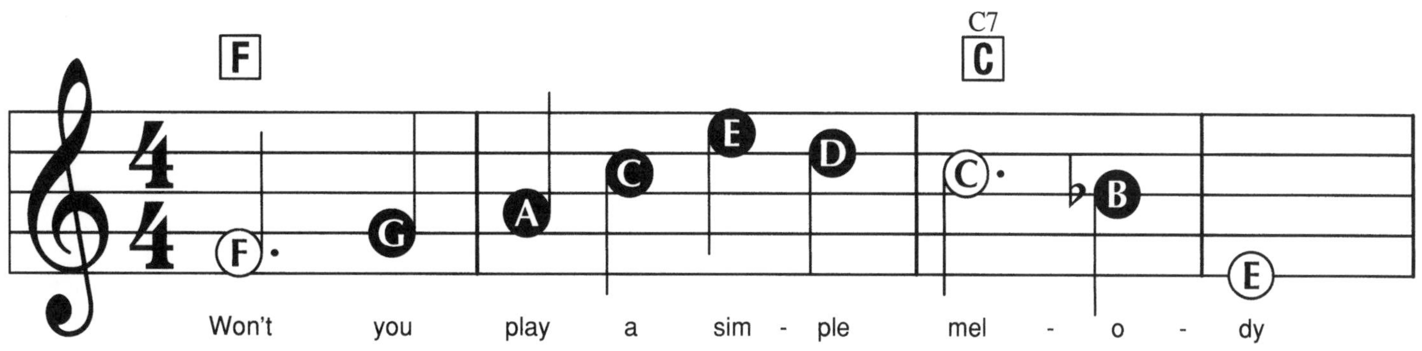

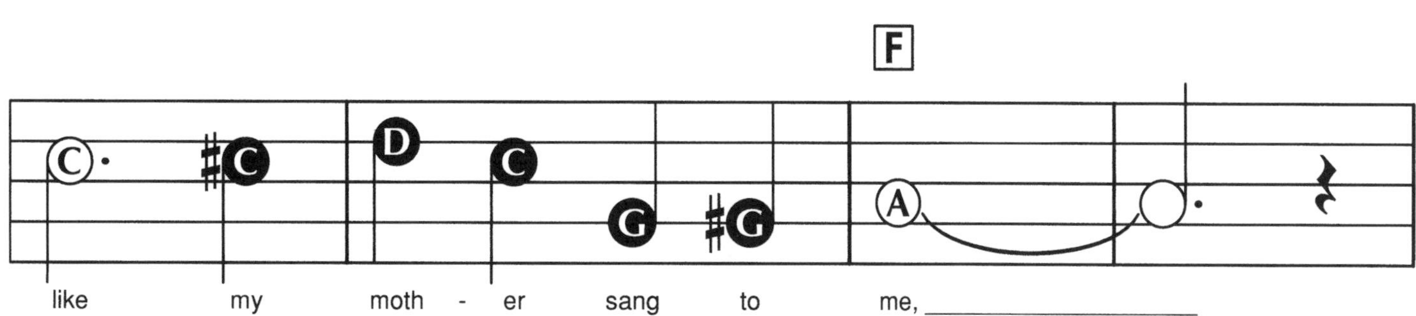

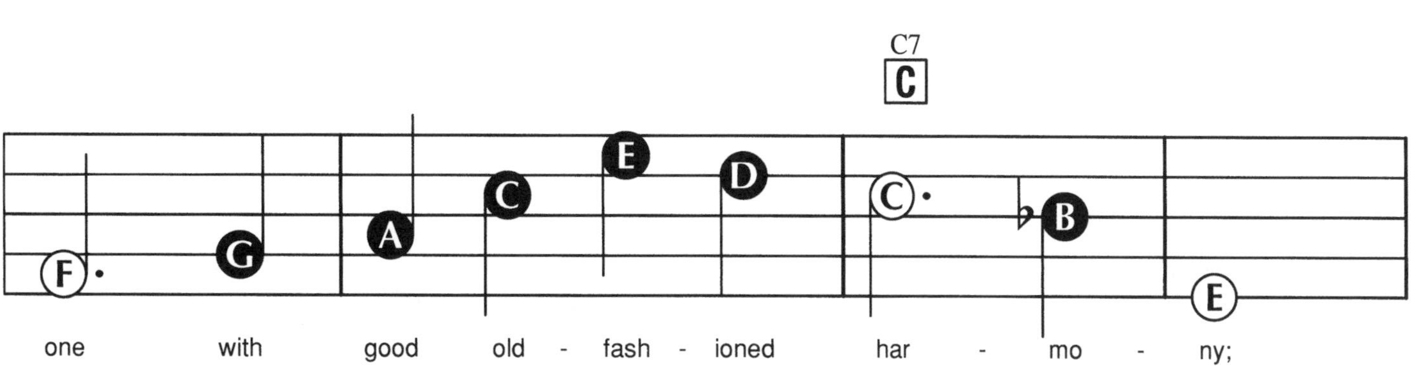

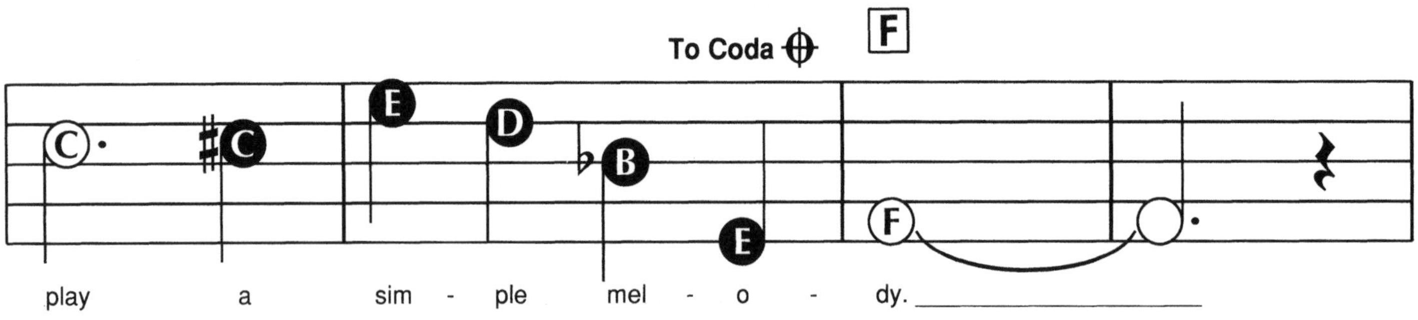
To Coda
F
C
C
E
D
B
E
F
play a sim - ple mel - o - dy.

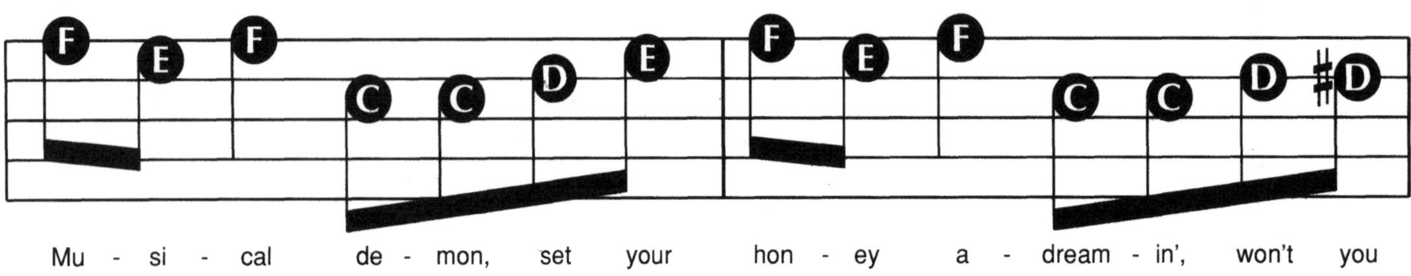
F E F C C D E F E F C C D D
Mu - si - cal de - mon, set your hon - ey a - dream - in', won't you

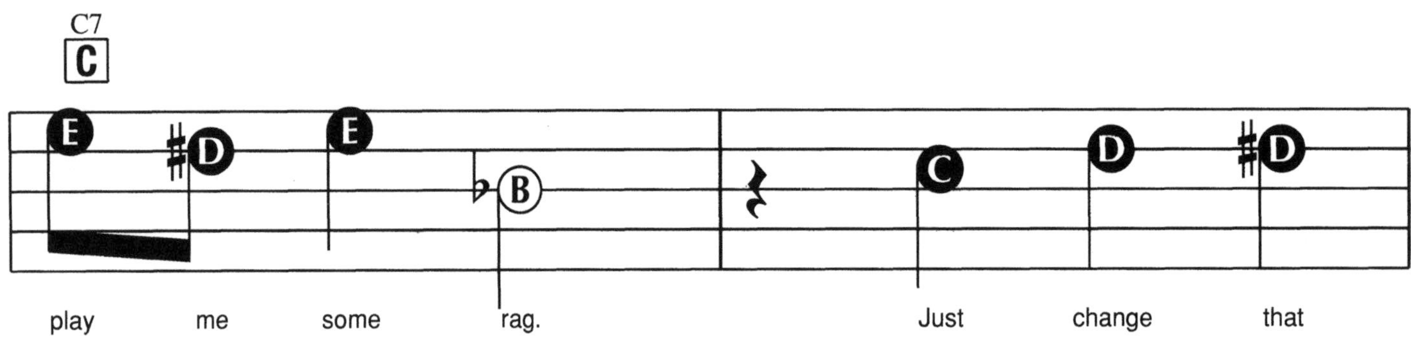
C7
C
E D E B C D D
play me some rag. Just change that

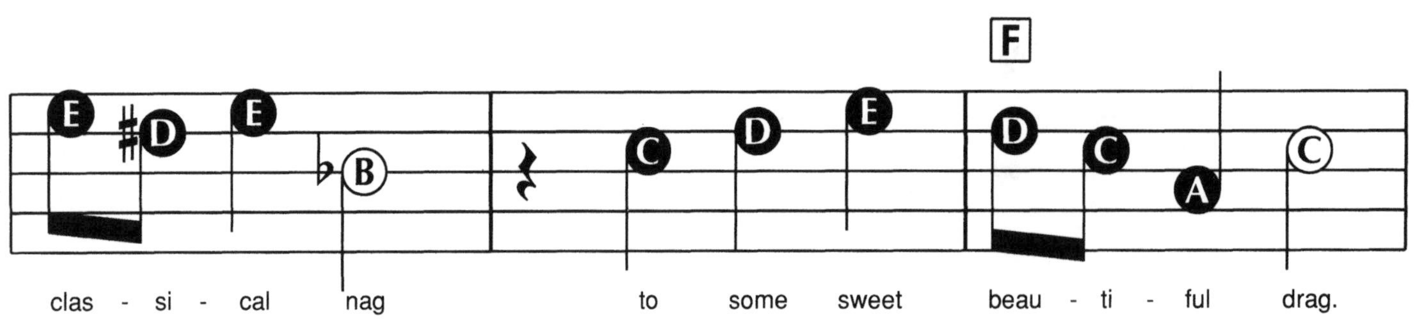
F
E D E B C D E D C A C
clas - si - cal nag to some sweet beau - ti - ful drag.

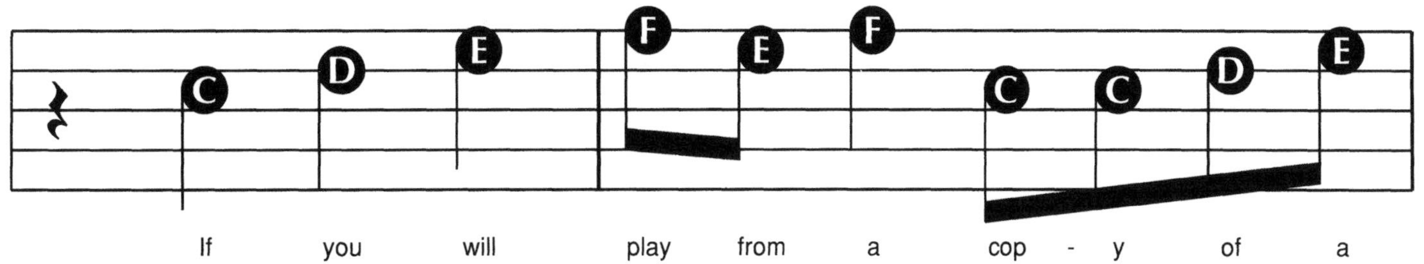
C
D
E
F
E
F
C
C
D
E
If you will play from a cop - y of a

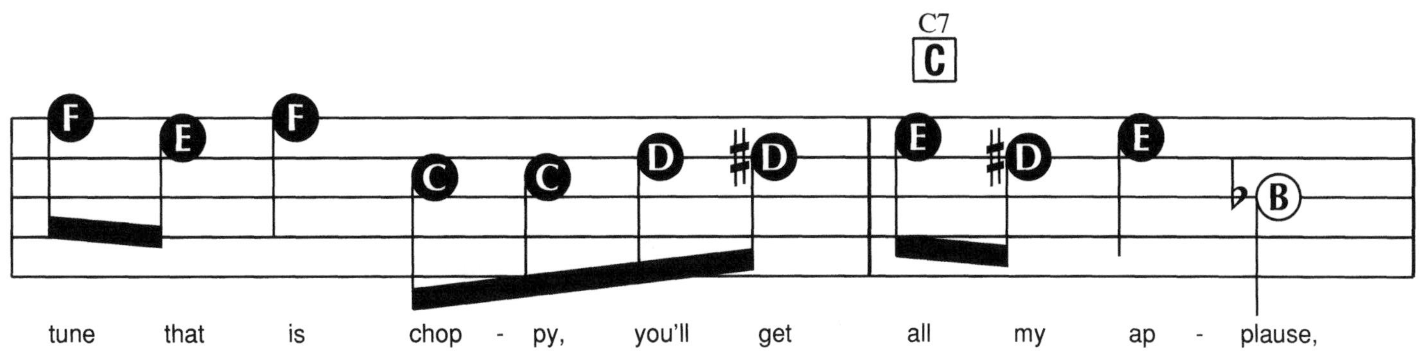
C7
C
F
E
F
C
C
D
♯D
E
♯D
E
♭B
tune that is chop - py, you'll get all my ap - plause,

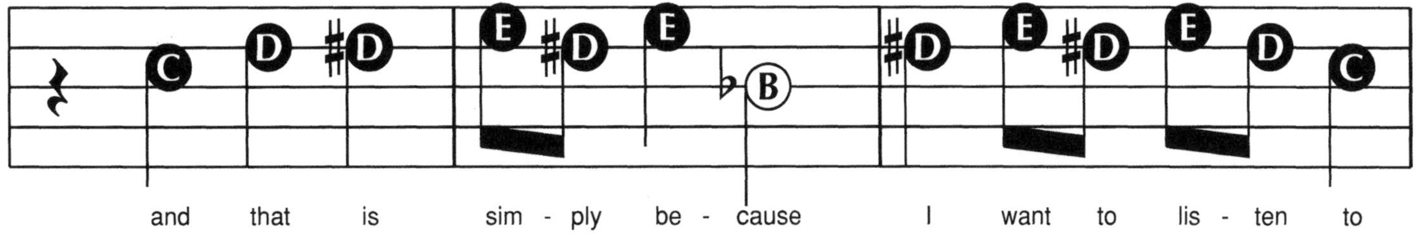
C
D
♯D
E
♯D
E
♭B
♯D
E
♯D
E
D
C
and that is sim - ply be - cause I want to lis - ten to

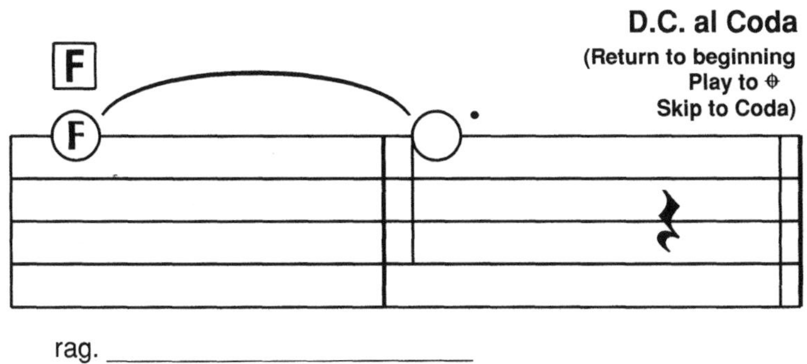
F
D.C. al Coda
(Return to beginning
Play to ⊕
Skip to Coda)
F
rag. ___

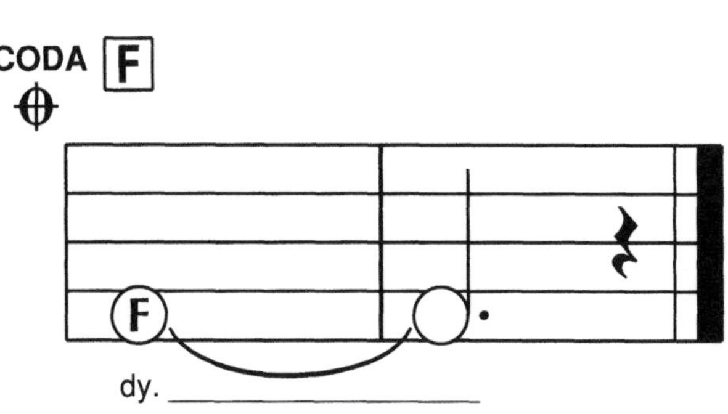
CODA
F
F
dy. ___

Meet Me Tonight in Dreamland

Registration 5
Rhythm: Waltz

Words by Beth Slater Whitson
Music by Leo Friedman

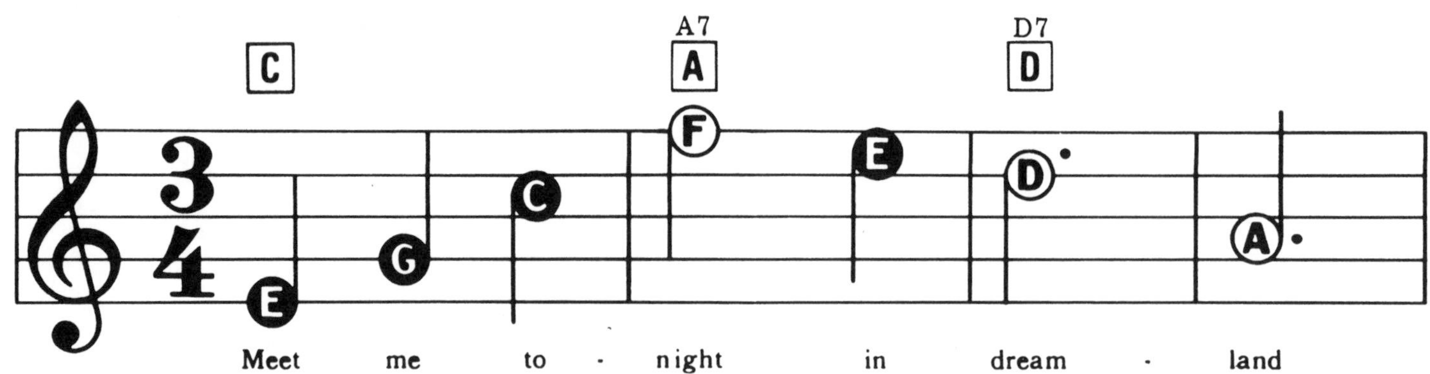

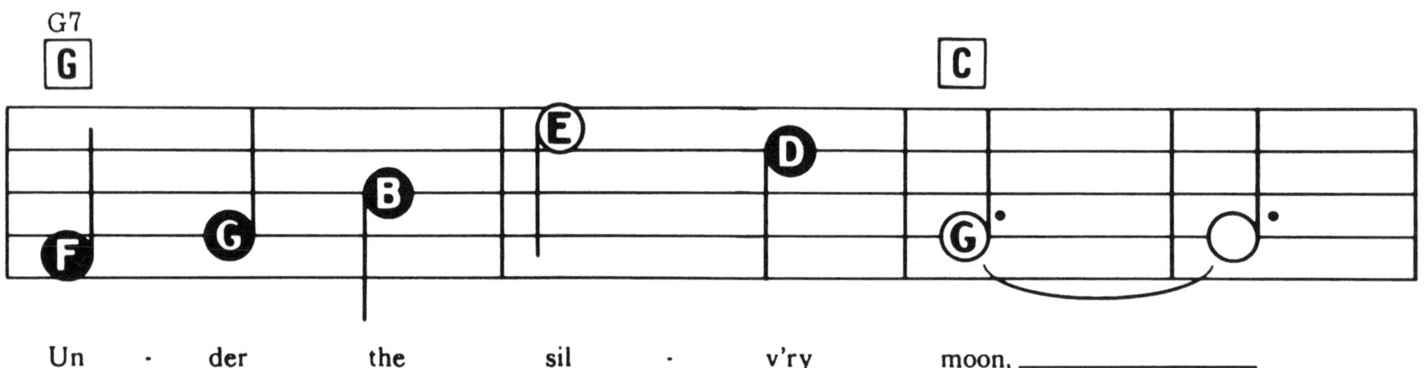

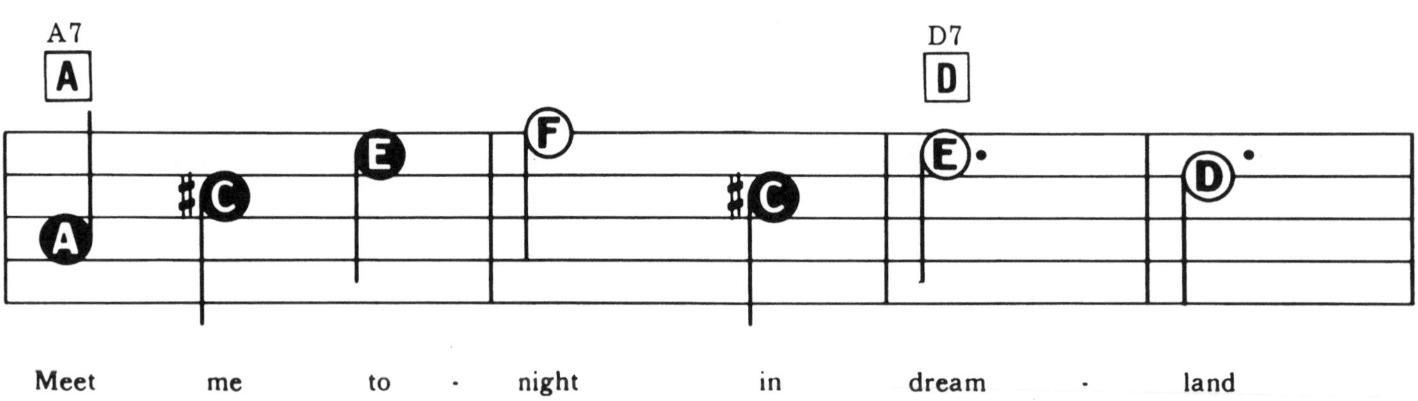

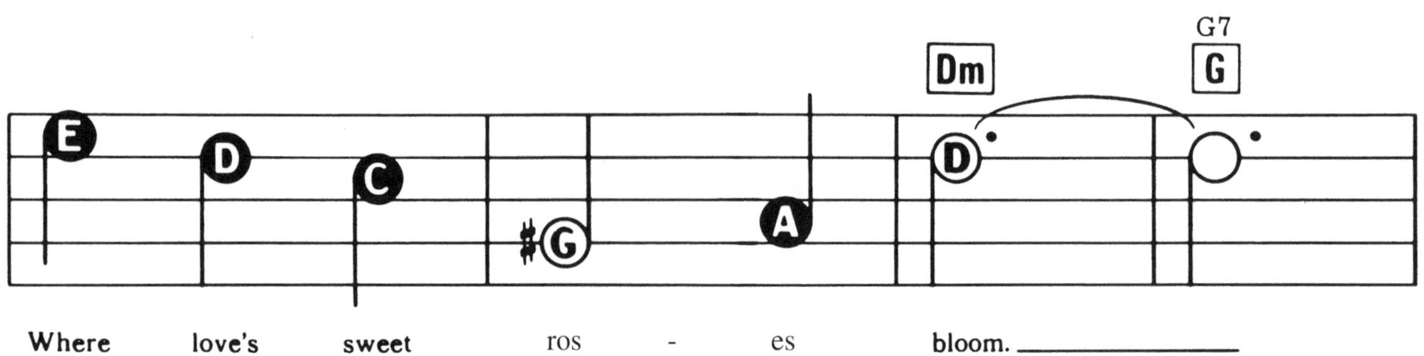

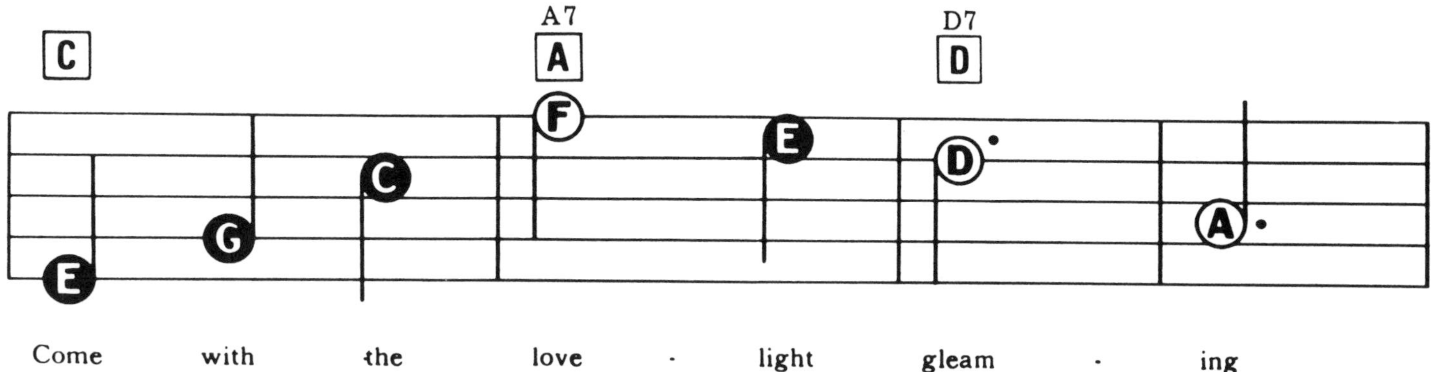
C
A7
A
D7
D
E
G
C
F
E
D
A
Come with the love - light gleam - ing

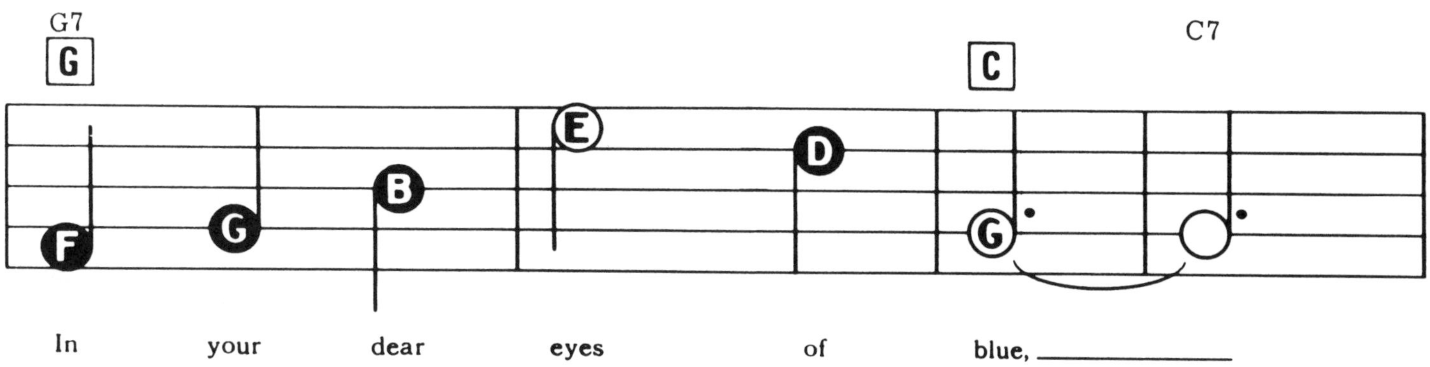
G7
G
C
C7
F
G
B
E
D
G
In your dear eyes of blue, ____

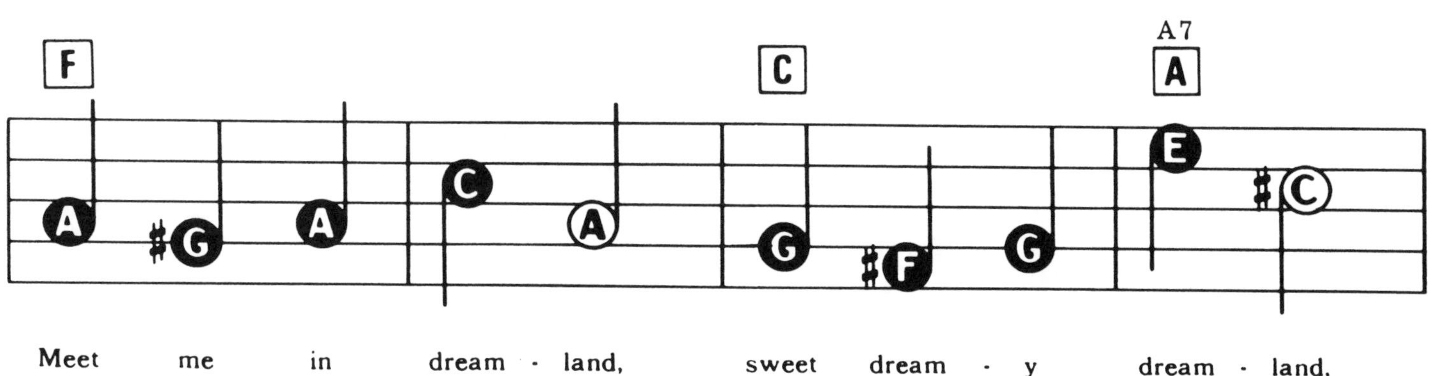
F
C
A7
A
A
G
A
C
A
G
F
G
E
C
Meet me in dream - land, sweet dream - y dream - land,

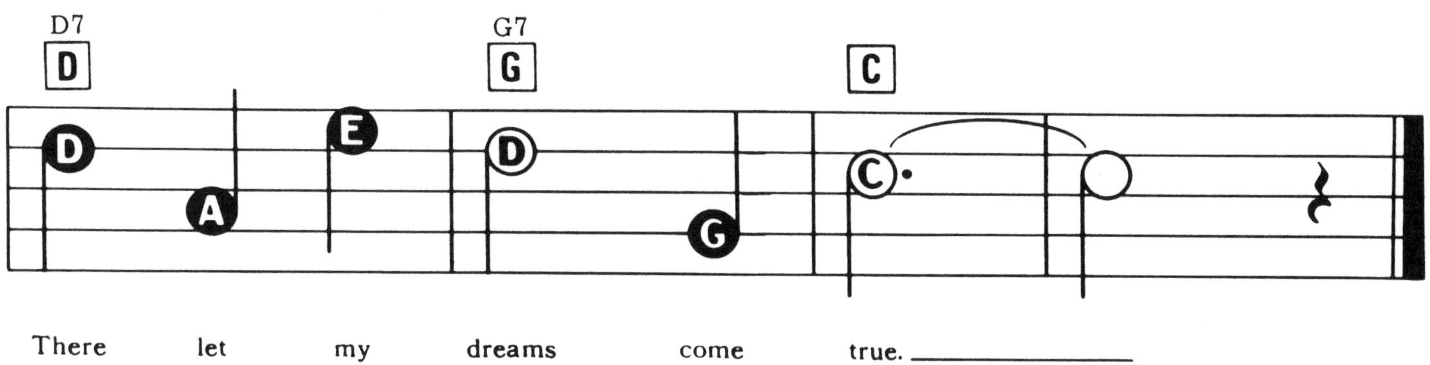
D7
D
G7
G
C
D
A
E
D
G
C
There let my dreams come true. ____

Moonlight Bay

Registration 2
Rhythm: Swing

Words by Edward Madden
Music by Percy Wenrich

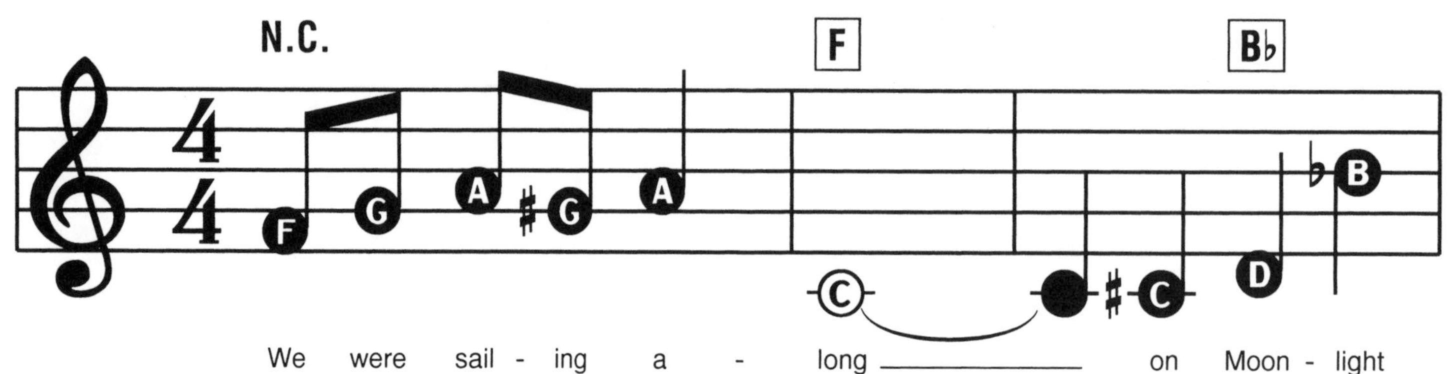

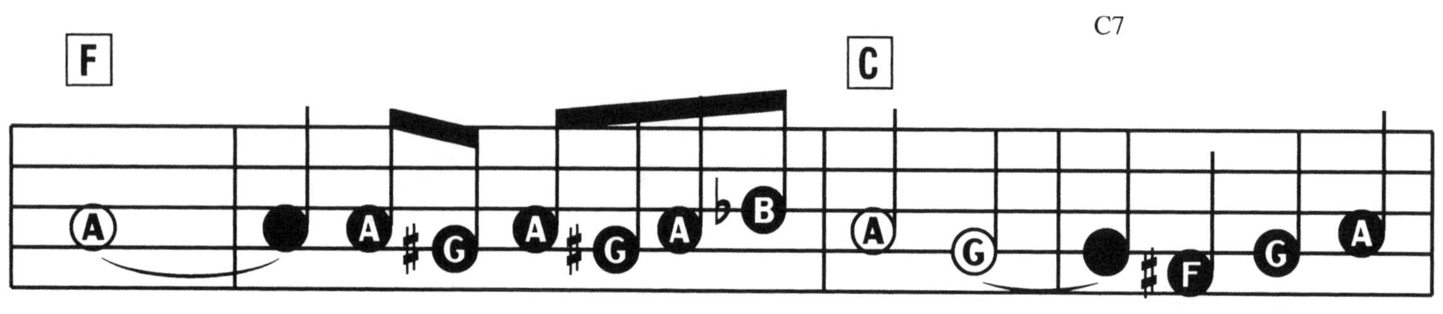

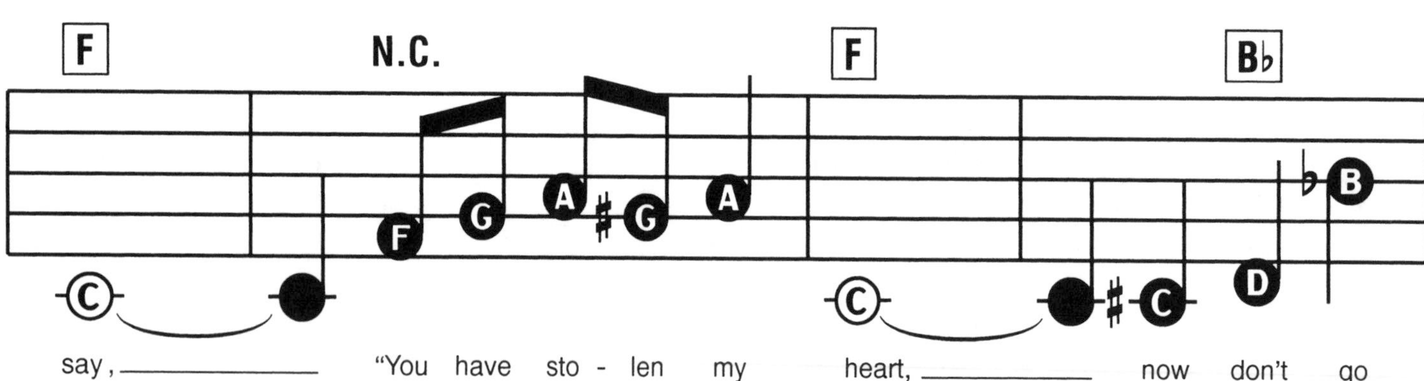

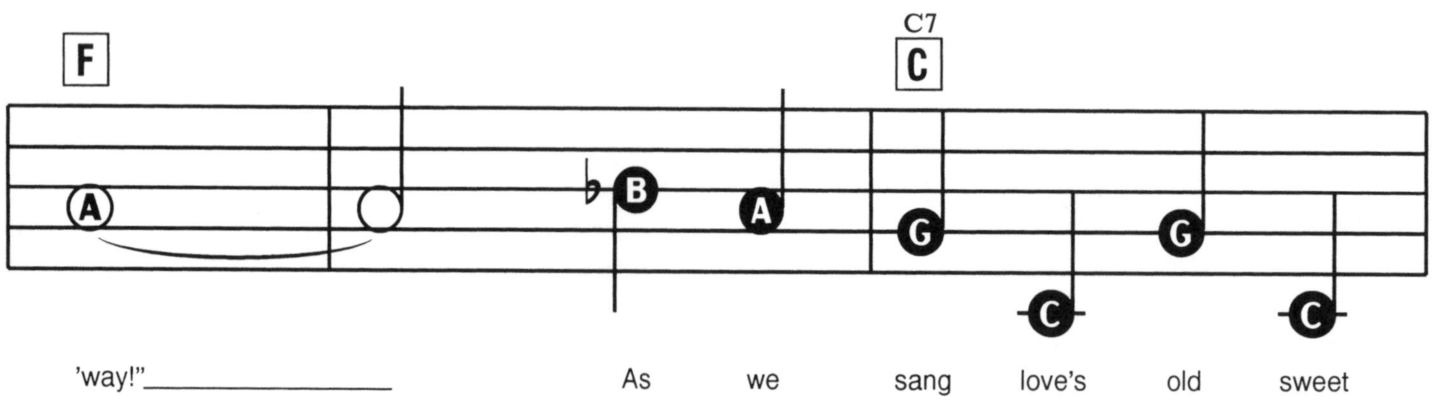

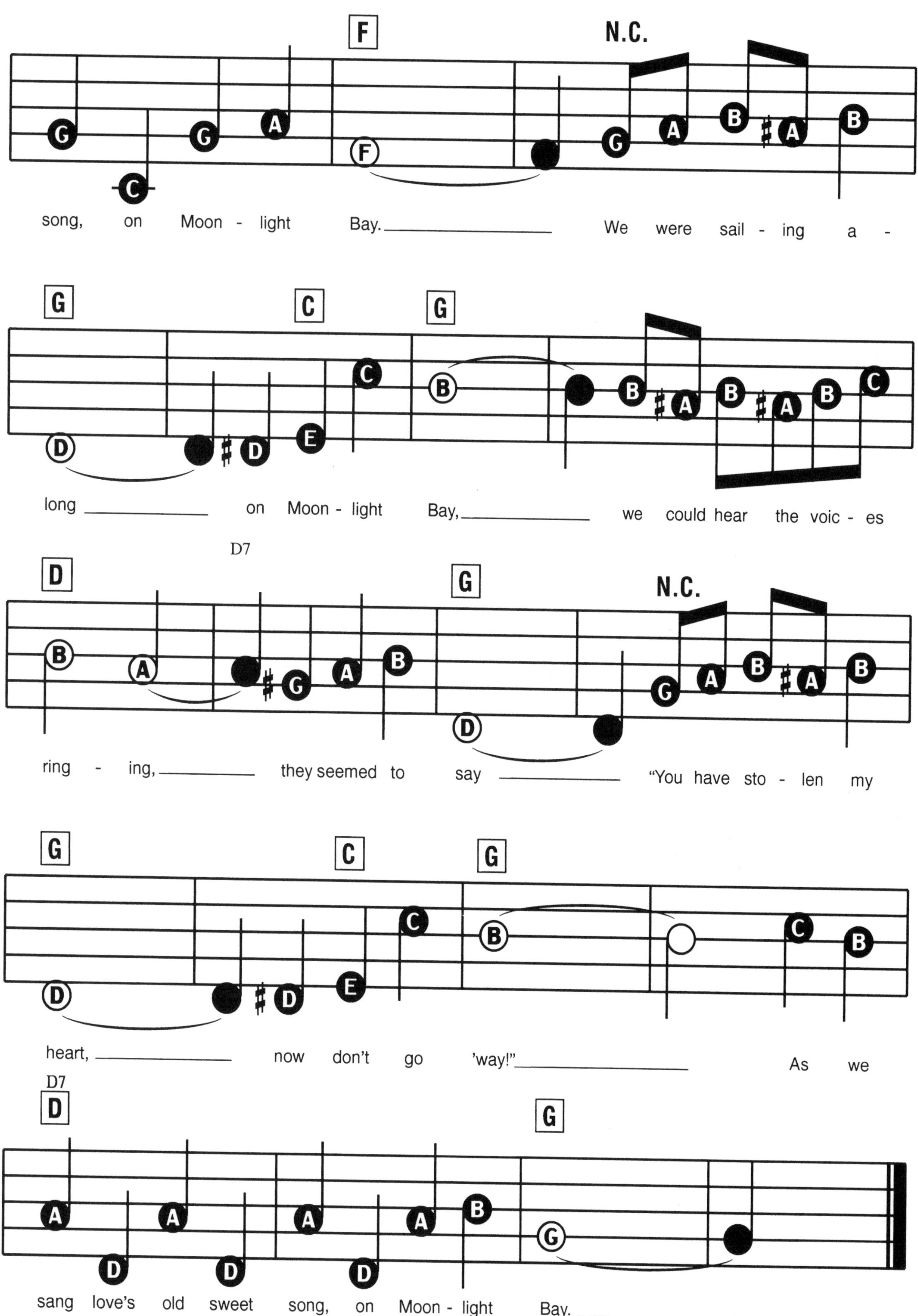
F
N.C.
song, on Moon - light Bay. We were sail - ing a -
G
C
G
long on Moon - light Bay, we could hear the voic - es
D
D7
G
N.C.
ring - ing, they seemed to say "You have sto - len my
G
C
G
heart, now don't go 'way!" As we
D7
D
G
sang love's old sweet song, on Moon - light Bay.

My Buddy

Registration 9
Rhythm: Waltz

Lyrics by Gus Kahn
Music by Walter Donaldson

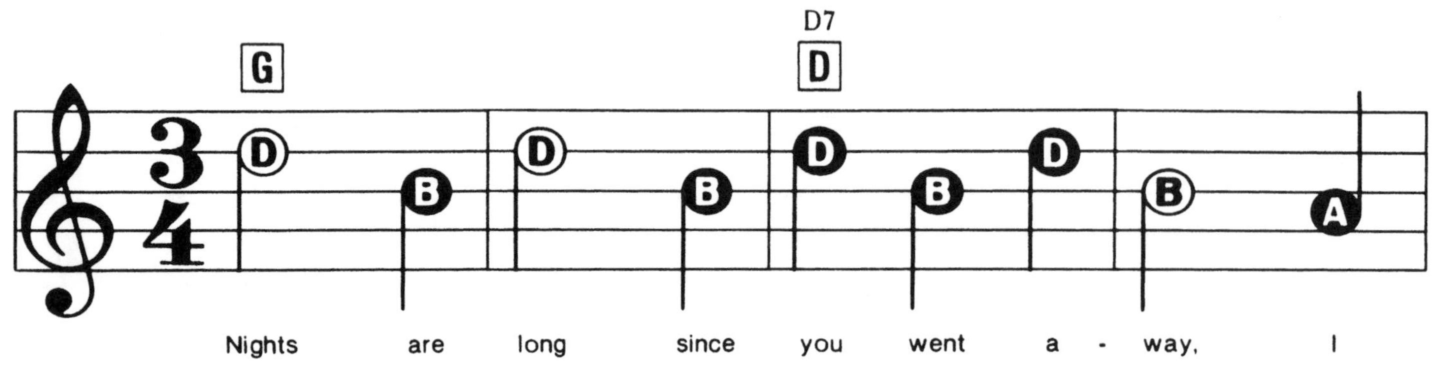

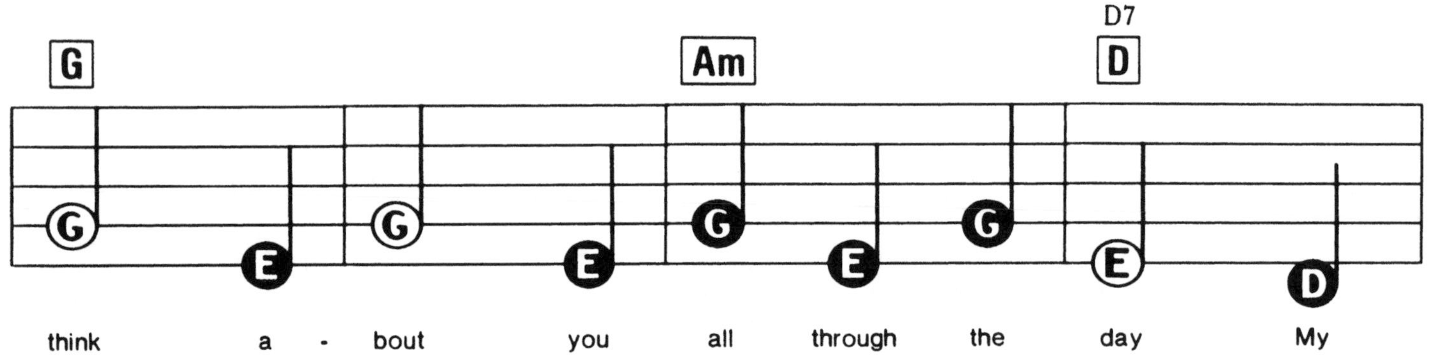

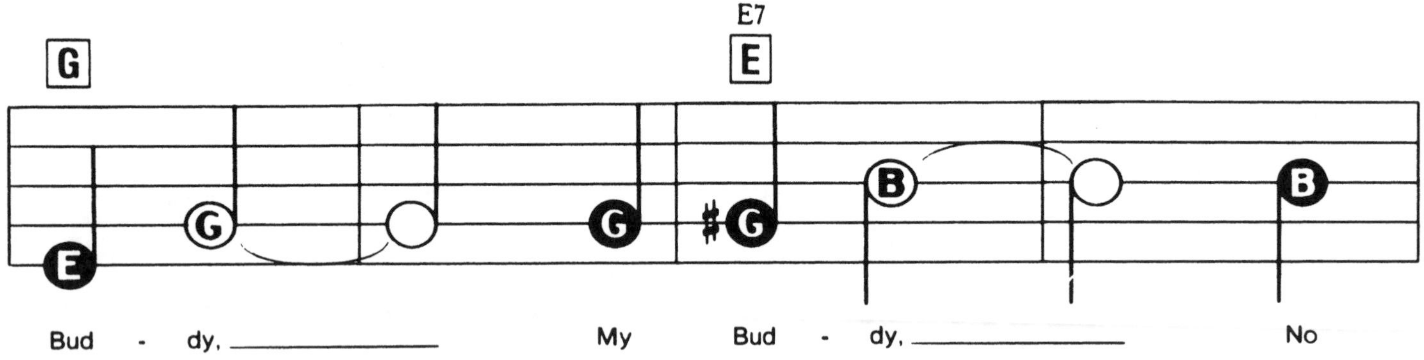

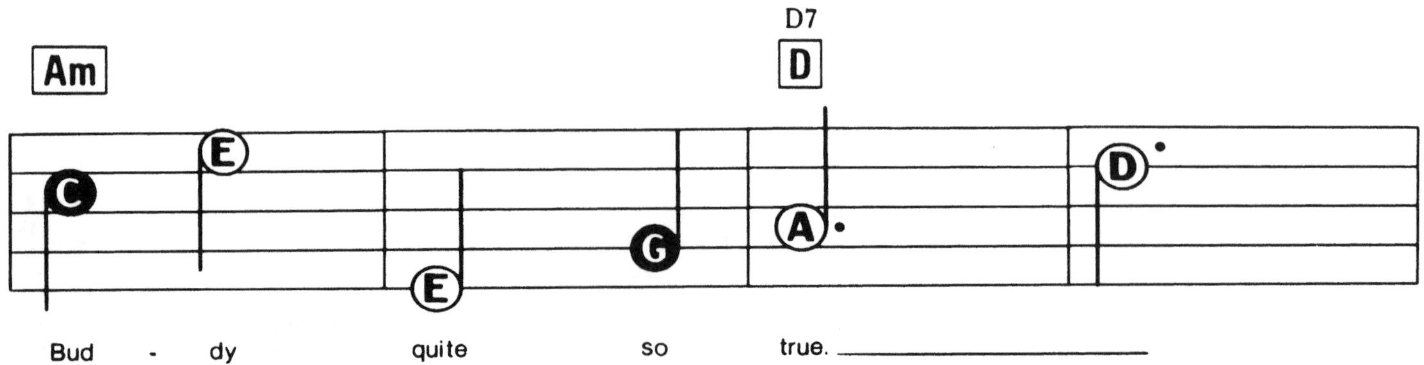

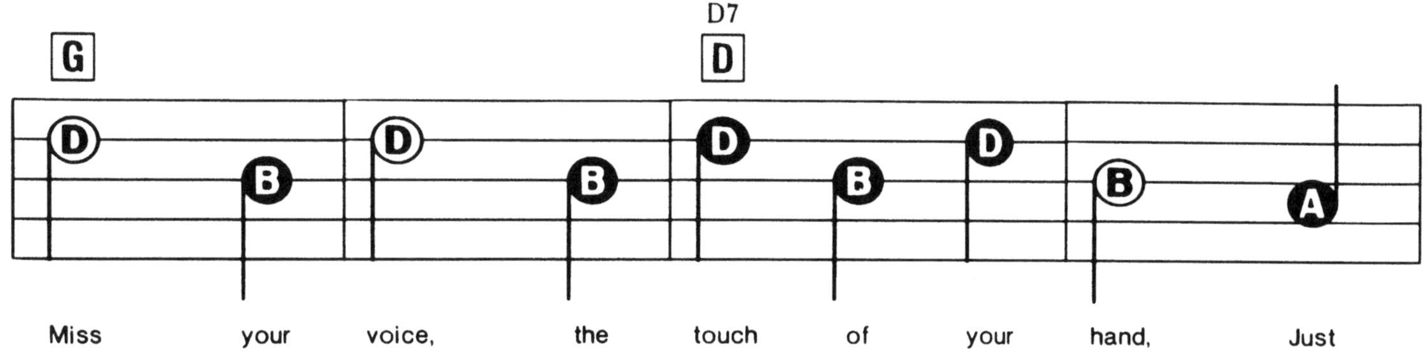
D7
G
D
D D B D B D B D B A
Miss your voice, the touch of your hand, Just

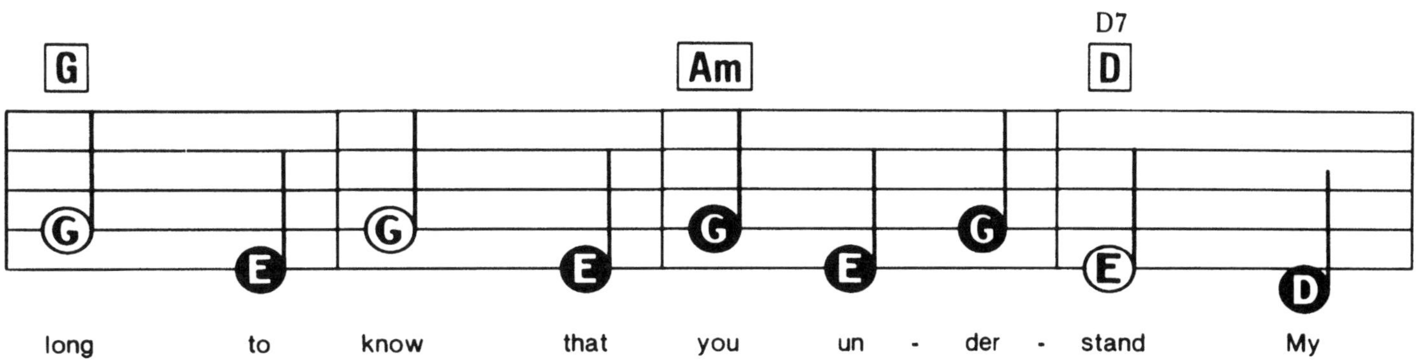
G
Am
D7
D
G E G E G E G E D
long to know that you un - der - stand My

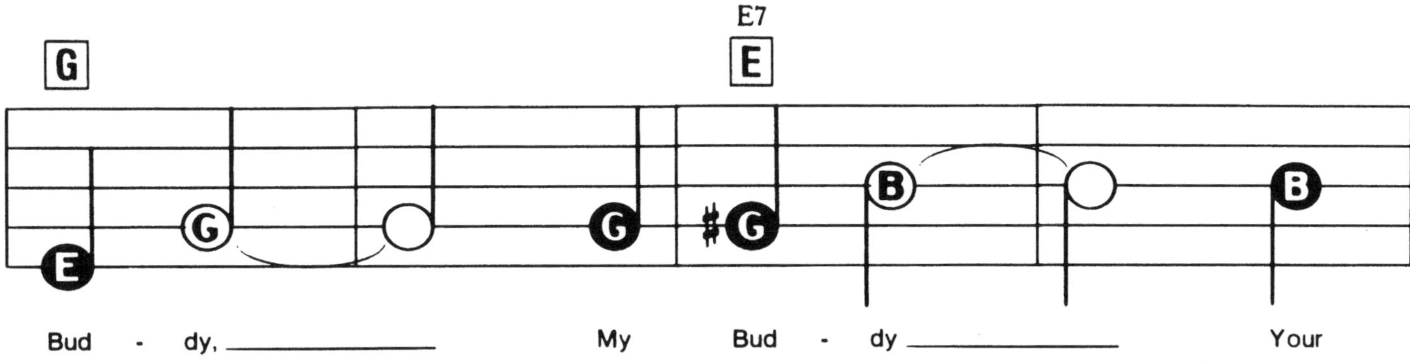
G
E7
E
E G G ♯G B B
Bud - dy, My Bud - dy Your

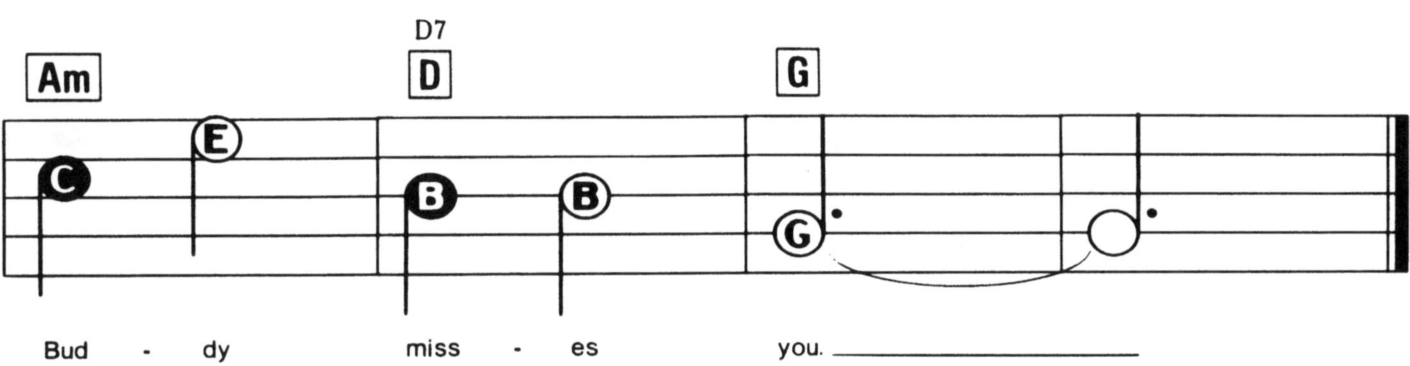
Am
D7
D
G
C E B B G
Bud - dy miss - es you.

My Wild Irish Rose

Registration 2
Rhythm: Waltz

Words and Music by
Chauncey Olcott

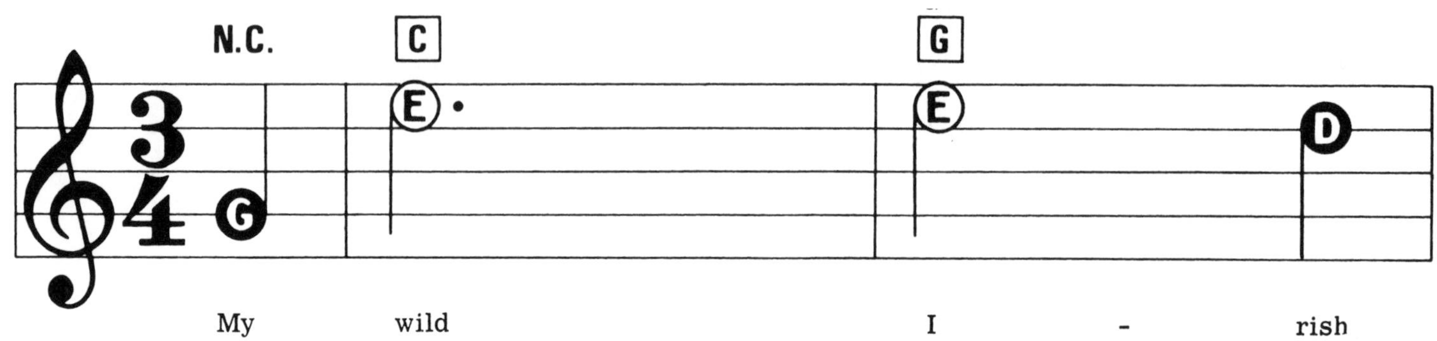

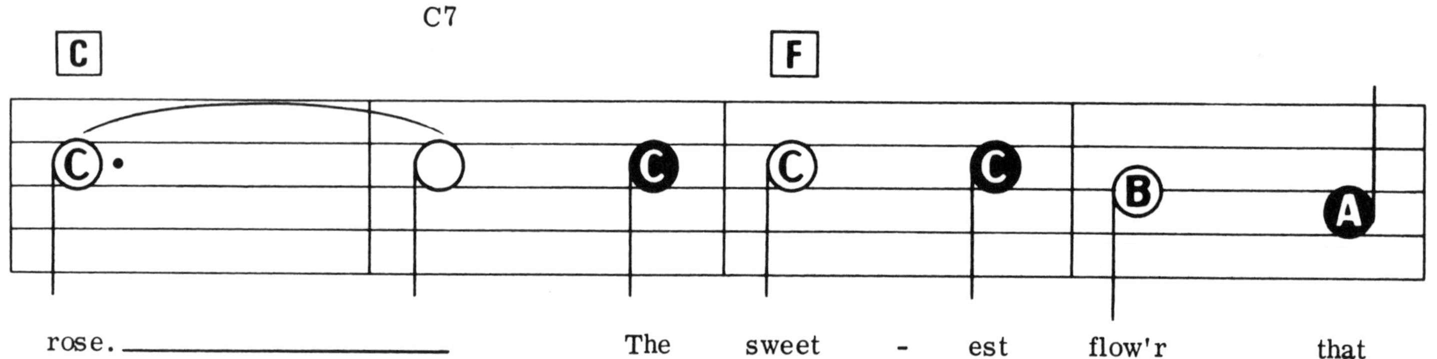

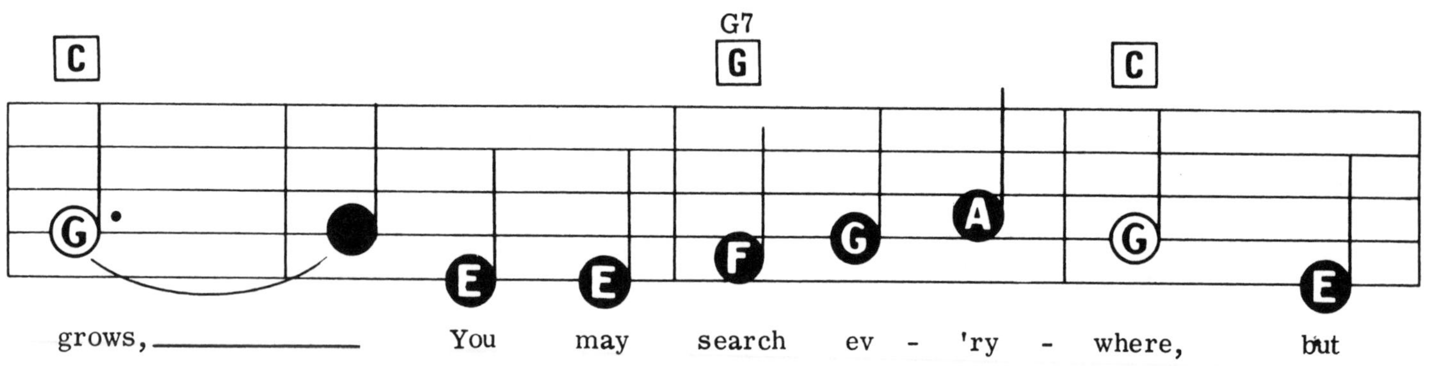

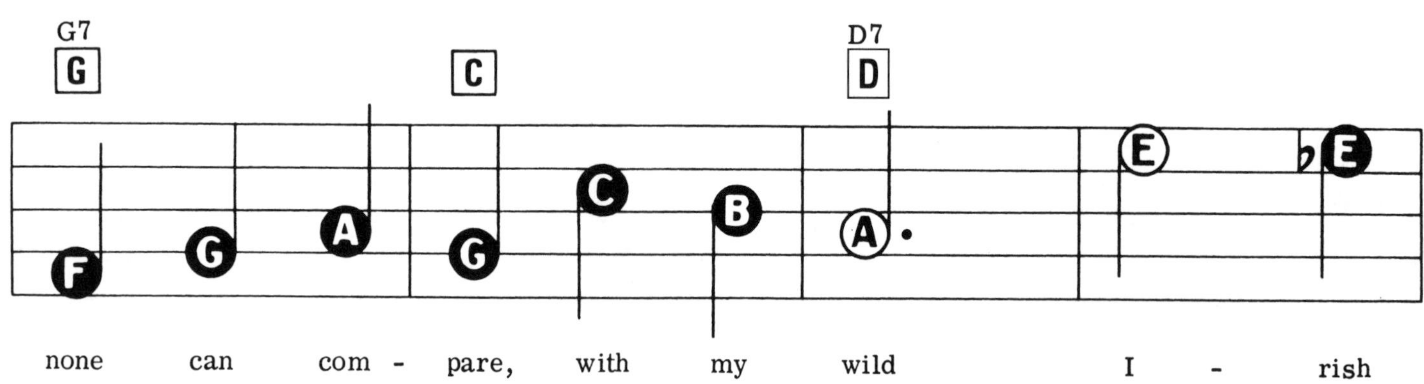

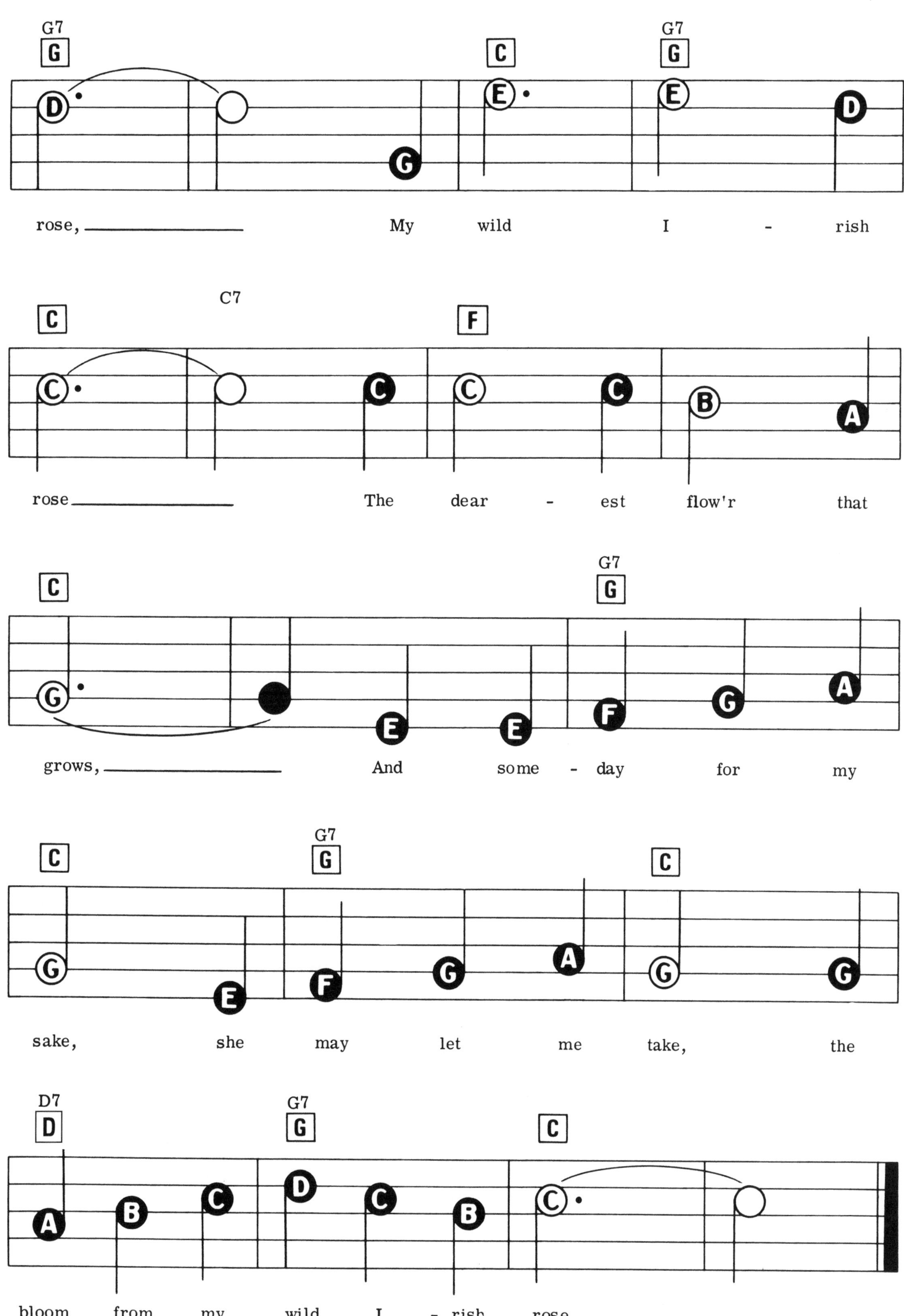
G7 G
C
G7 G
D E E D
G
rose, My wild I - rish
C
C7
F
C C C C B A
rose The dear - est flow'r that
C
G7 G
G E E F G A
grows, And some - day for my
C
G7 G
C
G E F G A G G
sake, she may let me take, the
D7 D
G7 G
C
A B C D C B C
bloom from my wild I - rish rose.

Oh! You Beautiful Doll

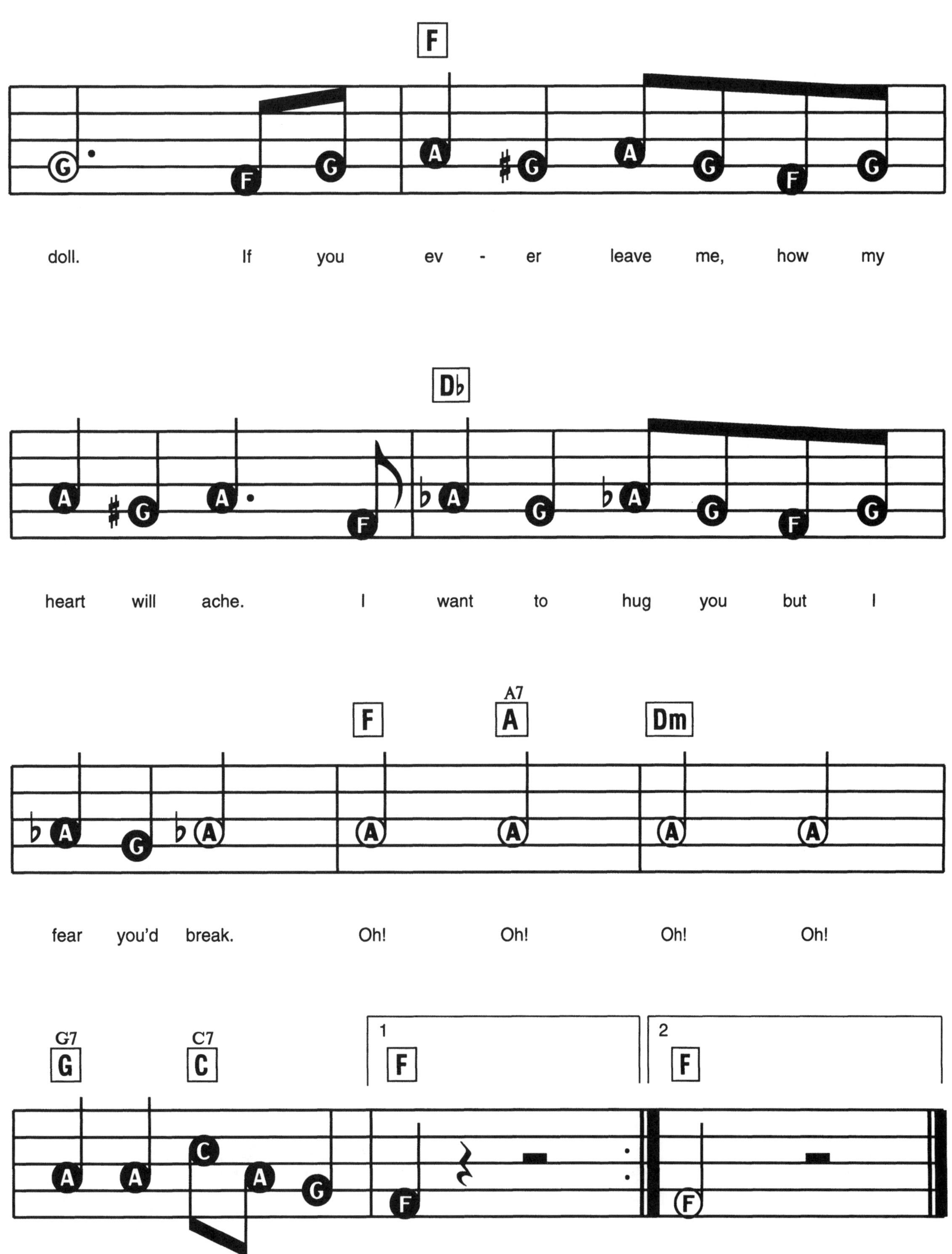
F
doll. If you ev - er leave me, how my
D♭
heart will ache. I want to hug you but I
F
A7
A
Dm
fear you'd break. Oh! Oh! Oh! Oh!
G7
G
C7
C
1
F
2
F
Oh! You beau - ti - ful doll! doll!

Paper Doll

Registration 4
Rhythm: Fox Trot or Swing

Words and Music by
Johnny S. Black

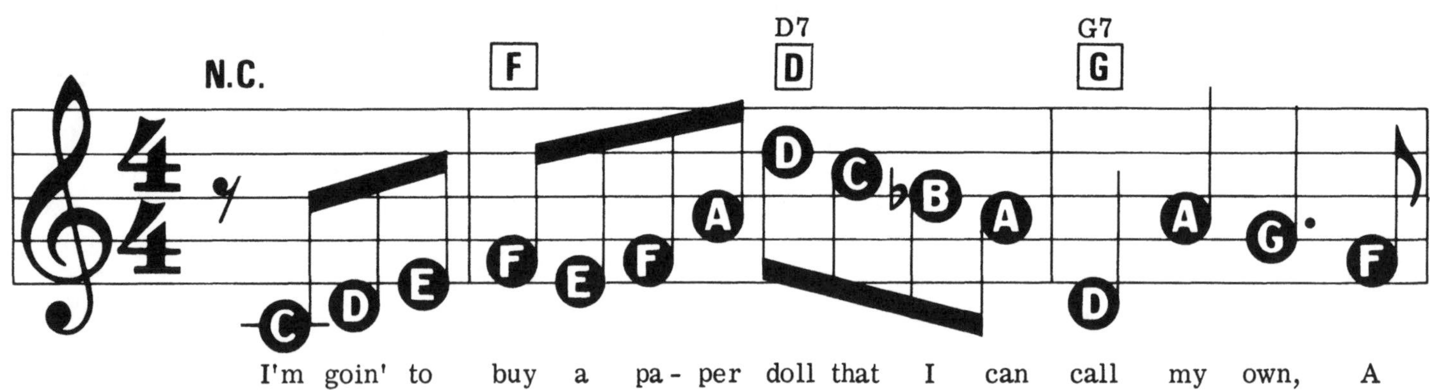

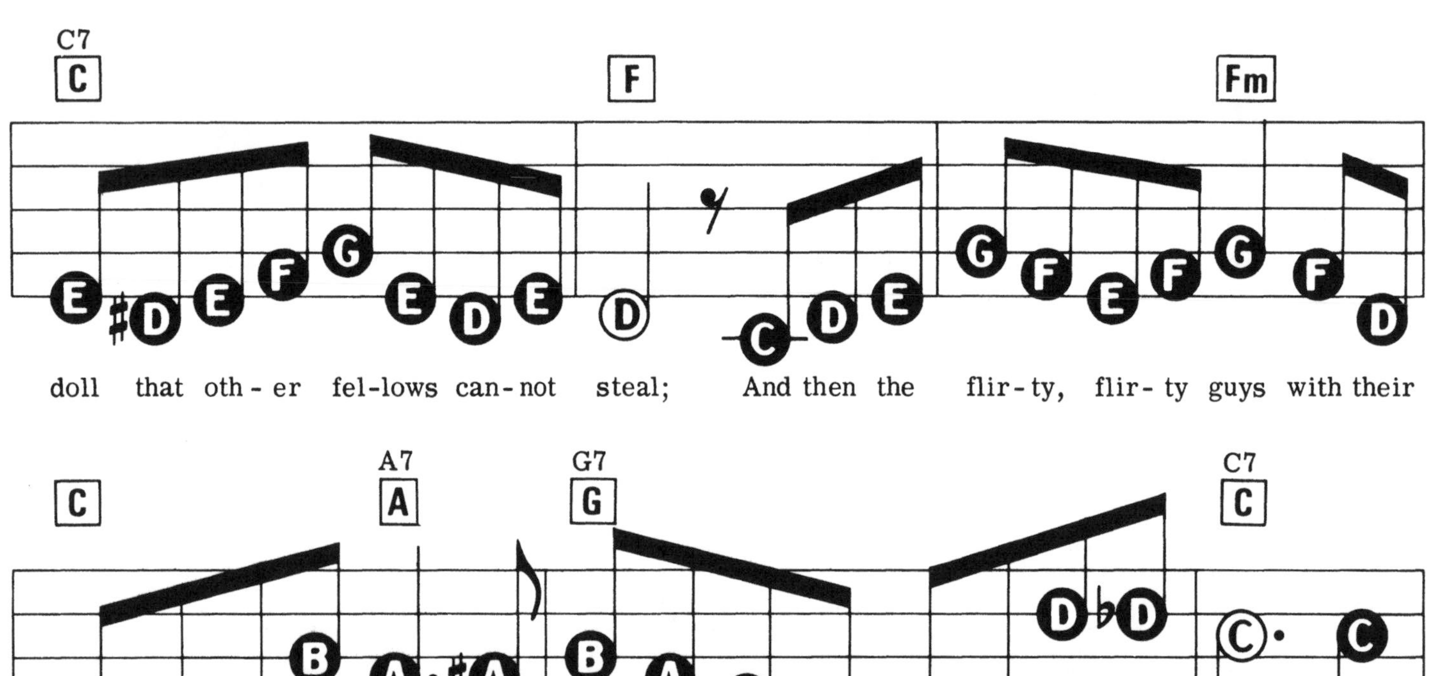

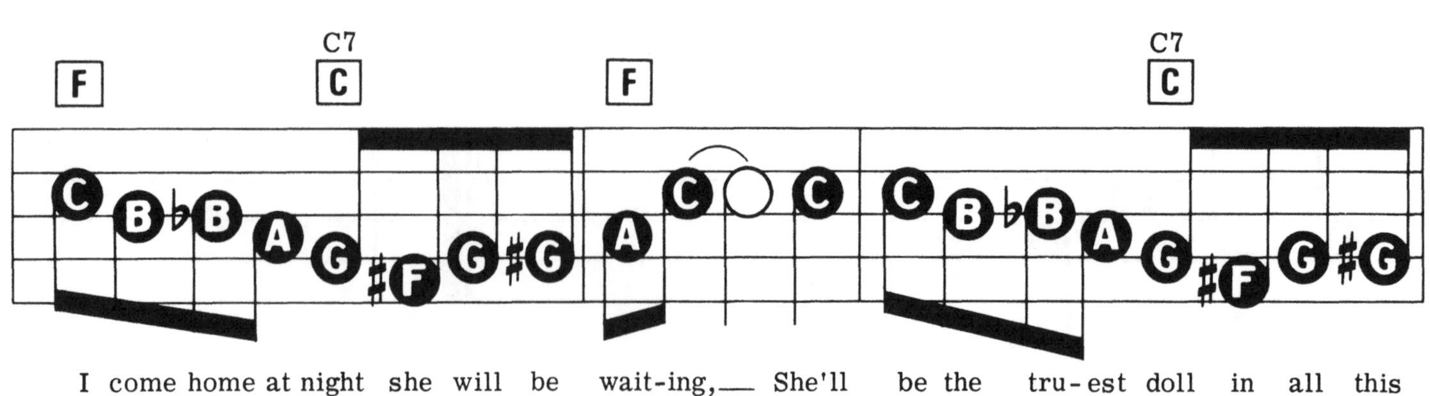

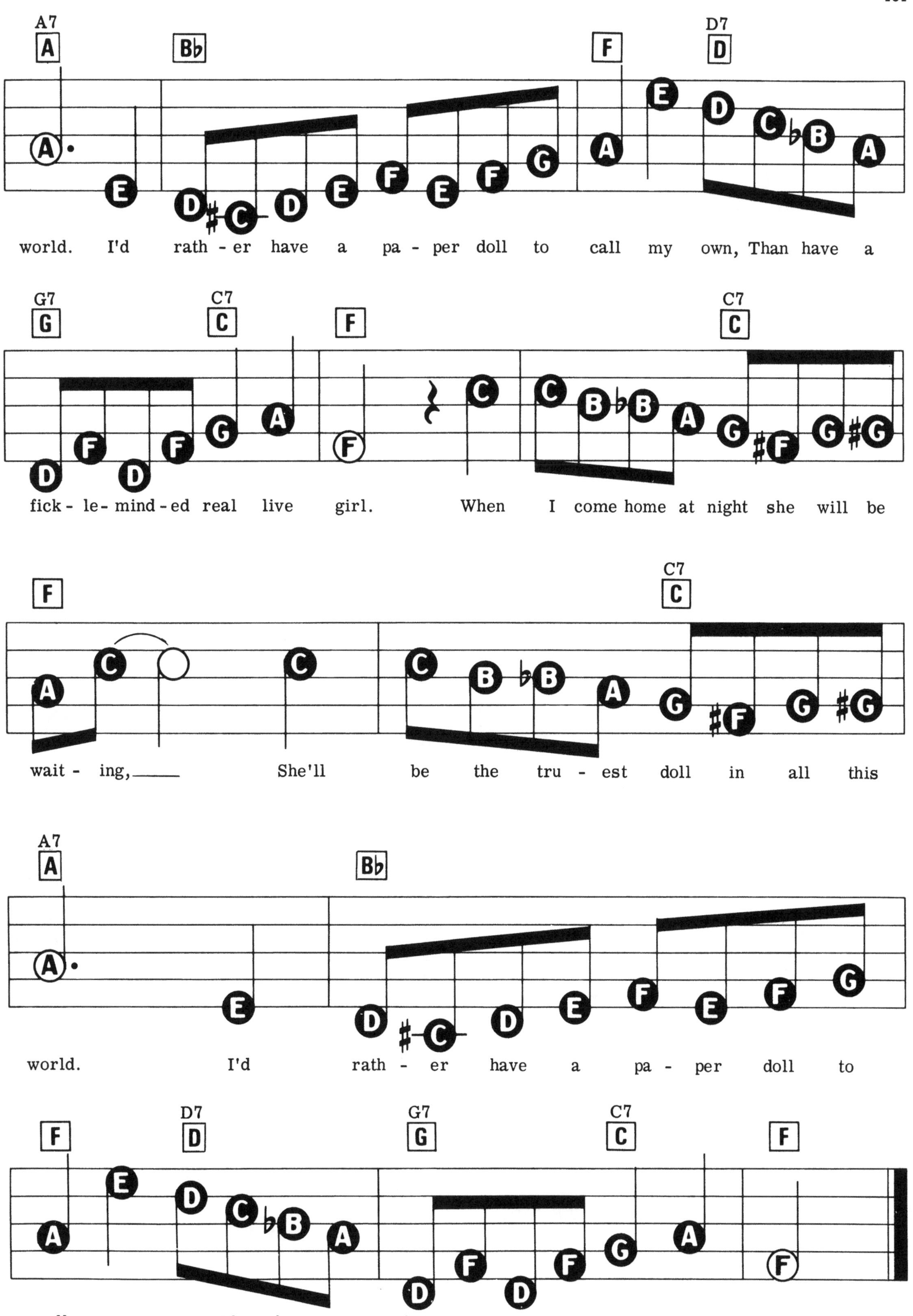
A7 A Bb F D7 D
world. I'd rath - er have a pa - per doll to call my own, Than have a
G7 G C7 C F C7 C
fick - le - mind - ed real live girl. When I come home at night she will be
F C7 C
wait - ing, She'll be the tru - est doll in all this
A7 A Bb
world. I'd rath - er have a pa - per doll to
F D7 D G7 G C7 C F
call my own, Than have a fick - le - mind - ed real live girl.

Pretty Baby

Registration 2
Rhythm: Swing

Words by Gus Kahn
Music by Egbert Van Alstyne and Tony Jackson

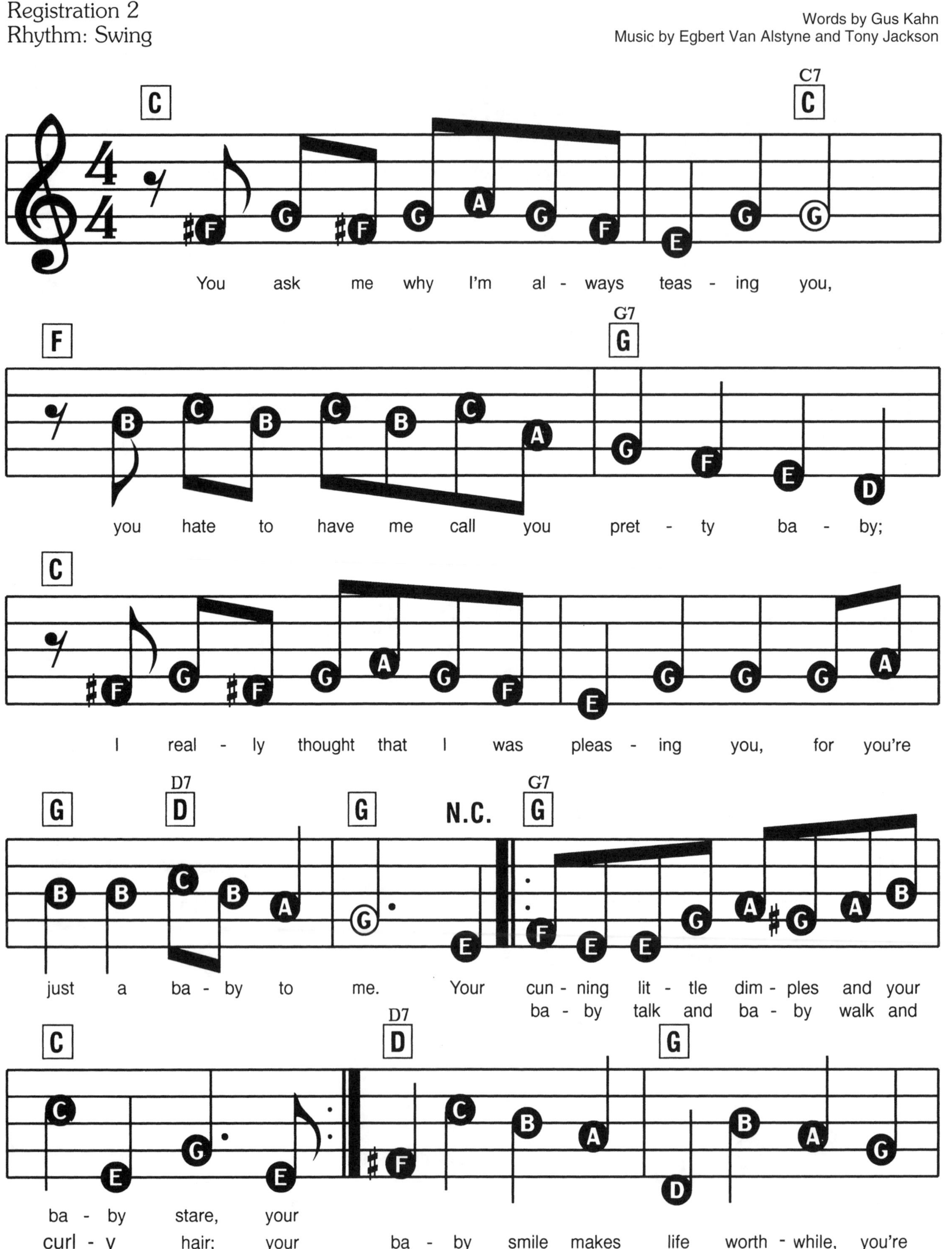

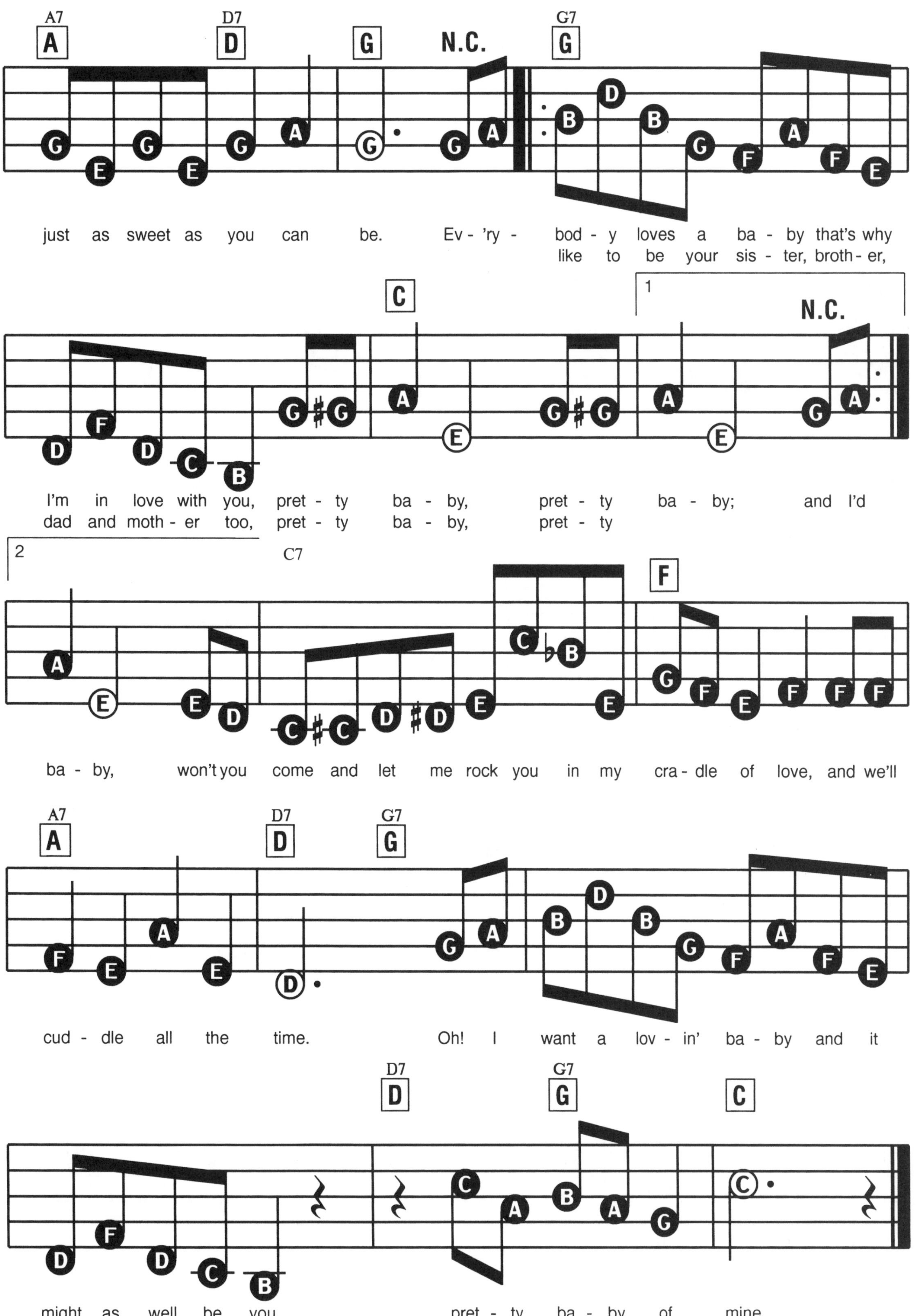
A7 D7 G7
N.C.
just as sweet as you can be. Ev - 'ry - bod - y loves a ba - by that's why
like to be your sis - ter, broth - er,
C
1
N.C.
I'm in love with you, pret - ty ba - by, pret - ty ba - by; and I'd
dad and moth - er too, pret - ty ba - by, pret - ty
2
C7
F
ba - by, won't you come and let me rock you in my cra - dle of love, and we'll
A7 D7 G7
cud - dle all the time. Oh! I want a lov - in' ba - by and it
D7 G7 C
might as well be you, pret - ty ba - by of mine.

A Pretty Girl Is Like a Melody

from the 1919 Stage Production ZIEGFELD FOLLIES

Registration 8
Rhythm: Fox Trot or Ballad

Words and Music by
Irving Berlin

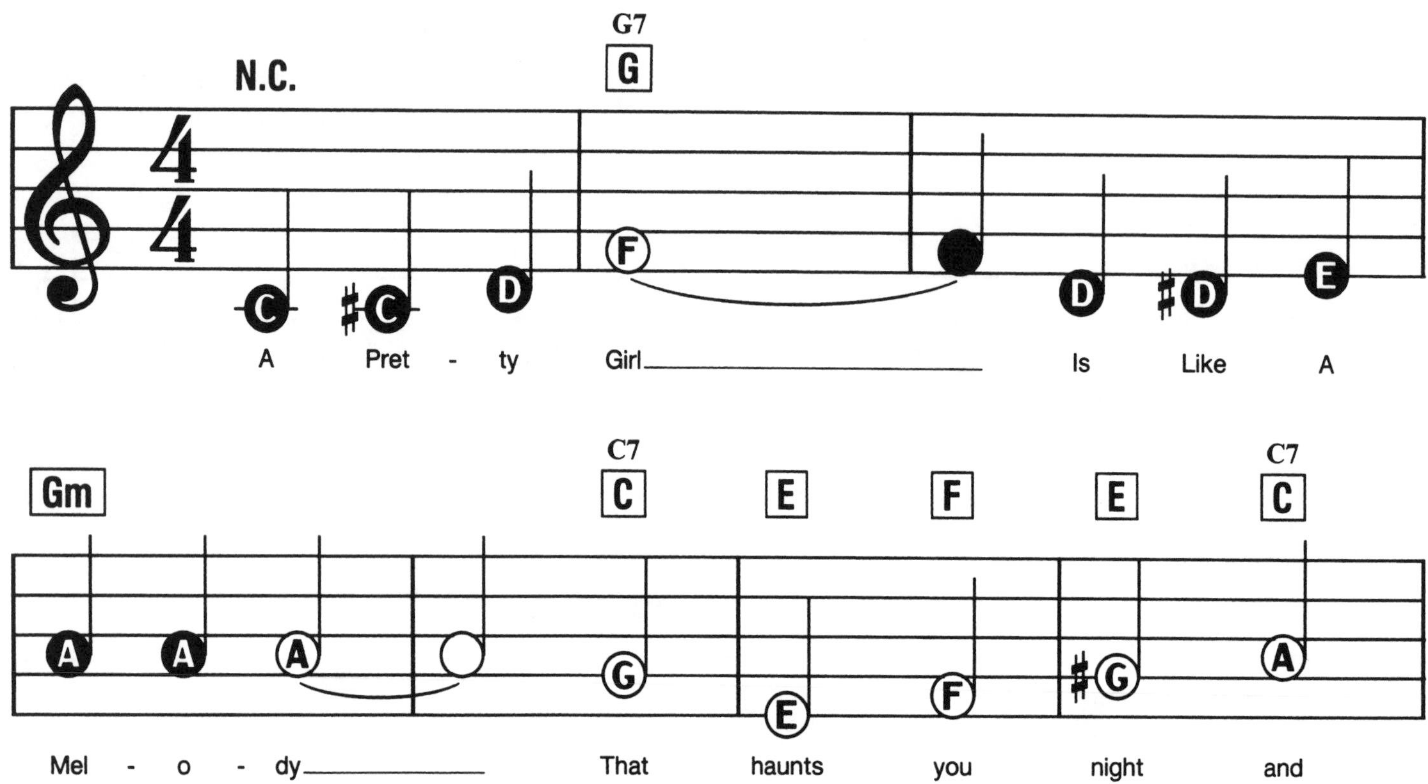

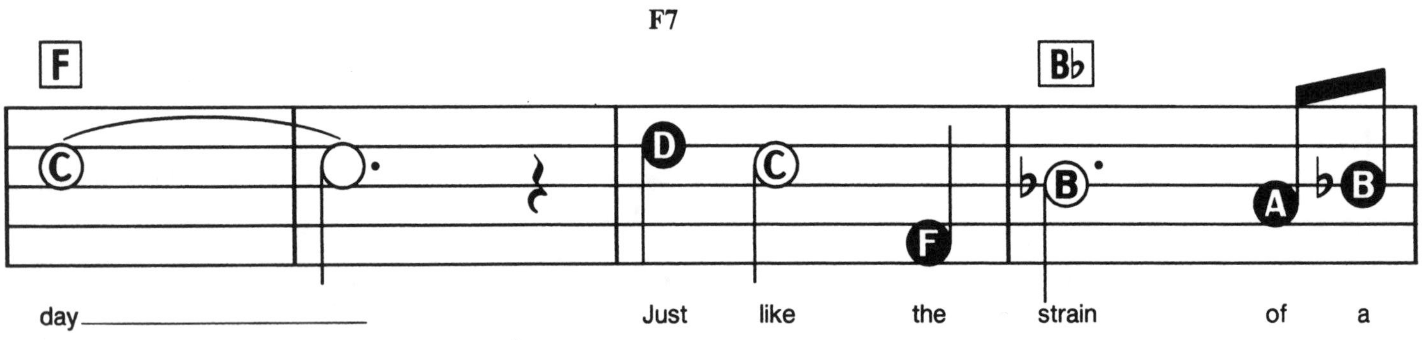

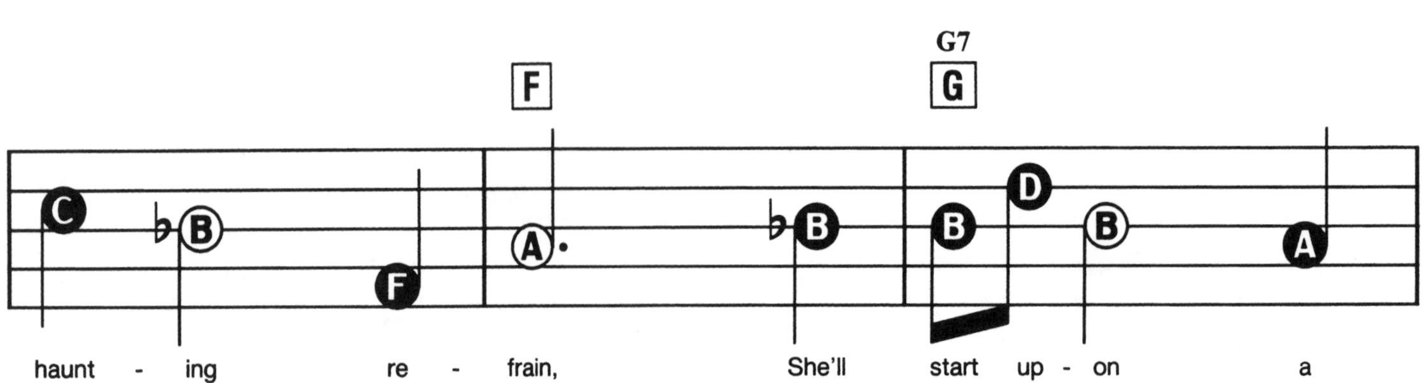

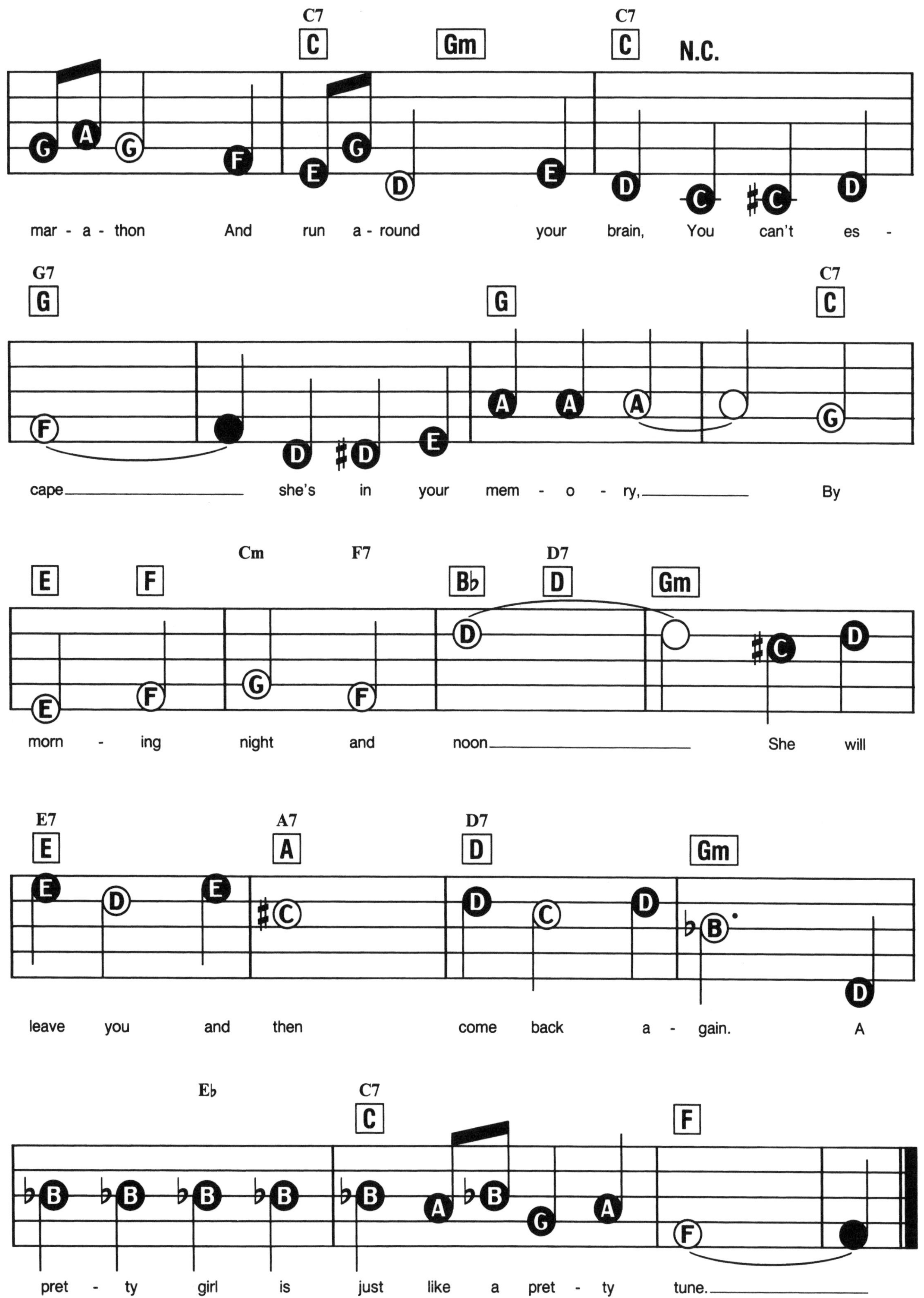
C7 C Gm C7 C N.C.
mar - a - thon And run a - round your brain, You can't es -
G7 G G C7 C
cape she's in your mem - o - ry, By
E F Cm F7 B♭ D7 D Gm
morn - ing night and noon She will
E7 E A7 A D7 D Gm
leave you and then come back a - gain. A
E♭ C7 C F
pret - ty girl is just like a pret - ty tune.

Put Your Arms Around Me, Honey

Registration 9
Rhythm: Fox Trot

Words by Junie McCree
Music by Albert von Tilzer

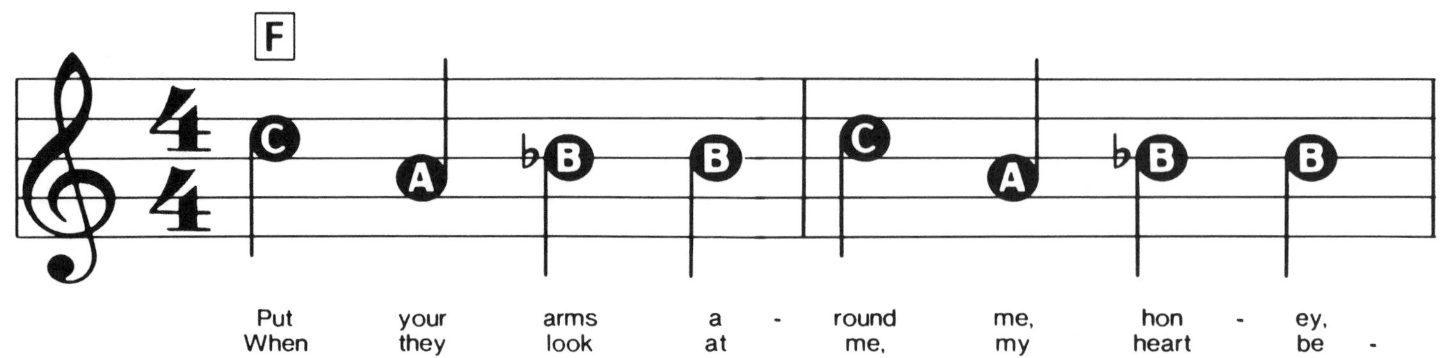

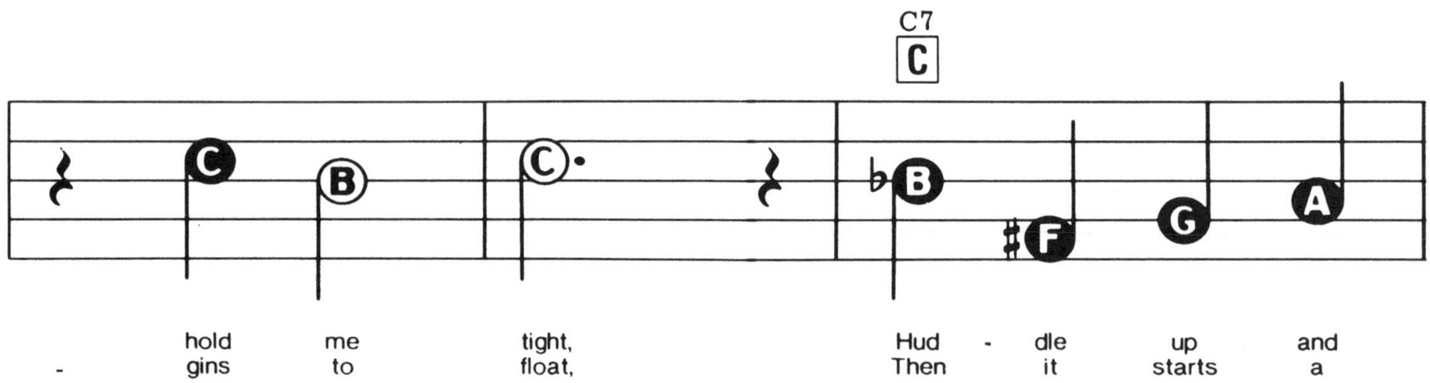

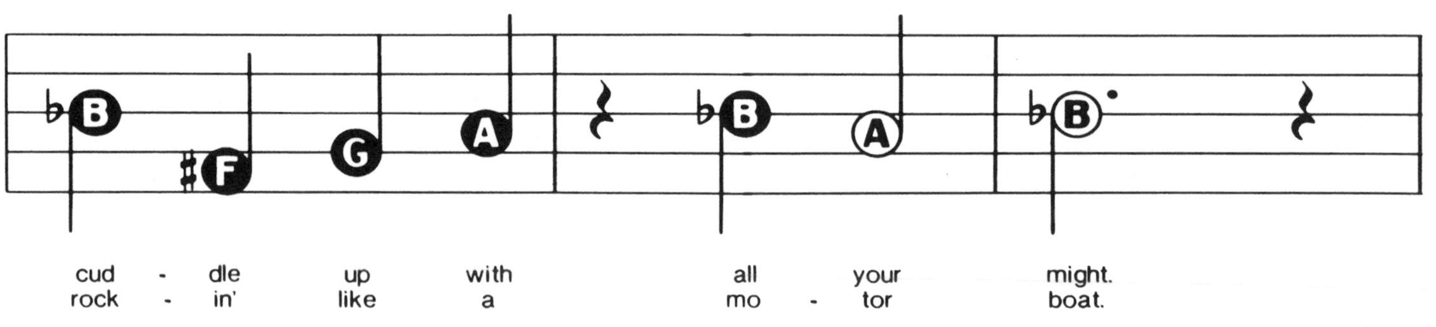

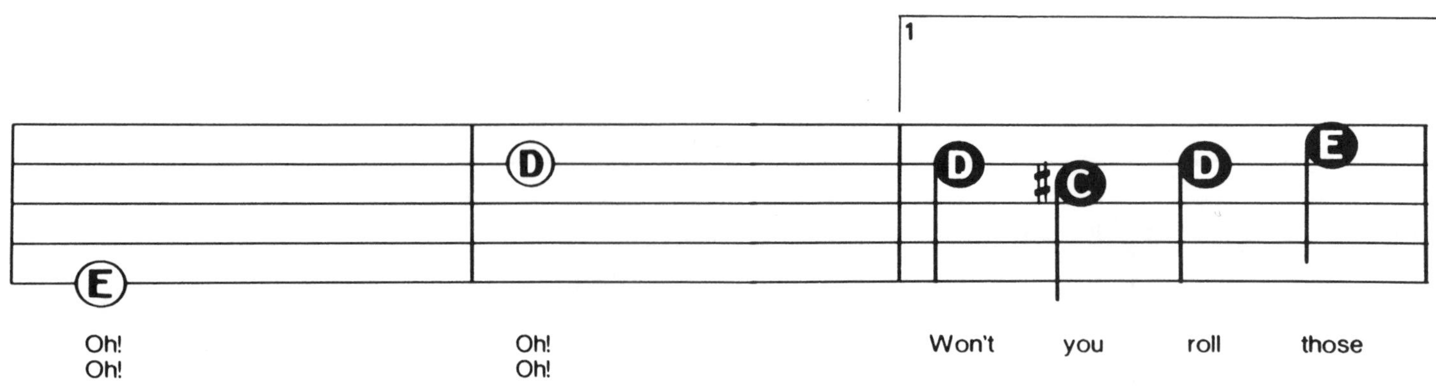

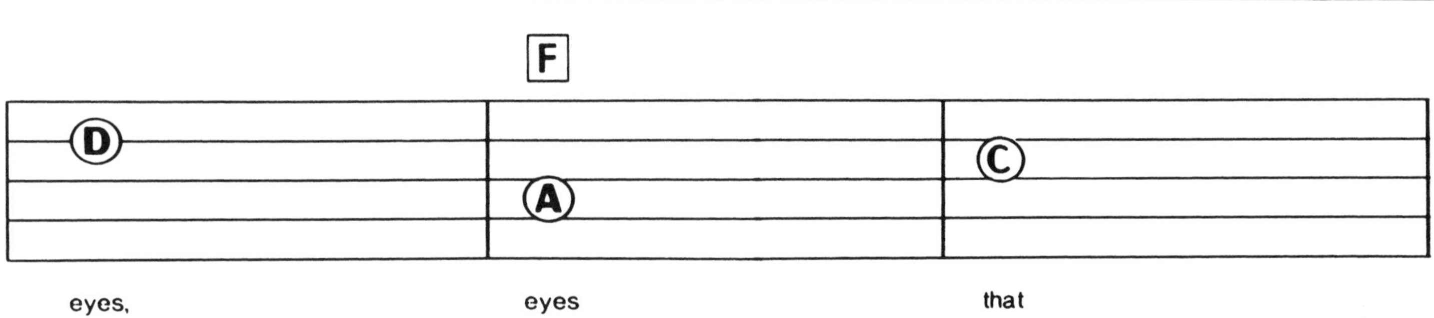
F
D
A
C
eyes,
eyes
that

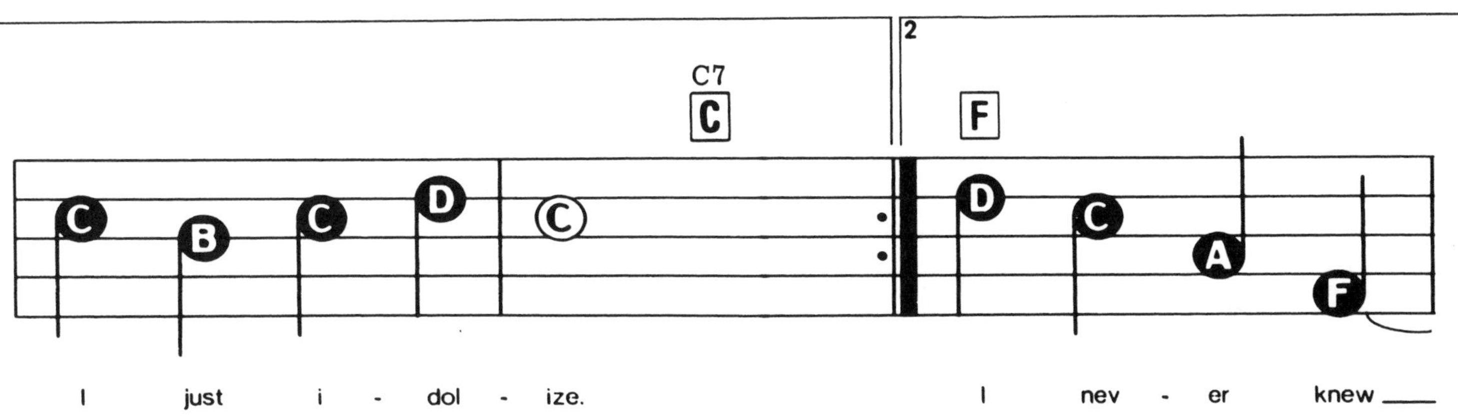
C7
C
2
F
C
B
C
D
C
D
C
A
F
I
just
i - dol - ize.
I
nev - er
knew

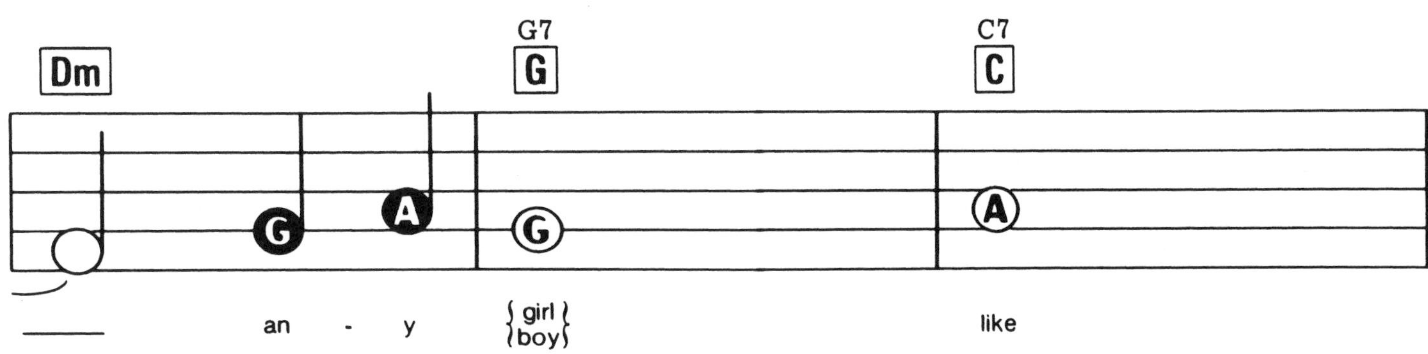
Dm
G7
G
C7
C
G
A
G
A
an - y
girl
boy
like

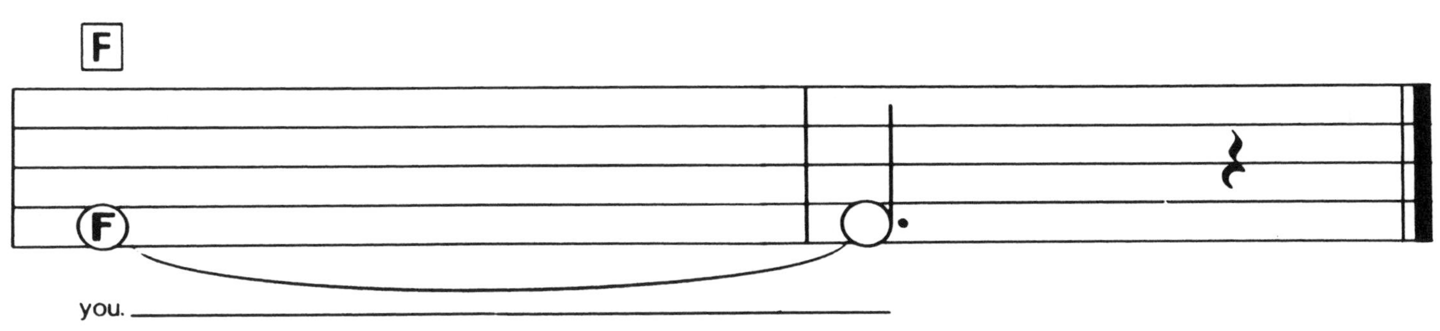
F
F
you.

Ragtime Cowboy Joe

Registration 5
Rhythm: Swing or Shuffle

Words and Music by Lewis F. Muir,
Grant Clarke and Maurice Abrahams

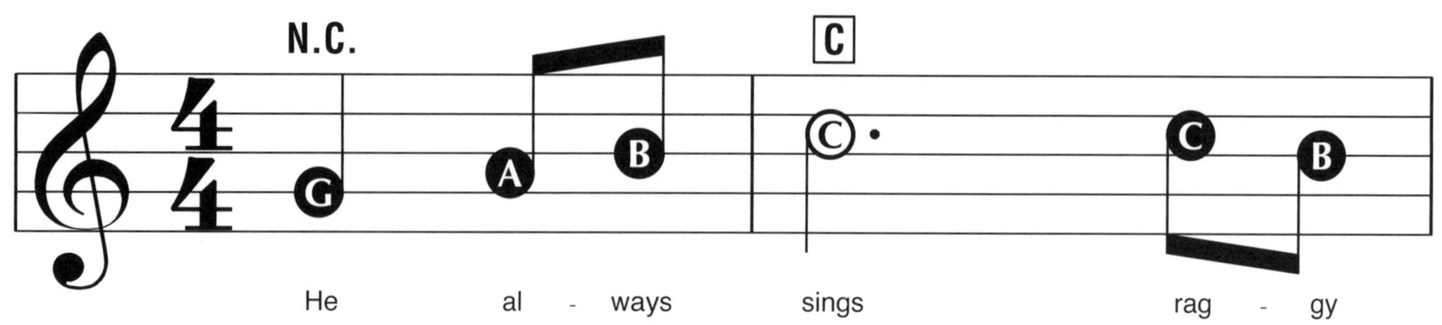

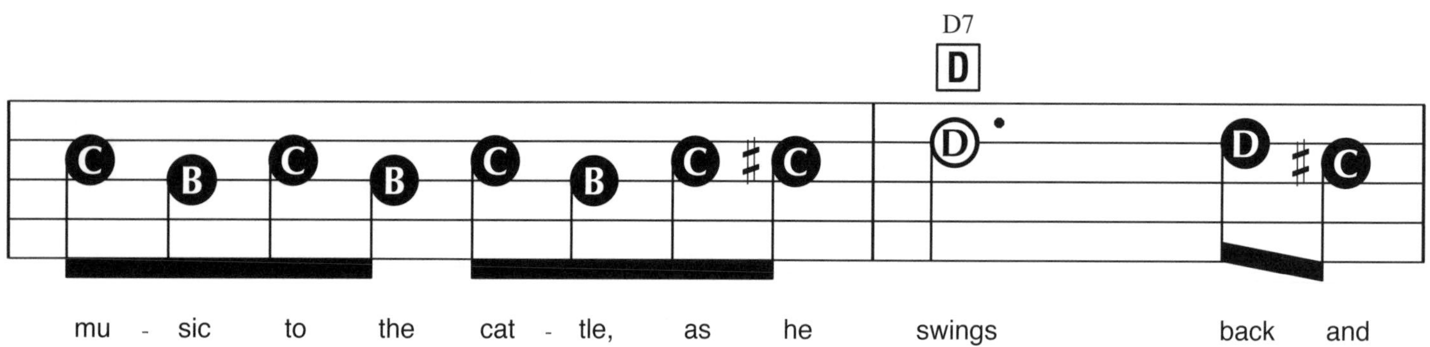

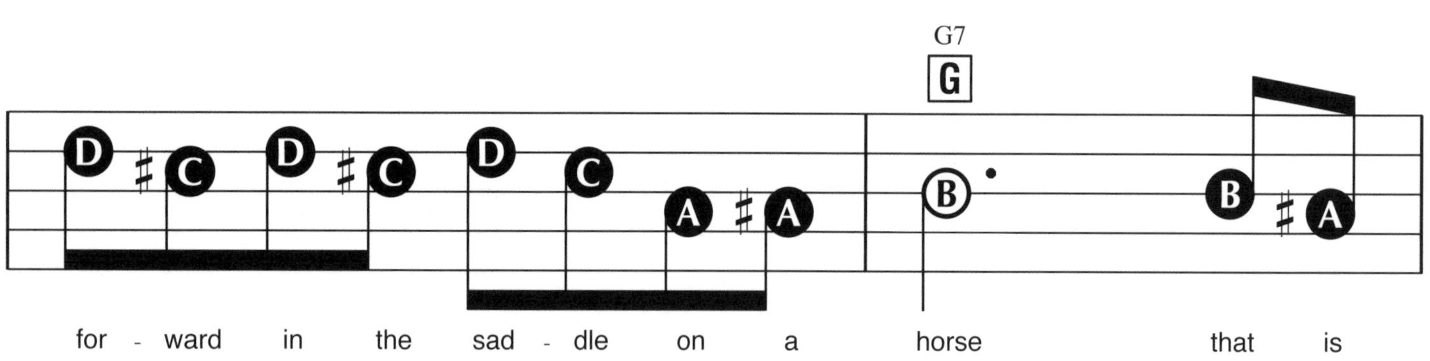

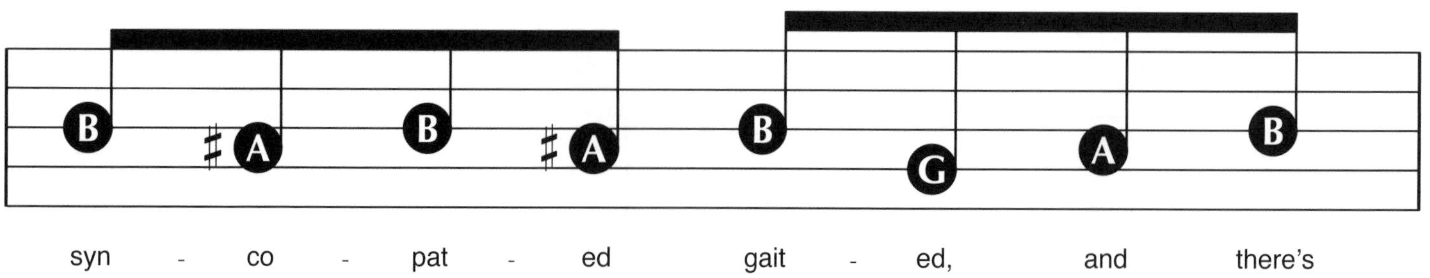

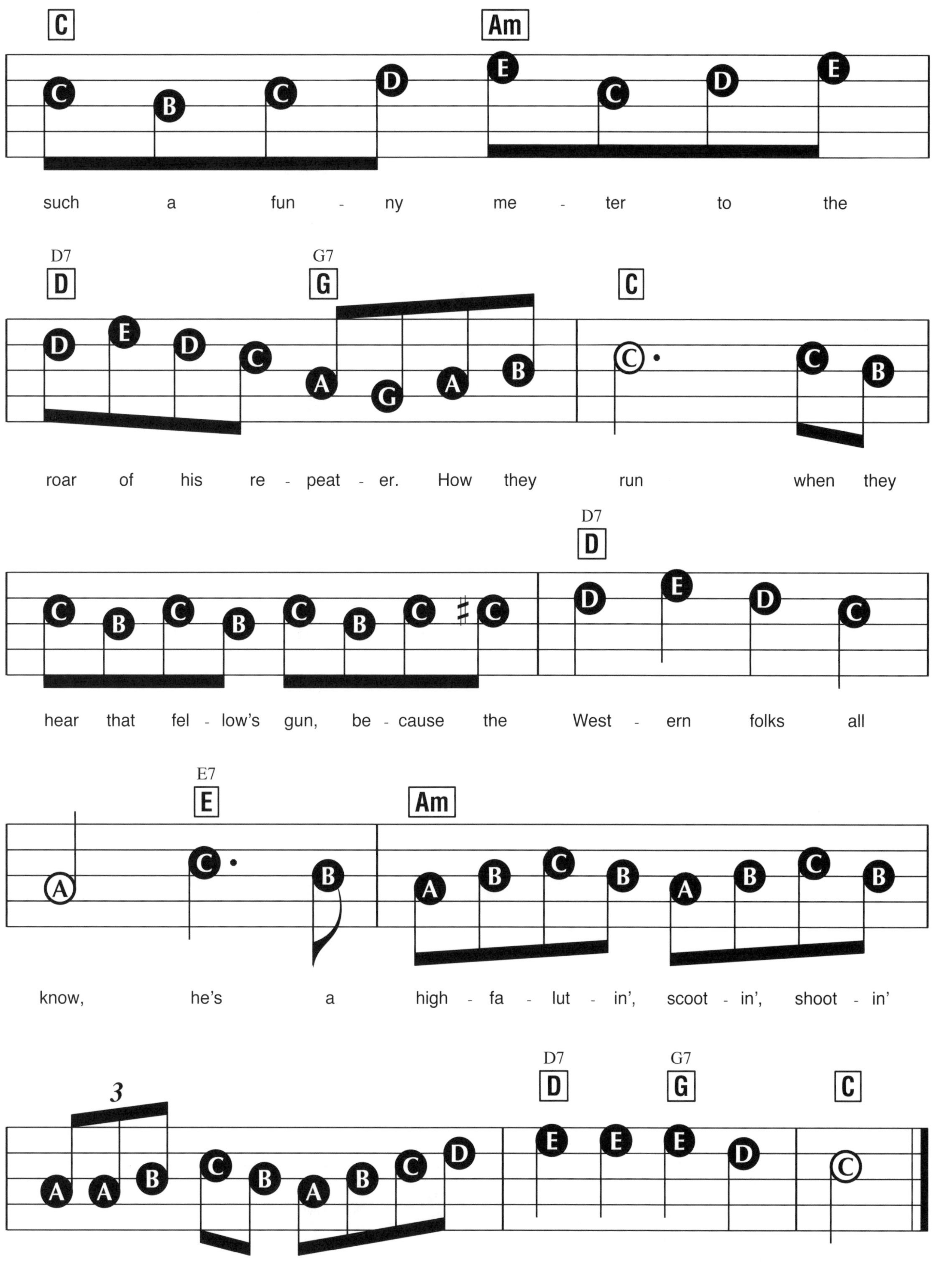
C
Am
such a fun - ny me - ter to the
D7 G7
D G C
roar of his re - peat - er. How they run when they
D7
D
hear that fel - low's gun, be - cause the West - ern folks all
E7
E Am
know, he's a high - fa - lut - in', scoot - in', shoot - in'
3
D7 G7
D G C
son - of - a - gun from Ar - i - zo - na, Rag - time Cow - boy Joe.

The Red River Valley

Registration 4
Rhythm: Swing

Traditional American Cowboy Song

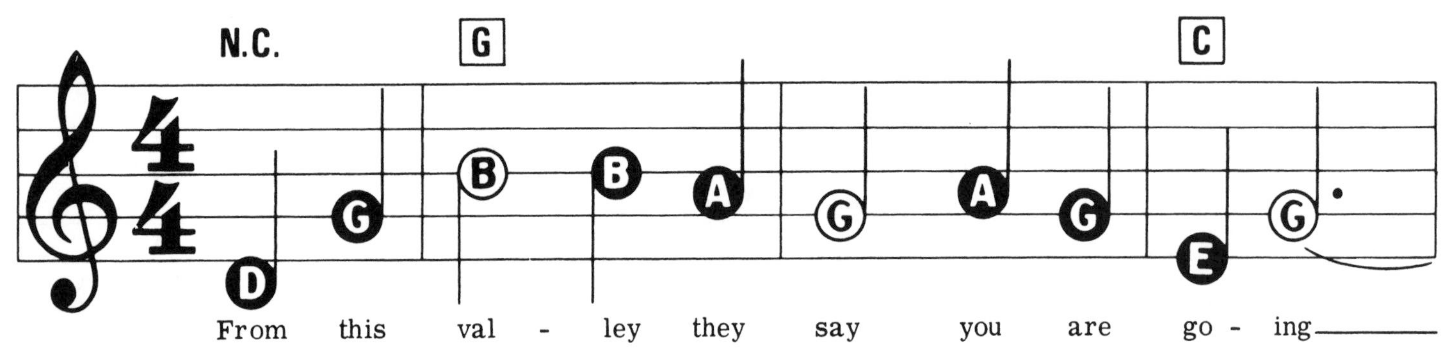

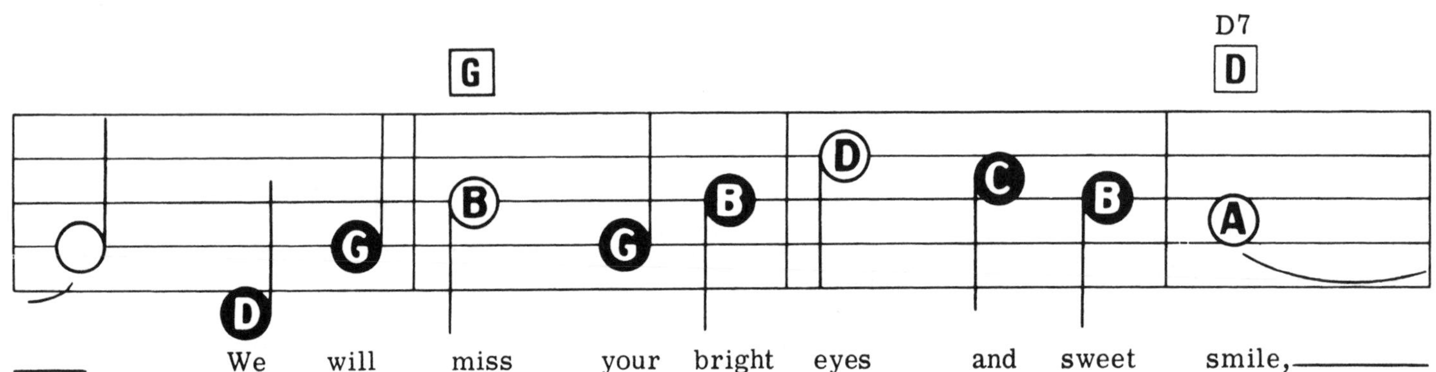

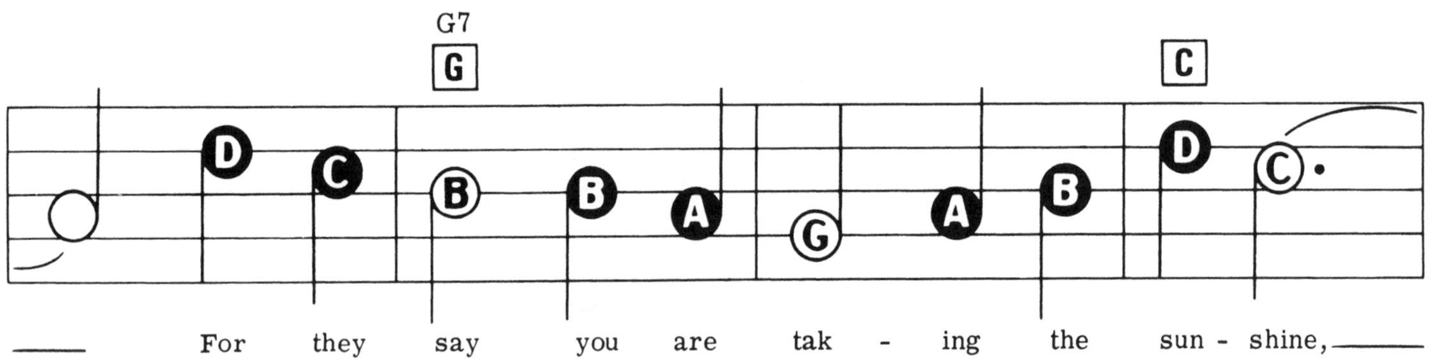

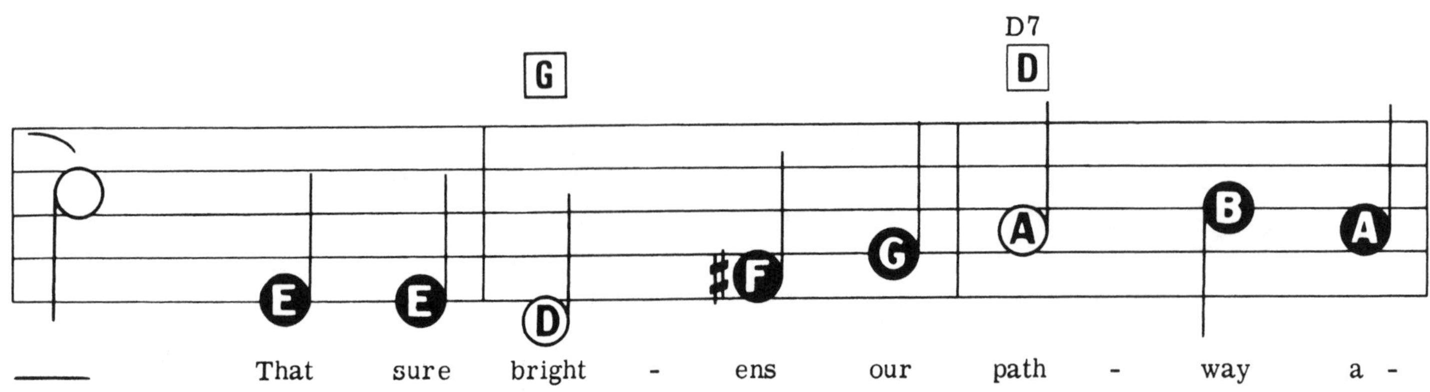

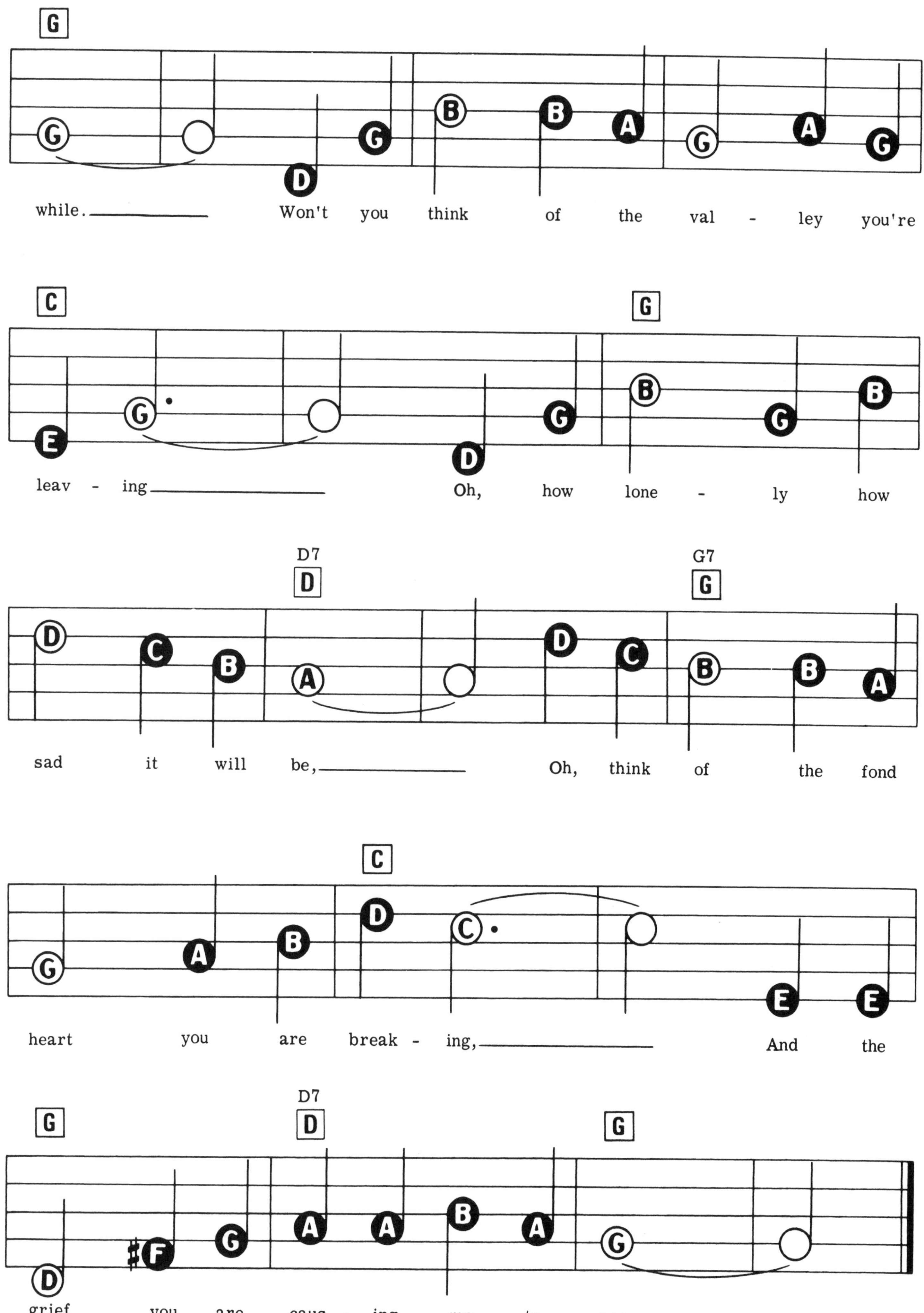
G
G
D
G
B
B
A
G
A
G
while.
Won't
you
think
of
the
val
-
ley
you're
C
G
E
G
D
G
B
G
B
leav
-
ing
Oh,
how
lone
-
ly
how
D7
D
G7
G
D
C
B
A
D
C
B
B
A
sad
it
will
be,
Oh,
think
of
the
fond
C
G
A
B
D
C
E
E
heart
you
are
break
-
ing,
And
the
G
D7
D
G
D
F
G
A
A
B
A
G
grief
you
are
caus
-
ing
me
to
see.

Schnitzelbank

Registration 2
Rhythm: None

German Folksong

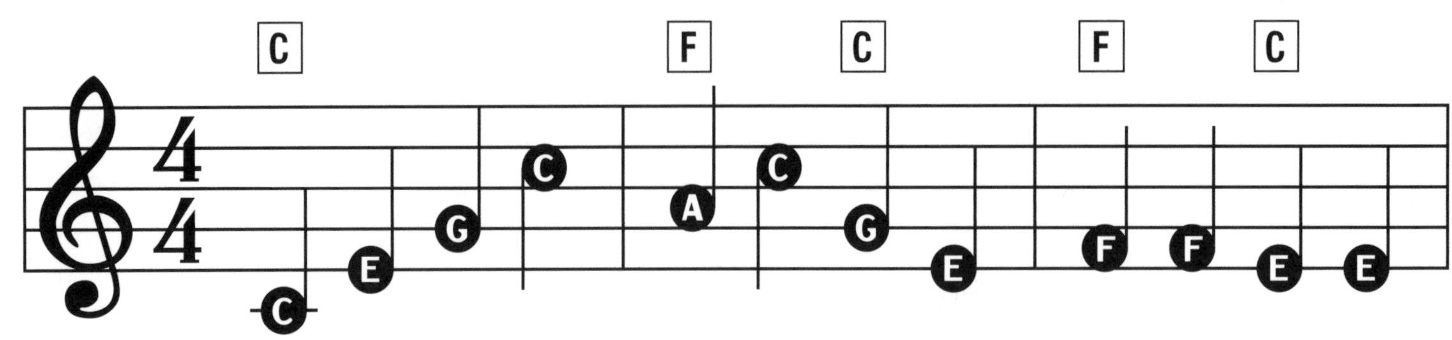

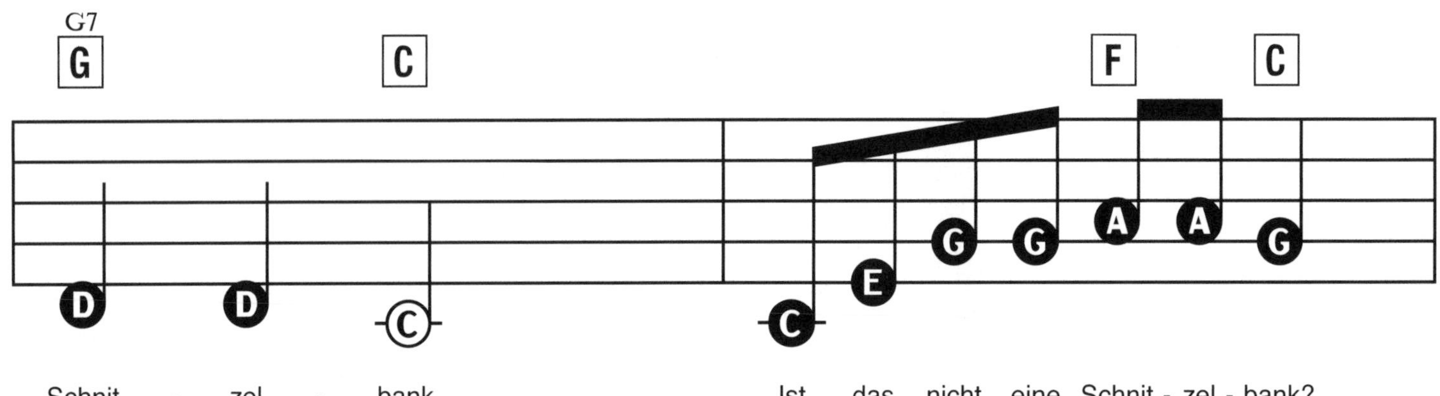

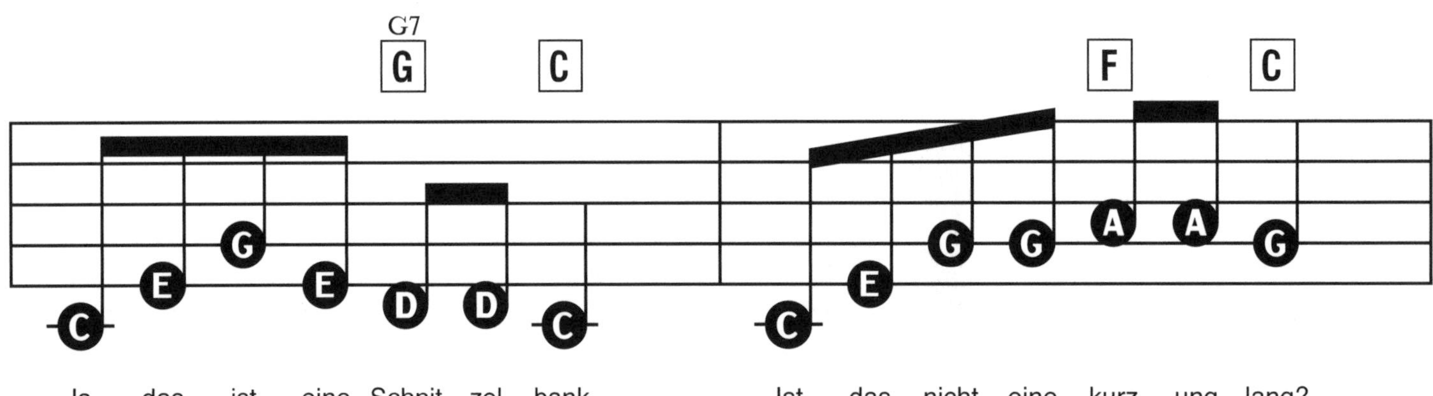

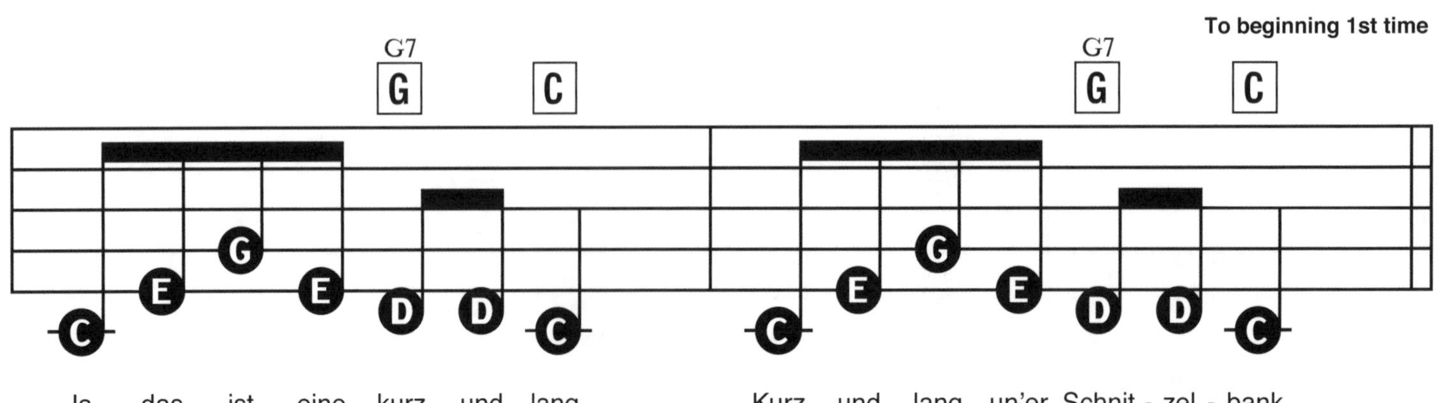

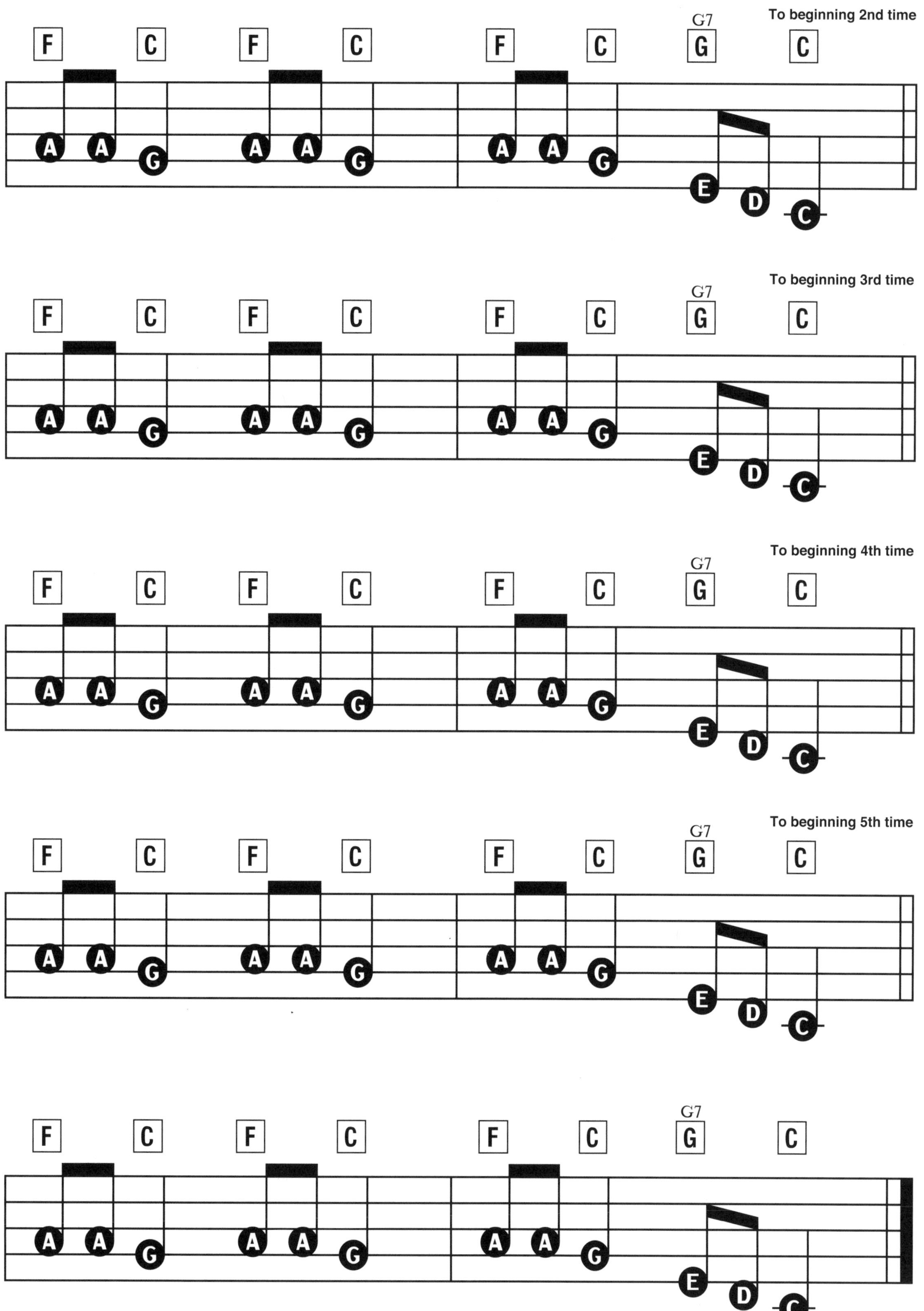
G7
To beginning 2nd time
F C F C F C G C
A A G A A G A A G E D C
G7
To beginning 3rd time
F C F C F C G C
A A G A A G A A G E D C
G7
To beginning 4th time
F C F C F C G C
A A G A A G A A G E D C
G7
To beginning 5th time
F C F C F C G C
A A G A A G A A G E D C
G7
F C F C F C G C
A A G A A G A A G E D C

Additional Lyrics

2. Ei du schöne, ei du schöne,
Ei du schöne Schnitzelbank.
Is das nicht ein Hin und Her?
Ja, das ist ein Hin und Her.
Ist das nicht eine Lichtputzschere?
Ja, das ist eine Lichtputzschere.
Lichtputzschere, Hin und Her,
Kurz und lang un'er Schnitzelbank.

3. Ei du schöne, ei du schöne,
Ei du schöne Schnitzelbank.
Is das nicht ein gold'ner Ring?
Ja, das ist ein gold'ner Ring.
Ist das nicht ein schönes Ding?
Ja, das ist ein schönes Ding.
Schönes Ding, gold'ner Ring, Lichtputzschere,
Hin und Her, Kurz und lang un'er Schnitzelbank.

4. Ei du schöne, ei du schöne,
Ei du schöne Schnitzelbank.
Is das nicht ein Krum und Grad?
Jas das ist ein Krum und Grad.
Ist das nicht ein Wagenrad?
Ja, das ist ein Wagenrad.
Wagenrad, Krum und Grad,
Schönes Ding, gold'ner Ring,
Lichtputzchere, Hin und Her,
Kurz und land un'er Schnitzelbank.

5. Ei du schöne, ei du schöne,
Ei du schöne Schnitzelbank.
Is das nicht ein Geisenbock?
Ja das ist ein Geisenbock.
Ist das nicht ein Reifenrock?
Jas das ist ein Reifenrock.
Reifenrock, Geisenbock, Wagengrad,
Krum und Grad, Schönes Ding,
Gold'ner Ring, Lichtputzschere, Hin und Her,
Kurz und lang un'er Schnitzelbank.

6. Ei du schöne, ei du schöne,
Ei du schöne Schnitzelbank.
Is das nicht eine gute Wurst?
Ja das ist eine gute Wurst.
Ist das nicht ein grosser Durst?
Jas das ist ein grosser Durst.
Grosser Durst, Gute Wurst,
Reifenrock,
Geisenbock, Wagenrad, Krum und
Grad,
Schönes Ding, gold'ner Ring,
Lichtputzchere, Hin und Her,
Kurz und land un'er Schnitzelbank.

Rock-a-Bye Your Baby with a Dixie Melody

from SINBAD

Registration 9
Rhythm: Fox Trot or Swing

Words by Sam M. Lewis and Joe Young
Music by Jean Schwartz

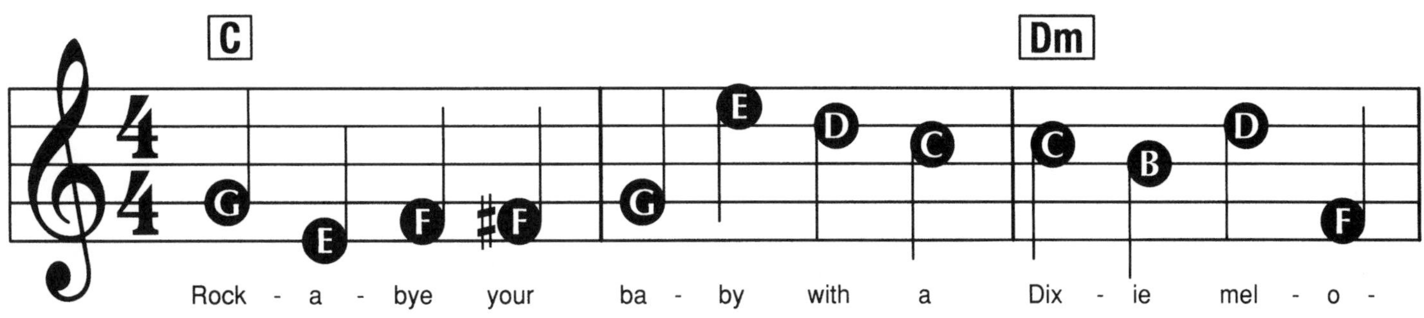

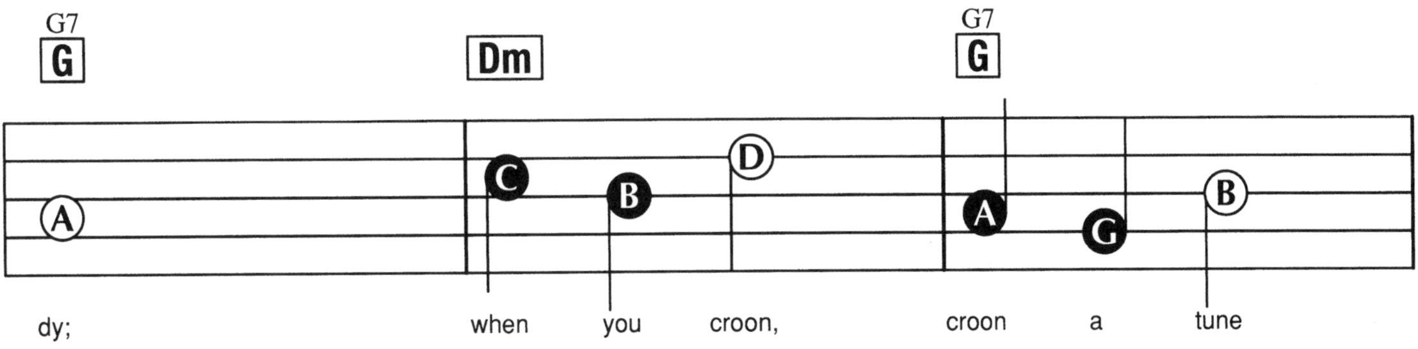

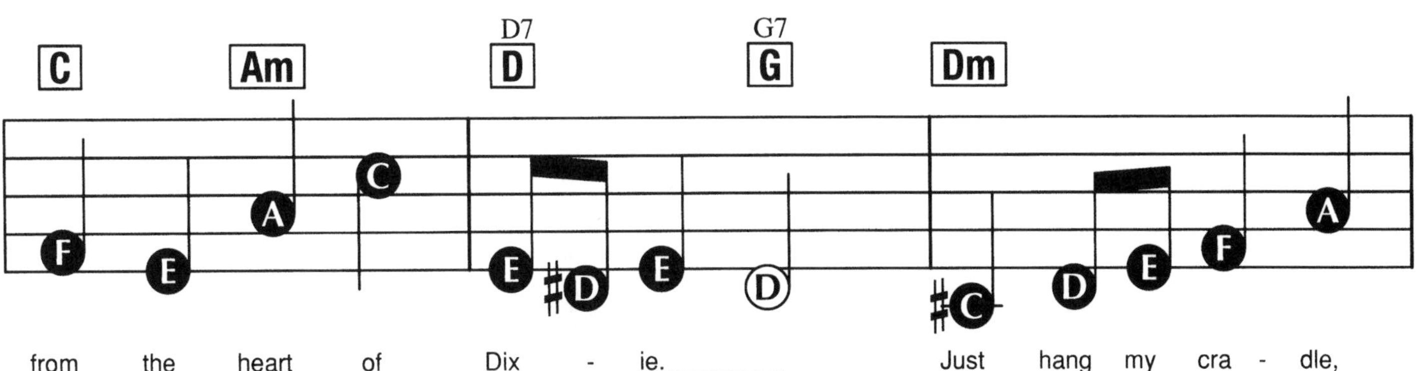

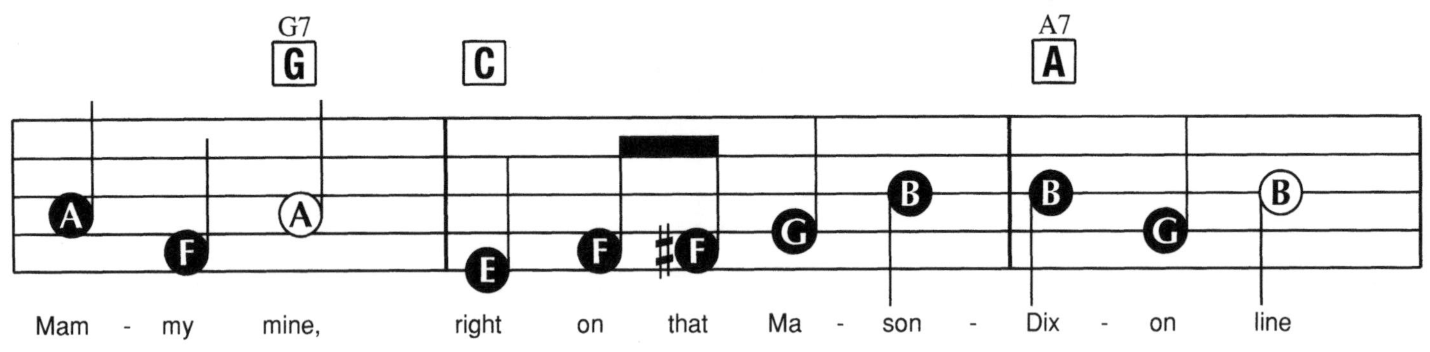
G7
G
C
A7
A
A F A E F F G B B G B
Mam - my mine, right on that Ma - son - Dix - on line

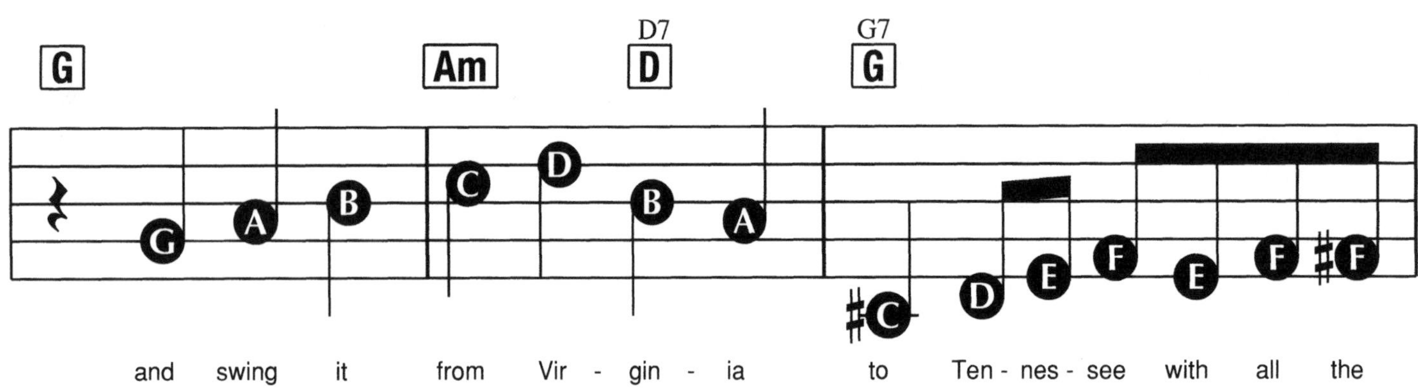
G
Am
D7
D
G7
G
G A B C D B A C D E F E F F
and swing it from Vir - gin - ia to Ten - nes - see with all the

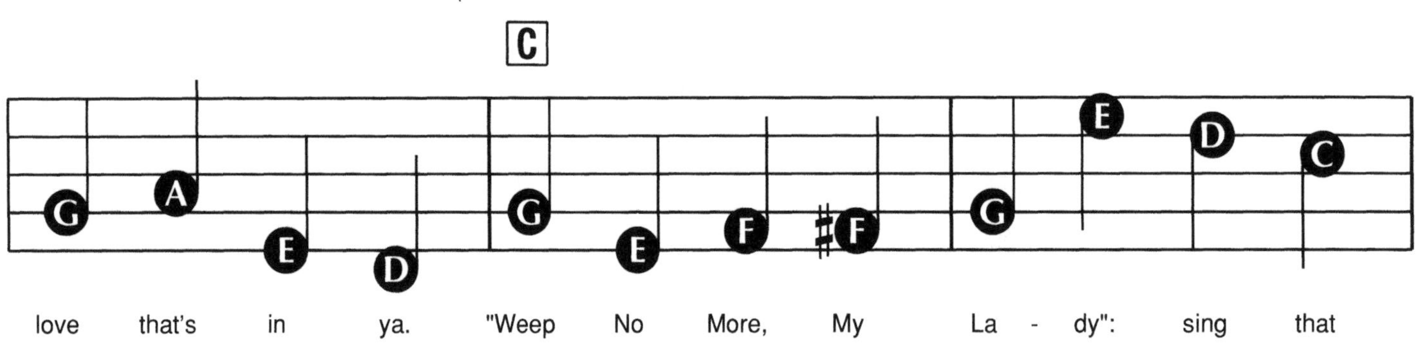
C
G A E D G E F F G E D C
love that's in ya. "Weep No More, My La - dy": sing that

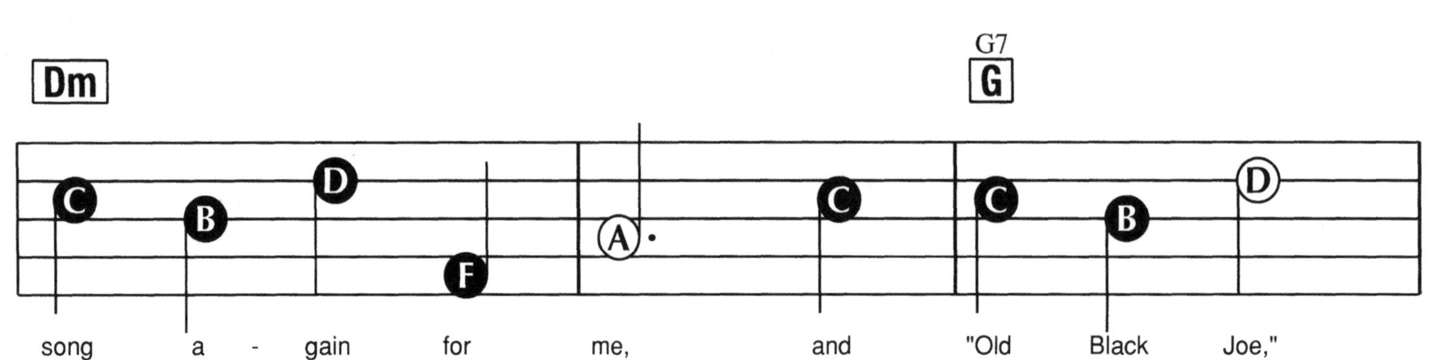
Dm
G7
G
C B D F A C C B D
song a - gain for me, and "Old Black Joe,"

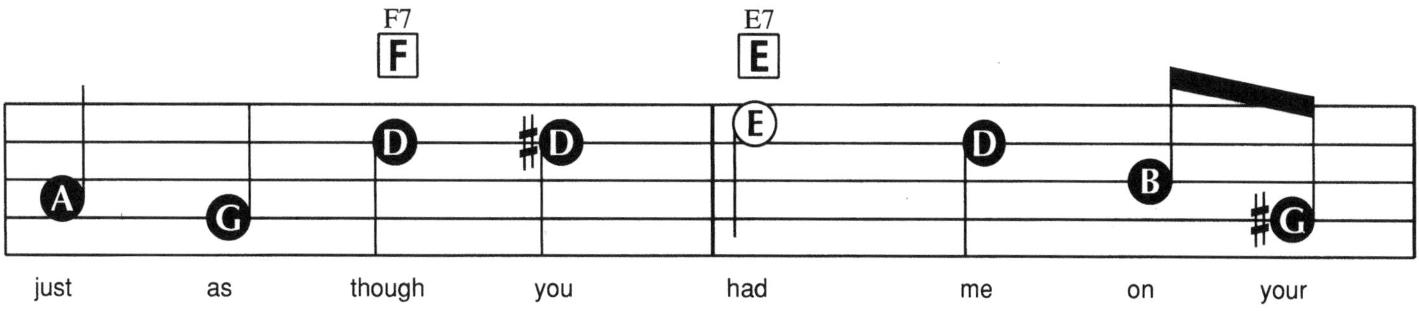
F7
F
E7
E
A G D ♯D E D B ♯G
just as though you had me on your

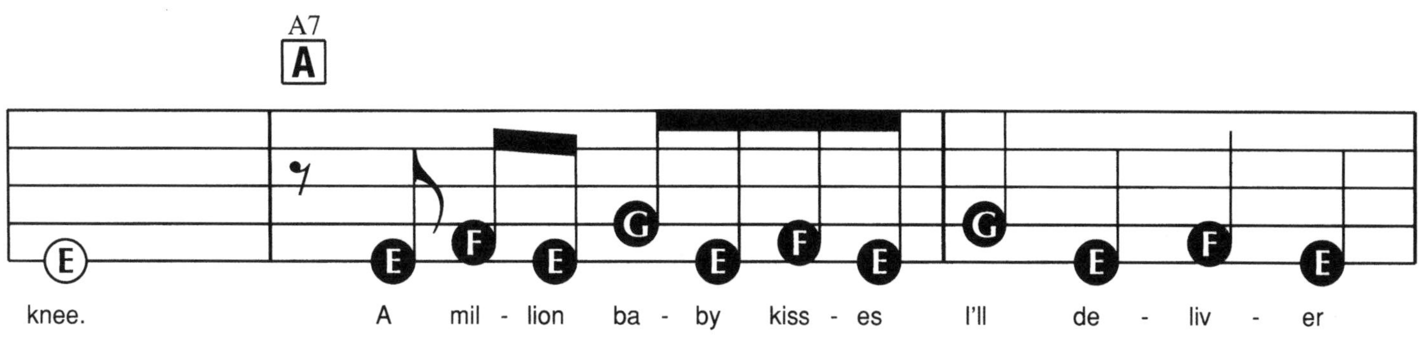
A7
A
E E F E G E F E G E F E
knee. A mil - lion ba - by kiss - es I'll de - liv - er

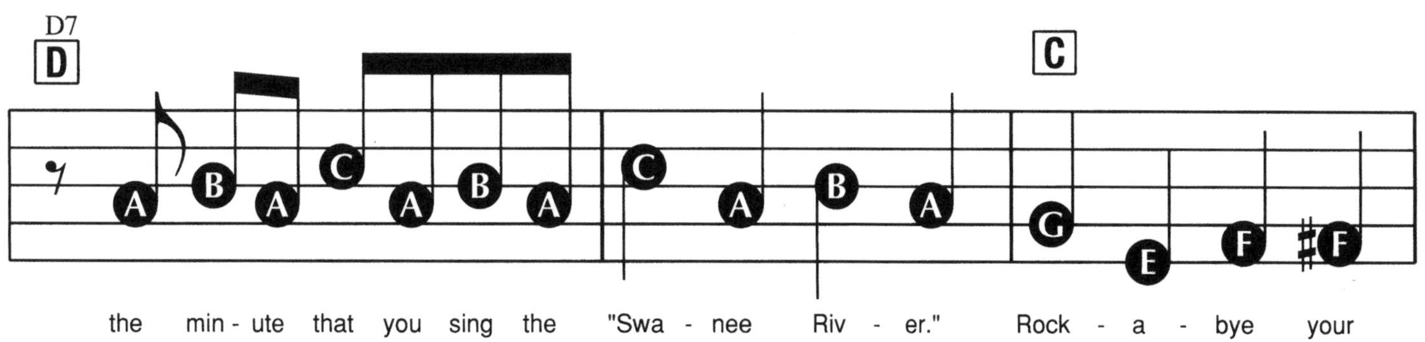
D7
D
C
A B A C A B A C A B A G E F ♯F
the min - ute that you sing the "Swa - nee Riv - er." Rock - a - bye your

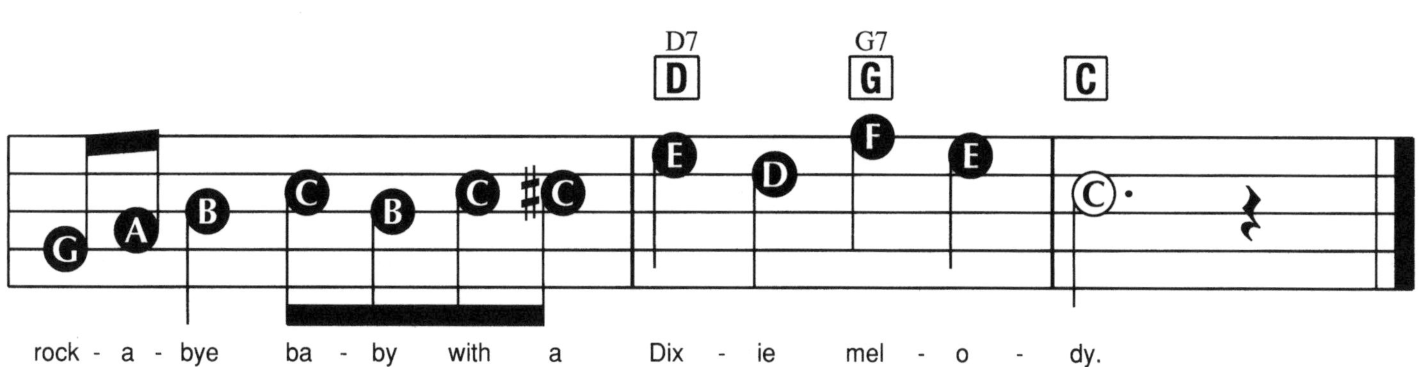
D7
D
G7
G
C
G A B C B C ♯C E D F E C
rock - a - bye ba - by with a Dix - ie mel - o - dy.

Scarborough Fair

Registration 3
Rhythm: Waltz

Traditional English

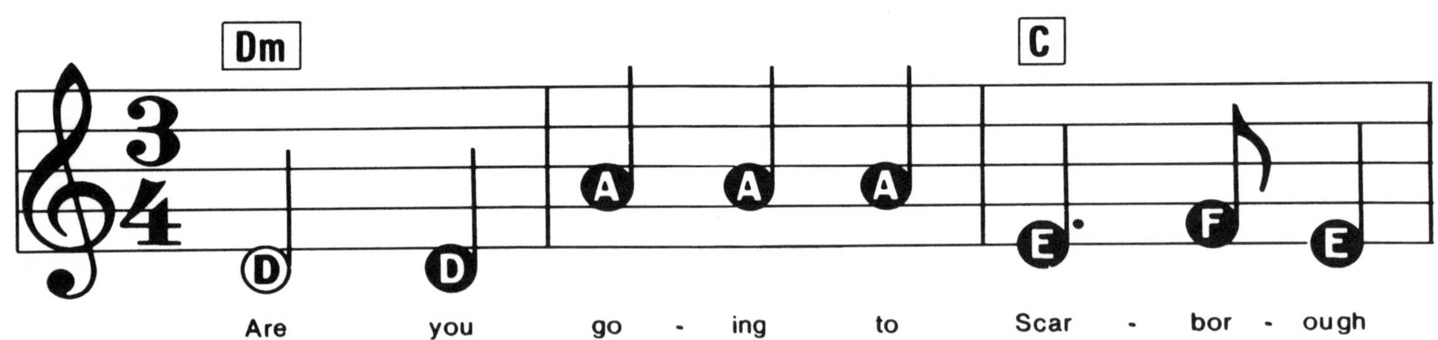

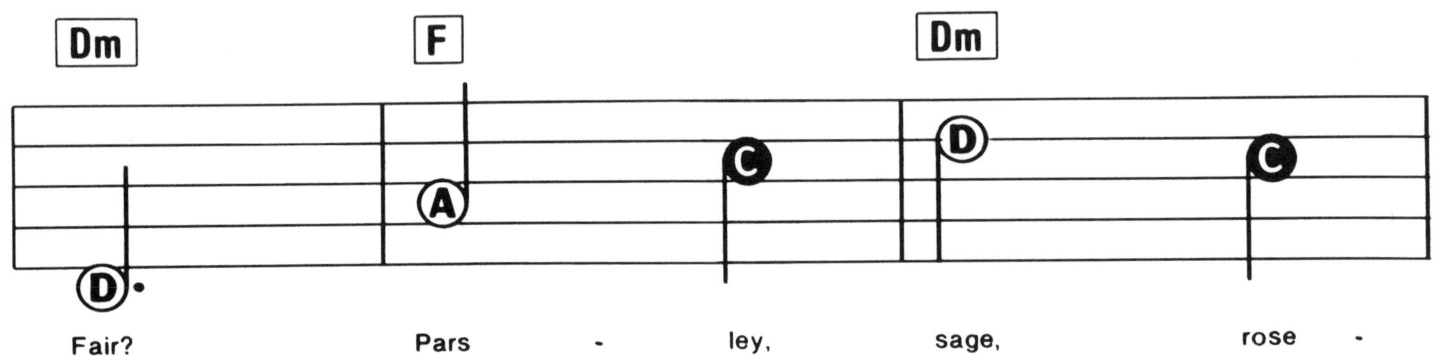

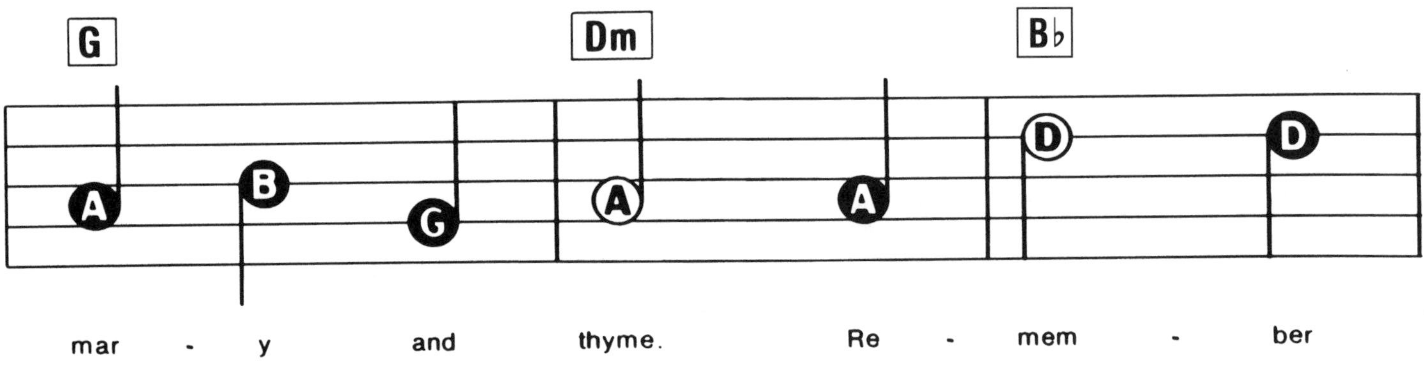

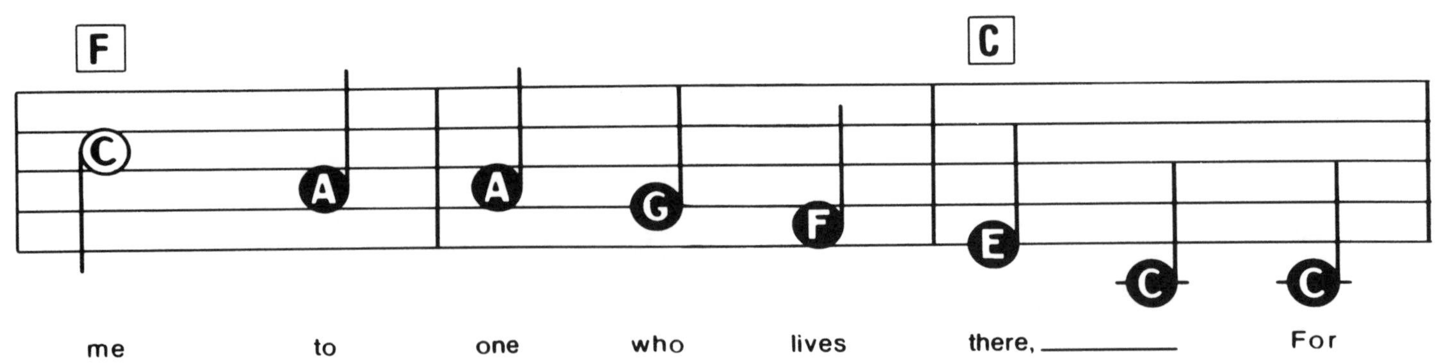

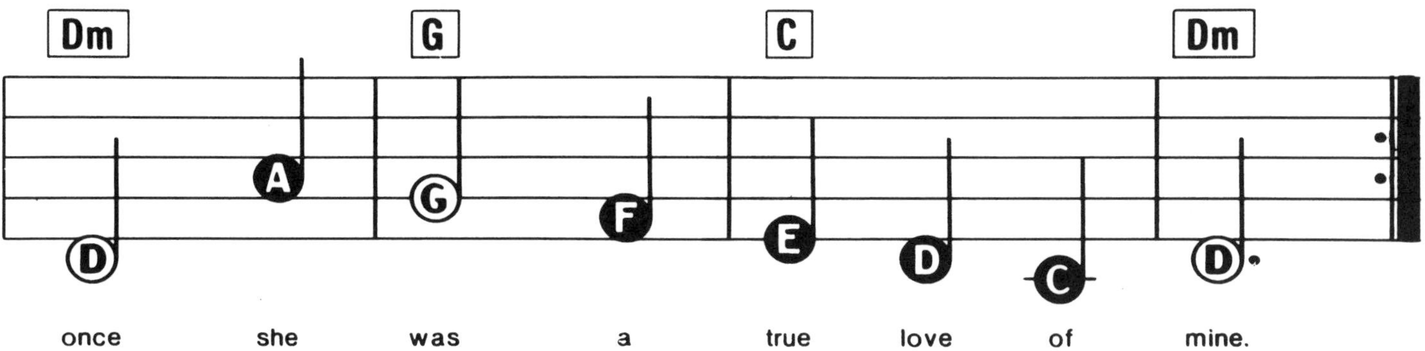

2. Tell her to make me a cambric shirt
   Parsley, sage, rosemary and thyme,
   Without any seam or fine needlework,
   For once she was a true love of mine.

3. Tell her to wash it in yonder dry well,
   Parsley, sage, rosemary and thyme.
   Where water ne'er sprung, nor drop of rain fell,
   For once she was a true love of mine.

4. Tell her to dry it on yonder thorn,
   Parsley, sage, rosemary and thyme,
   Which never bore blossom since Adam was born,
   For once she was a true love of mine.

5. Will you find me an acre of land,
   Parsley, sage, rosemary and thyme,
   Between the sea foam and the sea sand,
   For once she was a true love of mine.

6. Will you plough it with a lamb's horn,
   Parsley, sage, rosemary and thyme,
   And sow it all over with one peppercorn,
   For once she was a true love of mine.

7. Will you reap it with sickle of leather,
   Parsley, sage, rosemary and thyme,
   And tie it all up with a peacock's feather,
   For once she was a true love of mine.

8. When you've done and finished your work,
   Parsley, sage, rosemary and thyme,
   Then come to me for your cambric shirt,
   And you shall be a true love of mine.

She Wore a Yellow Ribbon

Registration 4
Rhythm: Swing or March

Words and Music by
George A. Norton

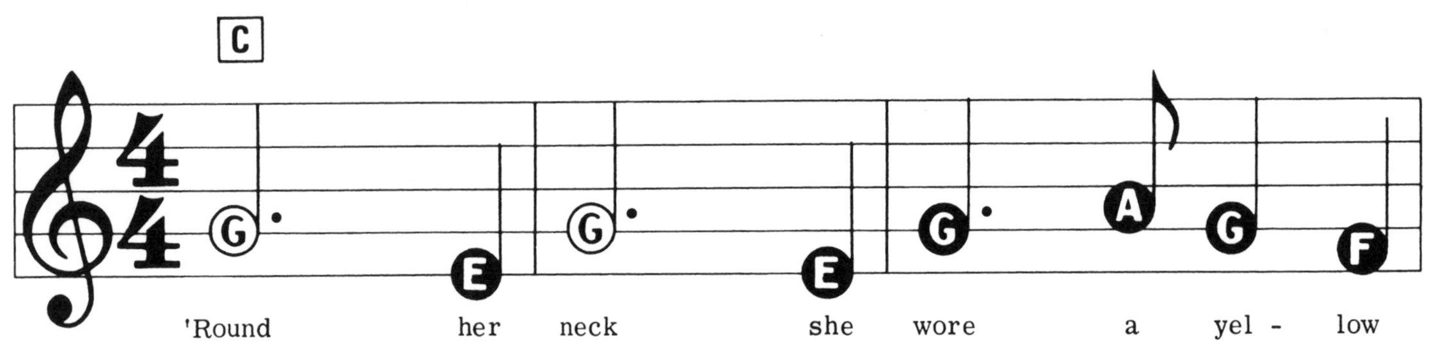

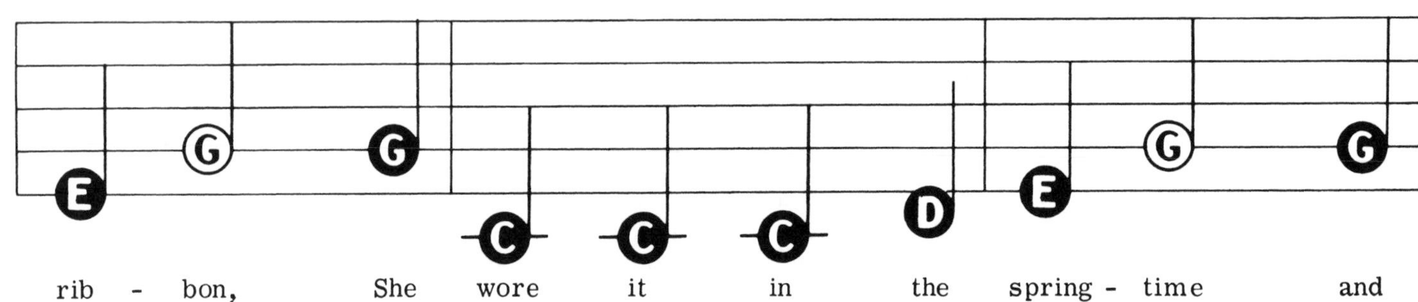

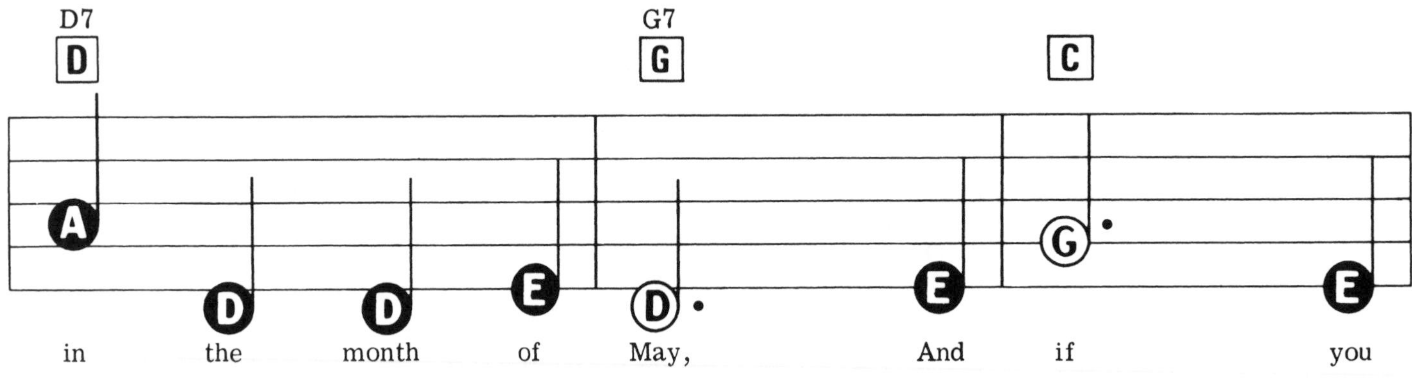

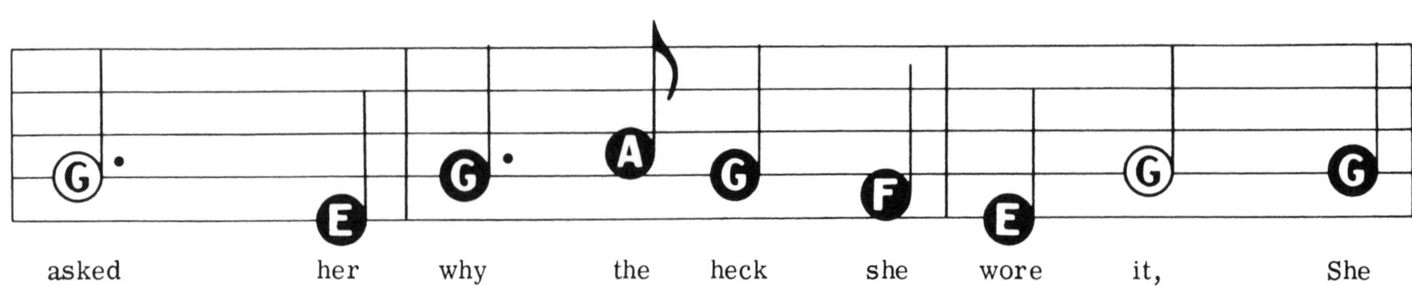

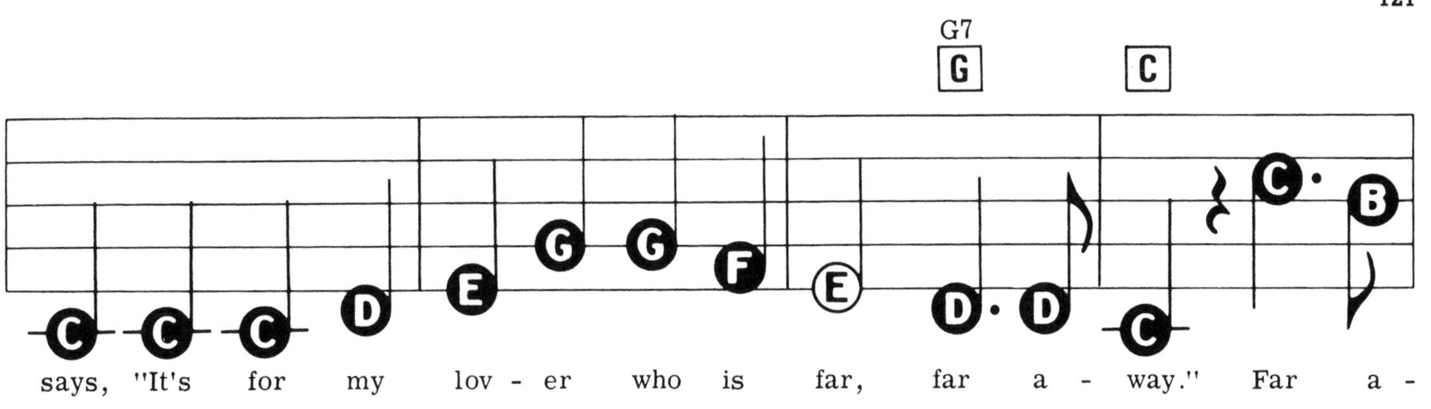
G7
G
C
C C C D E G G F E D D C C B
says, "It's for my lov - er who is far, far a - way." Far a -

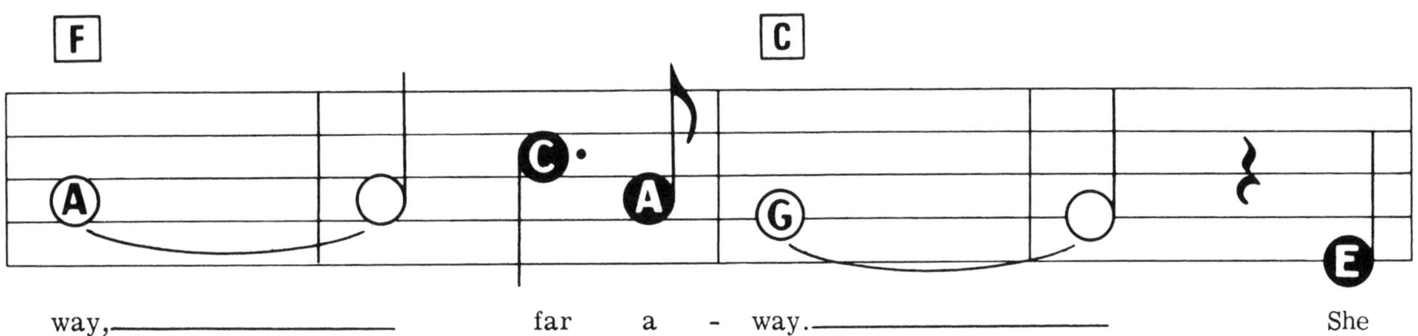
F
C
A C A G E
way, far a - way. She

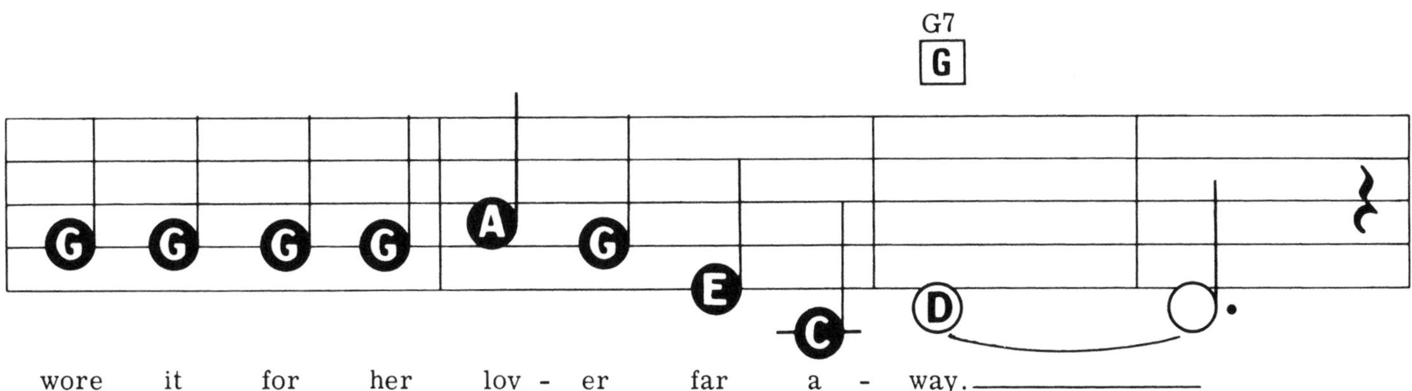
G7
G
G G G G A G E C D
wore it for her lov - er far a - way.

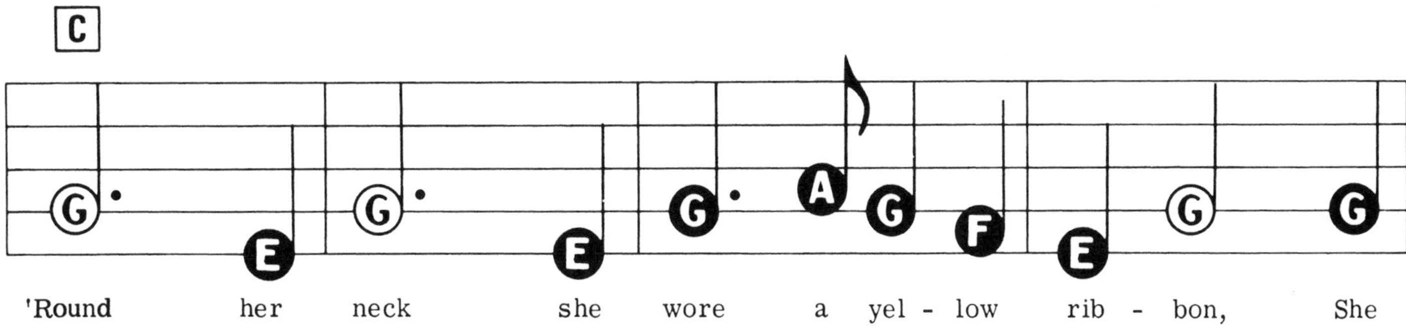
C
G E G E G A G F E G G
'Round her neck she wore a yel - low rib - bon, She

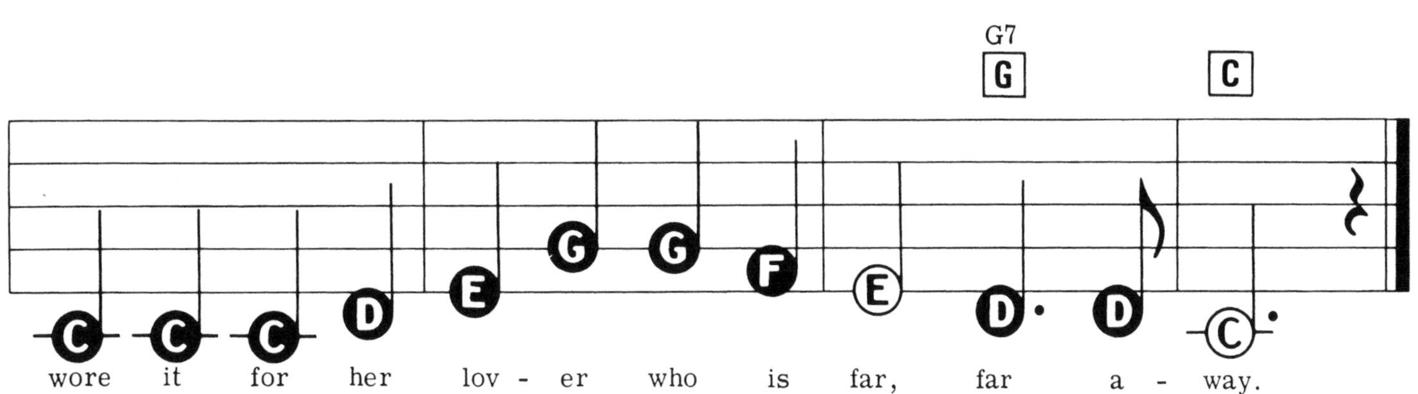
G7
G
C
C C C D E G G F E D D C
wore it for her lov - er who is far, far a - way.

Shine On, Harvest Moon

Registration 9
Rhythm: Fox Trot or Swing

Words by Jack Norworth
Music by Nora Bayes and Jack Norworth

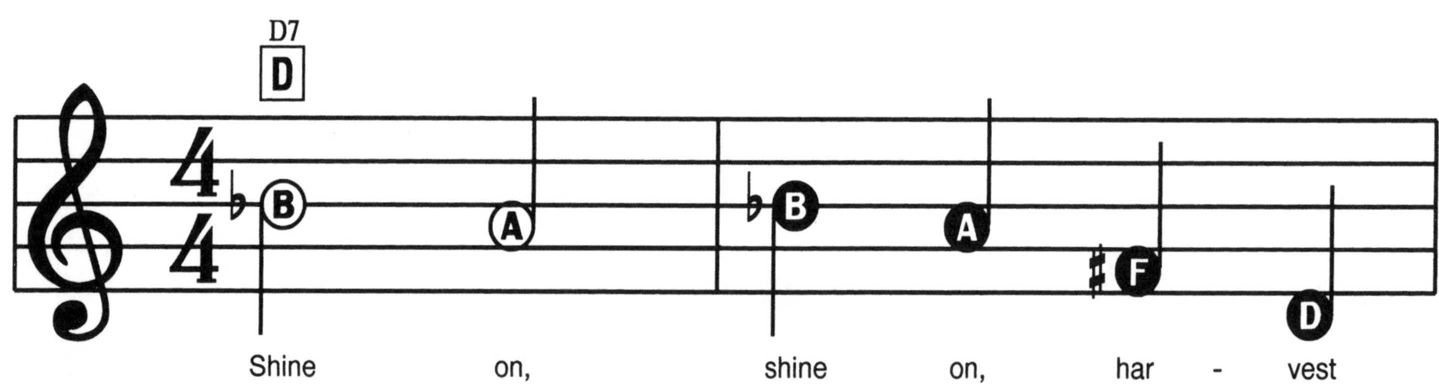

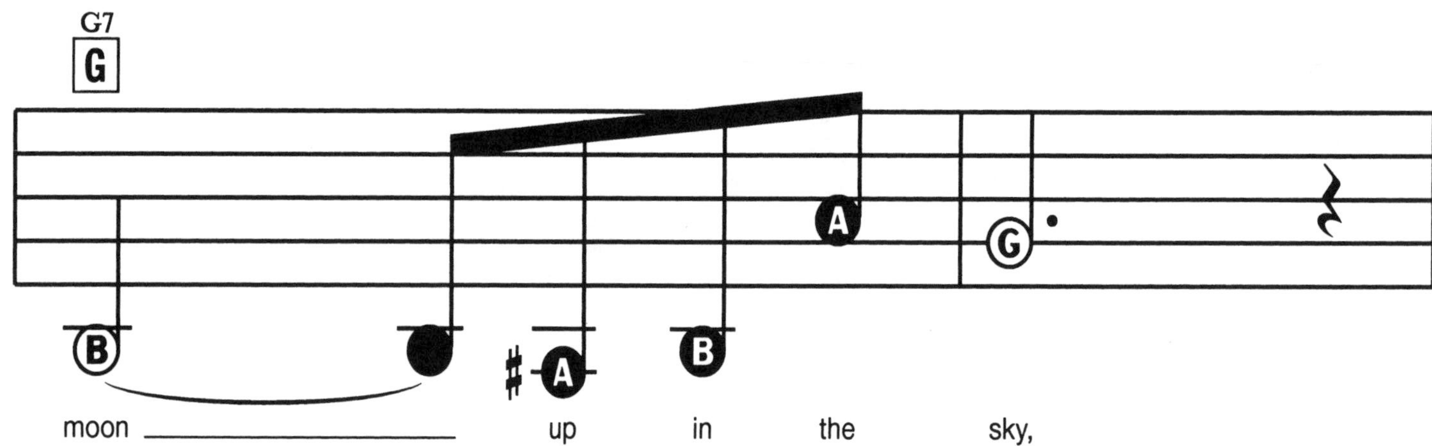

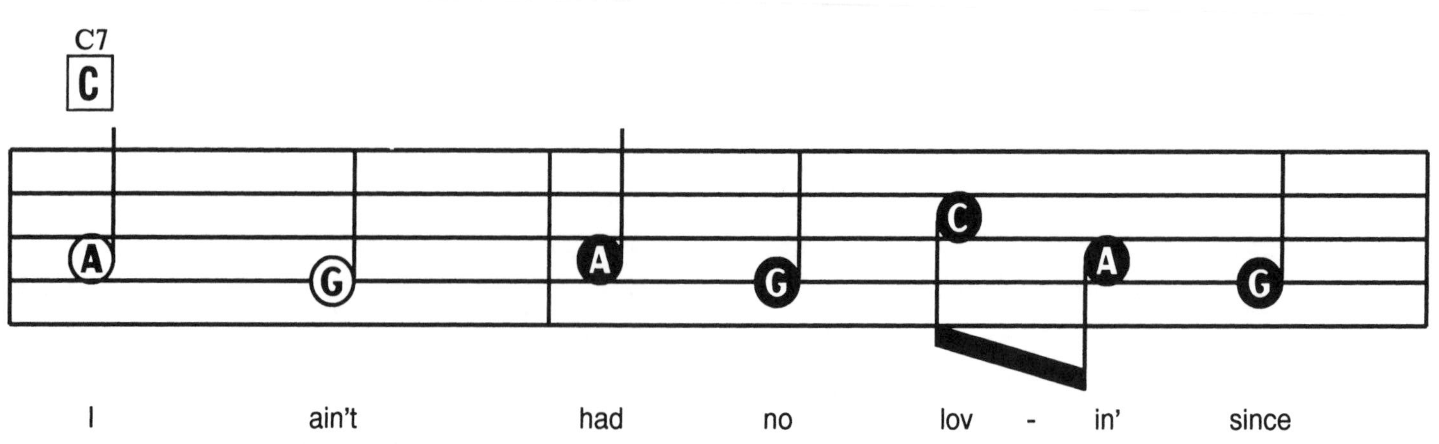

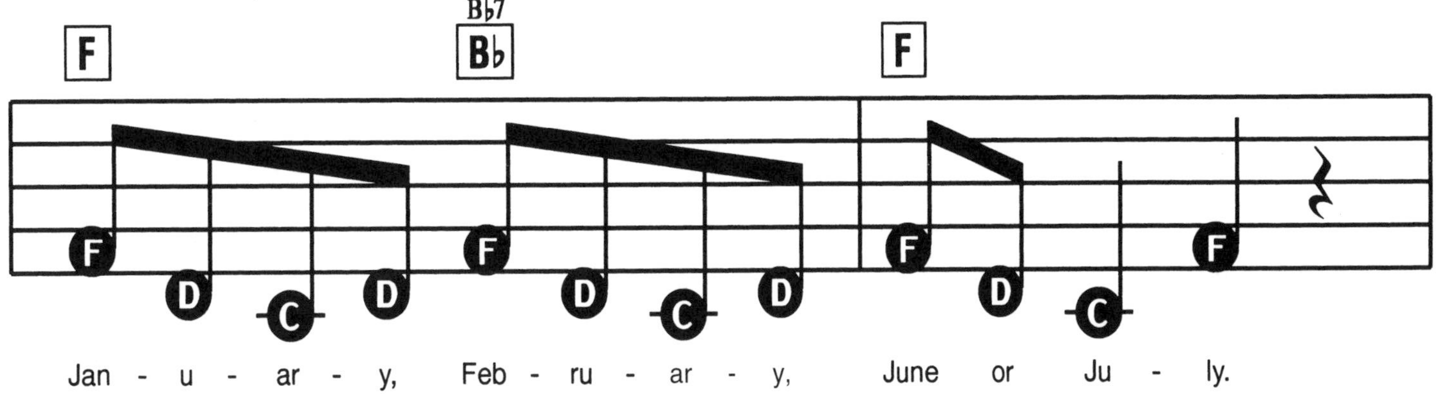
F
B♭7
B♭
F
F
D
C
D
F
D
C
D
F
D
C
F
Jan - u - ar - y, Feb - ru - ar - y, June or Ju - ly.

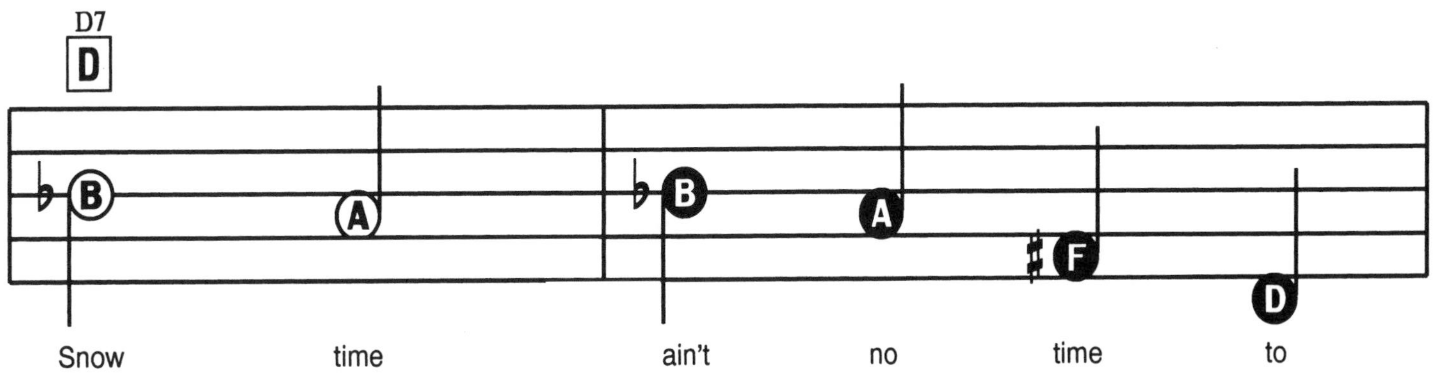
D7
D
B
A
B
A
F
D
Snow time ain't no time to

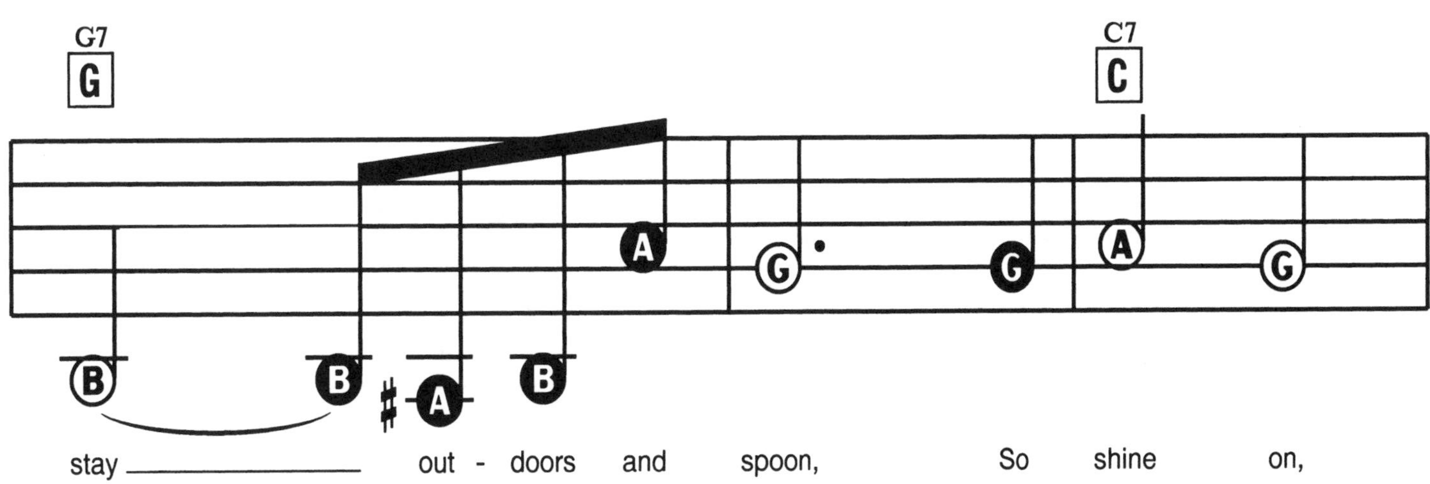
G7
G
C7
C
B
B
A
B
A
G
G
A
G
stay out - doors and spoon, So shine on,

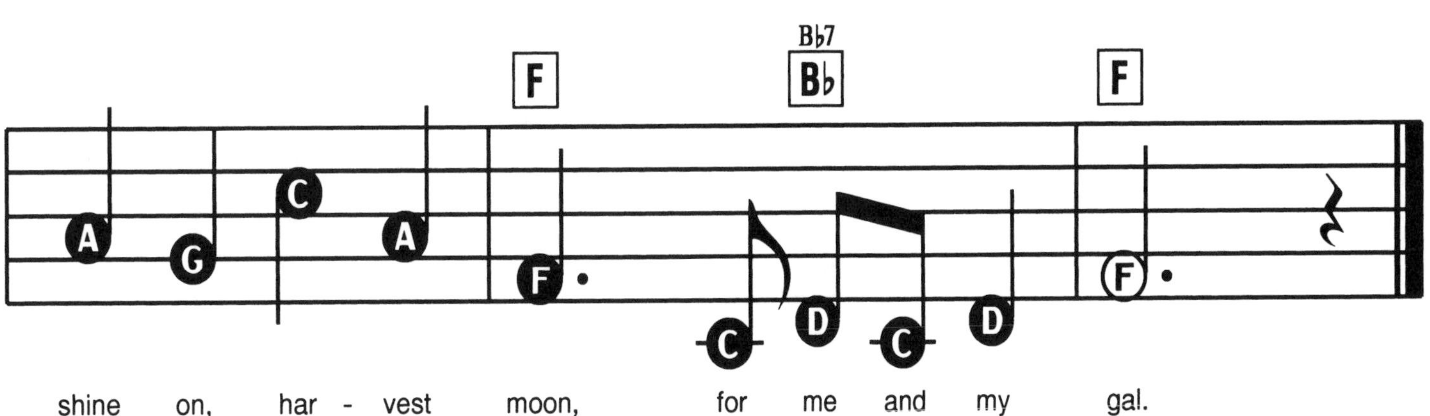
F
B♭7
B♭
F
A
G
C
A
F
C
D
C
D
F
shine on, har - vest moon, for me and my gal.

Smiles

Registration 2
Rhythm: Fox Trot

Words by J. Will Callahan
Music by Lee S. Roberts

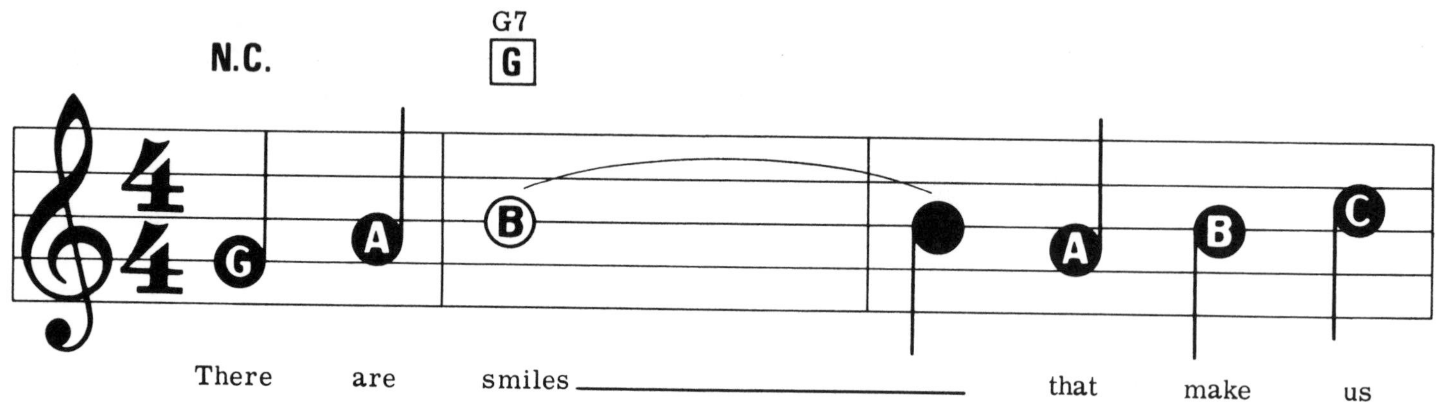

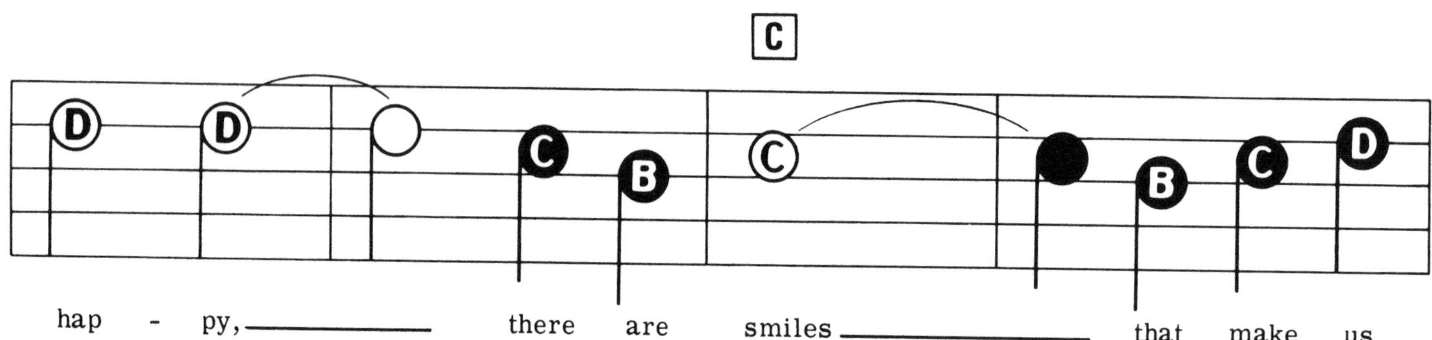

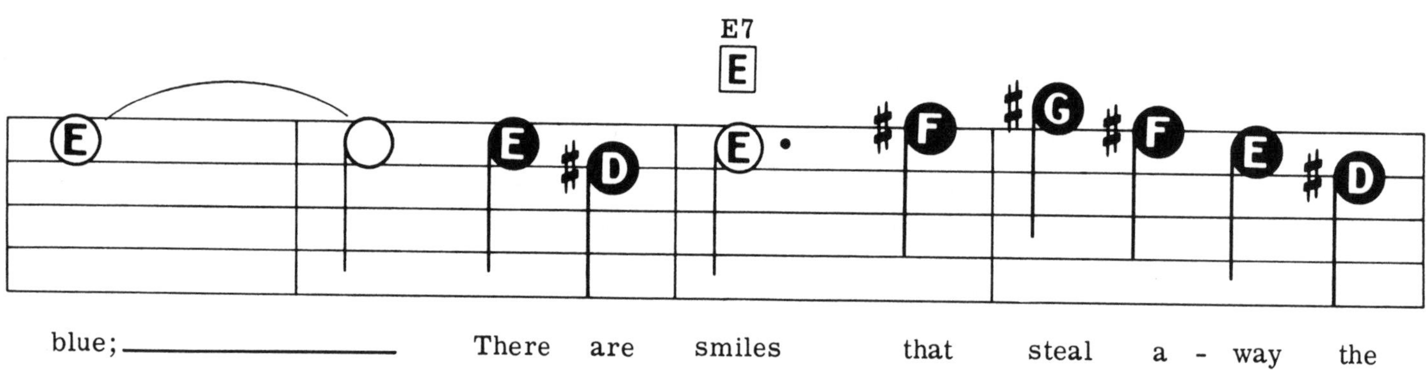

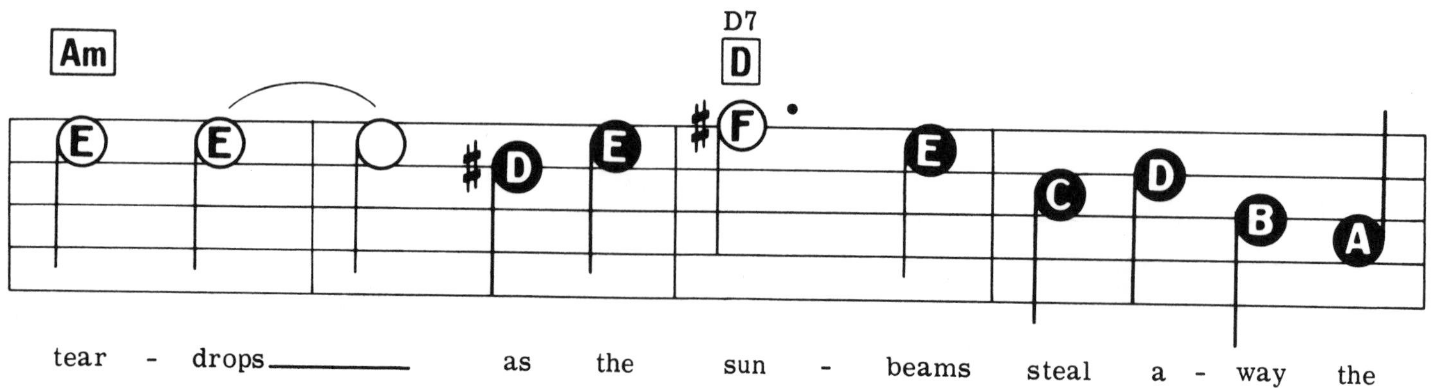

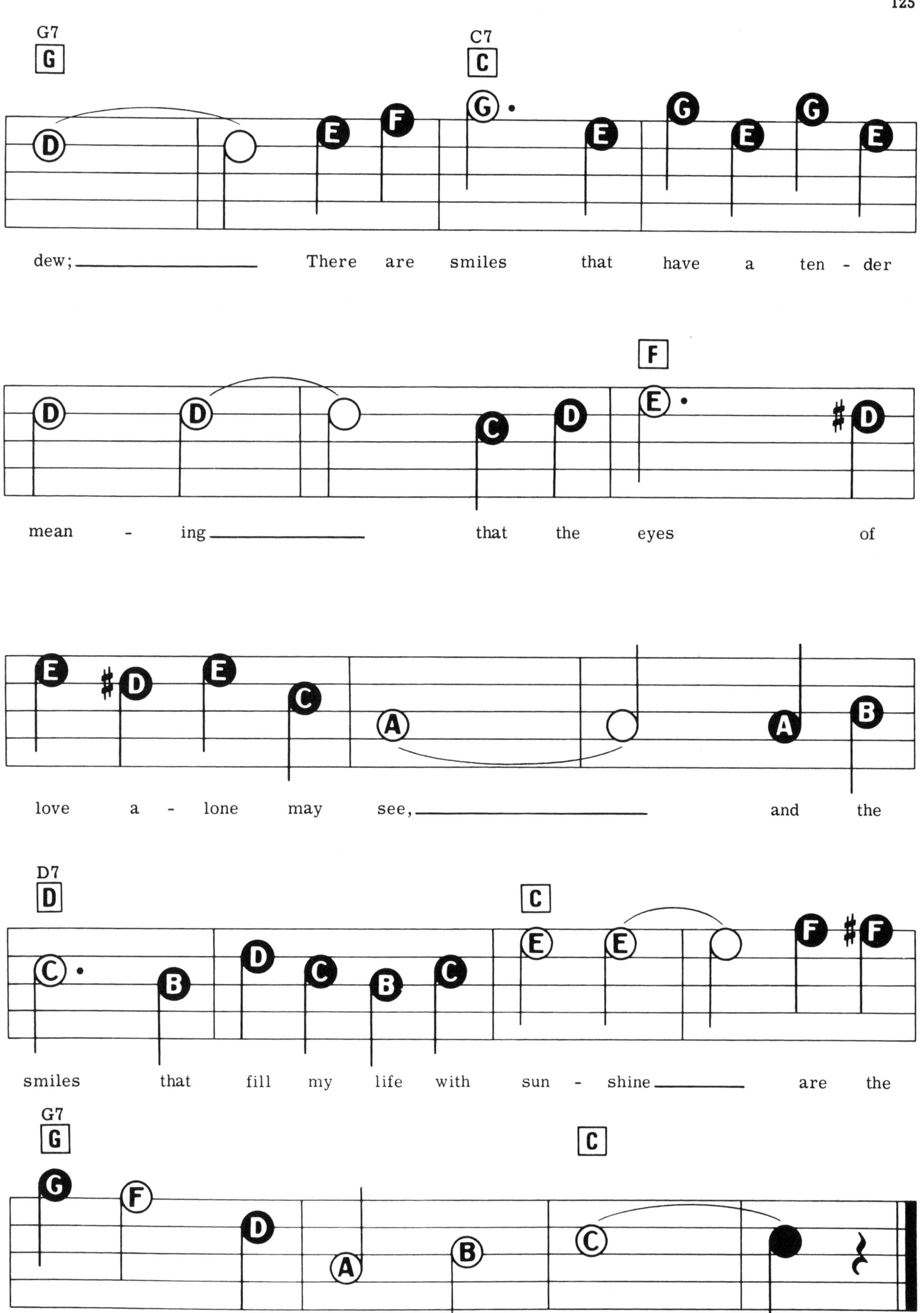
G7
G
C7
C
D
E
F
G
E
G
E
G
E
dew; There are smiles that have a ten - der
F
D
D
C
D
E
D
mean - ing that the eyes of
E
D
E
C
A
A
B
love a - lone may see, and the
D7
D
C
C
B
D
C
B
C
E
E
F
F
smiles that fill my life with sun - shine are the
G7
G
C
G
F
D
A
B
C
smiles that you give to me.

Swanee

Registration 9
Rhythm: Fox Trot or Swing

Words by Irving Caesar
Music by George Gershwin

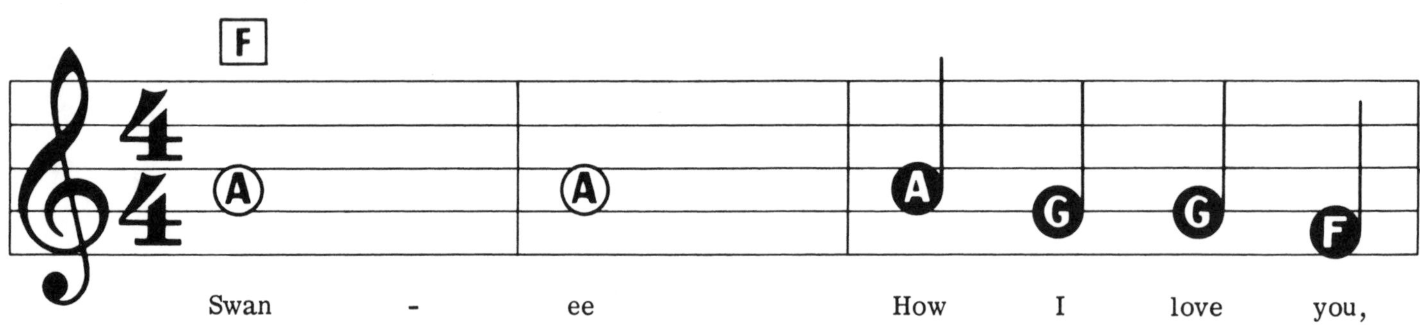

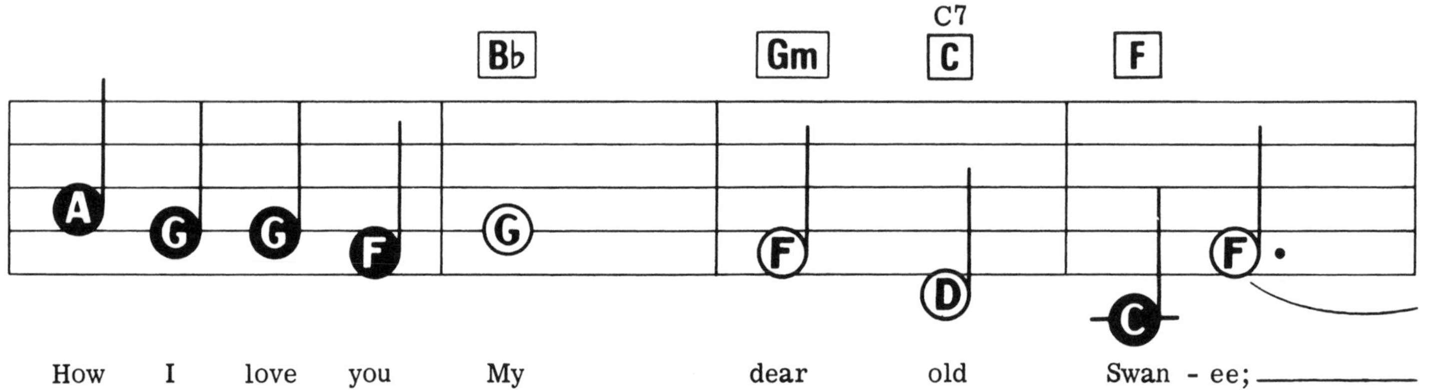

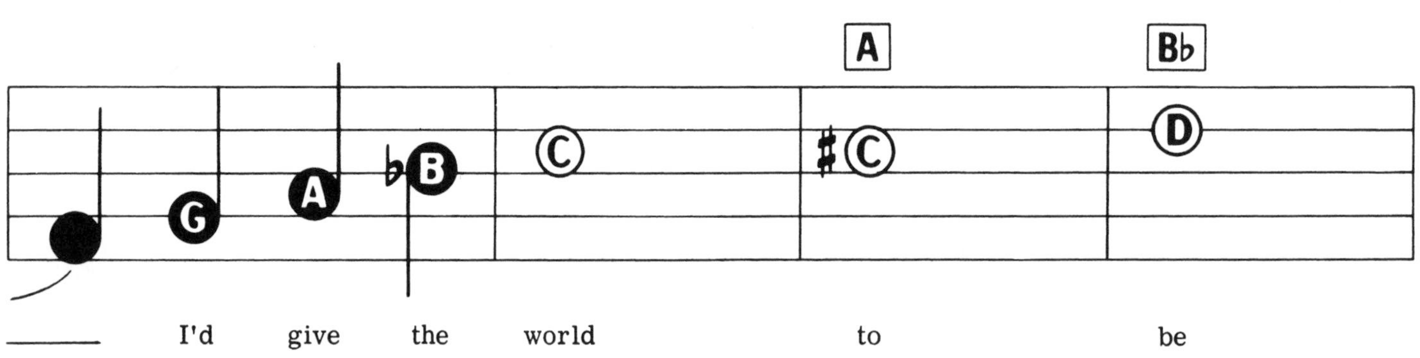

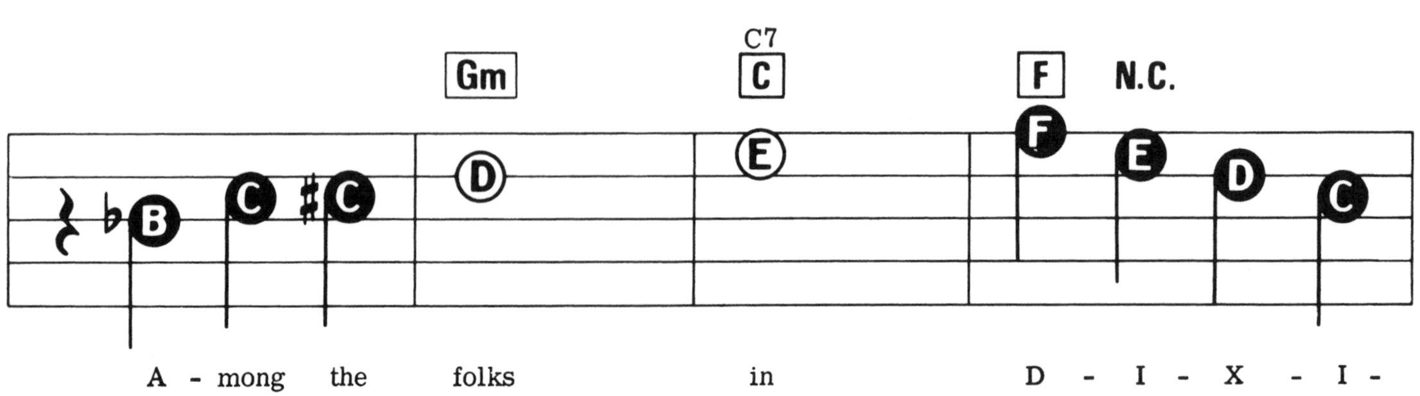

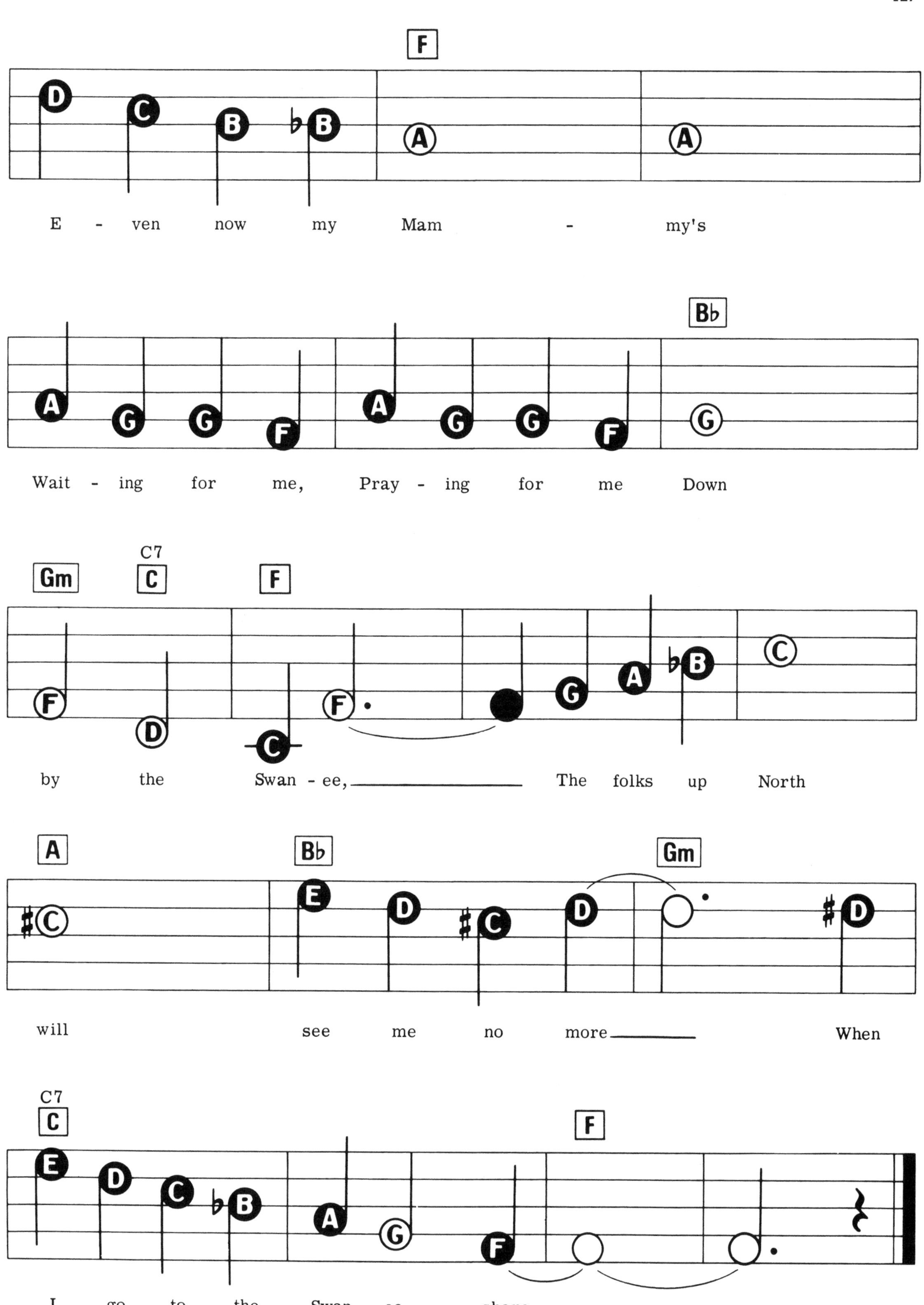
F
E - ven now my Mam - my's
Bb
Wait - ing for me, Pray - ing for me Down
Gm
C7
C
F
by the Swan - ee,
The folks up North
A
Bb
Gm
will see me no more
When
C7
C
F
I go to the Swan - ee shore.

Take Me Out to the Ball Game

Registration 4
Rhythm: Waltz

Words by Jack Norworth
Music by Albert von Tilzer

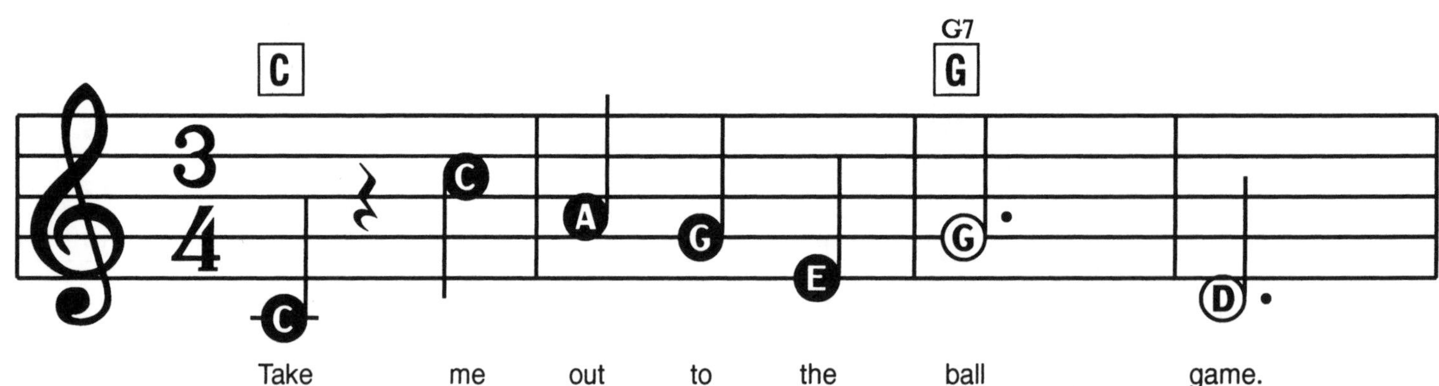

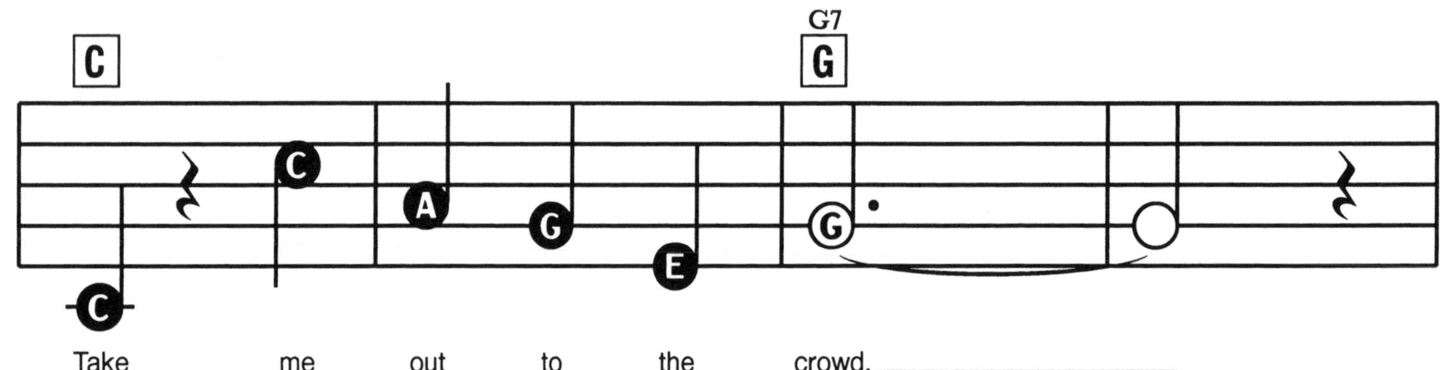

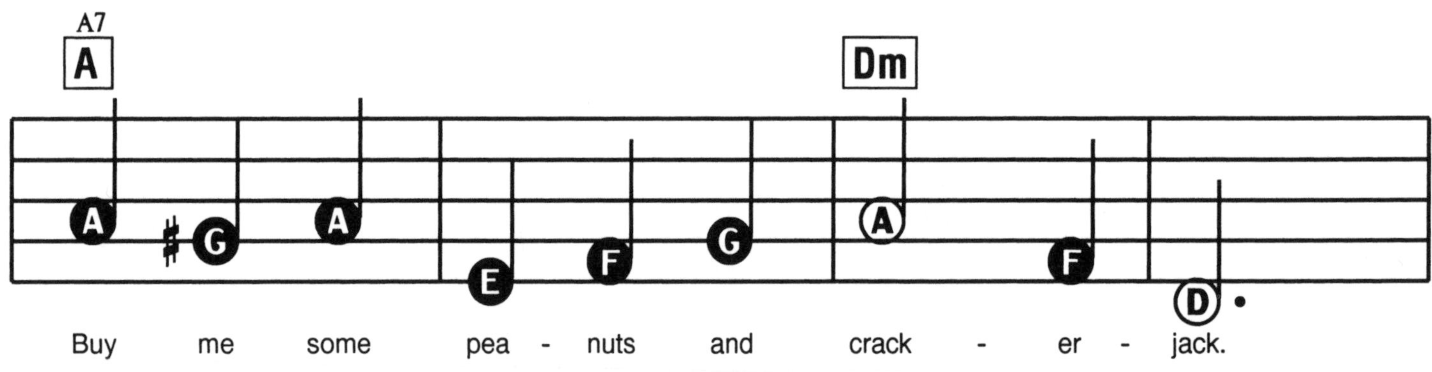

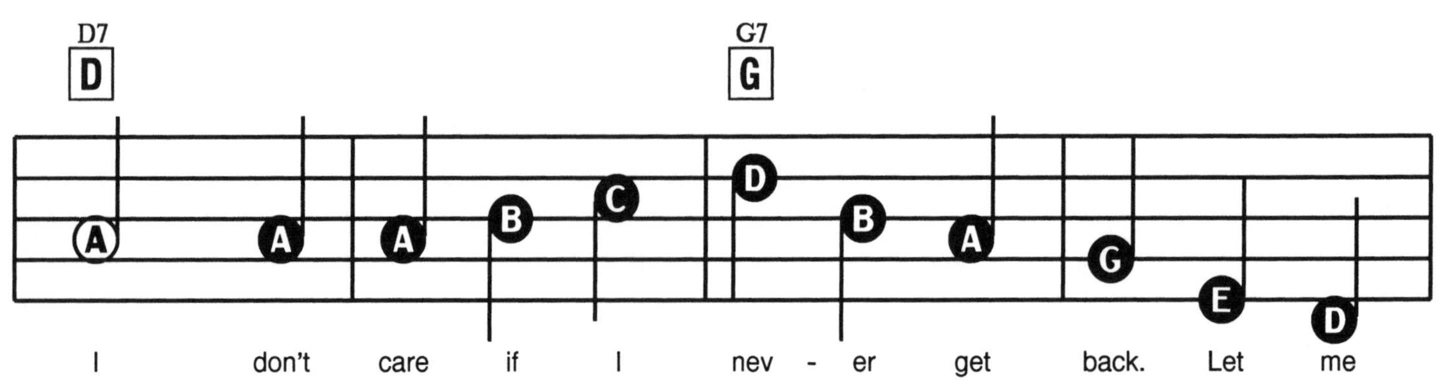

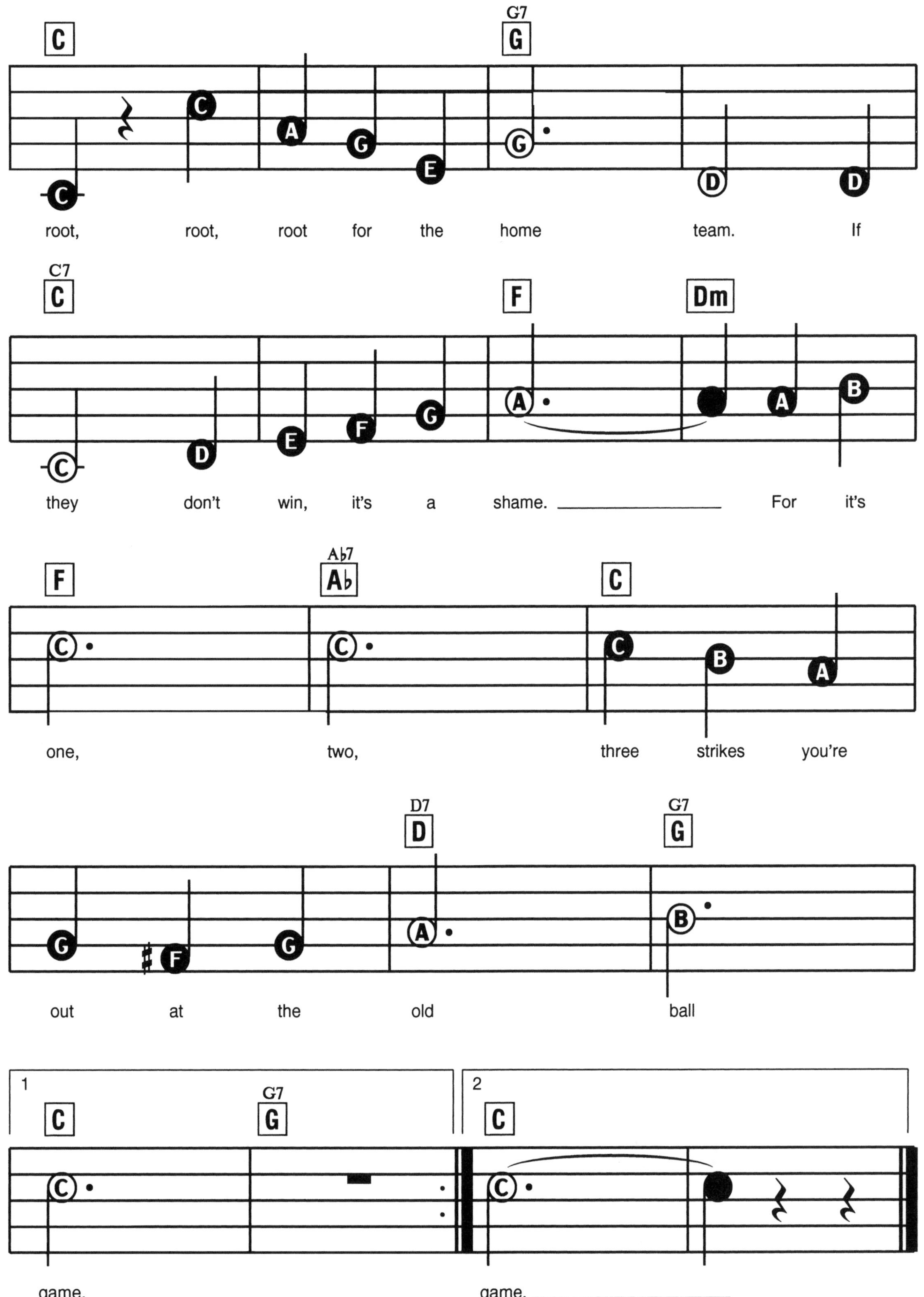
C
G7
G
C
A
G
E
G
D
D
root, root, root for the home team. If
C7
C
F
Dm
C
D
E
F
G
A
A
B
they don't win, it's a shame. For it's
F
Ab7
Ab
C
C
C
C
B
A
one, two, three strikes you're
D7
D
G7
G
G
F
G
A
B
out at the old ball
1
C
G7
G
C
2
C
C
game.
game.

There Is a Tavern in the Town

Registration 8
Rhythm: Fox Trot

Traditional Drinking Song

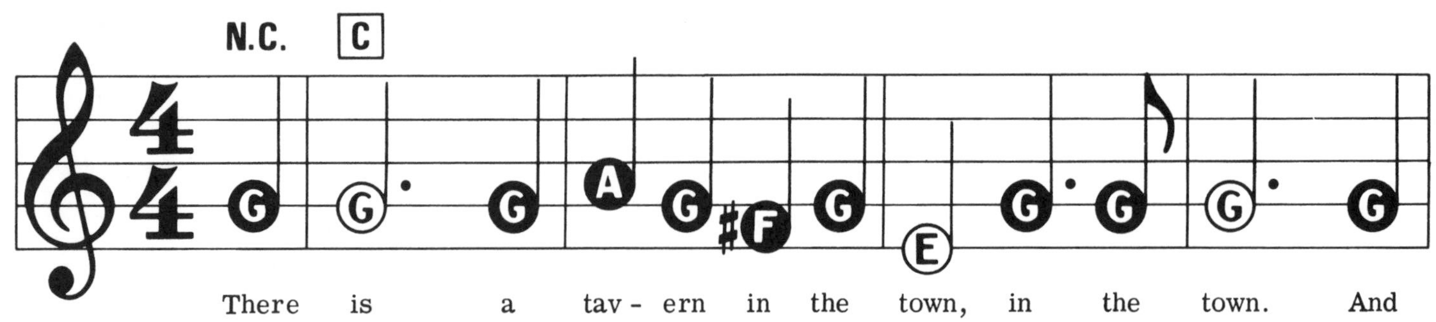

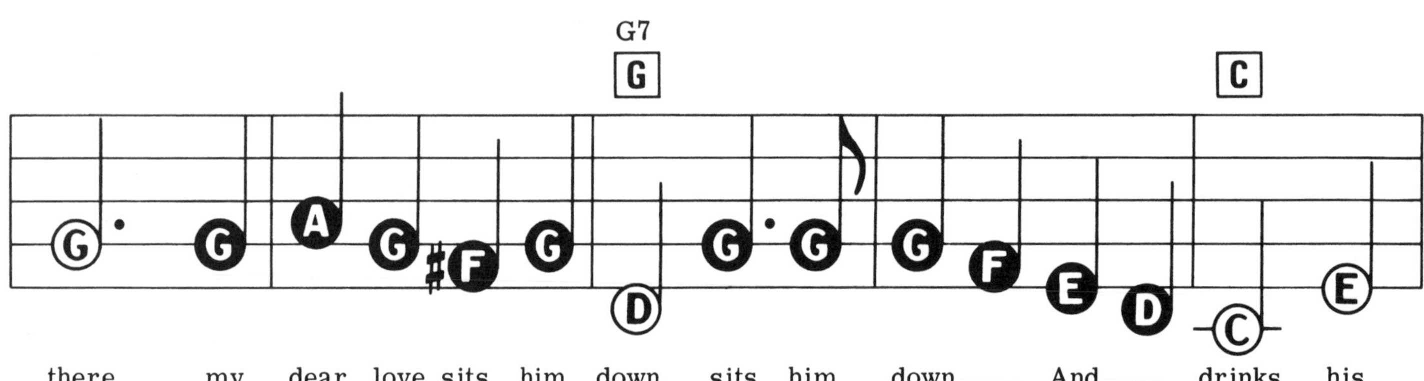

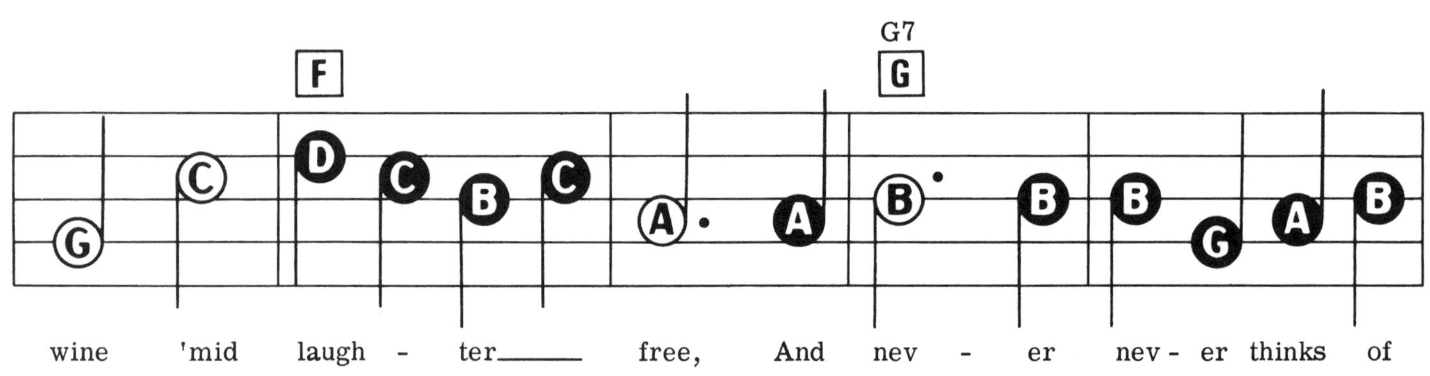

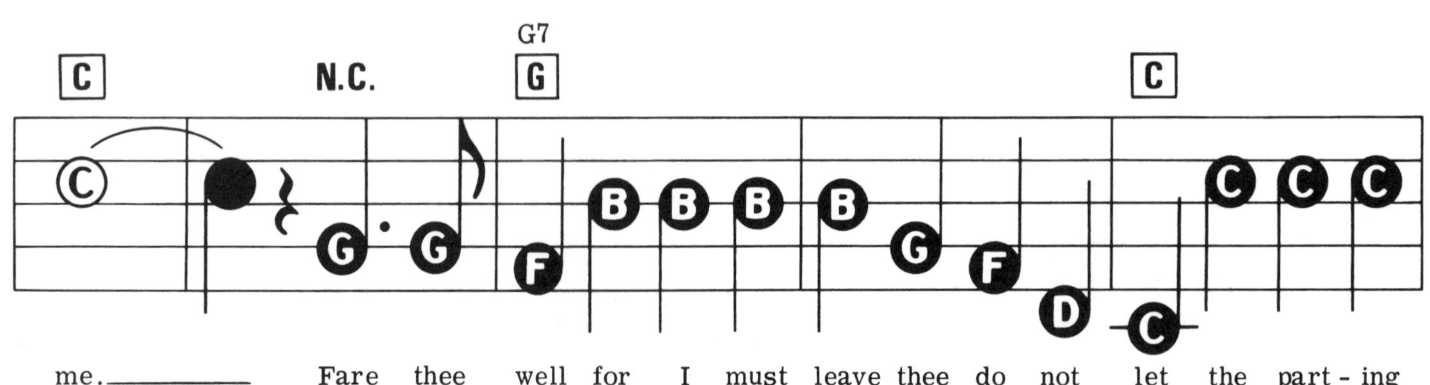

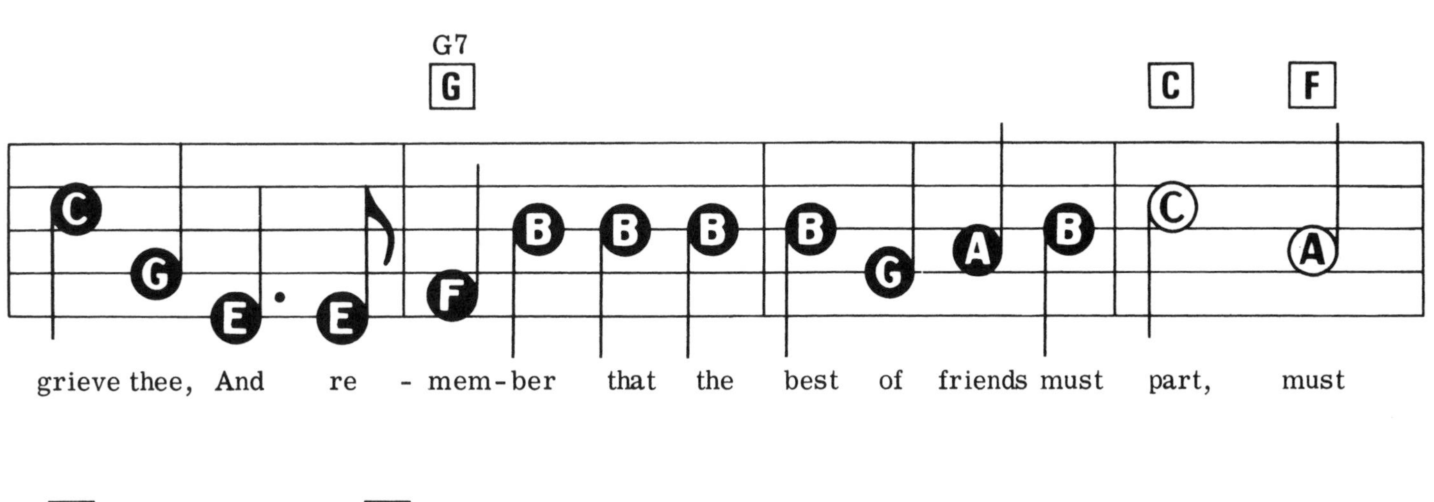
G7
G
C
F
C G E E F B B B B G A B C A
grieve thee, And re - mem-ber that the best of friends must part, must

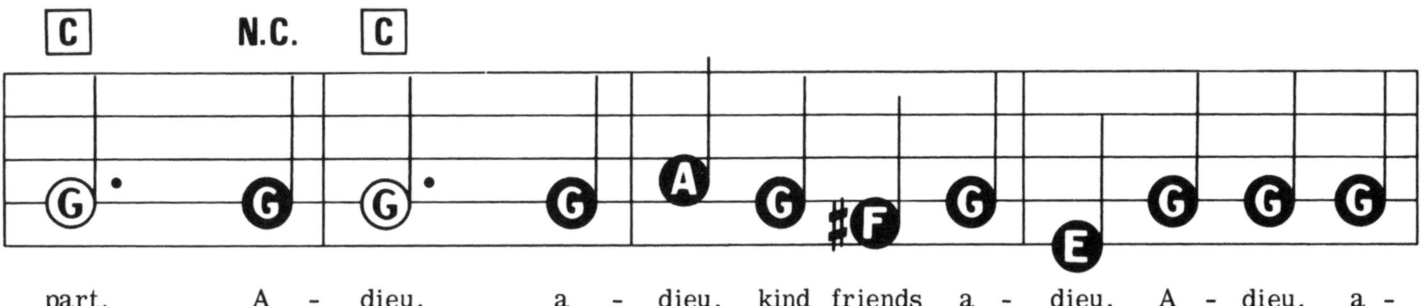
C
N.C.
C
G G G G A G #F G E G G G
part. A - dieu, a - dieu, kind friends a - dieu, A - dieu, a -

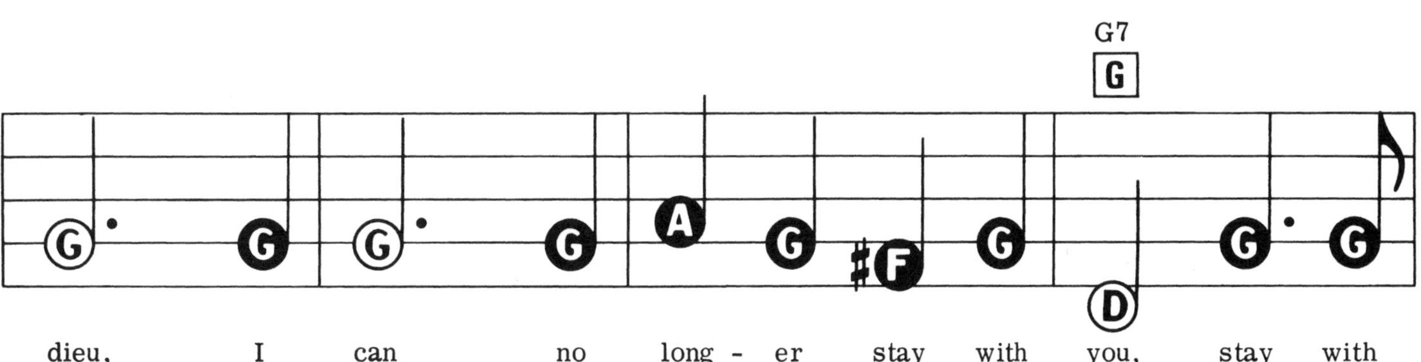
G7
G
G G G G A G #F G D G G
dieu, I can no long - er stay with you, stay with

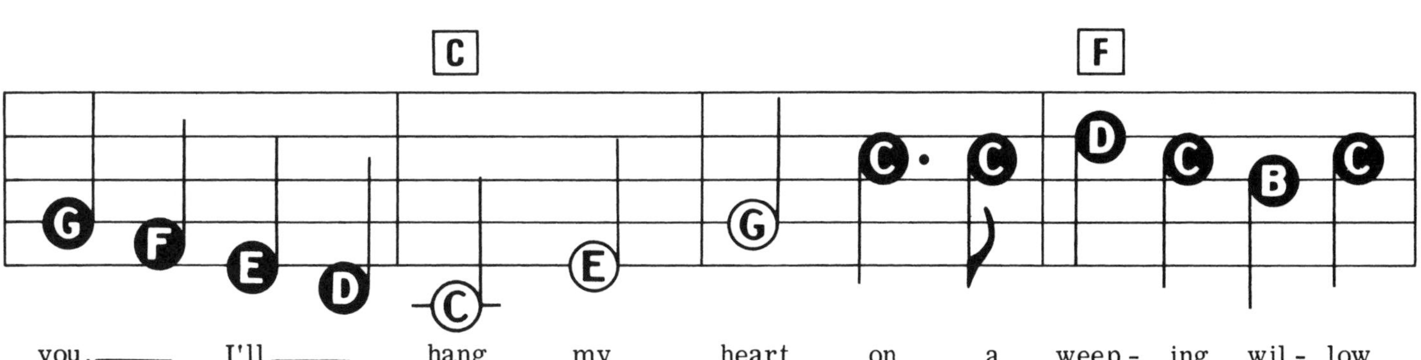
C
F
G F E D C E G C C D C B C
you, I'll hang my heart on a weep - ing wil - low

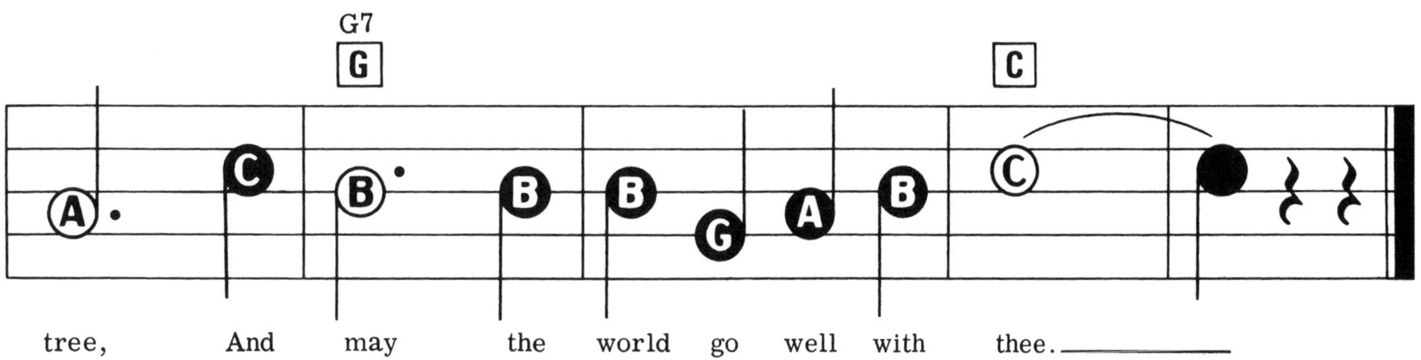
G7
G
C
A C B B B G A B C
tree, And may the world go well with thee.

Toot, Toot, Tootsie!
(GOOD-BYE!)
from THE JAZZ SINGER

Registration 4
Rhythm: Swing

Words and Music by Gus Kahn, Ernie Erdman,
Dan Russo and Ted Fiorito

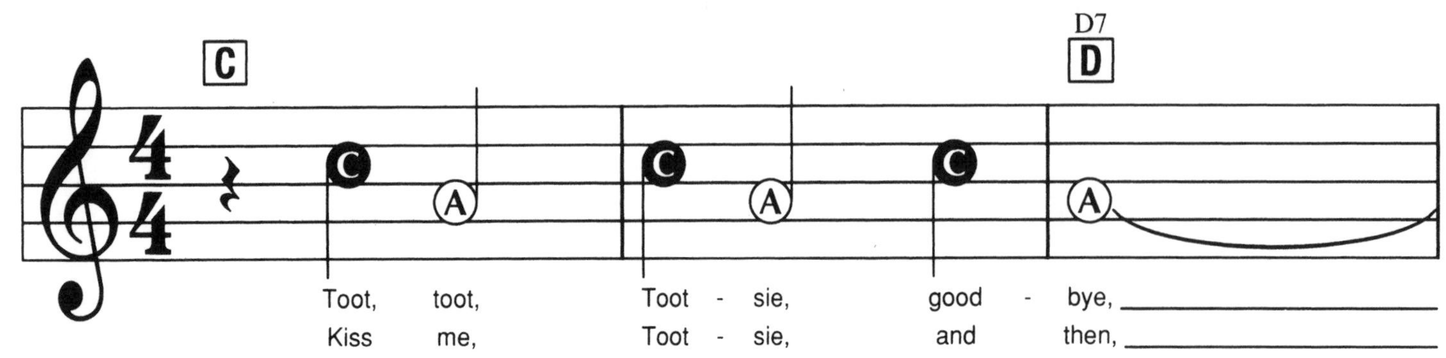

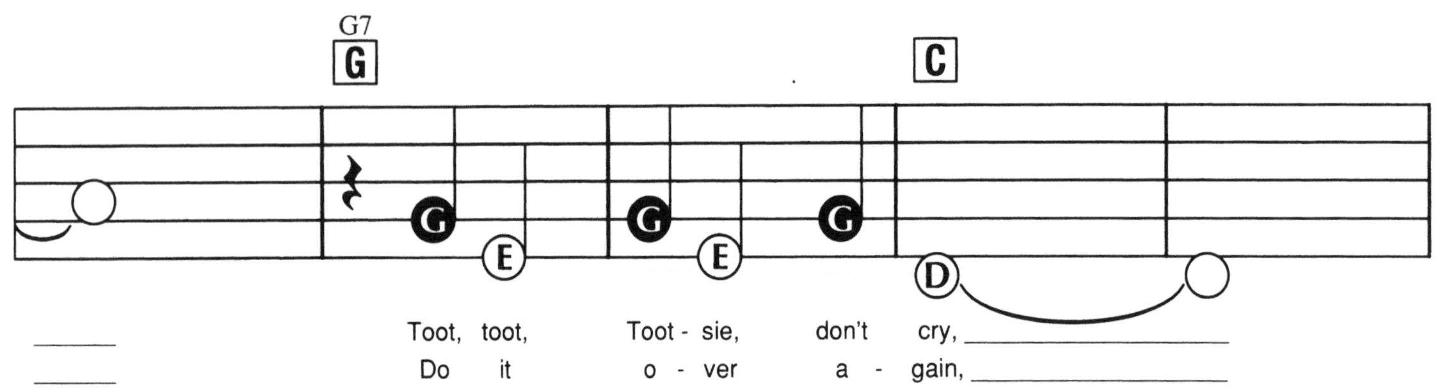

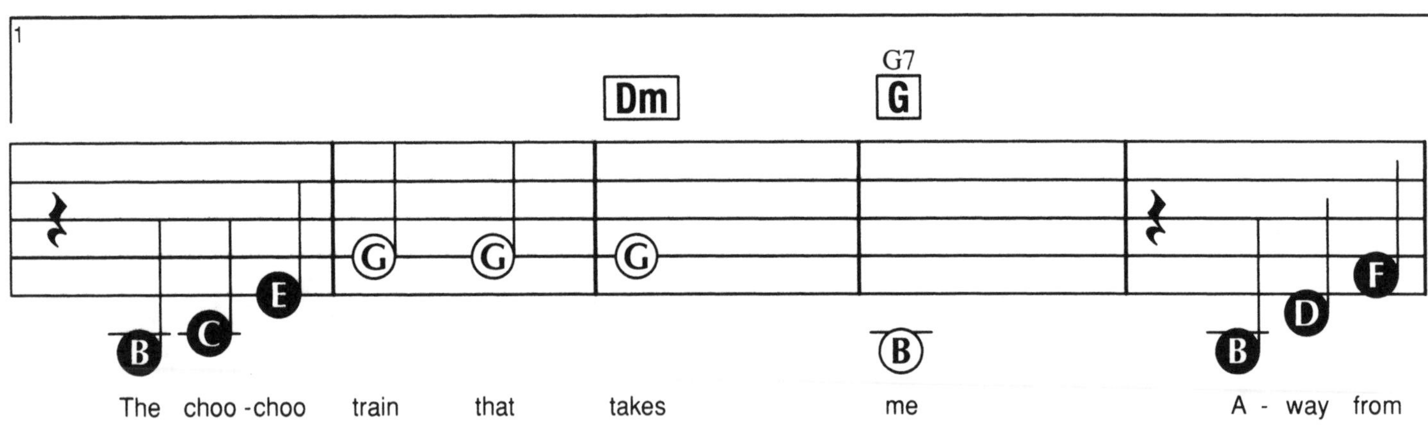

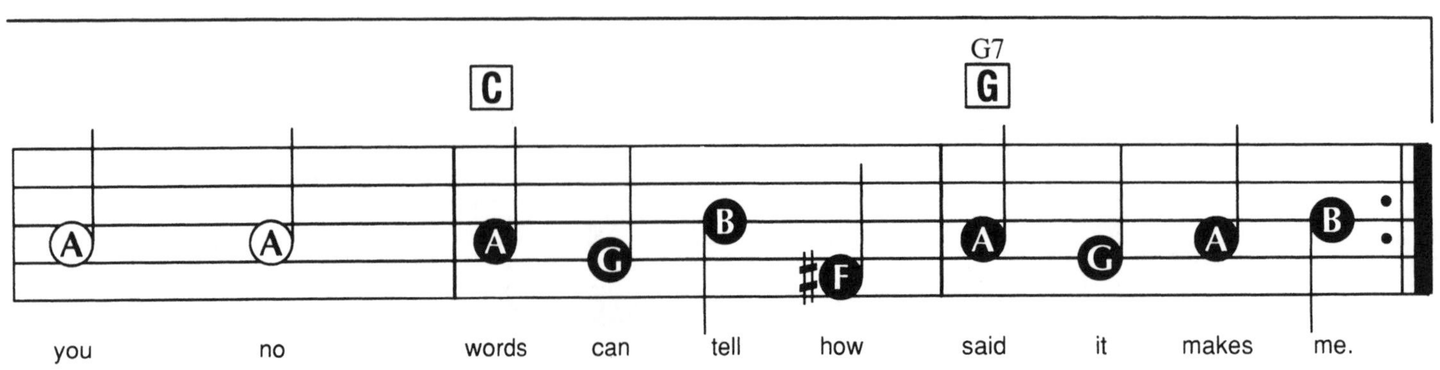

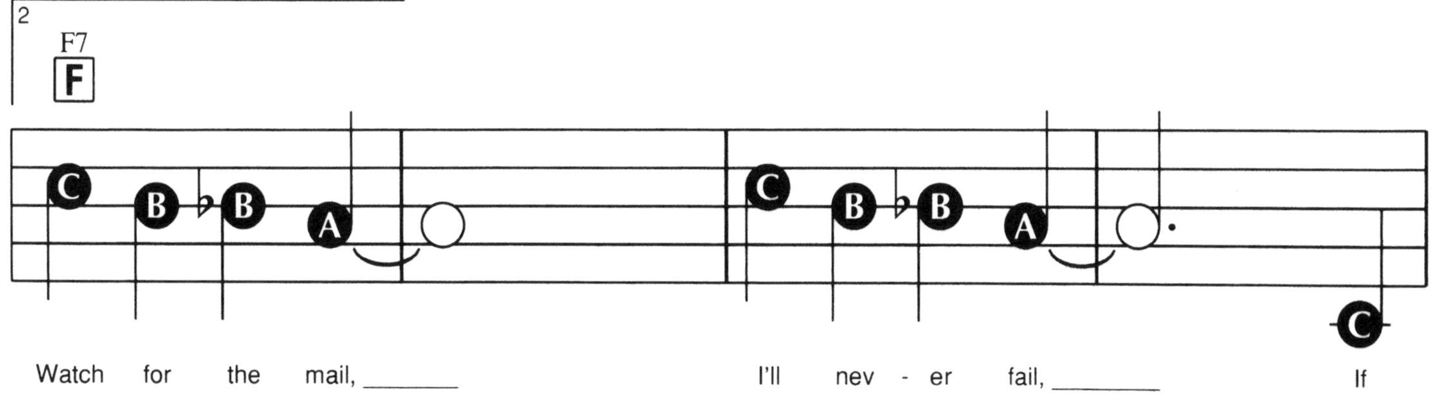
2
F7
F
C
B
B
A
C
B
B
A
C
Watch for the mail,
I'll nev - er fail,
If

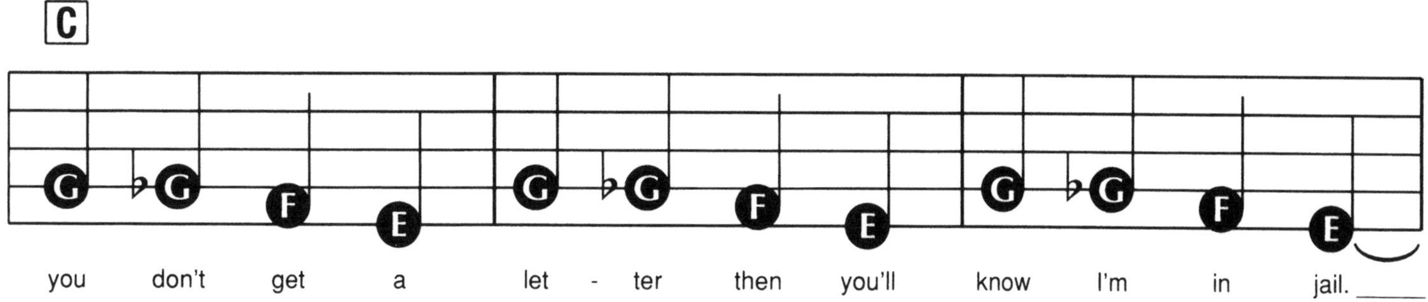
C
G
G
F
E
G
G
F
E
G
G
F
E
you don't get a
let - ter then you'll
know I'm in jail.

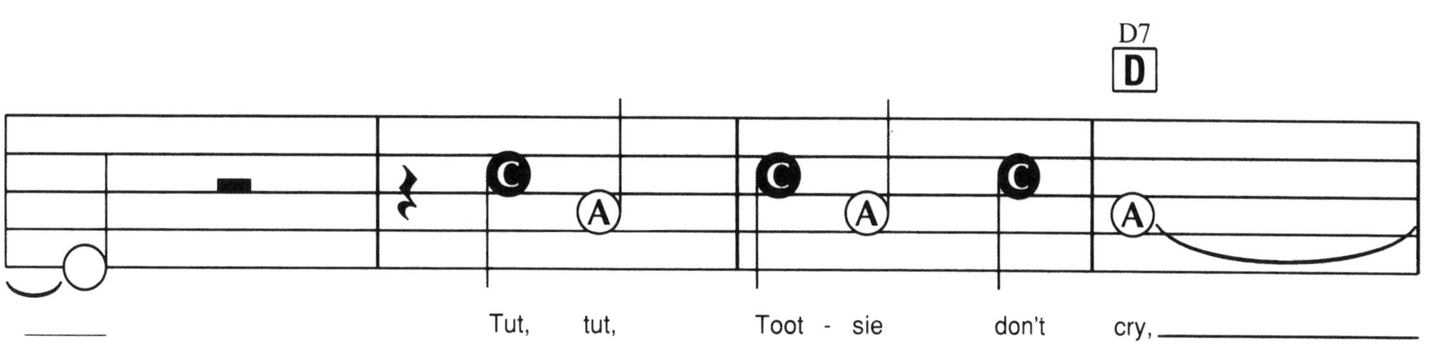
D7
D
C
A
C
A
C
A
Tut, tut,
Toot - sie
don't
cry,

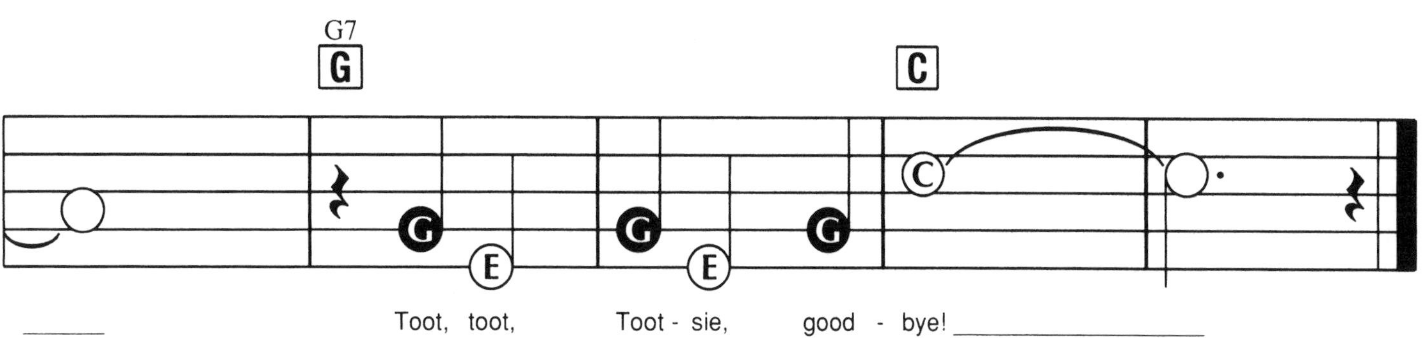
G7
G
C
G
E
G
E
G
C
Toot, toot,
Toot - sie,
good - bye!

Wait 'Til the Sun Shines, Nellie

Registration 2
Rhythm: Fox Trot

Words by Andrew B. Sterling
Music by Harry von Tilzer

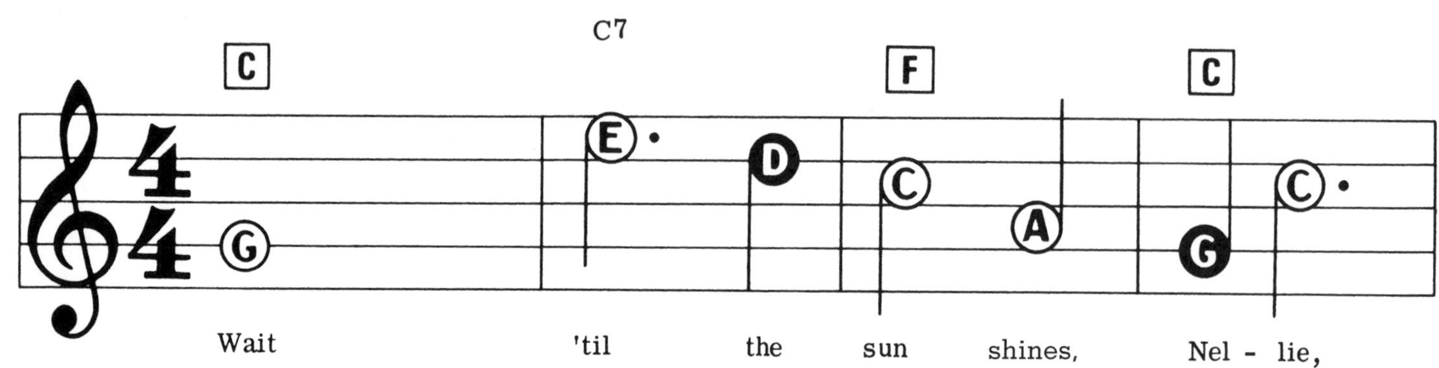

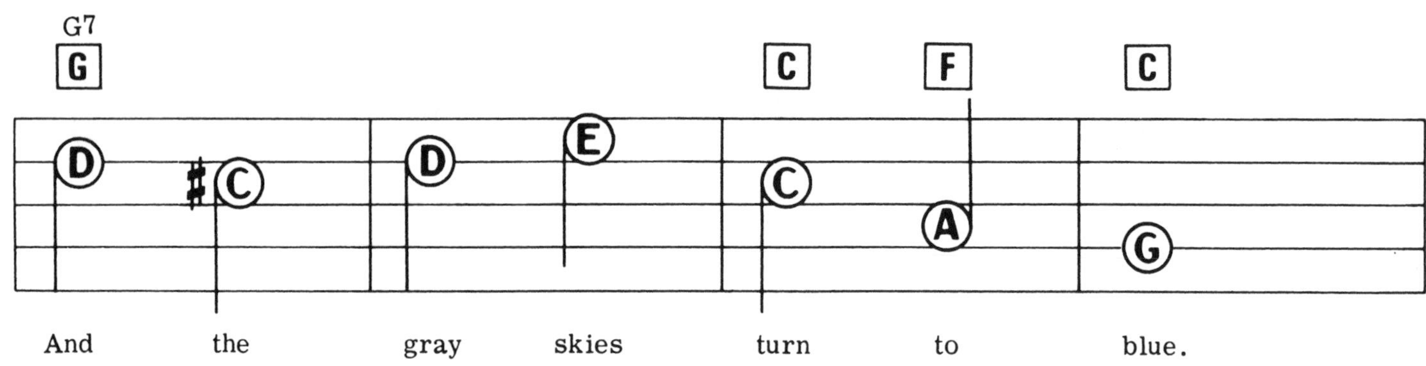

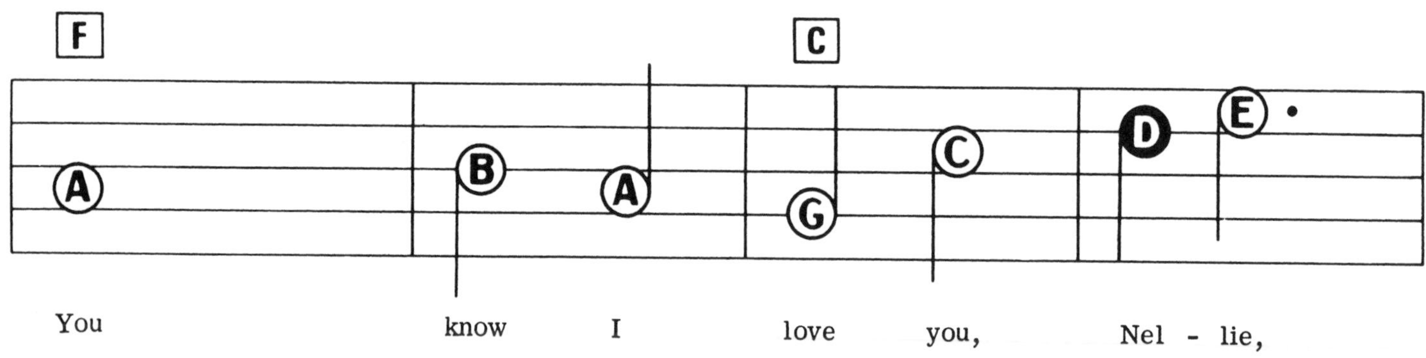

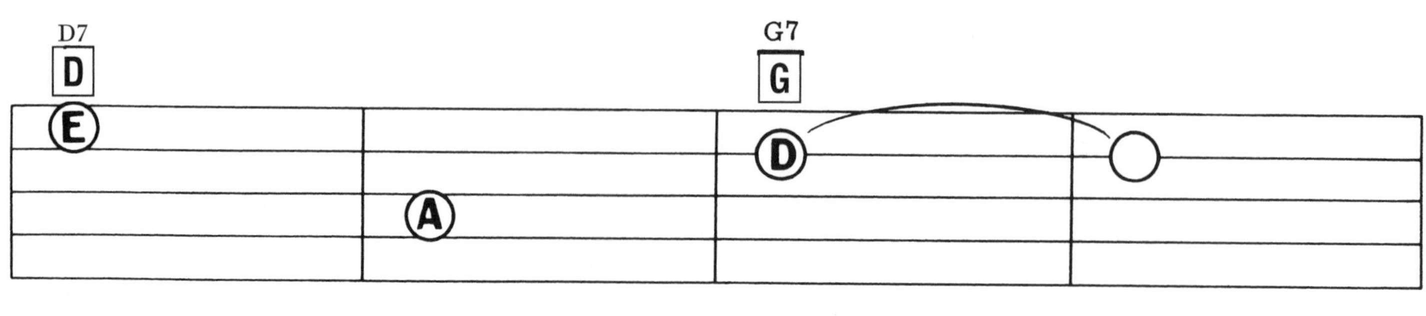

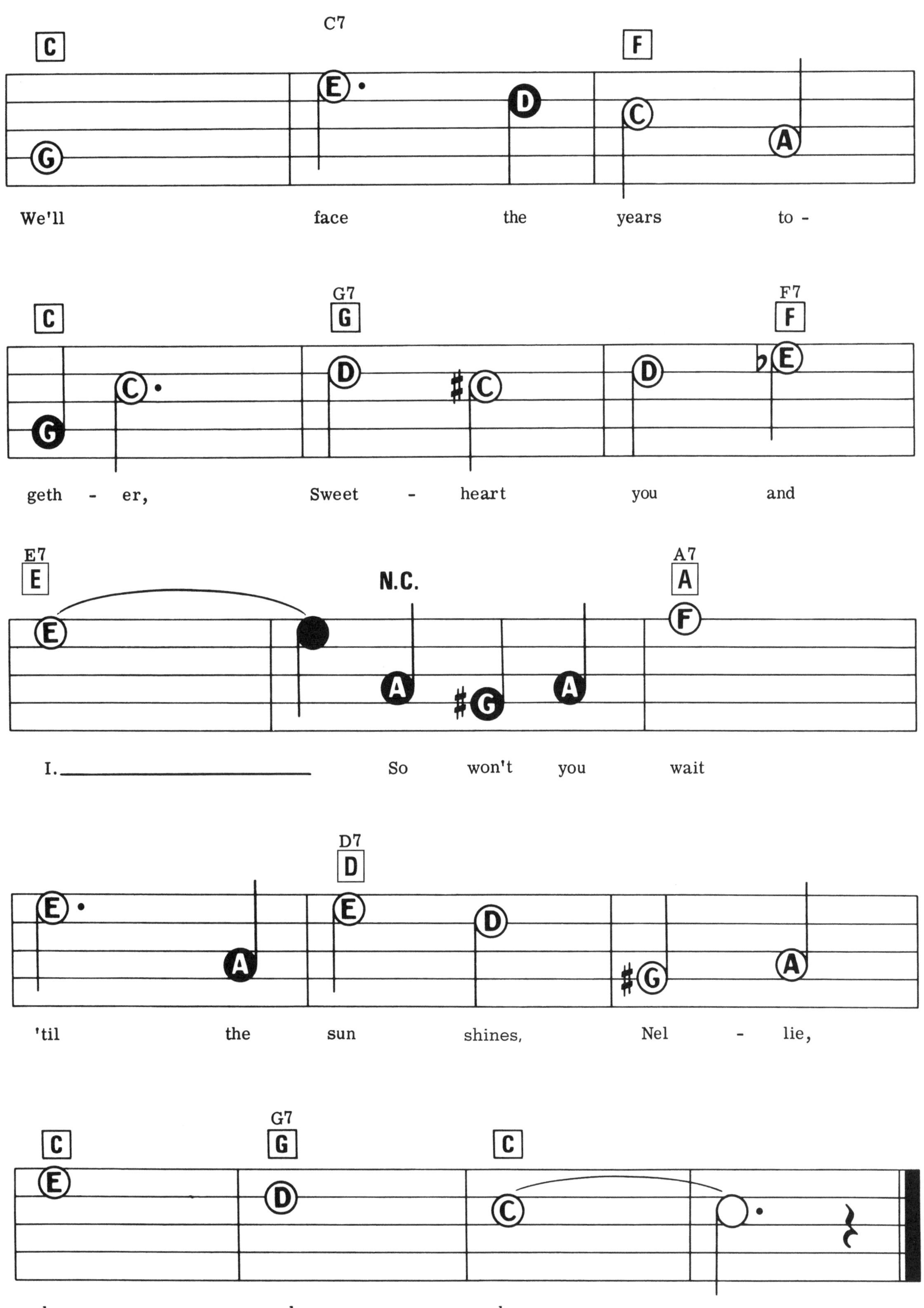
C
C7
F
We'll face the years to -
C
G7
G
F7
F
geth - er, Sweet - heart you and
E7
E
N.C.
A7
A
I. So won't you wait
D7
D
'til the sun shines, Nel - lie,
C
G7
G
C
by and by.

Waiting for the Robert E. Lee

Registration 3
Rhythm: Fox Trot or Jazz

Words by L. Wolfe Gilbert
Music by Lewis F. Muir

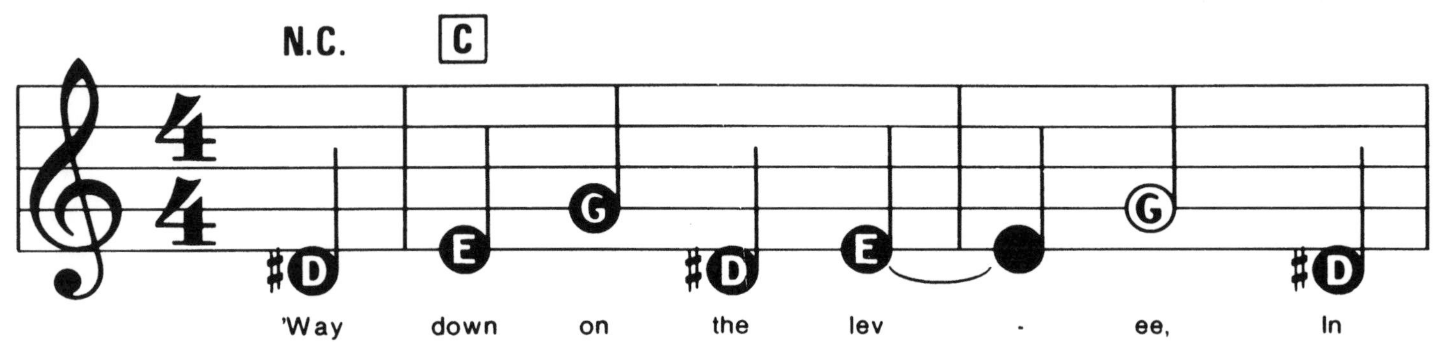

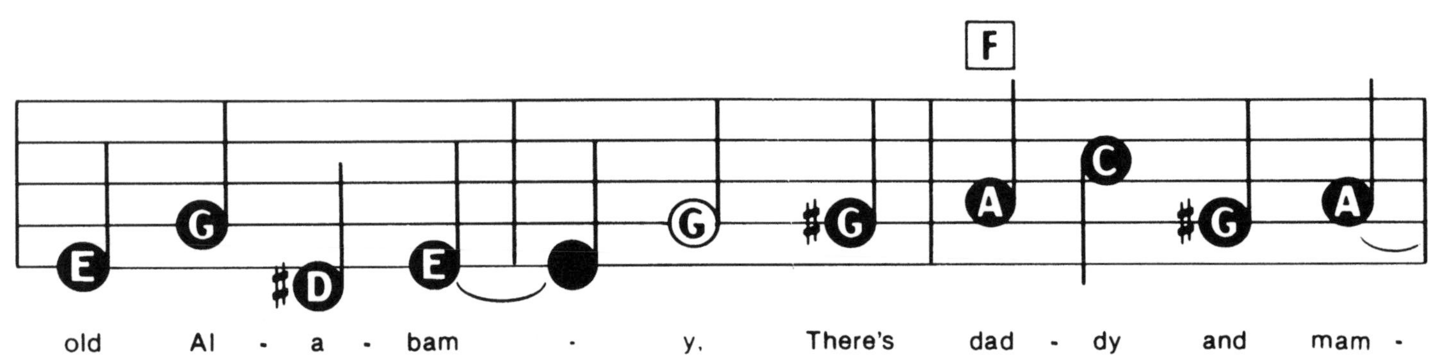

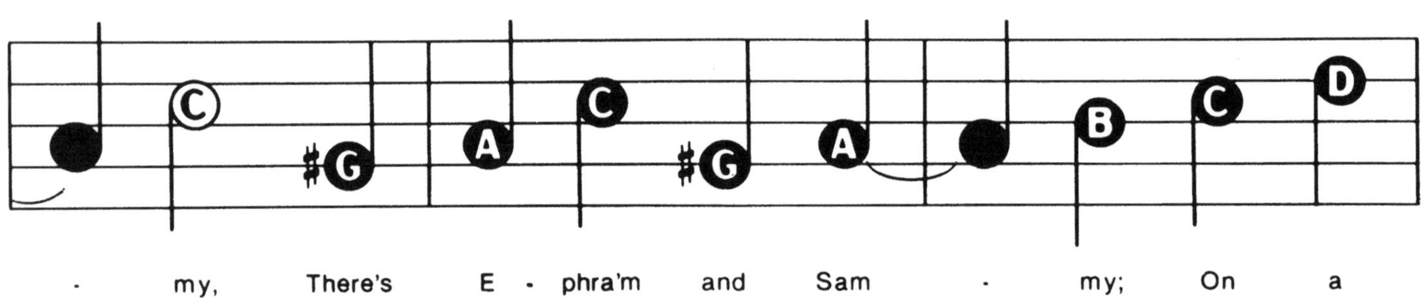

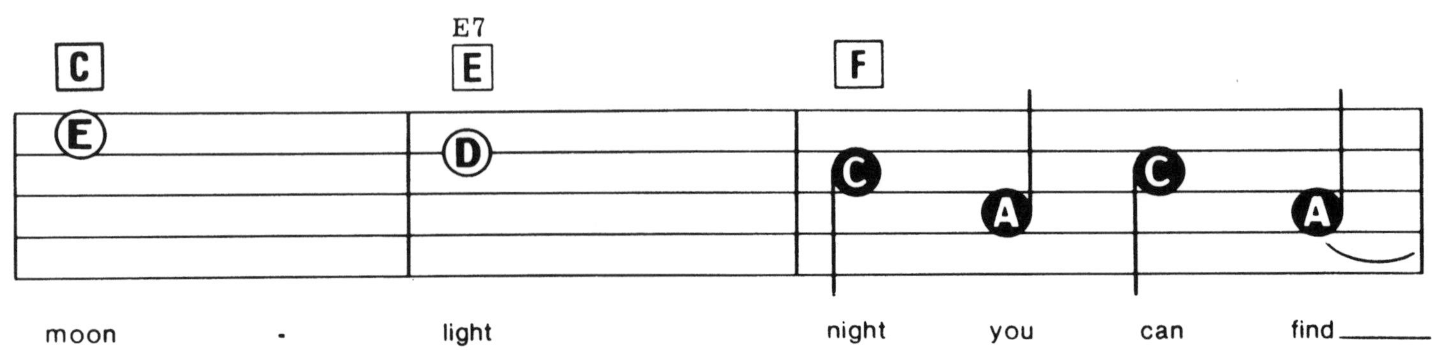

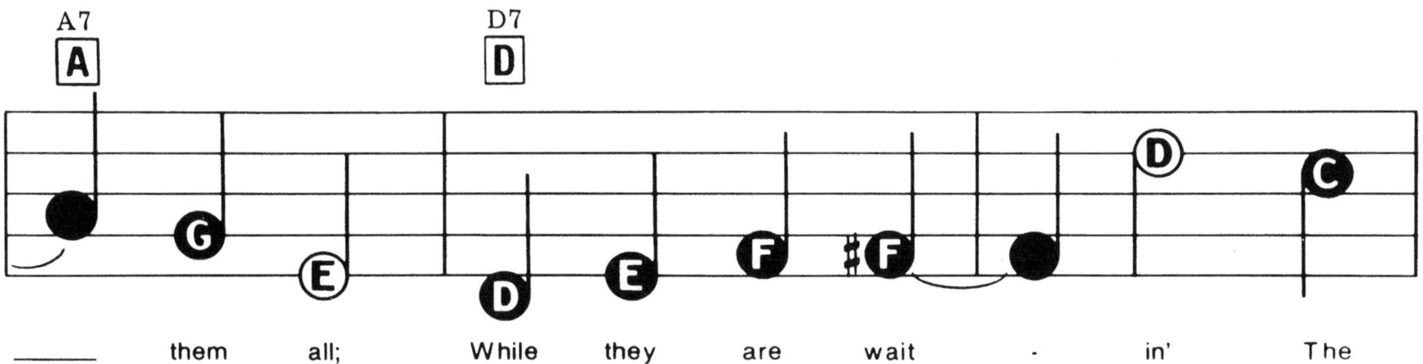
A7
A
D7
D
G
E
D
E
F
♯F
D
C
them all; While they are wait - in' The

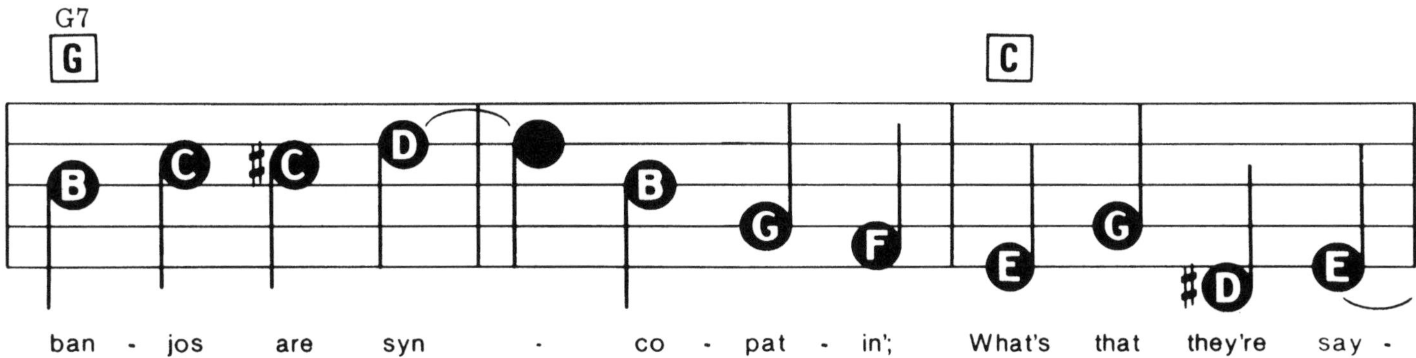
G7
G
C
B
C
♯C
D
B
G
F
E
G
♯D
E
ban - jos are syn - co - pat - in'; What's that they're say -

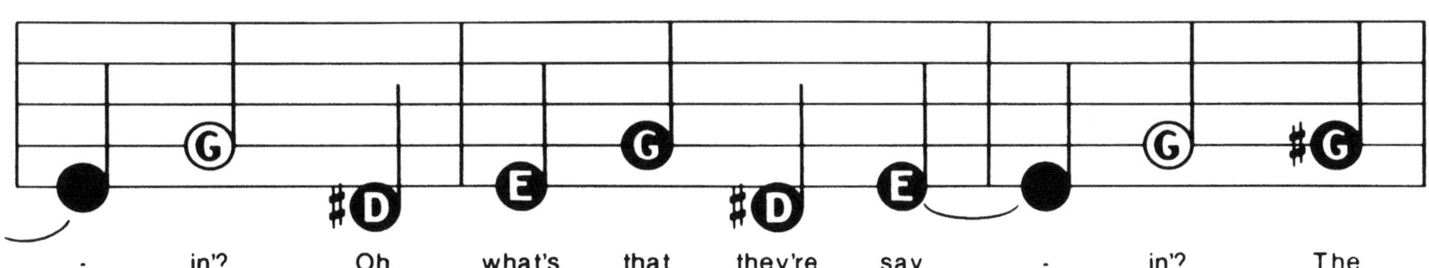
G
♯D
E
G
♯D
E
G
♯G
- in'? Oh, what's that they're say - in'? The

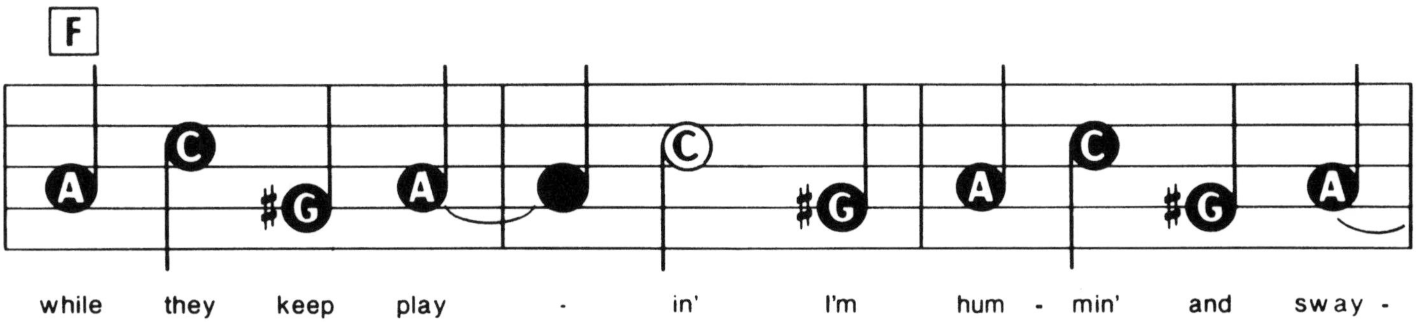
F
A
C
♯G
A
C
♯G
A
C
♯G
A
while they keep play - in' I'm hum - min' and sway -

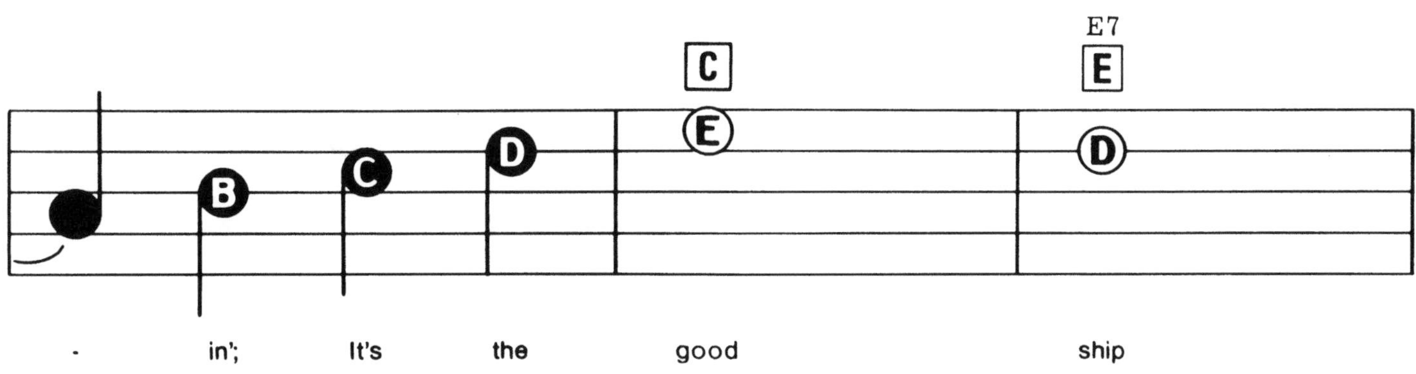
C
E7
E
B
C
D
E
D
- in'; It's the good ship

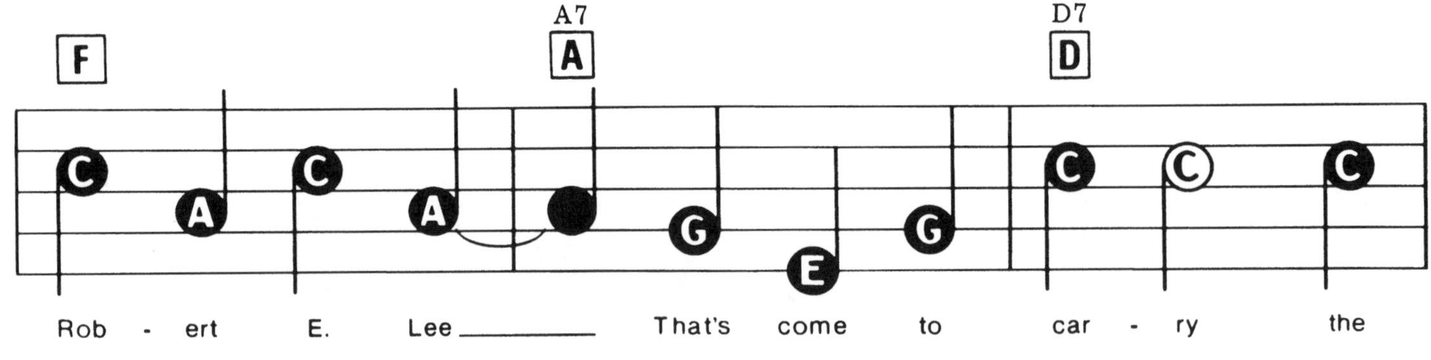
F
A7 A
D7 D
Rob - ert E. Lee That's come to car - ry the

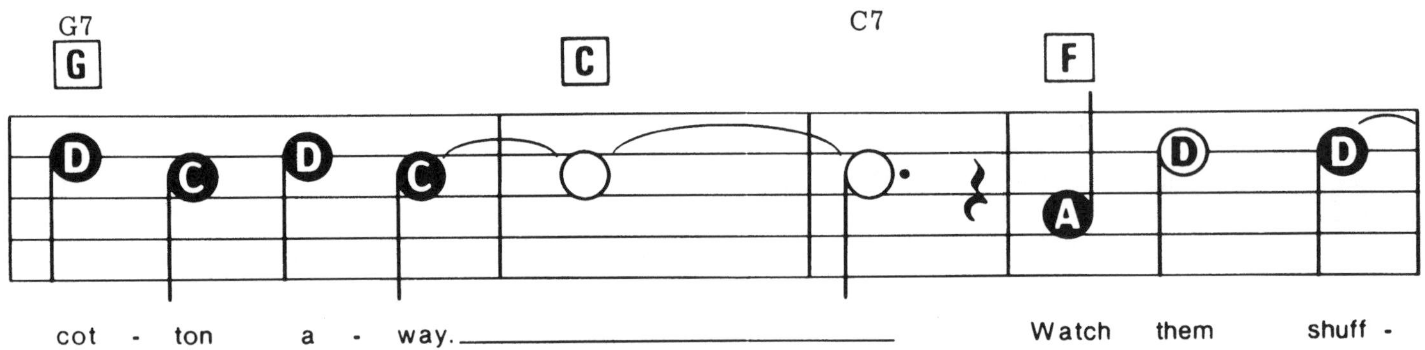
G7 G
C
C7
F
cot - ton a - way. Watch them shuff -

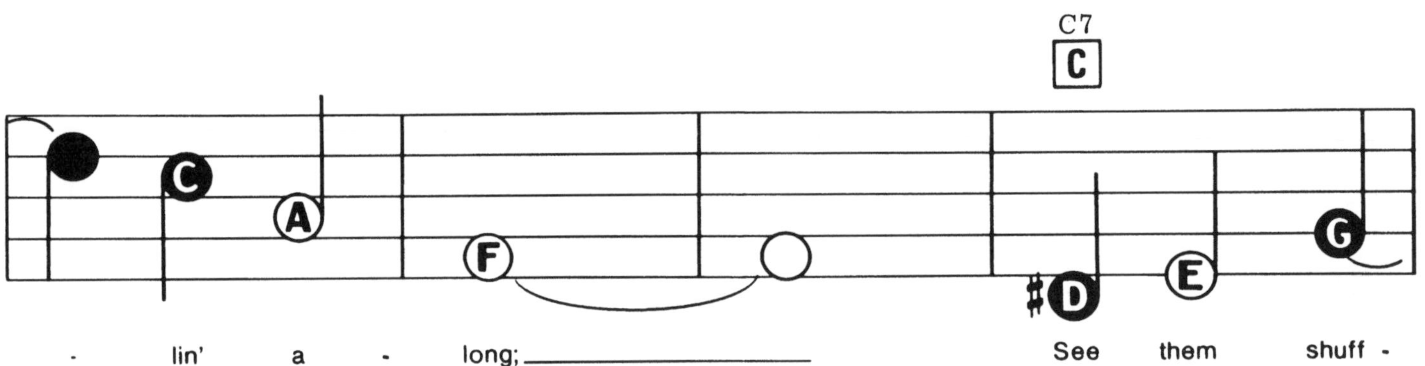
C7 C
- lin' a - long; See them shuff -

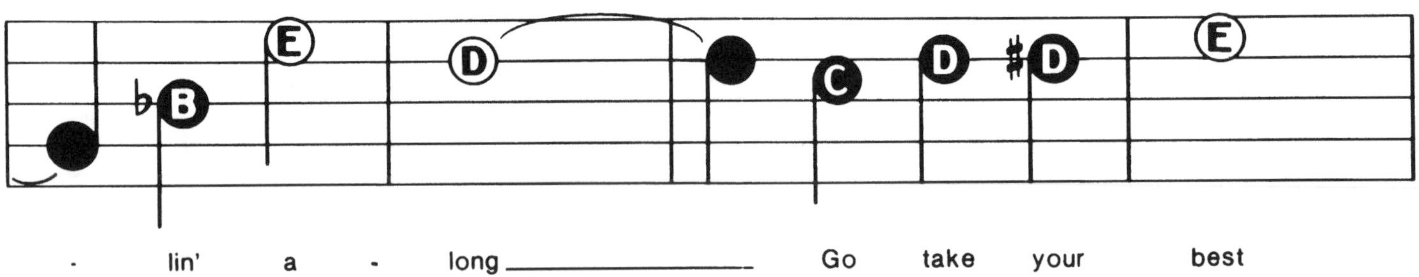
- lin' a - long Go take your best

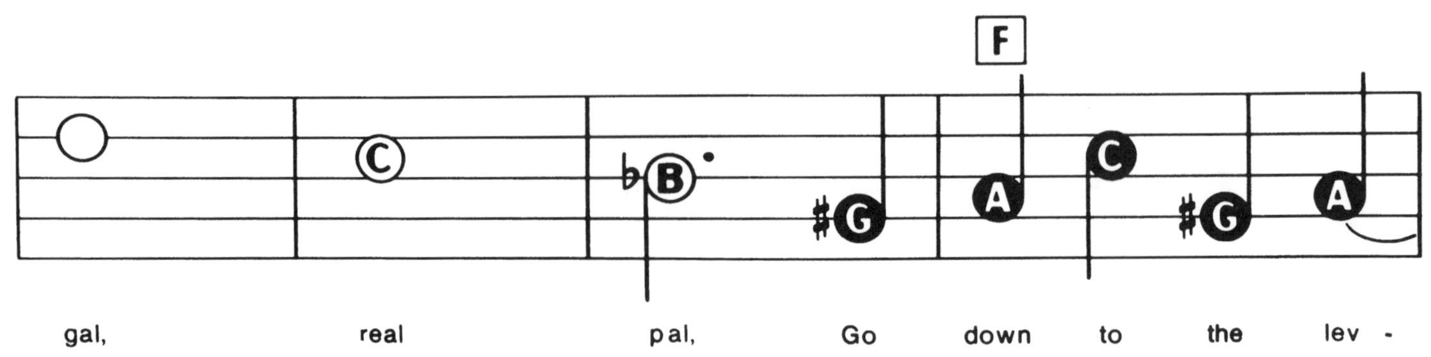
F
gal, real pal, Go down to the lev -

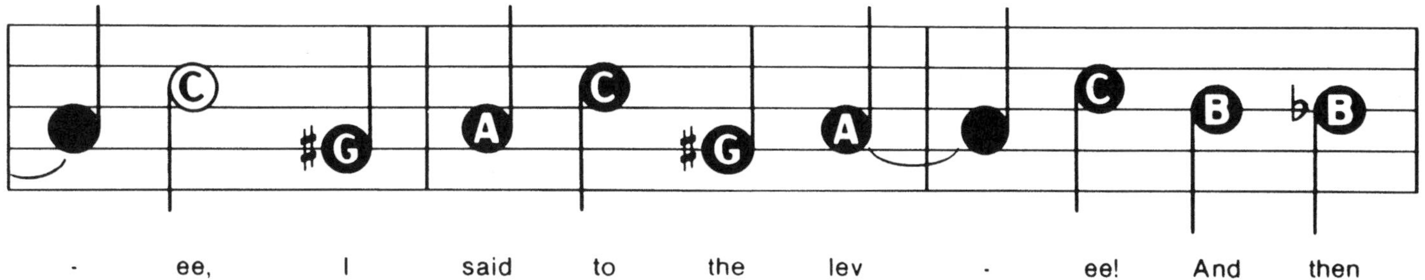
C
G
A
C
G
A
C
B
B
- ee, I said to the lev - ee! And then

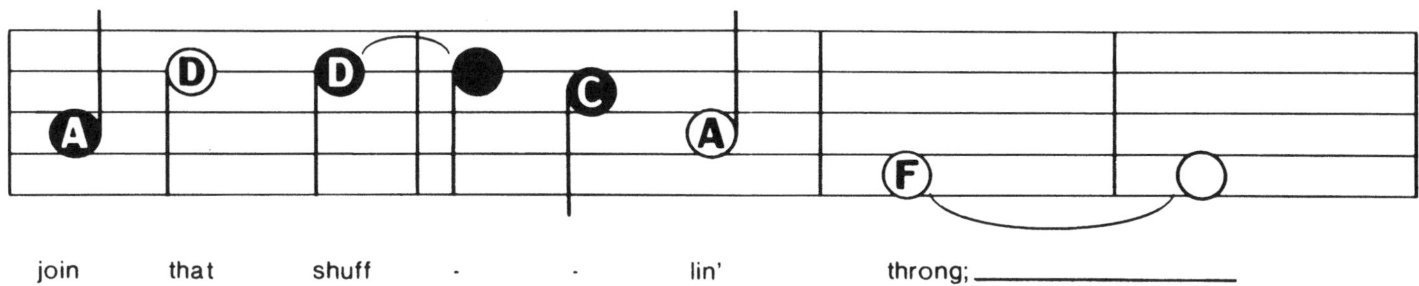
A
D
D
C
A
F
join that shuff - - lin' throng;

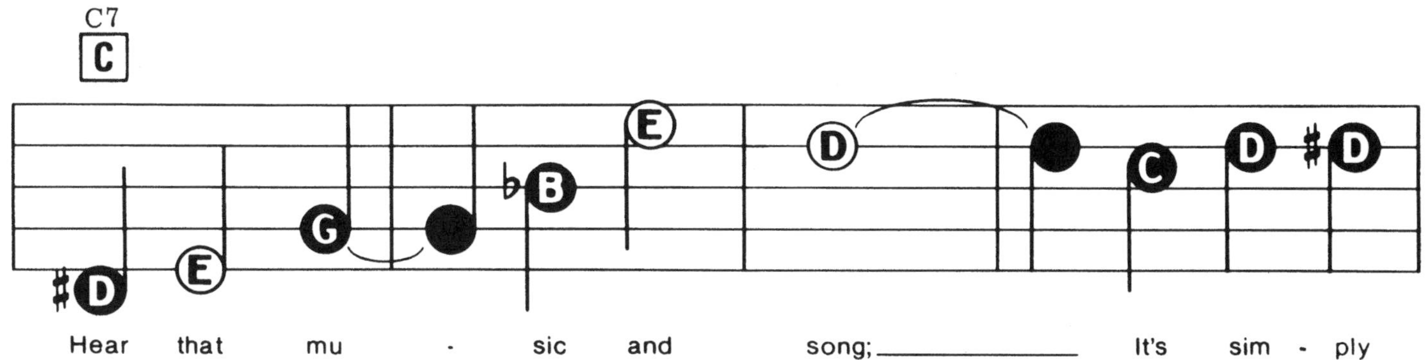
C7
C
D
E
G
B
E
D
C
D
D
Hear that mu - sic and song; It's sim - ply

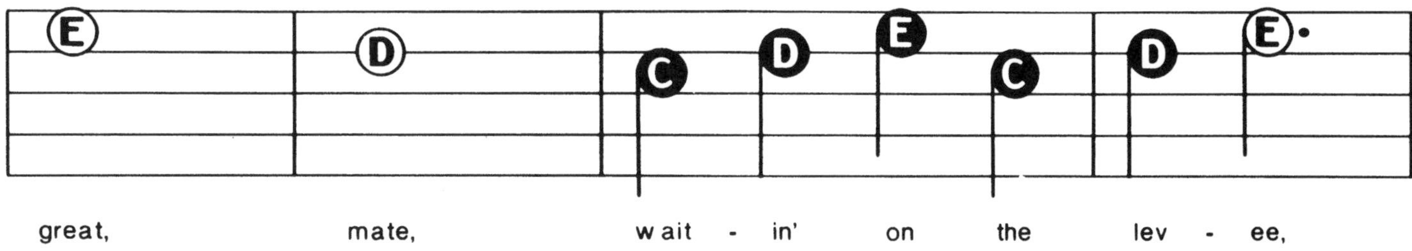
E
D
C
D
E
C
D
E
great, mate, wait - in' on the lev - ee,

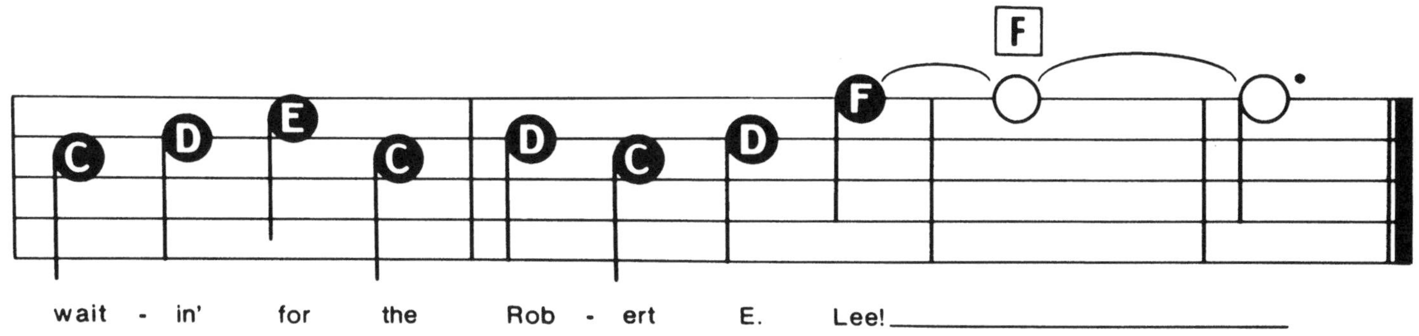
F
C
D
E
C
D
C
D
F
wait - in' for the Rob - ert E. Lee!

When Irish Eyes Are Smiling

Registration 3
Rhythm: Waltz

Words by Chauncey Olcott and George Grafg Jr.
Music by Ernest R. Ball

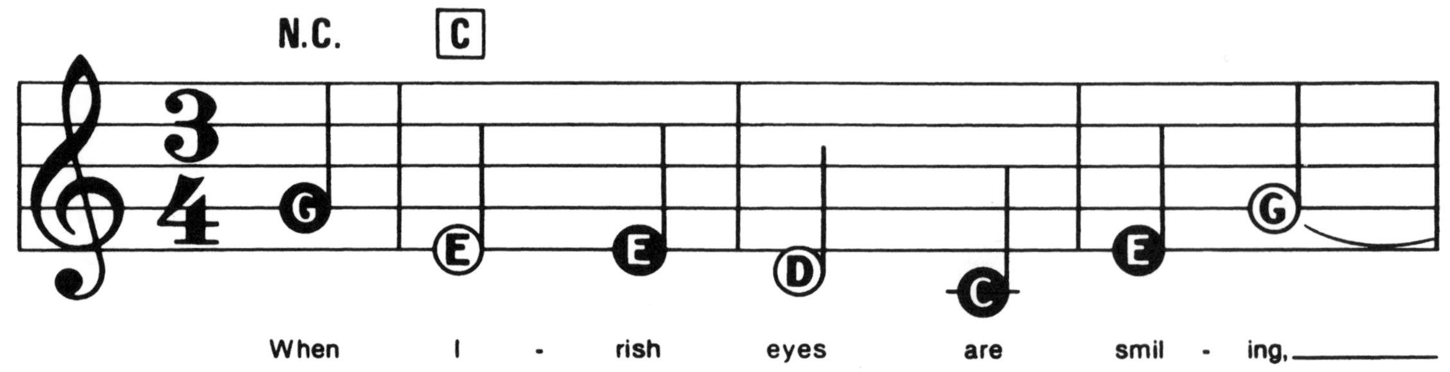

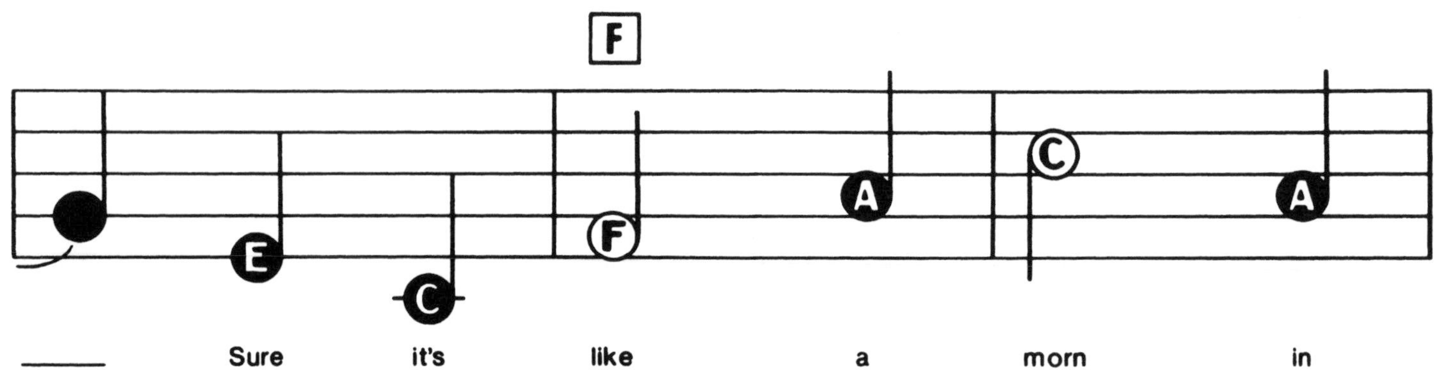

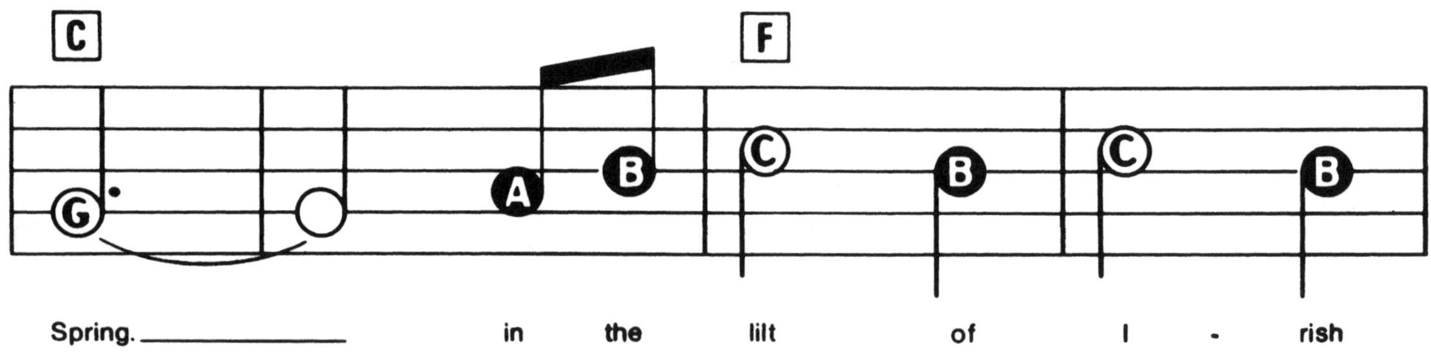

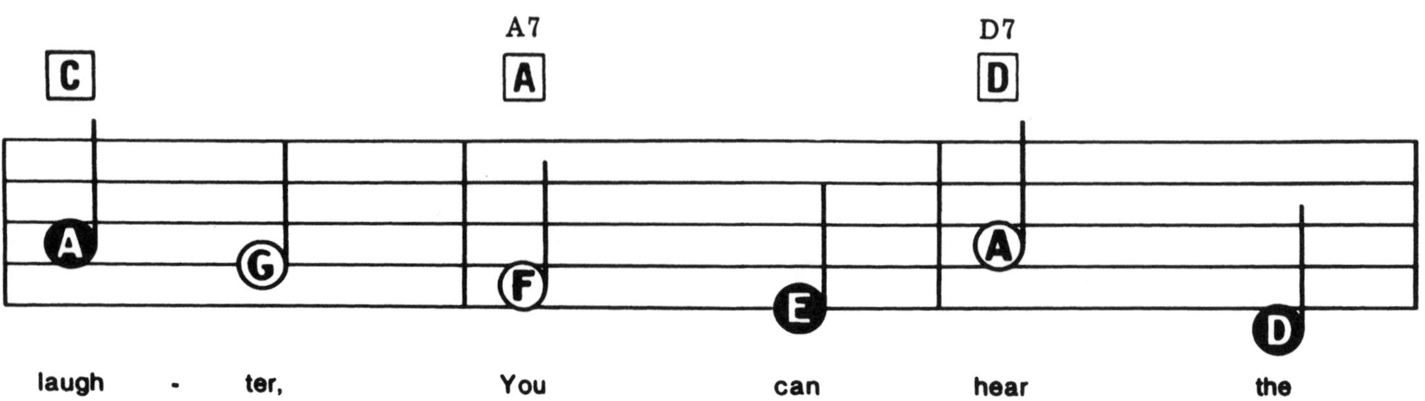

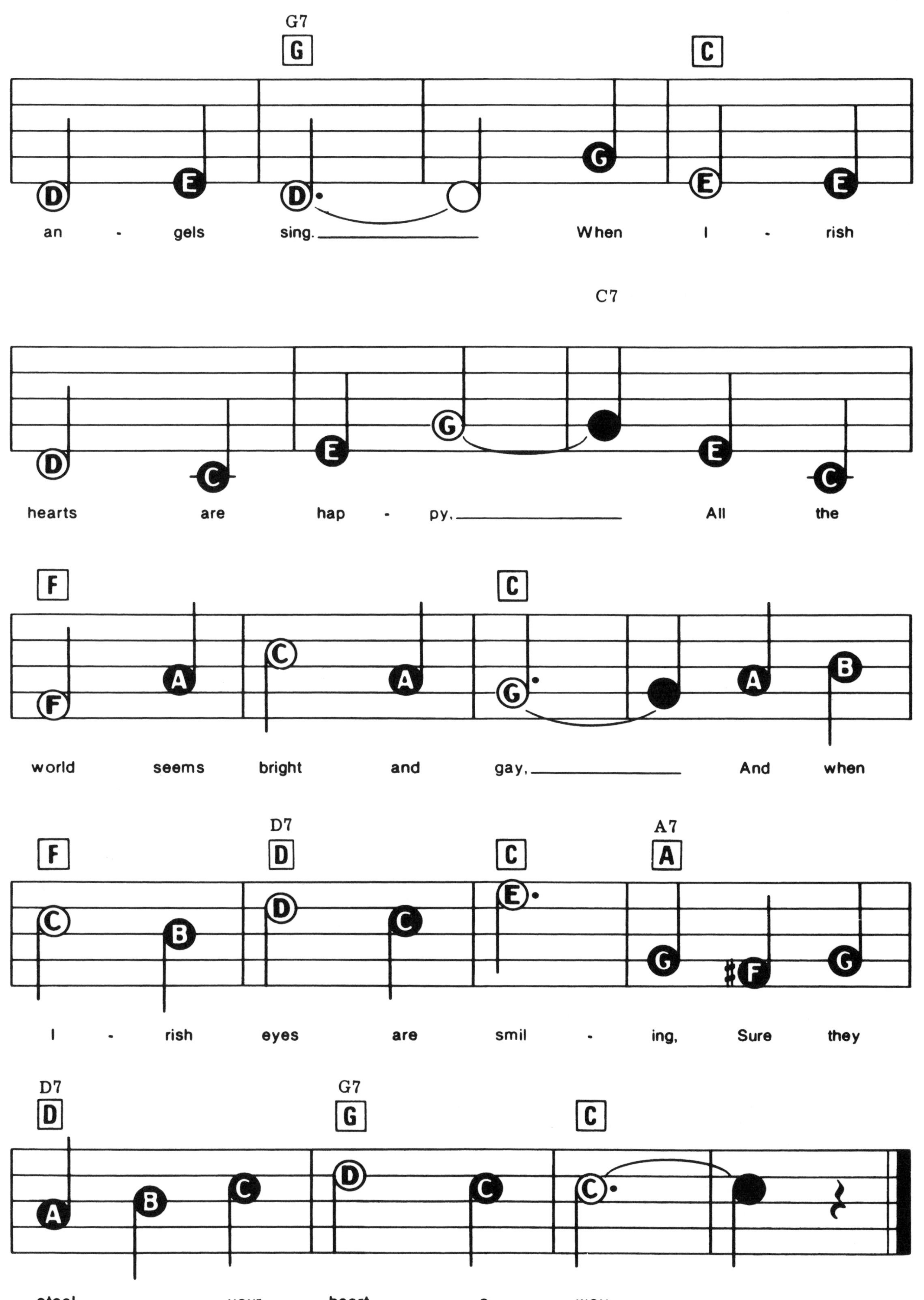
G7
G
C
D
E
D
G
E
E
an - gels sing.
When I - rish
C7
D
C
E
G
E
C
hearts are hap - py,
All the
F
C
F
A
C
A
G
A
B
world seems bright and gay,
And when
F
D7
D
C
A7
A
C
B
D
C
E
G
F
G
I - rish eyes are smil - ing,
Sure they
D7
D
G7
G
C
A
B
C
D
C
C
steal your heart a - way.

When Johnny Comes Marching Home

Registration 2
Rhythm: 6/8 March

Words and Music by
Patrick Sarsfield Gilmore

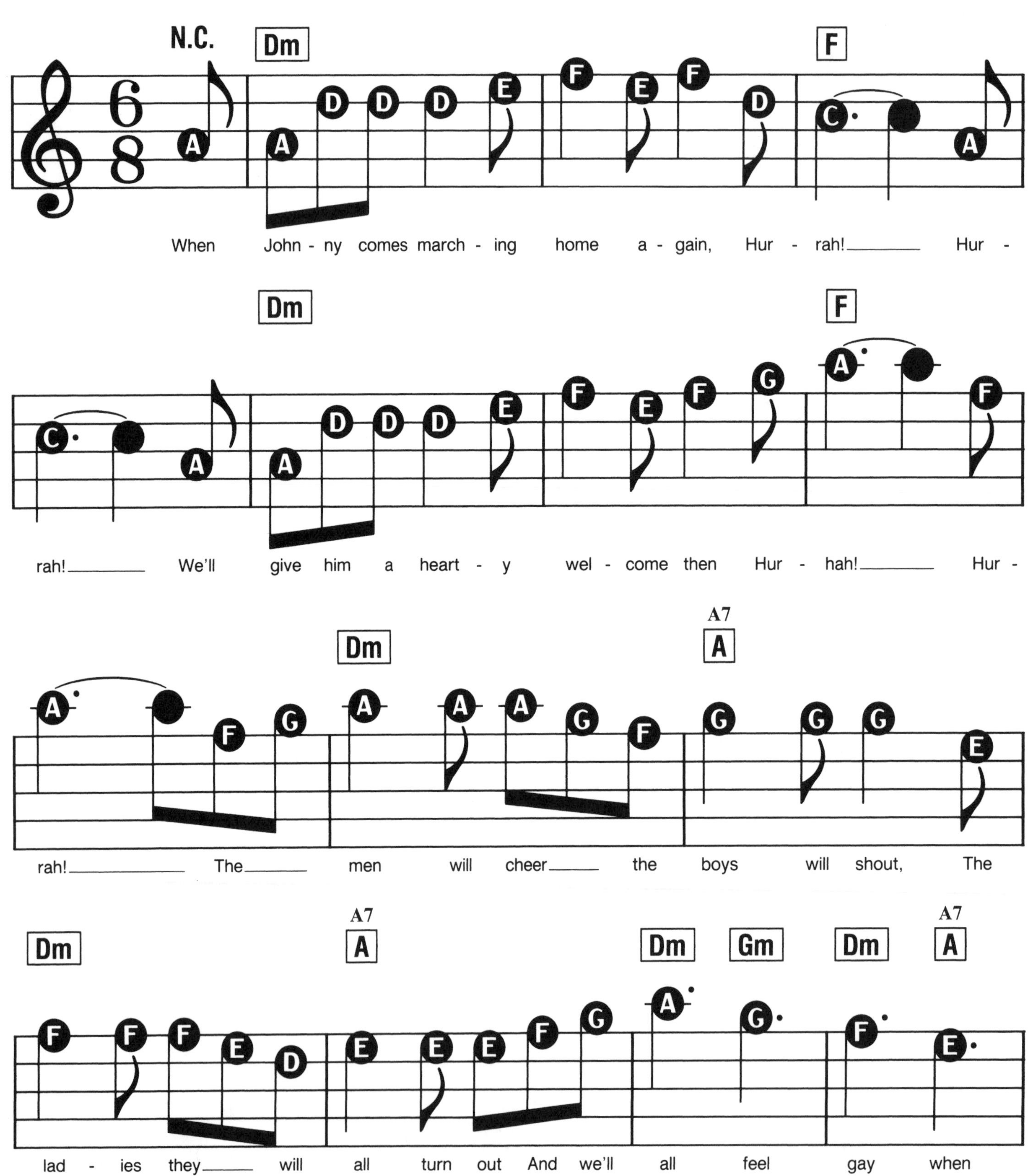

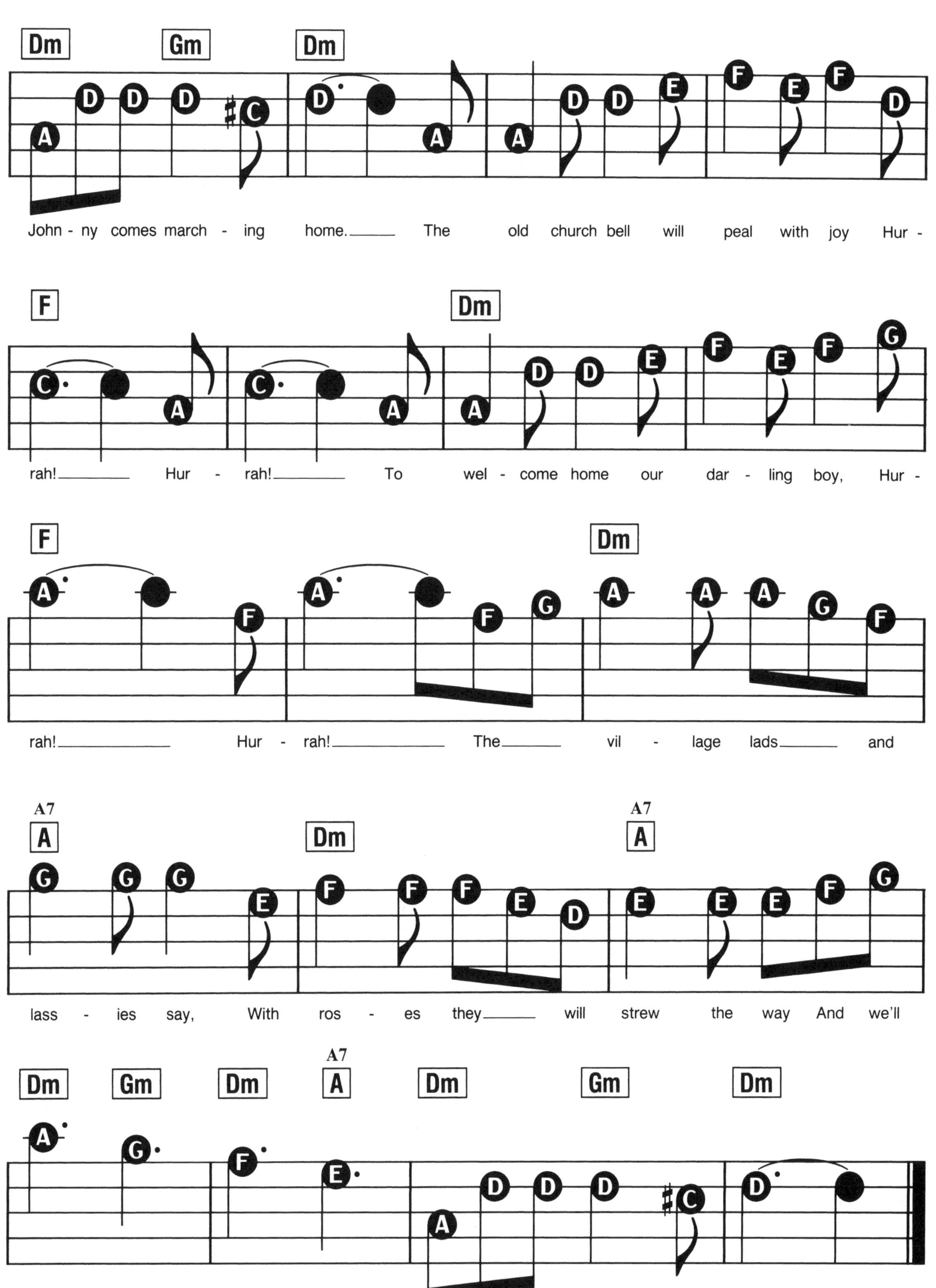
Dm Gm Dm
A D D D ♯C D A A D D E F E F D
John - ny comes march - ing home. The old church bell will peal with joy Hur -
F Dm
C A C A A D D E F E F G
rah! Hur - rah! To wel - come home our dar - ling boy, Hur -
F Dm
A F A F G A A A G F
rah! Hur - rah! The vil - lage lads and
A7 A Dm A7 A
G G G E F F F E D E E E F G
lass - ies say, With ros - es they will strew the way And we'll
Dm Gm Dm A7 A Dm Gm Dm
A G F E A D D D ♯C D
all feel gay when John - ny comes march - ing home.

When My Baby Smiles at Me

Registration 1
Rhythm: Fox Trot or Swing

Words and Music by harry von Tilzer,
Andrew B. Sterling, Bill Munro and Ted Lewis

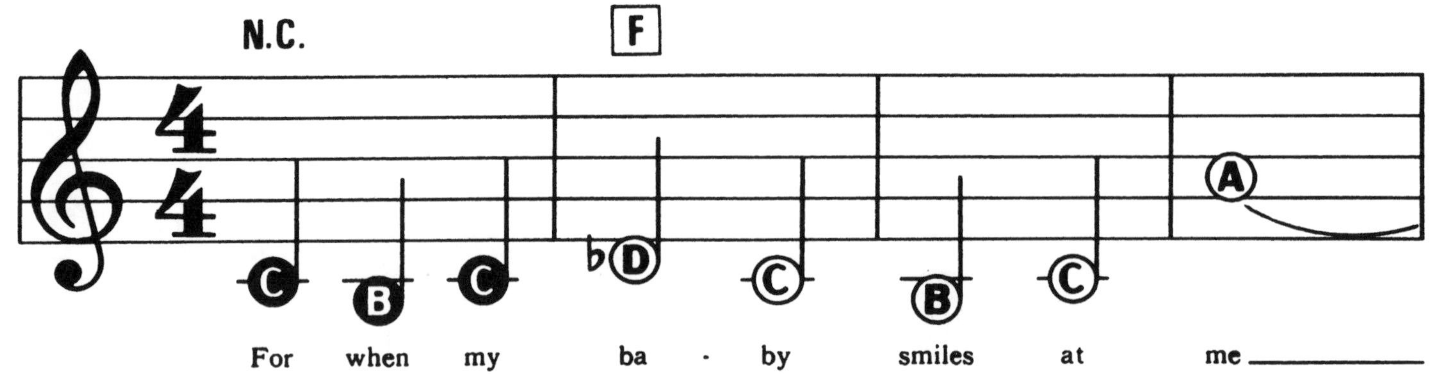

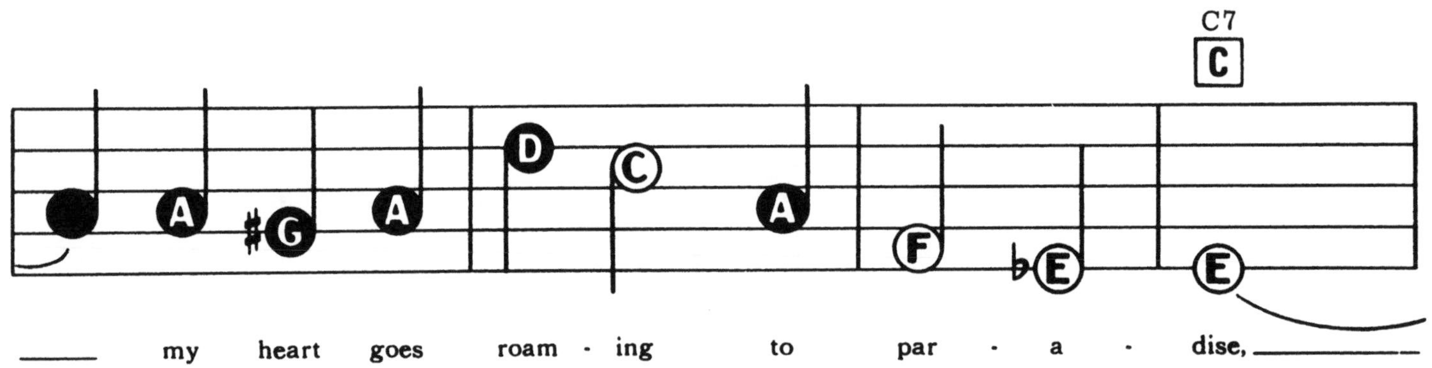

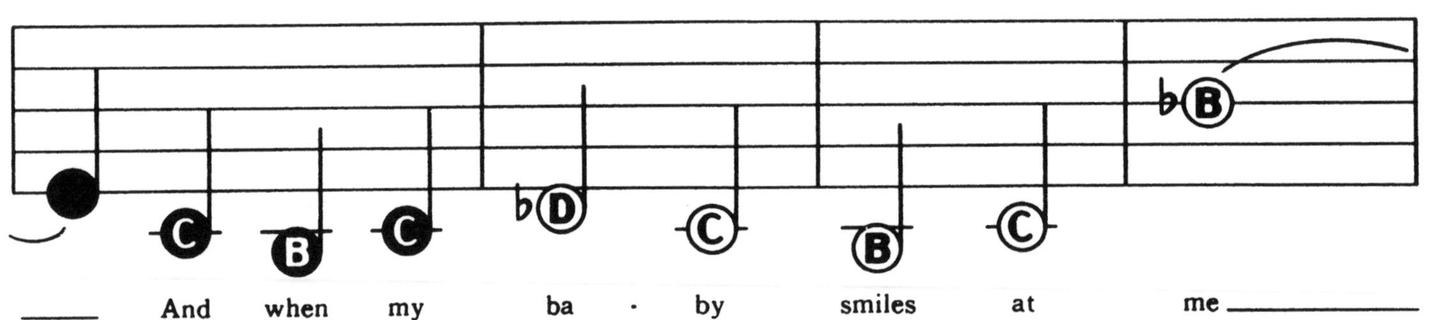

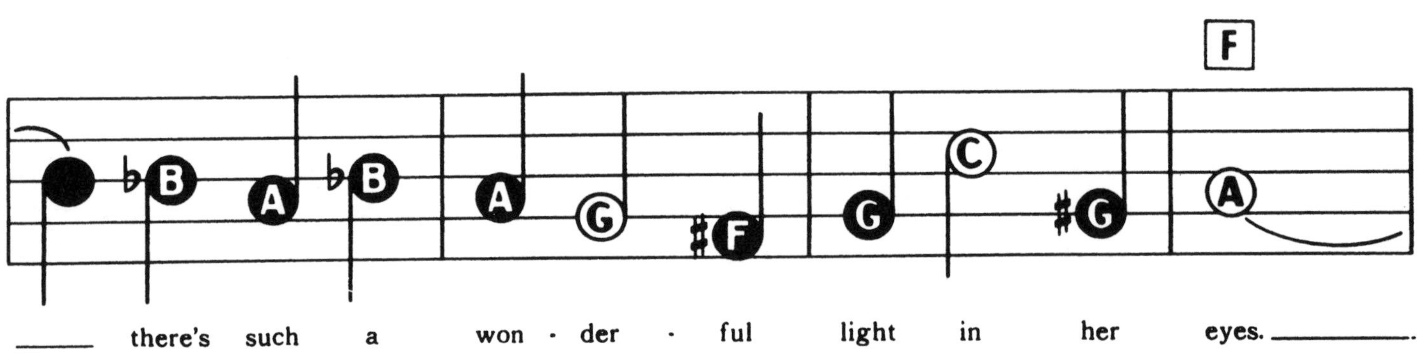

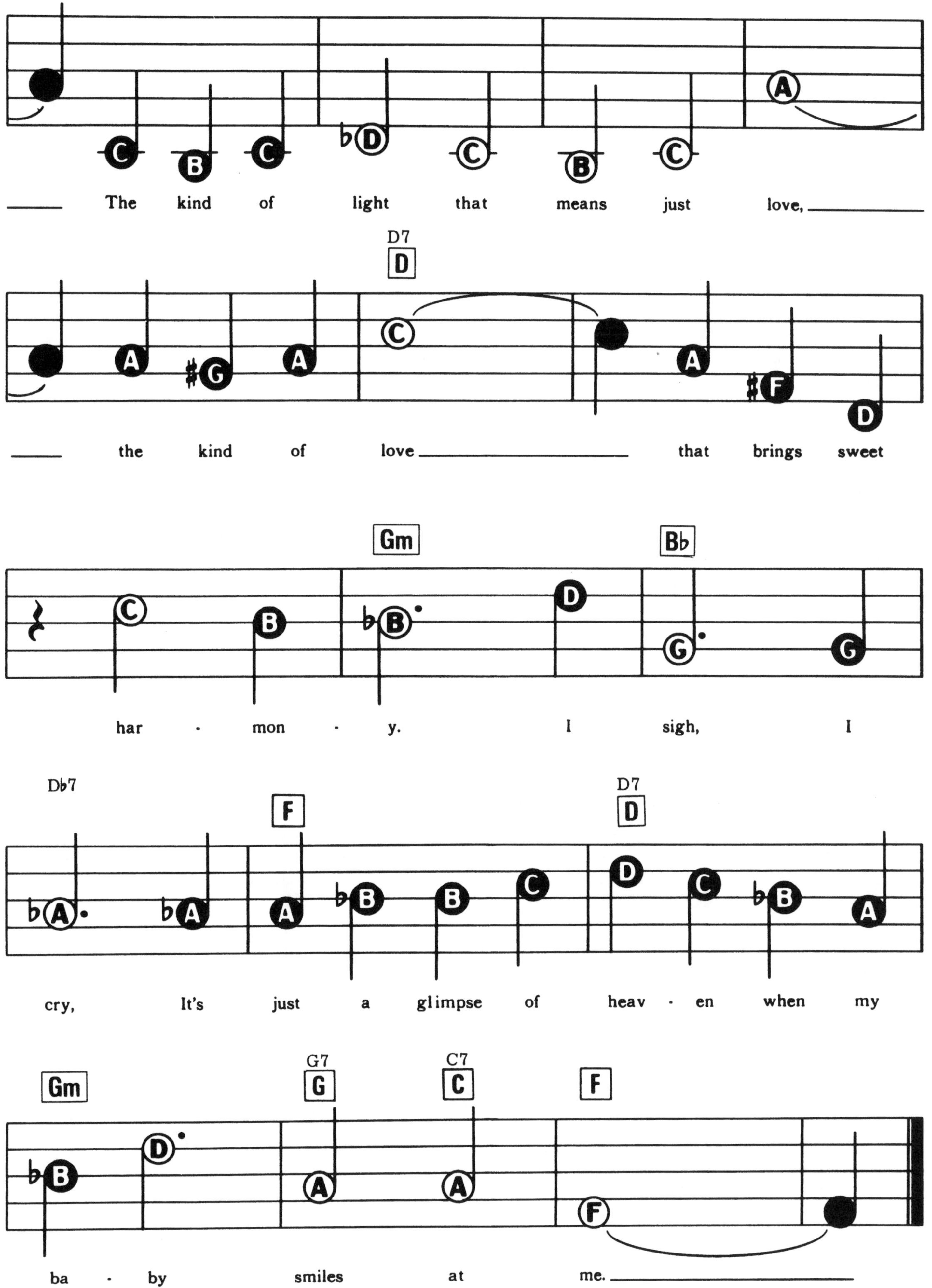
The kind of light that means just love,
D7
D
the kind of love that brings sweet
Gm
Bb
har - mon - y. I sigh, I
Db7
F
D7
D
cry, It's just a glimpse of heav - en when my
Gm
G7
G
C7
C
F
ba - by smiles at me.

When You Wore a Tulip
(And I Wore a Big Red Rose)

Registration 9
Rhythm: Fox Trot or Pops

Words by Jack Mahoney
Music by Percy Wenrich

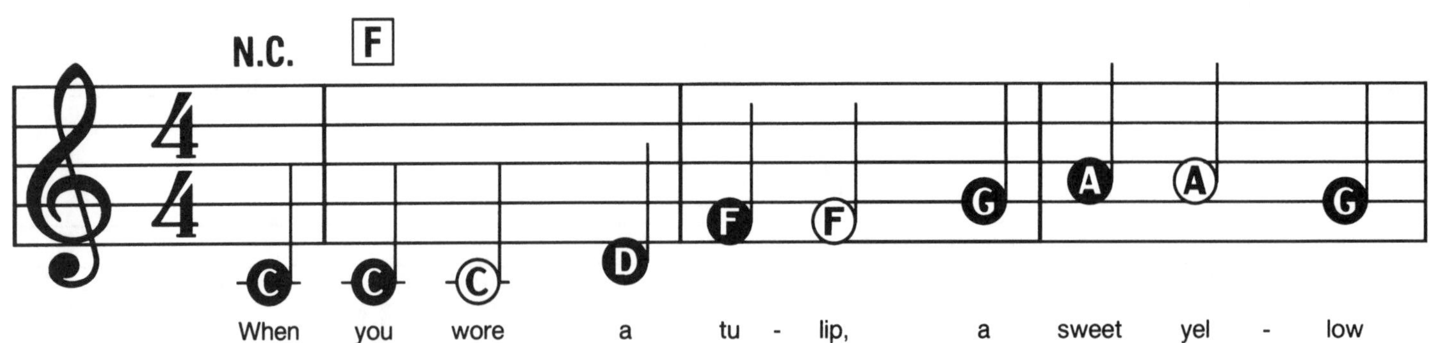

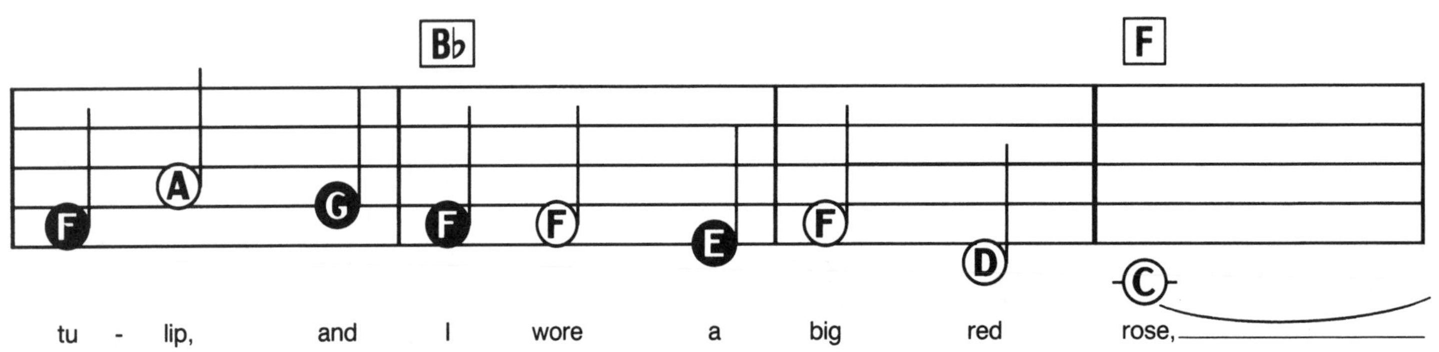

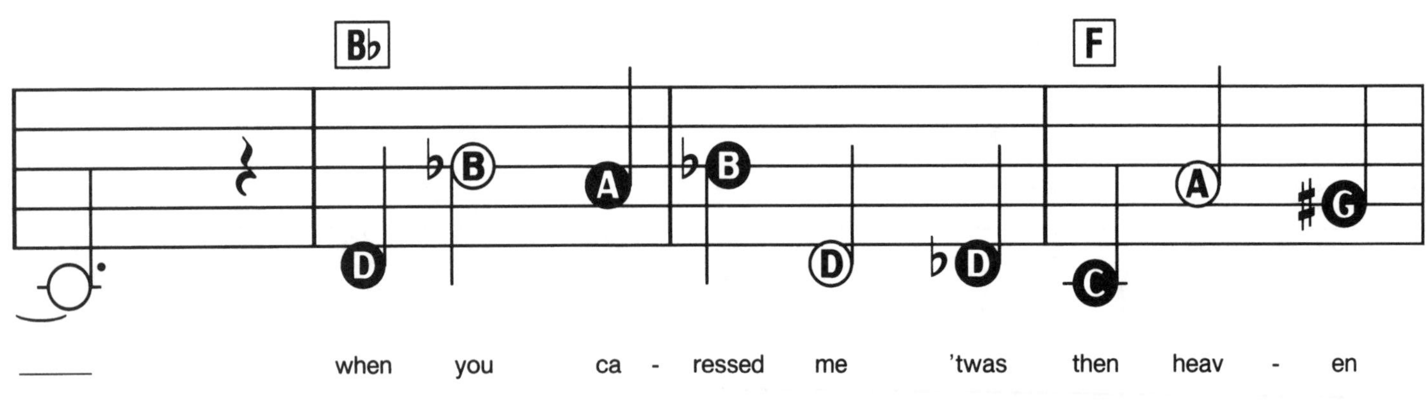

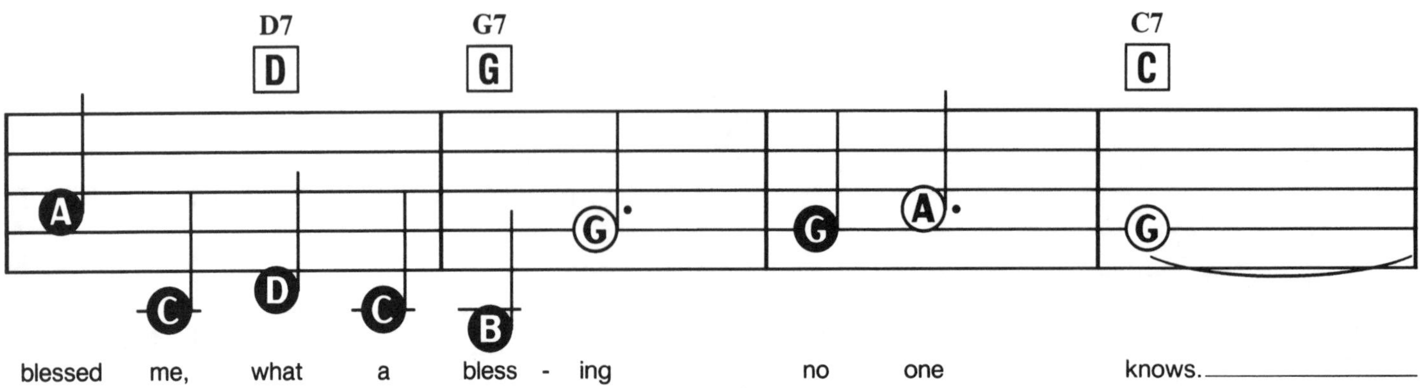

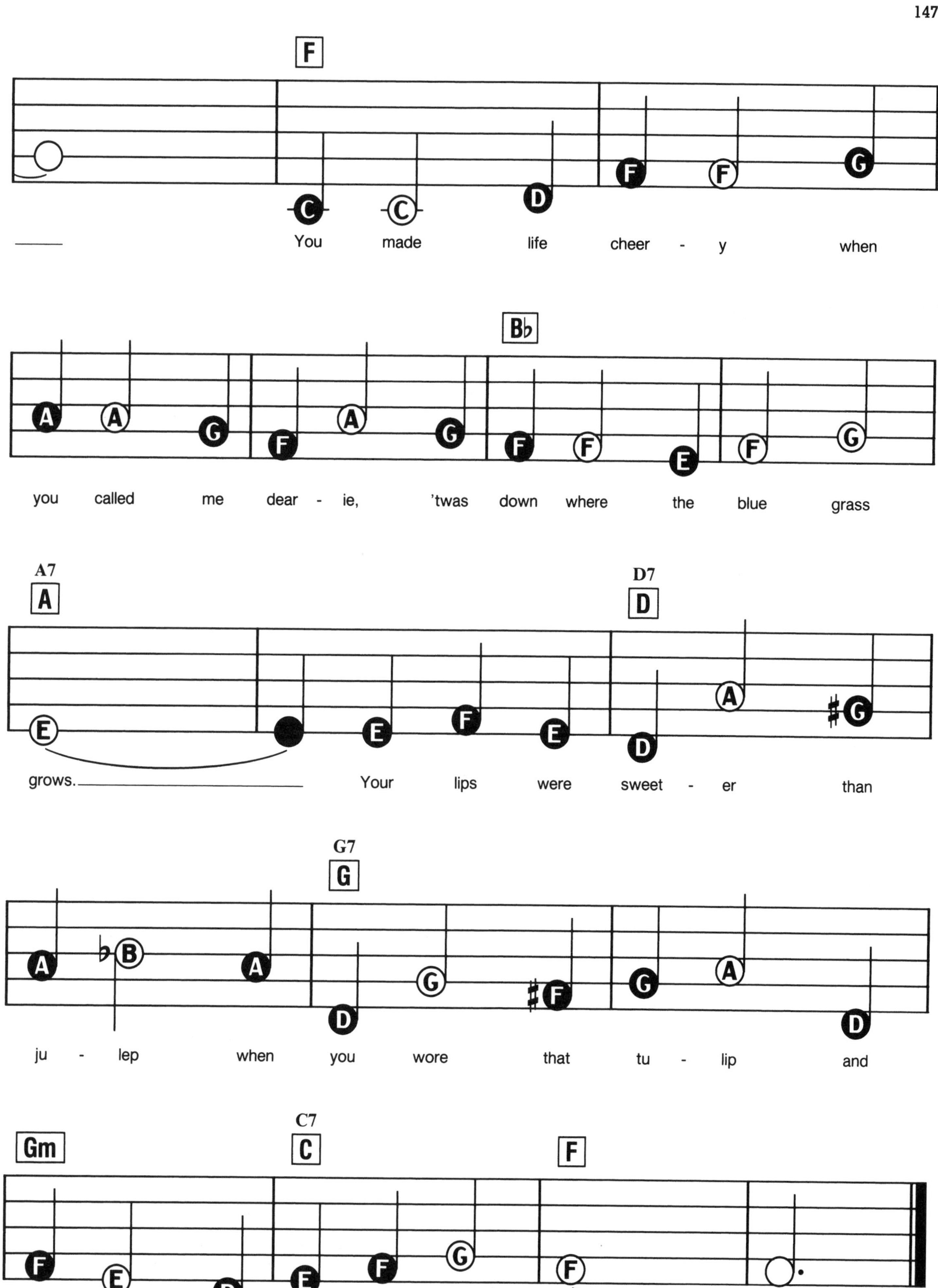
F
You made life cheer - y when
B♭
you called me dear - ie, 'twas down where the blue grass
A7
A
D7
D
grows. Your lips were sweet - er than
G7
G
ju - lep when you wore that tu - lip and
Gm
C7
C
F
I wore that big red rose.

While Strolling Through the Park One Day

Registration 2
Rhythm: Fox Trot

Words and Music by Ed Haley
and Robert A. Keiser

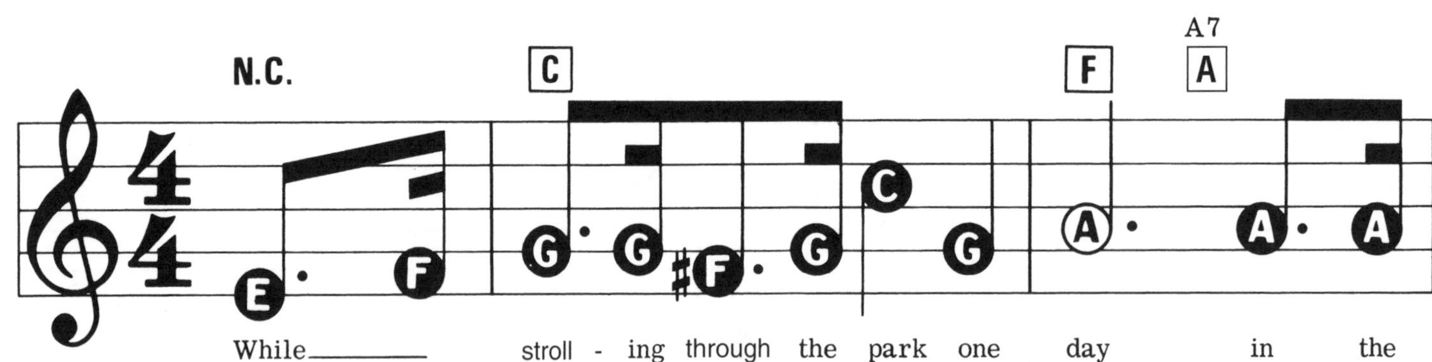

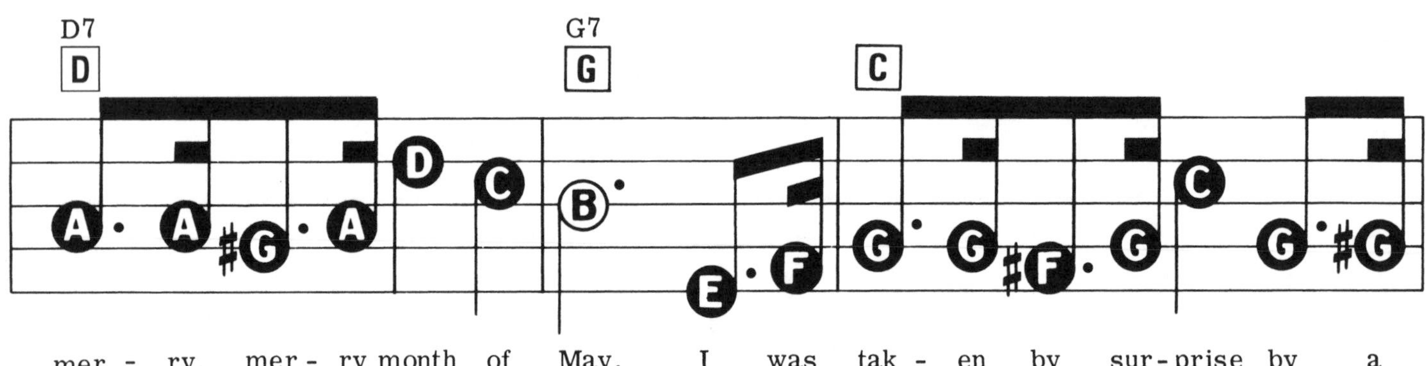

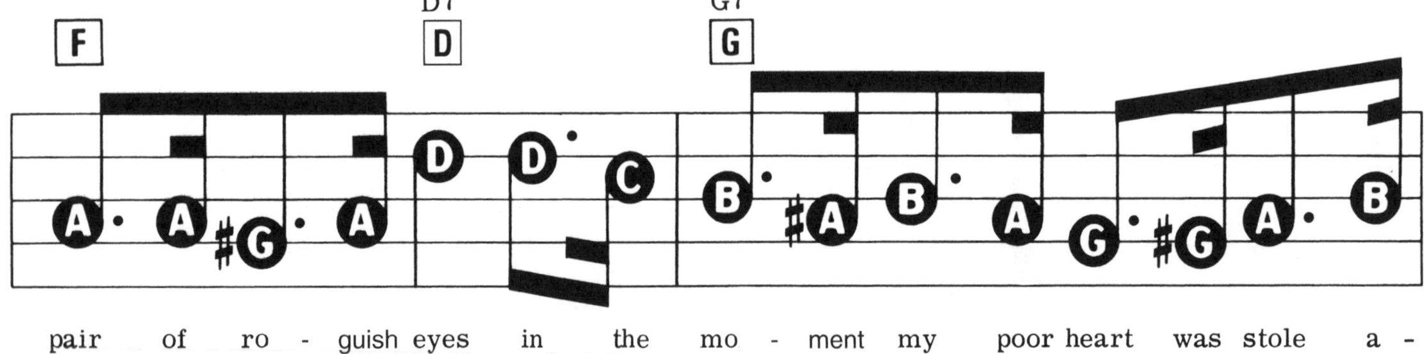

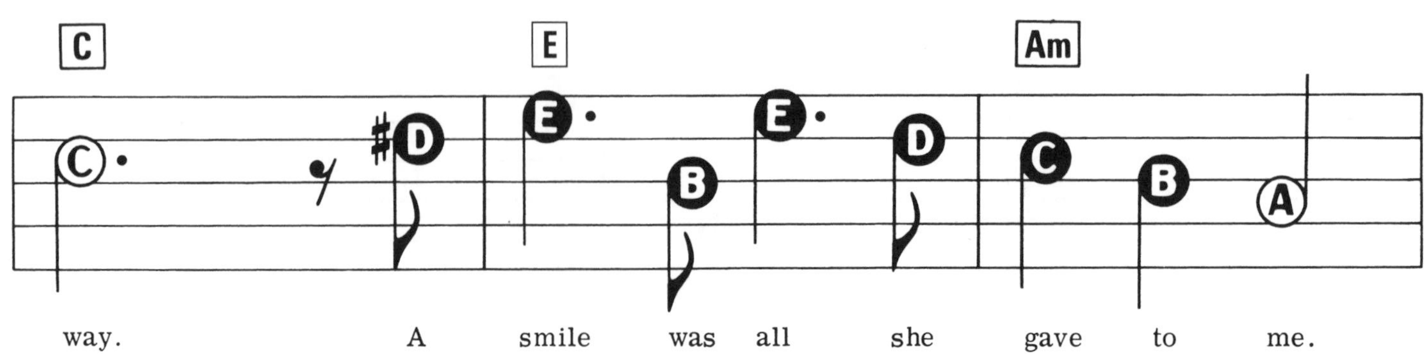

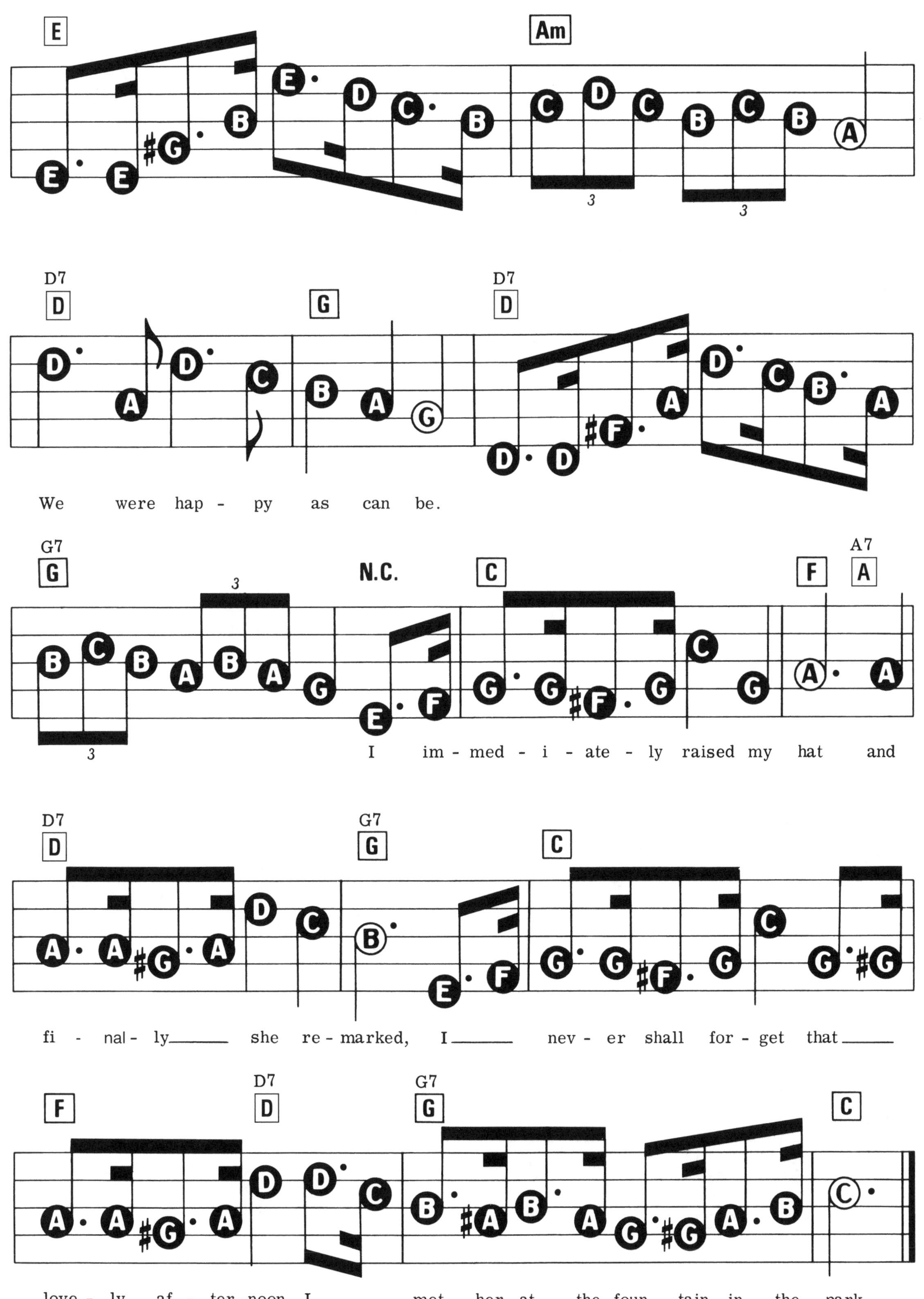
E
Am
D7 D
G
D7 D
We were hap - py as can be.
G7 G
N.C.
C
F
A7 A
I im - med - i - ate - ly raised my hat and
D7 D
G7 G
C
fi - nal - ly she re - marked, I nev - er shall for - get that
F
D7 D
G7 G
C
love - ly af - ter - noon I met her at the foun - tain in the park.

Whispering

Registration 1
Rhythm: Fox Trot

Words and Music by Richard Coburn,
John Schonberger and Vincent Rose

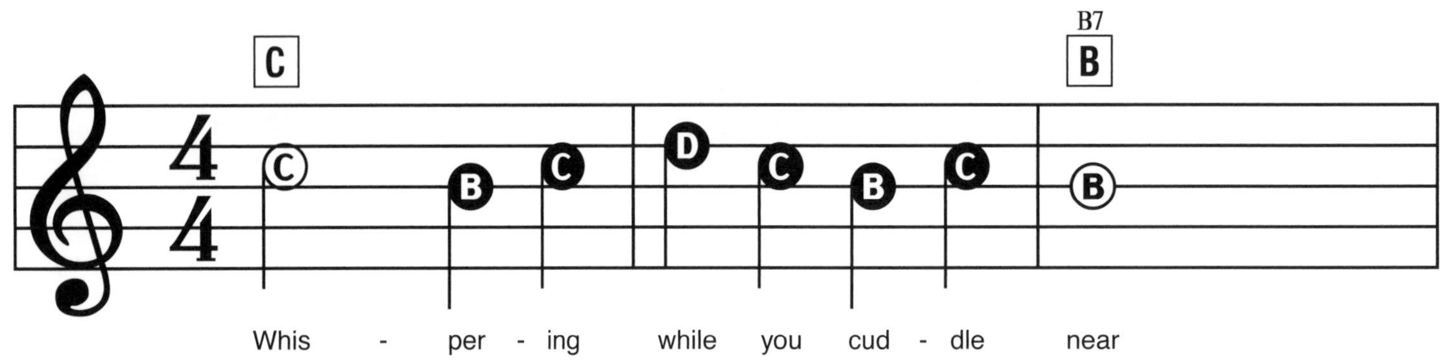

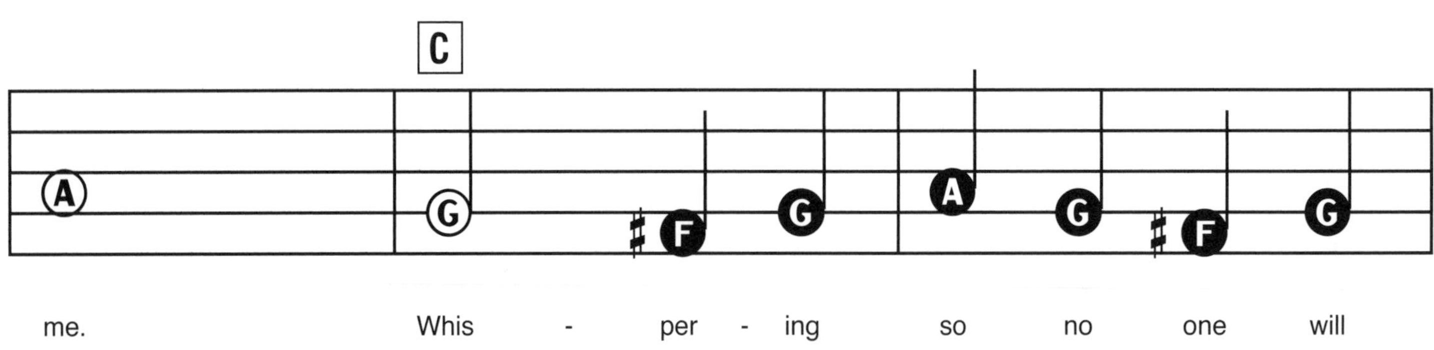

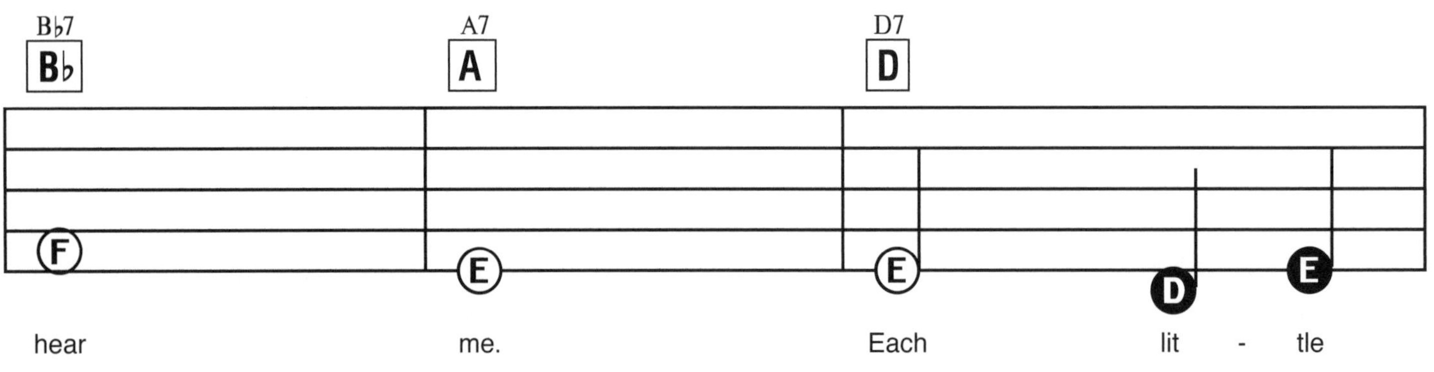

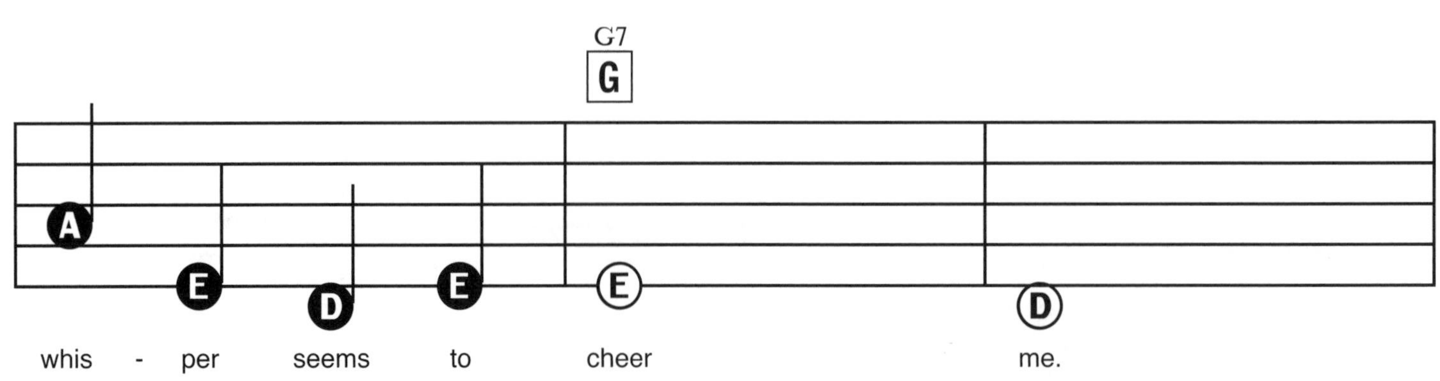

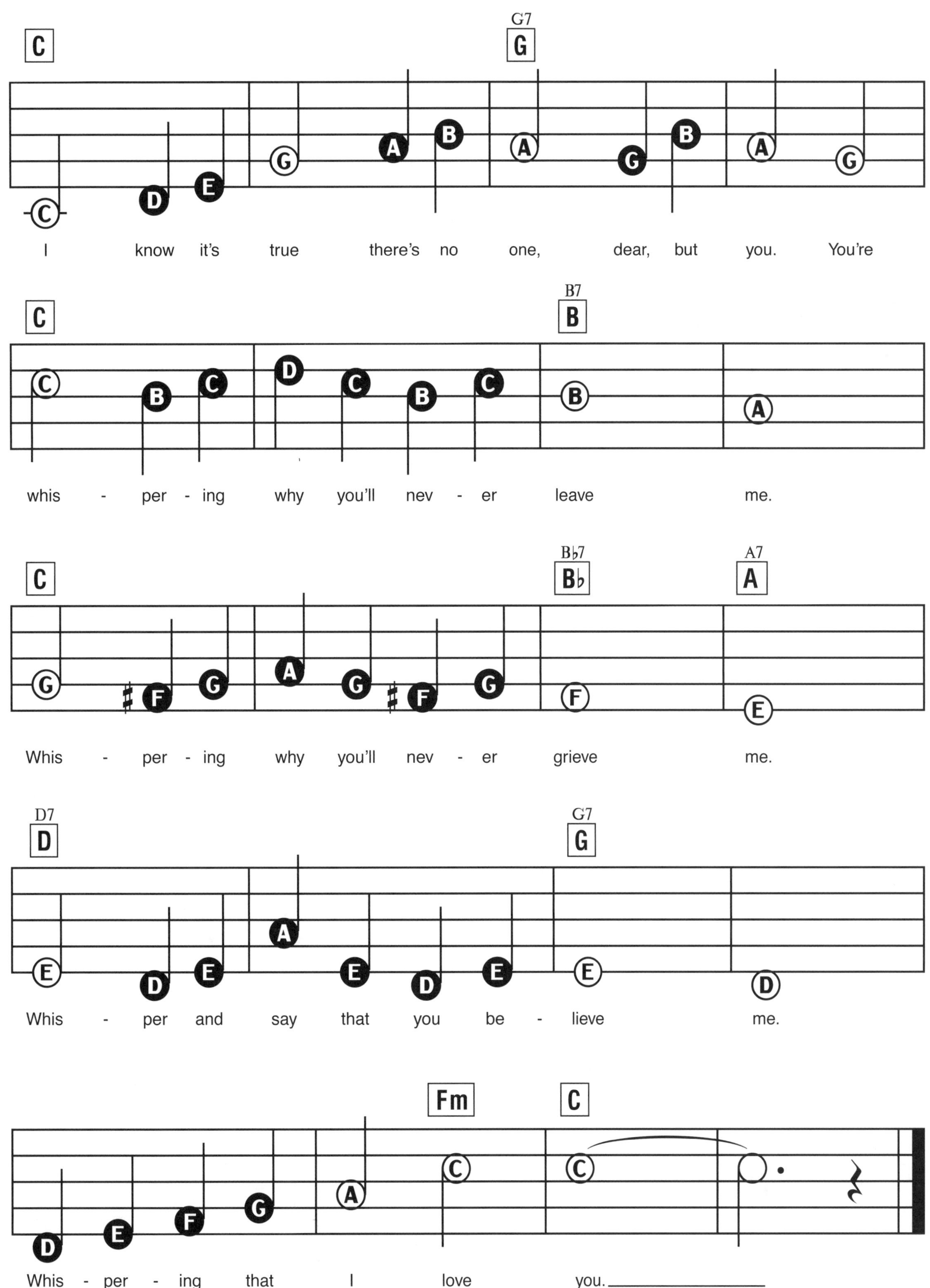
C
G7
G
C
D
E
G
A
B
A
G
B
A
G
I know it's true there's no one, dear, but you. You're
C
B7
B
C
B
C
D
C
B
C
B
A
whis - per - ing why you'll nev - er leave me.
C
B♭7
B♭
A7
A
G
♯
F
G
A
G
♯
F
G
F
E
Whis - per - ing why you'll nev - er grieve me.
D7
D
G7
G
E
D
E
A
E
D
E
E
D
Whis - per and say that you be - lieve me.
Fm
C
D
E
F
G
A
C
C
Whis - per - ing that I love you.

The World Is Waiting for the Sunrise

Registration 5
Rhythm: Fox Trot or Swing

Words by Eugene Lockhart
Music by Ernest Seitz

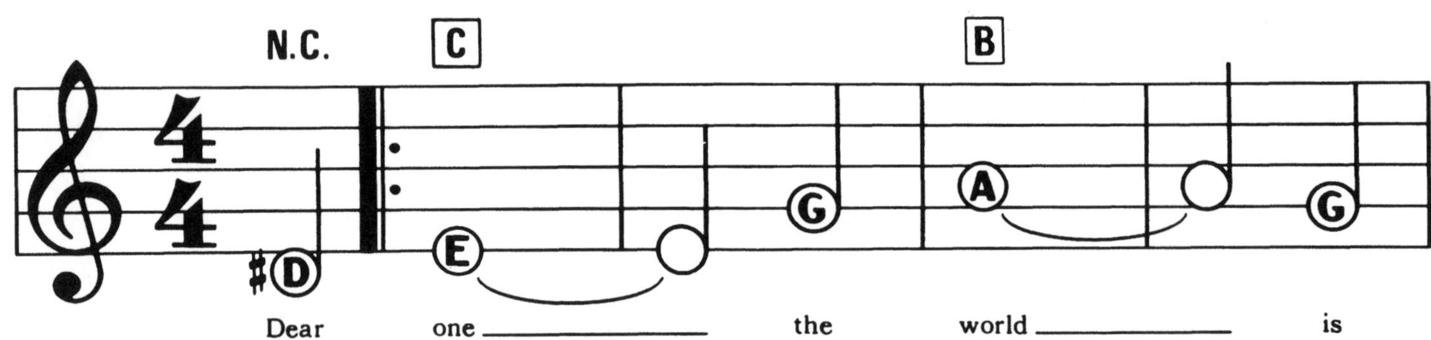

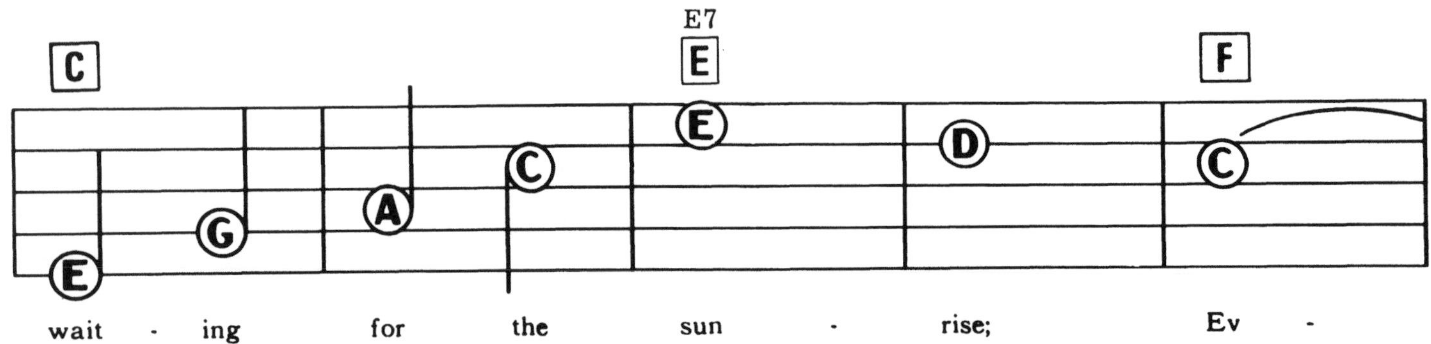

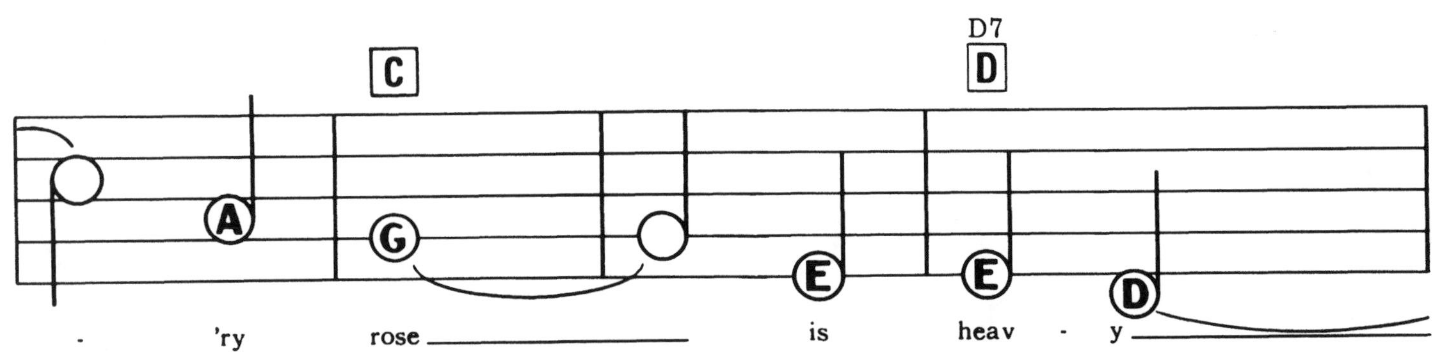

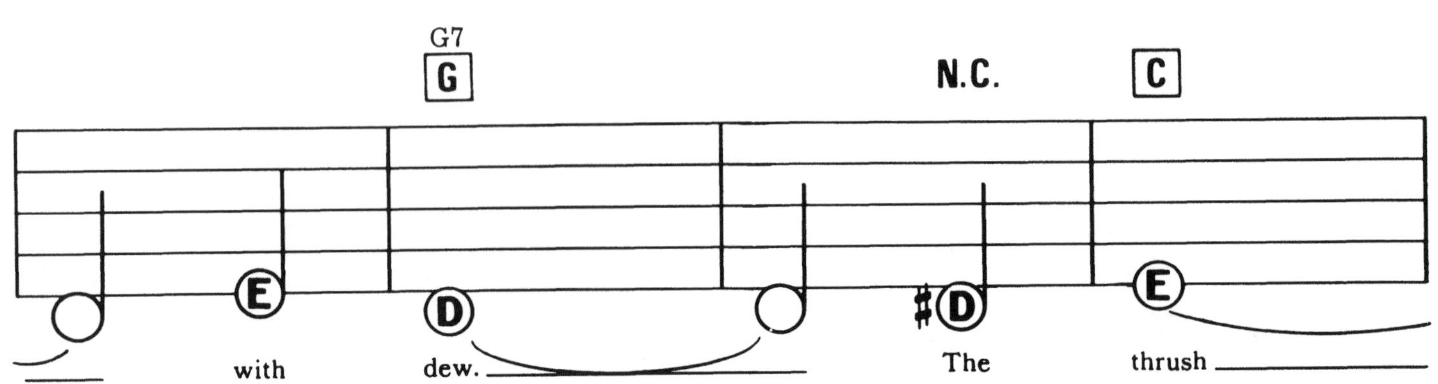

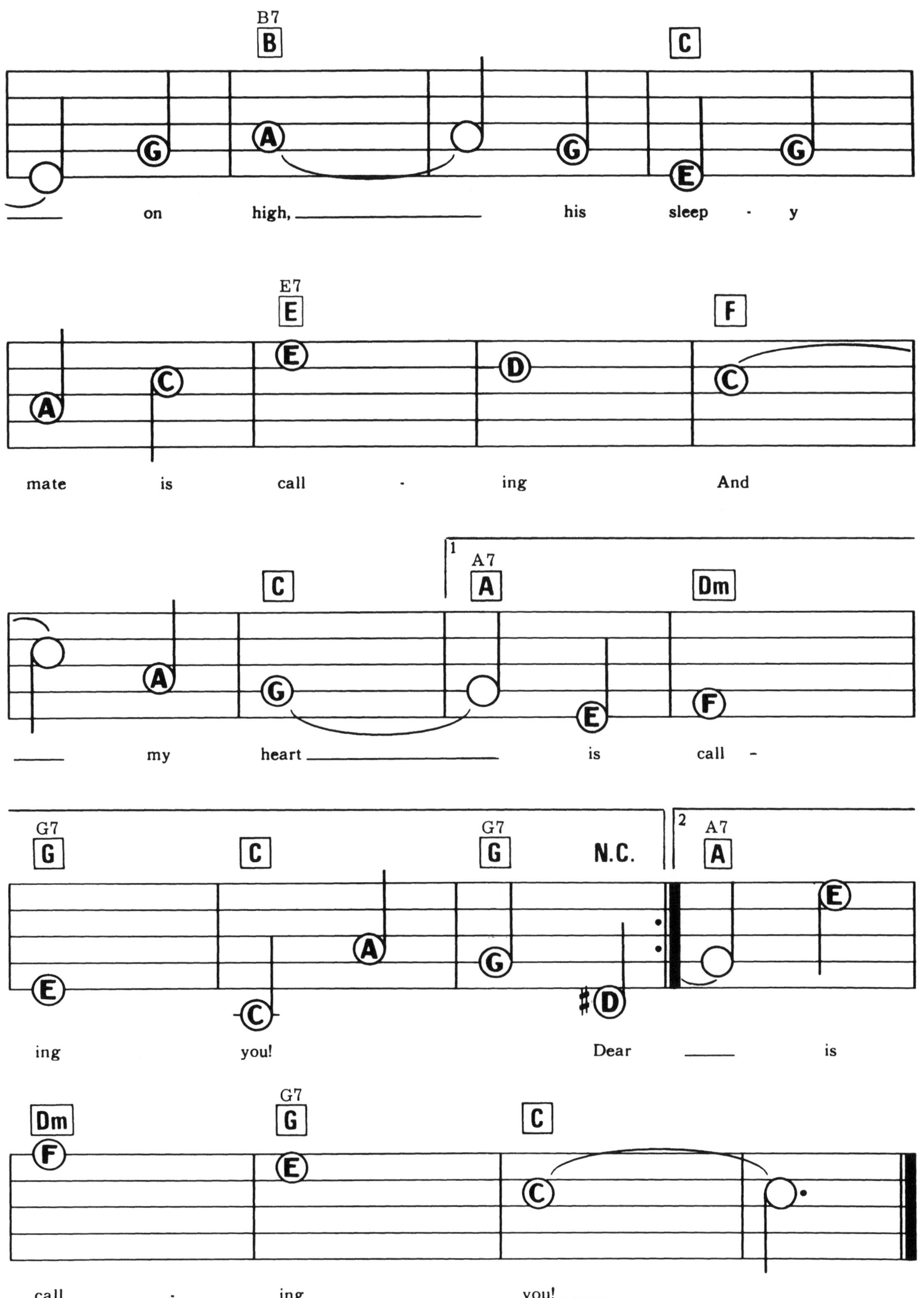

B7
B
C
G
A
G
E
G
on
high,
his
sleep
-
y
E7
E
F
A
C
E
D
C
mate
is
call
-
ing
And
1
A7
A
C
Dm
A
G
E
F
my
heart
is
call
-
G7
G
C
G7
G
N.C.
2
A7
A
E
C
A
G
D
E
ing
you!
Dear
is
Dm
G7
G
C
F
E
C
call
-
ing
you!

You Tell Me Your Dream

Registration 3
Rhythm: Waltz

Words by Seymour Rice and Albert H. Brown
Music by Charles N. Daniels

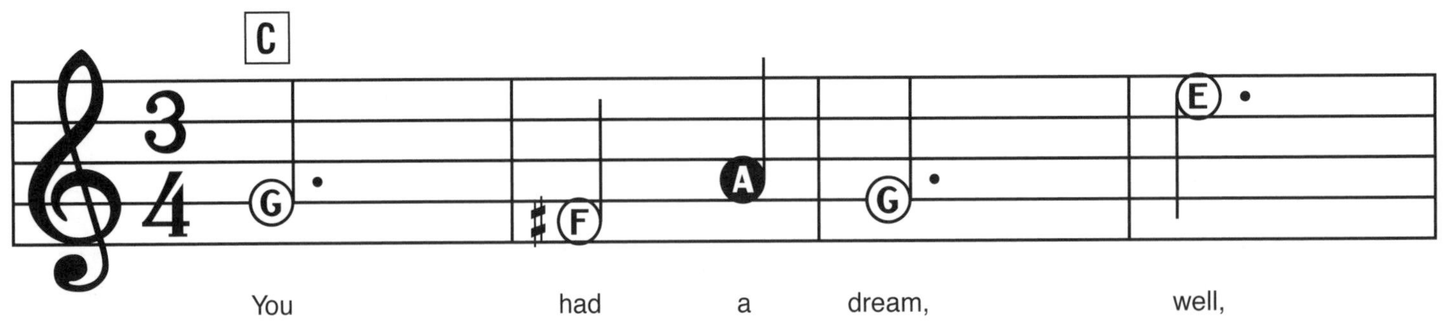

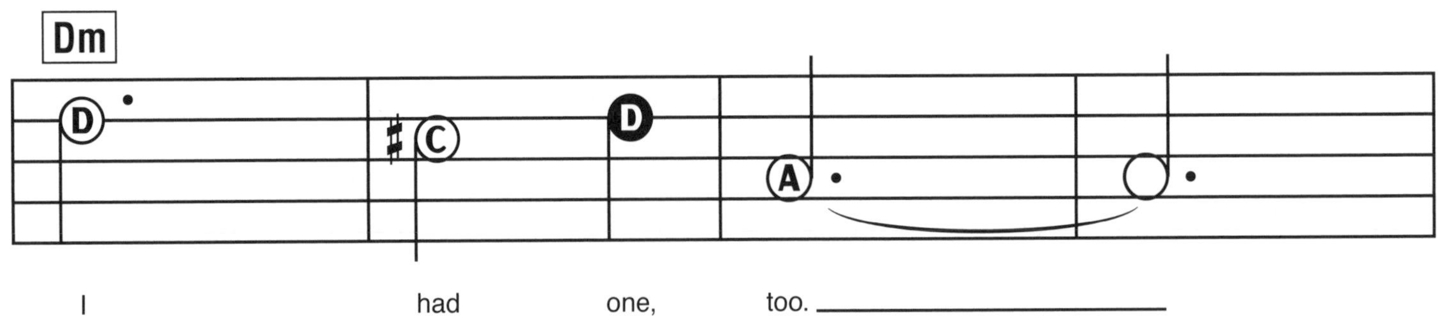

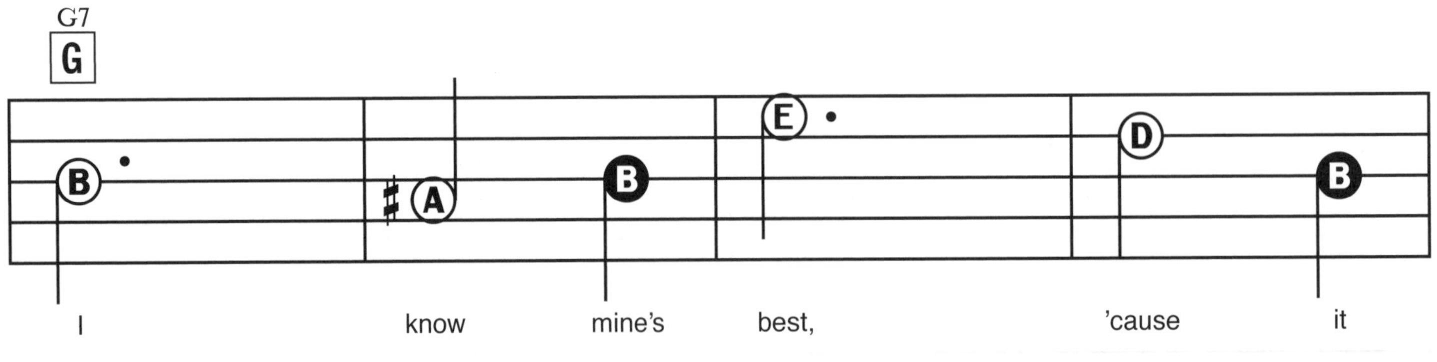

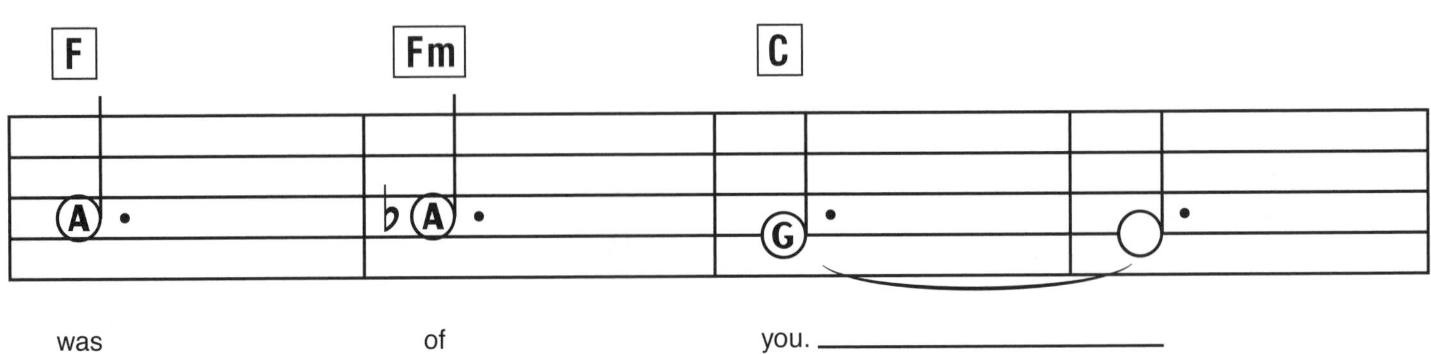

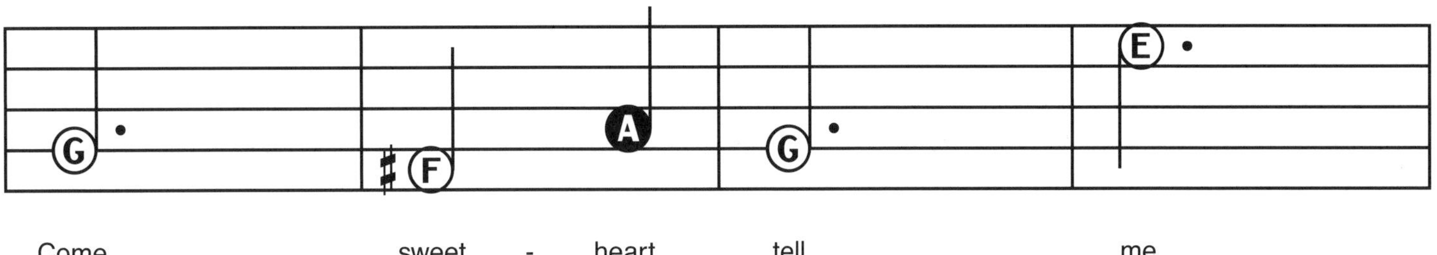
G
♯F
A
G
E
Come,
sweet - heart,
tell
me,

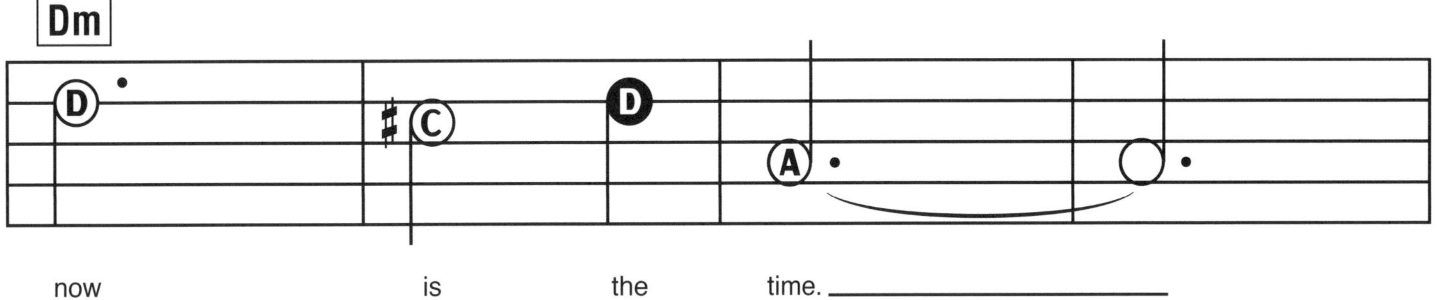
Dm
D
♯C
D
A
now
is
the
time.

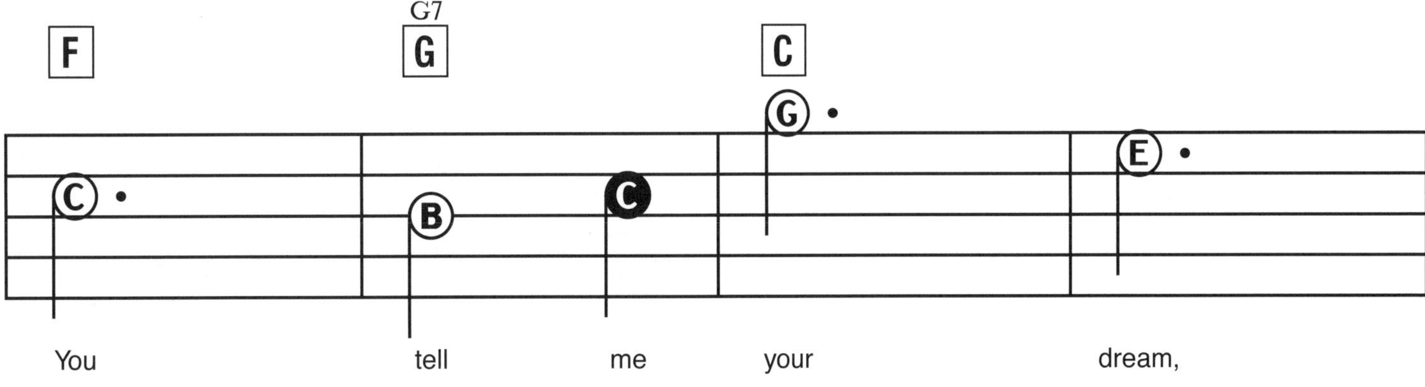
F
G7
G
C
C
B
C
G
E
You
tell
me
your
dream,

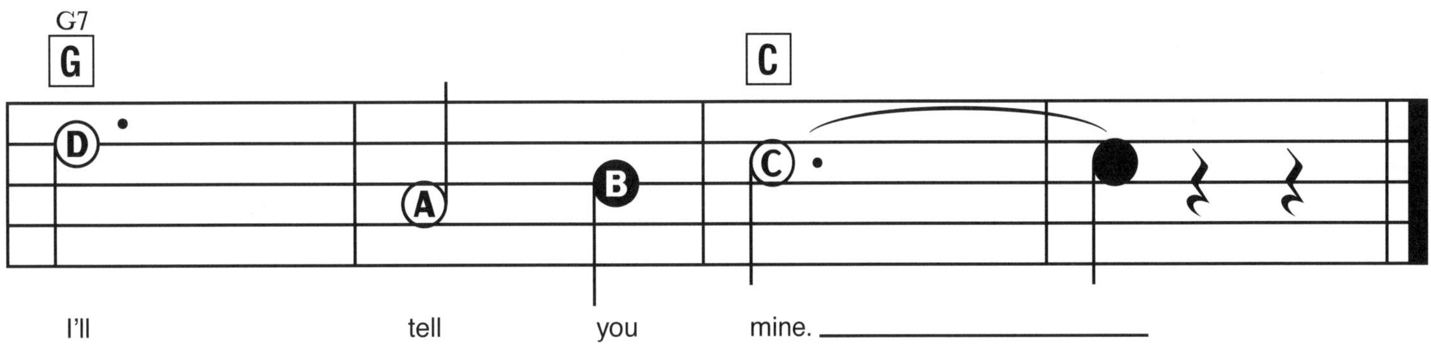
G7
G
C
D
A
B
C
I'll
tell
you
mine.

You Made Me Love You
(I Didn't Want to Do It)
from BROADWAY MELODY OF 1938

Registration 7
Rhythm: Fox Trot

Words by Joe McCarthy
Music by James V. Monaco

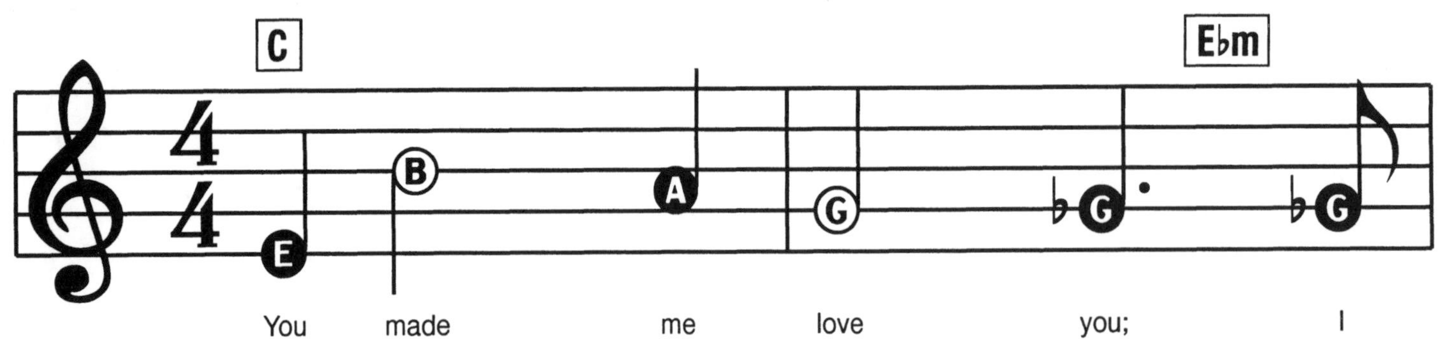

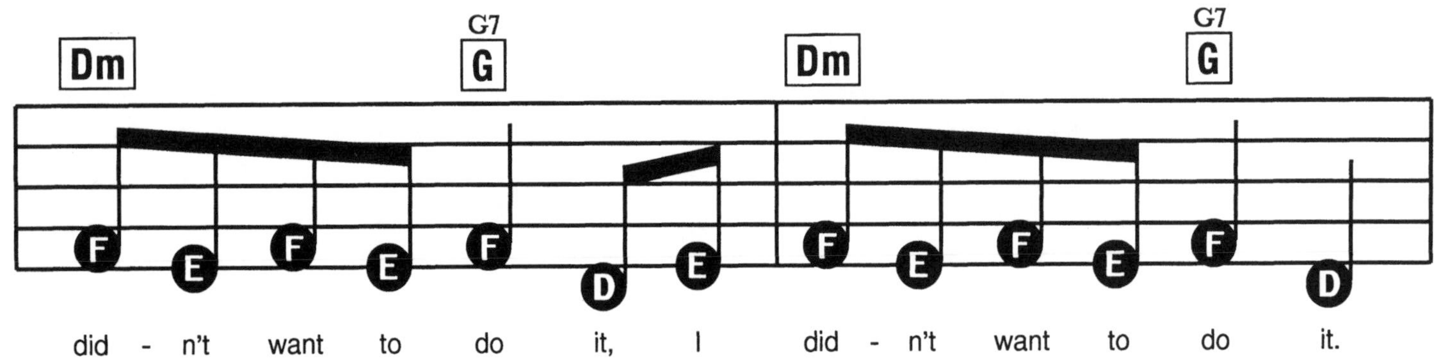

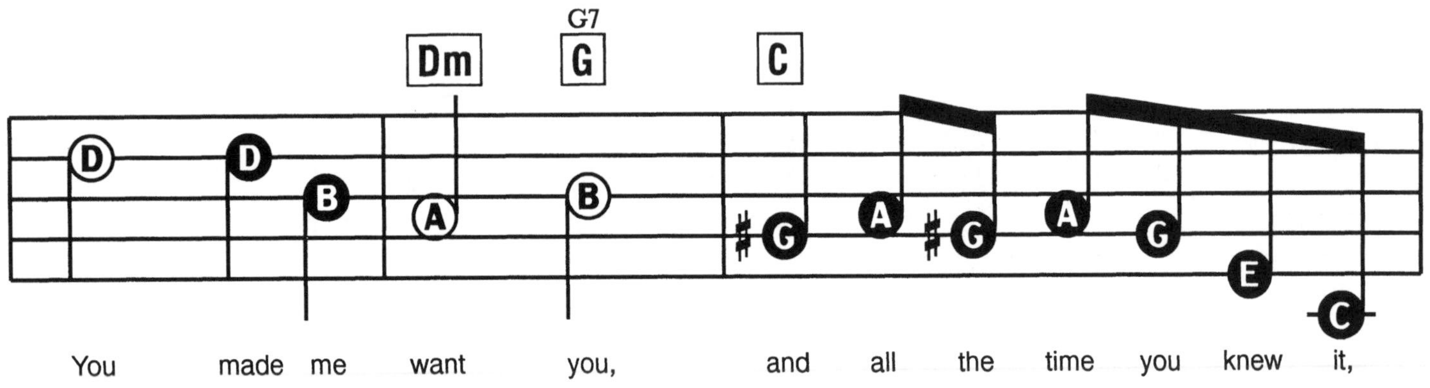

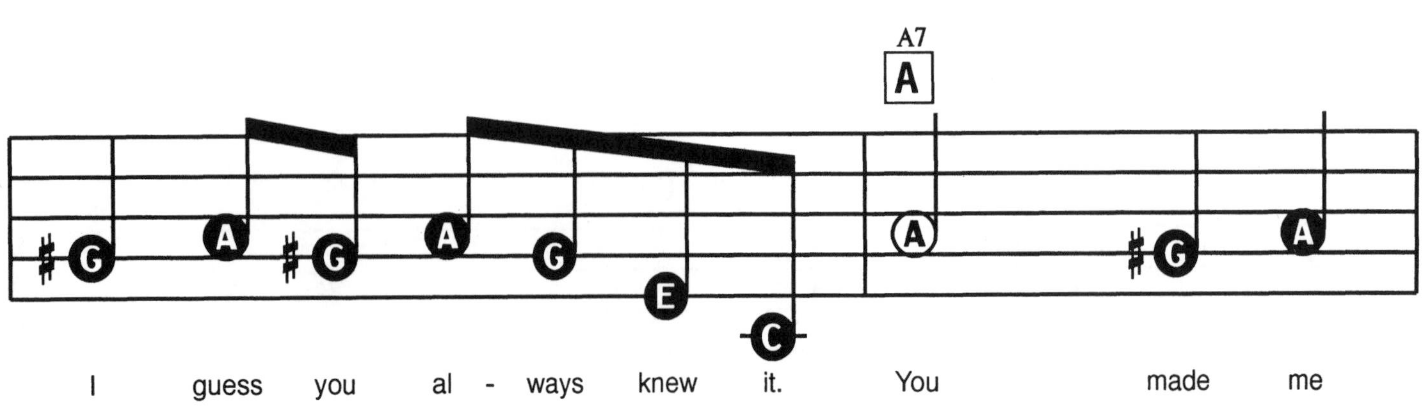

D7
D
Am
D7
D
hap - py some - times, you made me glad.
Am
D7
D
Dm
But there were times, dear, you made me feel so
G7
G
C
E♭m
bad. You made me sigh, for I
Dm
G7
G
Dm
G7
G
did - n't wan - na tell you, I did - n't wan - na tell you,
Dm
B7
B
I want some love that's

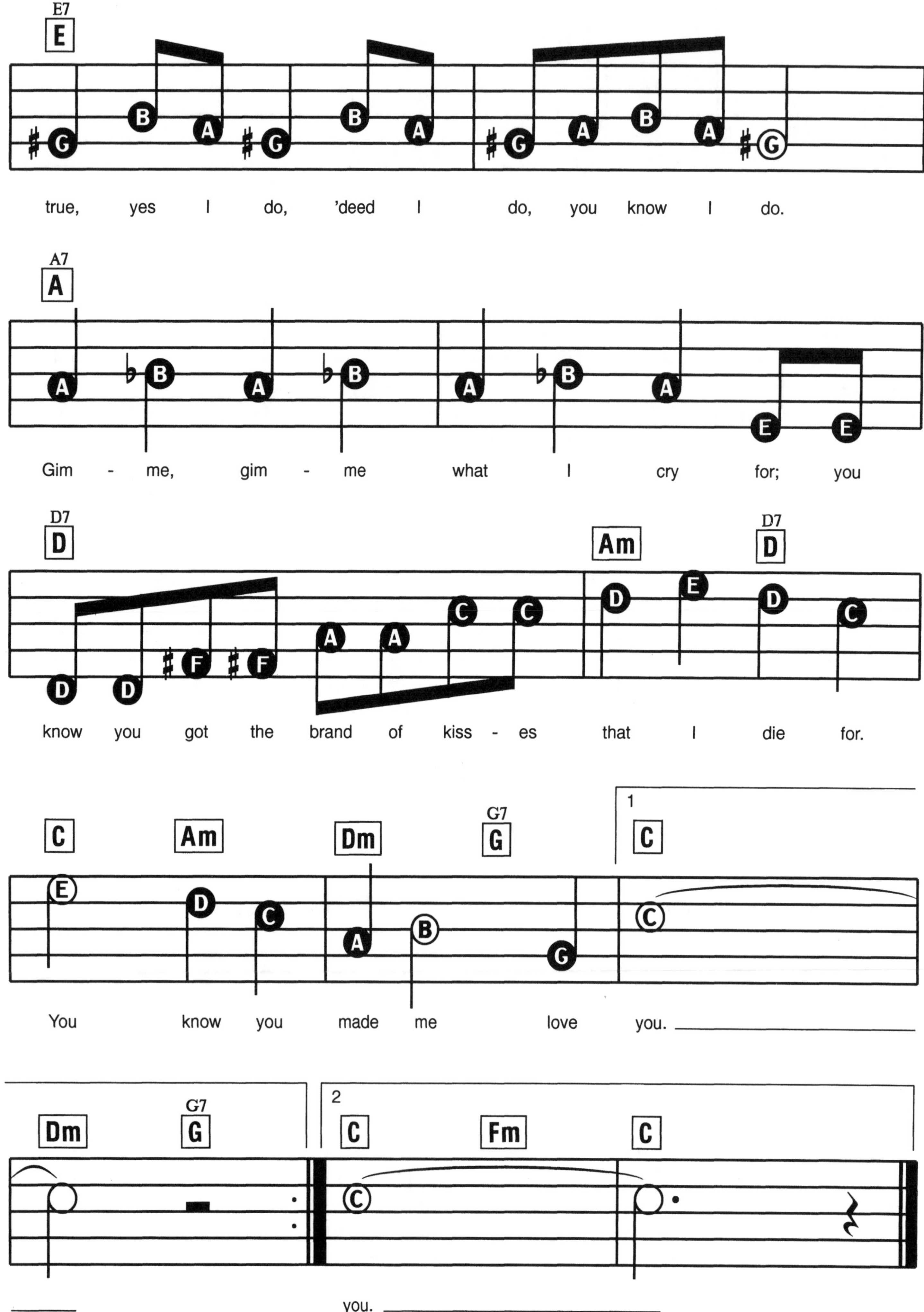
E7
E
G B A G B A G A B A G
true, yes I do, 'deed I do, you know I do.
A7
A
A B A B A B A E E
Gim - me, gim - me what I cry for; you
D7
D
Am
D7
D
D D F F A A C C D E D C
know you got the brand of kiss - es that I die for.
C
Am
Dm
G7
G
1
C
E D C A B G C
You know you made me love you.
Dm
G7
G
2
C
Fm
C
C
you.

Registration Guide

- Match the Registration number on the song to the corresponding numbered category below. Select and activate an instrumental sound available on your instrument.
- Choose an automatic rhythm appropriate to the mood and style of the song. (Consult your Owner's Guide for proper operation of automatic rhythm features.)
- Adjust the tempo and volume controls to comfortable settings.

Registration

1	Mellow	Flutes, Clarinet, Oboe, Flugel Horn, Trombone, French Horn, Organ Flutes
2	Ensemble	Brass Section, Sax Section, Wind Ensemble, Full Organ, Theater Organ
3	Strings	Violin, Viola, Cello, Fiddle, String Ensemble, Pizzicato, Organ Strings
4	Guitars	Acoustic/Electric Guitars, Banjo, Mandolin, Dulcimer, Ukulele, Hawaiian Guitar
5	Mallets	Vibraphone, Marimba, Xylophone, Steel Drums, Bells, Celesta, Chimes
6	Liturgical	Pipe Organ, Hand Bells, Vocal Ensemble, Choir, Organ Flutes
7	Bright	Saxophones, Trumpet, Mute Trumpet, Synth Leads, Jazz/Gospel Organs
8	Piano	Piano, Electric Piano, Honky Tonk Piano, Harpsichord, Clavi
9	Novelty	Melodic Percussion, Wah Trumpet, Synth, Whistle, Kazoo, Perc. Organ
10	Bellows	Accordion, French Accordion, Mussette, Harmonica, Pump Organ, Bagpipes

E-Z PLAY® TODAY PUBLICATION

The E-Z Play® Today songbook series is the shortest distance between beginning music playing fun! Check out this list of highlights and visit www.halleonard.com for a comp listing of all volumes and songlists.

Item	Title	Price
00102278	1. Favorite Songs with 3 Chords	$7.95
00100374	2. Country Sound	$8.95
00100167	3. Contemporary Disney	$16.99
00100382	4. Dance Band Greats	$7.95
00100305	5. All-Time Standards	$7.99
00100428	6. Songs of The Beatles	$10.99
00100442	7. Hits from Musicals	$7.99
00100490	8. Patriotic Songs	$8.99
00100355	9. Christmas Time	$7.95
00100435	10. Hawaiian Songs	$7.95
00110284	12. Star Wars	$7.99
00100248	13. Three-Chord Country Songs	$12.95
00100300	14. All-Time Requests	$8.99
00100370	15. Country Pickin's	$7.95
00100335	16. Broadway's Best	$7.95
00100362	18. Classical Portraits	$7.99
00102277	20. Hymns	$7.95
00100570	22. Sacred Sounds	$7.95
00100214	23. Essential Songs – The 1920s	$16.95
00100206	24. Essential Songs – The 1930s	$16.95
14041364	26. Bob Dylan	$12.99
00001236	27. 60 of the World's Easiest to Play Songs with 3 Chords	$8.95
00101598	28. Fifty Classical Themes	$9.95
00100135	29. Love Songs	$7.95
00100030	30. Country Connection	$8.95
00001289	32. Sing-Along Favorites	$7.95
00100253	34. Inspirational Ballads	$10.95
00100254	35. Frank Sinatra – Romance	$8.95
00100122	36. Good Ol' Songs	$10.95
00100410	37. Favorite Latin Songs	$7.95
00119955	40. Coldplay	$10.99
00100425	41. Songs of Gershwin, Porter & Rodgers	$7.95
00100123	42. Baby Boomers Songbook	$9.95
00100576	43. Sing-along Requests	$8.95
00102135	44. Best of Willie Nelson	$9.99
00100460	45. Love Ballads	$8.99
00100007	47. Duke Ellington – American Composer	$8.95
00100343	48. Gospel Songs of Johnny Cash	$7.95
00100043	49. Elvis, Elvis, Elvis	$9.95
00102114	50. Best of Patsy Cline	$9.95
00100208	51. Essential Songs – The 1950s	$17.95
00100209	52. Essential Songs – The 1960s	$17.95
00100210	53. Essential Songs – The 1970s	$19.95
00100211	54. Essential Songs – The 1980s	$19.95
00100342	55. Johnny Cash	$9.99
00100118	57. More of the Best Songs Ever	$17.99
00100285	58. Four-Chord Songs	$10.99
00100353	59. Christmas Songs	$8.95
00100304	60. Songs for All Occasions	$16.99
00102314	61. Jazz Standards	$10.95
00100409	62. Favorite Hymns	$6.95
00100360	63. Classical Music (Spanish/English)	$7.99
00100223	64. Wicked	$9.95
00100217	65. Hymns with 3 Chords	$7.95
00102312	66. Torch Songs	$14.95
00100218	67. Music from the Motion Picture Ray	$8.95
00100449	69. It's Gospel	$7.95
00100432	70. Gospel Greats	$7.95
00100117	72. Canciones Románticas	$7.99
00100568	75. Sacred Moments	$6.95
00100572	76. The Sound of Music	$8.95
00100489	77. My Fair Lady	$7.99
00100424	81. Frankie Yankovic – Polkas & Waltzes	$7.95
00100286	87. 50 Worship Standards	$14.99
00100287	88. Glee	$9.99
00100577	89. Songs for Children	$7.95
00290104	90. Elton John Anthology	$16.99
00100034	91. 30 Songs for a Better World	$8.95
00100288	92. Michael Bublé – Crazy Love	$10.99
00100036	93. Country Hits	$10.95
00100139	94. Jim Croce – Greatest Hits	$8.95
00100219	95. The Phantom of the Opera (Movie)	$10.95
00100263	96. Mamma Mia – Movie Soundtrack	$7.99
00109768	98. Flower Power	$16.99
00100125	99. Children's Christmas Songs	$7.95
00100602	100. Winter Wonderland	$8.95
00001309	102. Carols of Christmas	$7.99
00119237	103. Two-Chord Songs	$9.99
00100256	107. The Best Praise & Worship Songs Ever	$16.99
00100363	108. Classical Themes (English/Spanish)	$6.95
00102232	109. Motown's Greatest Hits	$12.95
00101566	110. Neil Diamond Collection	$14.99
00100119	111. Season's Greetings	$14.95
00101498	112. Best of The Beatles	$19.95
00100134	113. Country Gospel USA	$10.95
00101612	115. The Greatest Waltzes	$9.95
00100136	118. 100 Kids' Songs	$12.95
00100433	120. Gospel of Bill & Gloria Gaither	$14.95
00100333	121. Boogies, Blues and Rags	$7.95
00100146	122. Songs for Praise & Worship	$8.95
00100001	125. Great Big Book of Children's Songs	$14.99
00101563	127. John Denver's Greatest Hits	$9.95
00116947	128. John Williams	$10.99
00116956	130. Taylor Swift Hits	$10.99
00102318	131. Doo-Wop Songbook	$10.95
00100306	133. Carole King	$9.99
00100171	135. All Around the U.S.A.	$10.95
00001256	136. Christmas Is for Kids	$8.99
00100144	137. Children's Movie Hits	$7.95
00100038	138. Nostalgia Collection	$14.95
00100289	139. Crooners	$19.99
00101956	140. Best of George Strait	$12.95
00100314	142. Classic Jazz	$14.99
00101946	143. The Songs of Paul McCartney	$8.99
00100597	146. Hank Williams – His Best	$7.95
00116916	147. Lincoln	$7.99
00100003	149. Movie Musical Memories	$10.95
00101548	150. Best Big Band Songs Ever	$16.95
00100152	151. Beach Boys – Greatest Hits	$8.95
00101592	152. Fiddler on the Roof	$9.99
00101549	155. Best of Billy Joel	$10.99
00001264	157. Easy Favorites	$7.99
00100315	160. The Grammy Awards Record of the Year 1958-2010	$16.99
00100293	161. Henry Mancini	$9.99
00100049	162. Lounge Music	$10.95
00100295	163. The Very Best of the Rat Pack	$12.99
00101530	164. Best Christmas Songbook	$9.95
00101895	165. Rodgers & Hammerstein Songbook	$9.95
00100148	169. A Charlie Brown Christmas™	$10.99
00101900	170. Kenny Rogers – Greatest Hits	$9.95
00101537	171. Best of Elton John	$7.95
00100321	173. Adele – 21	$10.99
00100149	176. Charlie Brown Collection™	$7.99
00102325	179. Love Songs of The Beatles	$10.99
00101610	181. Great American Country Songbook	$12.95
00001246	182. Amazing Grace	$12.95
00450133	183. West Side Story	$9.99
00100151	185. Carpenters	$10.99
00101606	186. 40 Pop & Rock Song Classics	$12.95
00100155	187. Ultimate Christmas	$17.95
00102276	189. Irish Favorites	$7.95
00100053	191. Jazz Love Songs	$8.95
00101998	192. 65 Standard Hits	$15.95
00123123	193. Bruno Mars	$10.99
00124609	195. Opera Favorites	$8.99
00101609	196. Best of George Gershwin	$14.99
00100057	198. Songs in 3/4 Time	$9.95
00119857	199. Jumbo Songbook	$24.99
00101539	200. Best Songs Ever	$19.95
00101540	202. Best Country Songs Ever	$17.95
00101541	203. Best Broadway Songs Ever	$17.99
00101542	204. Best Easy Listening Songs Ever	$17.95
00101543	205. Best Love Songs Ever	$17.95
00100058	208. Easy Listening Favorites	$7.95
00100059	210. '60s Pop Rock Hits	$12.95
14041777	211. The Big Book of Nursery Rhymes & Children's Songs	$12.99
00126895	212. Frozen	$9.99
00101546	213. Disney Classics	$14.95
00101533	215. Best Christmas Songs Ever	$19.95
00100156	219. Christmas Songs with 3 Chords	$8.99
00102080	225. Lawrence Welk Songbook	$9.95
00101931	228. Songs of the '20s	$13.95
00101932	229. Songs of the '30s	$13.95
00101933	230. Songs of the '40s	$14.95
00101935	232. Songs of the '60s	$14
00101936	233. Songs of the '70s	$14
00101581	235. Elvis Presley Anthology	$15
00290170	239. Big Book of Children's Songs	$14
00290120	240. Frank Sinatra	$14
00100158	243. Oldies! Oldies! Oldies!	$10
00290242	244. Songs of the '80s	$14
00100041	245. Best of Simon & Garfunkel	$8
00100269	247. Essential Songs – Broadway	$17
00100296	248. The Love Songs of Elton John	$12
00100175	249. Elv1s – 30 #1 Hits	$9
00102113	251. Phantom of the Opera (Broadway)	$14
00100301	255. Four-Chord Hymns	$8
00100203	256. Very Best of Lionel Richie	$8
00100302	258. Four-Chord Worship	$9
00100178	259. Norah Jones – Come Away with Me	$9
00102306	261. Best of Andrew Lloyd Webber	$12
00100063	266. Latin Hits	$7
00100062	269. Love That Latin Beat	$7
00100179	270. Christian Christmas Songbook	$14
00101425	272. ABBA Gold – Greatest Hits	$7
00102248	275. Classical Hits – Bach, Beethoven & Brahms	$6
00100186	277. Stevie Wonder – Greatest Hits	$9
00100237	280. Dolly Parton	$9
00100068	283. Best Jazz Standards Ever	$15
00100244	287. Josh Groban	$10
00100022	288. Sing-a-Long Christmas	$10
00100023	289. Sing-a-Long Christmas Carols	$9
00102124	293. Movie Classics	$9
00100069	294. Old Fashioned Love Songs	$9
00100303	295. Best of Michael Bublé	$12
00100075	296. Best of Cole Porter	$7
00102130	298. Beautiful Love Songs	$7
00001102	301. Kid's Songfest	$9
00102147	306. Irving Berlin Collection	$14
00102182	308. Greatest American Songbook	$9
00100194	309. 3-Chord Rock 'n' Roll	$8
00001580	311. The Platters Anthology	$7
02501515	312. Barbra – Love Is the Answer	$10
00100196	314. Chicago	$8
00100197	315. VH1's 100 Greatest Songs of Rock & Roll	$19
00100080	322. Dixieland	$7
00100277	325. Taylor Swift	$10
00100082	327. Tonight at the Lounge	$7
00100092	333. Great Gospel Favorites	$7
00100278	338. The Best Hymns Ever	$19
00100279	340. Anthology of Jazz Songs	$19
00100280	341. Anthology of Rock Songs	$19
00100281	342. Anthology of Broadway Songs	$19
00100282	343. Anthology of Love Songs	$19
00100283	344. Anthology of Latin Songs	$19
00100284	345. Anthology of Movie Songs	$19
00102235	346. Big Book of Christmas Songs	$14
00100292	347. Anthology of Country Songs	$19
00100095	359. 100 Years of Song	$17
00100096	360. More 100 Years of Song	$19
00100103	375. Songs of Bacharach & David	$7
00100107	392. Disney Favorites	$19
00100108	393. Italian Favorites	$7
00100111	394. Best Gospel Songs Ever	$17
00100114	398. Disney's Princess Collections	$10
00100115	400. Classical Masterpieces	$10

7777 W. Bluemound Rd. P.O. Box 13819 Milwaukee, WI 53213